Workers' Paradise Lost

Workers' Paradise Lost

Fifty Years of Soviet Communism: A Balance Sheet

Eugene Lyons

FUNK & WAGNALLS

NEW YORK

This book is dedicated to
THE PEOPLES OF RUSSIA
the first and worst victims of communism

ACKNOWLEDGMENTS

I am indebted to many people for help with research on this book and checking of the manuscript, too many to be listed. But I want to express special appreciation for their generous and scholarly cooperation to Dr. Leo Dudin and Dr. Anatol Popluiko of the Radio Liberty Committee, Joseph A. Gwyer of the Library of Congress, and Professor Albert Parry, Chairman of the Department of Russian Studies at Colgate University.

E.L.

Contents

PART I

Verdict
of Five Decades

On November 7, 1917, a handful of Bolsheviks under Vladimir Ilyich Lenin and Leon Trotsky seized control of the Russian state, not from the Romanoff monarchy, but from the democratic Provisional Government set up about eight months earlier. On November 7, 1967, therefore, Soviet communism will have rounded out a half century of existence.*

This is a dramatic milestone not only in the history of Russia, but in world history. Because international communism has been in essence an extension of Soviet power and messianic zeal, the impact of the Bolshevik *coup d'état* on all mankind can scarcely be overstated. The Kremlin's self-proclaimed leadership of the "world proletariat" in an unswerving drive for One Communist World has been and remains a prime force in shaping our twentieth century.

The Soviet experience has been called a Great Experiment. The formula is unfair if not cynical, in that it seems to equate the Russian people with guinea pigs and laboratory dogs. Yet Russia has in fact provided the longest, most intensive test of a set of social theories in all history, conducted by steel-nerved fanatics in a laboratory comprising a sixth of the earth's surface, endowed with vast population and natural resources.

In today's fast-moving fast-changing world, fifty years are equivalent to several centuries in the past. No one can reasonably plead, as some did in the first decades, that the Soviet enterprise is too

* Under the old Julian calendar then in use in Russia, the corresponding date for November 7 was October 25. In communist usage, the event is therefore known as the October Revolution.

young to have proven itself one way or the other. The time is ripe for some clear and definitive judgments.

Has Soviet communism "succeeded"? To what extent has it reached the objectives set forth in 1917; objectives indeed, set forth continually since 1848, when Karl Marx and Friedrich Engels launched their *Communist Manifesto?* Does socialism—not as a theory but in its concrete embodiment in the USSR—offer a rational model for emulation by the rest of the world, in particular by peoples and countries caught up in the so-called revolution of rising expectations? What are the realities behind the communist rhetoric and hyperbolic claims?

I am not proposing anything new. A great debate on these questions has been under way throughout the fifty years. Perhaps no other phenomenon in modern times has been so thoroughly described, analyzed, documented, and argued about; books on Soviet Russia, adulatory and critical and in-between, would fill a good-sized library. Winston Churchill's notion that Russia is an impenetrable enigma is far from the facts.

Yet the completion of the half-century is a convenient point in time for other and more current appraisals.

Soviet leaders and their partisans give us their own clearcut verdict, substantially the same one we have heard for at least thirty years. Soviet communism, they insist, has long ceased to be an experiment. It is magnificently "victorious" and just what Marx and Lenin ordered. "Socialism [has] triumphed in the Soviet Union, completely and finally," according to the latest official *Program of the Communist Party,* adopted by its Twenty-second Congress in 1961. A "classless society" marches resolutely and happily toward full communism in some dim future. The masses everywhere have only to follow in the footsteps of the Soviet Union, under the Marxist-Leninist banner, to achieve the same results.

Already that verdict is being trumpeted to the world. A long, turgid resolution by the Central Committee of the ruling party, on January 9, 1967, declared that year the "jubilee year" of communism triumphant. Running to nearly two close-printed pages in all Soviet newspapers, the resolution ordered the whole country, in town and village, to begin at once to mobilize for the greatest celebration in history on the anniversary. No doubt the entire world-wide communist apparatus has been instructed to do no less. A full year in advance of the event, for instance, the mouthpiece of the American Communist Party, *The Worker,* promised "the biggest rip-roaring celebration in history."

The resolution is an extraordinary document. In florid, billowing clichés, it hailed the final achievement of socialism, without defining it concretely. It spread-eagled all the familiar claims and boasts: the abolition of poverty, the glories of industrialization and collectivized farming, the defeat of the "world of private property, individualism, egotism." But there is little substance under the blaring boastfulness.

In the thousands of words there are few specific facts or figures on any phase of Soviet society, only flamboyant rhetoric and sweeping generalizations about their "new world" and its happy life. The grim realities of the half-century are evaded and bypassed. Karl Marx, the prophet, is named directly three or four times; for the rest, he figures only as part of the hybrid abstraction of Marxism-Leninism. There is not so much as a mention of Joseph Stalin and Nikita Khrushchev who, between them, dominated two-thirds of the fifty-year period. And this is presented as a summation of the whole history of Soviet communism.*

Whatever else the Kremlin may or may not have accomplished, everyone agrees that it has perfected a global propaganda machine without precedent for size and penetrative power. With that machine having gone into high gear for the fiftieth birthday, our planet will be flooded with claims that socialism—or what Moscow calls socialism—has been demonstrated to be a superior system of social and economic organization, with miraculous achievements in all departments of life.

This claim will be spread to all corners of the earth, not only by the Soviet Union and its captive regimes in Europe and Cuba, by some eighty Moscow-oriented communist parties, but by swarms of fellow travelers and sympathizers. Who are these unaffiliated supporters of everything Soviet, millions in the aggregate, and what moves them to various degrees of fervor?

For the most part they are middle-class intellectuals, not proletarians. Some of them sense in communism a path to heady personal power; in the fantasies that excite them they see themselves

---

* An expanded resolution, on June 25, did include some big statistics and slanting reference to Stalin.

always among the elite of an iron dictatorship, never in the gray mass of those dictated to. Others are driven by hatred of their own capitalist or colonial environment, a hatred too often justified, but of an emotional intensity that precludes a sensible assessment of *all* the alternatives. The great majority, however, are enlightened liberals and progressives sincerely concerned for their fellow men, but so bemused by communist terminology and slogans—"workers' state . . . classless society . . . achievements without match in history . . . national planning . . . universal brotherhood"—that they cannot always look with unblinking eyes on the one nation that has tried to implement them for half a century.

Key Questions

"In an exact sense, Soviet Russia has become the opiate of the progressives," the liberal historian Arthur M. Schlesinger, Jr., wrote in *The Vital Center*. While Schlesinger was talking of progressives in the United States, his statement applies even more aptly to their counterparts in the new or emerging nations, the underdeveloped nations, if only because their problems are more urgent and the temptations of a supposedly quick and "efficient" solution more compelling. Politically young, excited by their new opportunities, distrustful and envious of the capitalist West, these new elites have shown themselves especially vulnerable to communist enticements, with their easy-to-follow recipes of a vulgarized Marxism.

In the end, of course, each nation will find its own road, without slavishly imitating ready-made models. But in the search for guidance it can hardly avoid comparing relatively free and open societies such as the United States with totally regimented, one-party societies such as the USSR. The questions it asks are almost as important as the answers. Unless they are directed to basic, factual realities, the searchers may find themselves bogged down in doctrinal disputations about theoretical heavens-on-earth.

Granting that there are faults and contradictions in all human institutions—are ordinary persons, from peasants to intellectuals, more oppressed and exploited in the United States or in the USSR? Where do they have stronger, more independent labor unions to defend their rights as wage-earners? Where do people enjoy more freedom of speech, press and assembly, more influence on the conduct of their government? Where can they count on more freedom of thought, beliefs, opinions, and dissent? The less developed continents being predominantly agricultural, in which country do the tillers of the soil suffer more "feudal" controls, whether exercised by individuals or by a state-landlord?

I have not suggested economic questions; first, because they are always asked without prompting, and second, because more fundamental considerations, relating to the *person*, his dignity and his rights, are the essence of the contrast. If industrial output and rocketry were the proofs of a superior society, then Hitler's Germany was an unqualified success. After all, no sane human being would knowingly settle for slavery or a fascist police-state, even if it could guarantee a full stomach for everybody.

Yet economic factors do have an important place in the comparison. Nikita Khrushchev in his time of power repeatedly stressed that the improvement of living conditions is the "socialist bloc" and their deterioration in the free-economy world would be an *object lesson to developing nations*. Things have not worked out as he expected but the object lesson remains valid.

Honest leaders of opinion cannot in good conscience ignore, in this connection, the implications of the forty-year-old Soviet slogan: *dognat' i peregnat'*, to overtake and outdistance the leading capitalist countries. As of 1967, the slogan is being muted in Moscow, because the economic gap, far from being closed, is widening. The Soviets, after fifty years of travail, are still striving to reach the levels of economic well-being, which other systems have long ago attained. The plain truth is that in terms of material well-being the superiority of the United States over the USSR is too apparent to require, at this point, statistical support.

We need not derogate material goals to believe that human and spiritual values, age-old ethical principles, justice and mercy and reverence for life must take precedence. One proof of this is that millions under communism yearn for these rejected values, thousands constantly try to escape from dehumanized regimentation to the freer world. It is not for bread alone that they risk their lives—most of them are from the better-off classes—but for freedom, faith, dignity, conscience.

Despite the pseudo-scientific pretensions of Marxism, socialism has become in our century a formless concept, meaning different things to different schools of advocates. It ranges from the diluted socialism of the Scandinavian countries and England to the total species in Soviet Russia and China, and under different labels it has included, in all logic, managed societies like Mussolini's corporate state in Italy and National Socialism (Nazism) in Hitler's Germany.

Leaders or would-be leaders who consider themselves socialists, especially in Asia, Africa, and Latin America, therefore, owe it to themselves and their followers to define their aims with some precision. The line between so called "scientific socialism" and socialist voodoo is hard to trace.

The Meaning of Durability

On January 24, 1918, a small man in rumpled clothes, with an aggressively jutting reddish beard and a gleaming bald head, was addressing hundreds of delegates from all over Russia in an ornate but unheated hall in Petrograd. This was the forty-eight-year-old Vladimir Ilyich Ulyanov—Lenin to history—reporting on the young regime he headed to an All-Russian Congress of Soviets.

The country was hungry and in economic collapse, torn by civil war and crumbling under the attacks of German armies on its western borders. But Lenin began on a note of triumph. Happily, a bit incredulously, he announced a new historical record. "Two months and fifteen days having elapsed since the establishment of Soviet power," he said, it had already survived "five days more" than the Paris Commune of 1871, the only other communist government of an entire nation in modern times. (Actually it was seven days more, but Lenin was counting not from November 7, when he took the power, but from November 9, when his new government was formally proclaimed.)

It was evident that neither he nor his comrades expected their fledgling regime to live very long—unless some major industrial nation, such as Germany, also went communist.

A number of their most important associates (Zinoviev, Rykov, Kamenev, and others) had publicly warned Lenin and Trotsky that the revolution would founder if they refused to share power with other socialist parties and failed to retain a modicum of democracy. "The preservation of a purely Bolshevik government by political terror," they declared in a joint statement, could only lead to "an irresponsible regime, the loss of the revolution."

The regime did survive to celebrate its fiftieth anniversary. This is a remarkable fact. More remarkable, however, is the wide belief that the mere staying power of a revolution proves its merits, establishes an irresistible wave of the future, and qualifies it to serve as a model for other nations.

Those who argue that its sheer survival demonstrates the "success" and even superiority of Soviet communism forget that its predecessor, the Romanoff dynasty, persisted for three hundred years. Latin American history is replete with examples of oligarchies that ruled for a generation or more under a single strongman. The Franco setup in Spain is well on its way toward a ripe old age. The Middle Ages and feudalism, the despotism of the Pharaohs in ancient Egypt and the Byzantine Empire in closer times, all prevailed for many centuries.

The idea that durability somehow connotes excellence is especially curious when held by people who abhor capitalism, though it has endured in various forms since the decline and fall of feudalism. Capitalism was pronounced moribund by the *Communist Manifesto* one hundred twenty years ago. "The Western bourgeoisie," Lenin wrote in 1912, "has decayed and is already confronted by its grave-diggers—the proletariat." Khrushchev was repeating a moldy cliché, to be found in every Soviet political text these fifty years, when he boasted, "We will bury you!"

These happy auguries have not been fulfilled. Thus far, capitalism has remained alive and flourished, especially where it is most capitalistic. As for the appointed grave-diggers, they are otherwise engaged, busily enlarging their share of goods and rights in ever more affluent societies.

Durability in itself, in short, proves nothing about the *quality* of a way of life or rule. With respect to the USSR, the decisive question is *what* has endured. Is it the promised classless society or a society dominated by a new ruling class? Is it the promised "withering" state or a new breed of absolutism? "Normally the fact that a tyranny has long endured is hardly a recommendation for it, but rather a stronger ground for criticism," Sidney Hook, Professor of Philosophy at New York University, remarked in a recent article. If the dream with which the Great Experiment started has turned into a nightmare, then survival *per se* is not a "victory" but a calamity.

Referring to the anniversary, an able analyst and historian of communism, the Frenchman Boris Souvarine, wrote: "The Soviet regime has indeed endured, by renouncing its initial program, its founding principles, and even its reason for existing." Those close associates of Lenin who "did not believe in the durability of a strictly Bolshevik regime," Souvarine contends, "were perfectly right, for they did not attribute to their political opponents any design to endure through endless, limitless terror."

What has emerged and entrenched itself is not the kind of socialism that Marx or the earliest Bolsheviks envisioned, not the kind that most self-styled socialists anywhere today would acknowledge as such. Before and since the Revolution, orthodox Marxists foresaw total control of an economy through nationalization of the means of production—not the total nationalization of the bodies, minds, and even souls of the entire population. That *had* been foreseen and foretold, with startling accuracy, but only by critics and opponents of Marxism, from Herbert Spencer and Hilaire Belloc to Ludwig von Mises.

What, in truth, are the Soviet Union and its world-wide apparatus celebrating? Not communism, surely, since that has been consigned to a remote and problematical future. Nor the existing socialism, at a time when it is admittedly in deep trouble and trying to extricate itself with capitalist devices. They are celebrating, in the final analysis, merely political staying power—the retention of sole authority by the same group that seized it half a century ago.

If Soviet longevity has demonstrated anything, it is the awesome efficacy of modern totalitarianism, as developed first and most completely in the USSR. Its German variant, too, might well have endured for fifty years had not Hitler, in his madness, gambled his "thousand-year Reich" on a premature war. All regimes and social systems survive until they are overthrown or die of old age. To turn this truism into proof of the superiority of any of them is unworthy of a clear mind.

Promise and Performance

Can the fifty-year-old Soviet Union be reasonably accepted at its own estimate, as a "success story"? The problem in historical accounting is to weigh the constructive against the destructive, the end-product against the human investments; to ascertain whether equivalent or better results could have been obtained by more humane and more moral means.

Russia under Soviet communism has been industrialized to the point where it is second only to the United States, although the distance between them remains enormous. It has built a mighty military machine and is on a par with America in space exploration. Russia has scored high on literacy and in promoting education. It has introduced an array of social services, such as health clinics and old-age pensions. Real wages, the basic index to living standards, have finally, in the last fifteen years or so, reached the levels that prevailed just before World War I and before the Revolution, and since then, though with occasional setbacks, have been rising marginally.

To call these "spectacular achievements" and "miracles of progress" is gibberish. Two all-important facts must be borne in mind:

1. All other major nations have made similar and in most cases greater progress in the same fifty years, without expunging essential political and intellectual freedoms.
2. Russia itself, under a relatively democratic and constitutional government, plus a measure of private enterprise, would unquestionably have done as well; its record in the decades before 1917, as we shall see, leaves little doubt in this respect.

The point is that *there is nothing specifically and exclusively Marxist-Leninist about the real and purported accomplishments,* nothing that has not been attained elsewhere and could not have been attained in Russia without benefit of the Marxist analysis and Soviet methods. It is incumbent on apologists for the Kremlin to prove that communism and communism alone is the magic ingredient capable of such progress.

Actually, as many Western scholars have argued, the vaunted

advances in many areas of Soviet life have been made *despite* communism—despite the built-in handicaps, the paralysis of personal incentives, the wastage of physical and human resources, the drains of mammoth bureaucracies, the priorities assigned to political-ideological over economic imperatives.

The communist contempt for life, to cite one example, operated to destroy large professional and intellectual elites—engineers, scientists, agronomists, professors, administrators—whose brains and expertise the country sorely needed. It was a blunder in practical terms. The Sovietized Russia was obliged to start from scratch, like the most primitive of countries, in many areas where it had at hand —but itself destroyed—inherited resources of knowledge, talent, and experience. Even today the Kremlin is plagued by a paucity of superior people for command posts as it seeks to meet the demands of a more sophisticated technology.

Another example: Deliberately, the communist leaders have punished their impoverished society by stamping out valuable economic activities that could not be forced into collectivist strait jackets. They suppressed the small private artisan and service shops —tailors, shoemakers, tinsmiths, plumbers, etc.—which would have eased existence for a goods-starved population. Once flourishing Russian enterprises, such as family handicraft and cottage industries, were ruled out because they did not lend themselves to total state management. For forty years, billions of man-hours of labor represented by peasant idleness between harvests and new sowings were thrown away; only now are efforts being made to revive village crafts.

A common-sense appraisal of an undertaking, moreover, must take into account its original direction and goals. These, after all, have been the standard excuse for Soviet crimes and deceptions, euphemistically called "great sacrifices." Anyone who sets out for the balmy tropics and ends up in the frozen Arctic, then proclaims the journey a tremendous success, can scarcely be taken seriously. Even if the misdirected expedition brings some incidental benefits and showy trophies, say gaudy marble subways, the blunderers should be denied any medals.

We need only sample the glowing promises to the Russian peoples and the world made before and since the revolution to realize how far Bolshevism has strayed from its charted course. Perfection being beyond mortal grasp, one does not blame communism for failing to reach paradise, but it cannot be held blameless for coming so close to an inferno.

The central promises were explicit in Lenin's pre-Revolutionary writings. He demanded unrestricted mobility for the peasant, release of all political prisoners, severe punishment for officials who make arbitrary arrests or imprison anyone without trial. "Until freedom of assembly, of speech and the press is declared," he said, there would be persecution of "unofficial faith, unofficial opinion, unofficial doctrines." He insisted on the elimination of the death penalty and of the internal passport.

In the months before the October *coup*, the Bolshevik press and speeches recapitulated these pledges and heaped more upon them for good measure. The Soviets, when entrusted with all power, would be "fully democratic," allowing peaceful struggle among all non-bourgeois parties. They would assure "genuine freedom of the press for all." All the nationalities in the country would enjoy self-determination; in Lenin's words, "full restitution of freedom to Finland, the Ukraine, White Russia, the Moslems, etc., . . . including even freedom to secede."

On the brink of the dictatorship, Lenin dared to promise that the state will fade away, since "all need of force will vanish." Not in some remote future, but at once: "The proletarian state begins to wither immediately after its triumph, for in a classless society a state is unnecessary and impossible. . . . Soviet power is a new type of state, in which there is no bureaucracy, no police, no standing army." Also: "So long as the state exists, there is no freedom. When there is freedom, there will be no state."

Within a few months after they attained power, most of the tsarist practices the Leninists had condemned were revived, usually in more ominous forms: political prisoners, convictions without trial and without the formality of charges, savage persecution of dissenting views, death penalties for more varieties of crime than in any other modern nation. The rest were put into effect in the following years, including the suppression of all other parties, restoration of the internal passport, a state monopoly of the press, along with repressive practices the monarchy had outlived for a century or more.

A decree issued immediately after launching the Soviet regime asserted that "workers' control shall be exercised by all the workers and employees of an enterprise." Lenin ordered: "All officials and every kind of deputy must be subjected not only to election but also to recall at any time. Their pay must not exceed that of a competent workman."

His aim, Lenin assured H. G. Wells and others, was "a regime of justice." There would be no more classes, no more "exploitation of man by man," no more rich and poor, plenty for all, equitably distributed, equality and more equality: "The privileges of wealth, of bourgeois education, of social connections, etc., . . . all this disappears under the Soviet organization."

This suggests the flavor of the teeming commitments. I do not wish to imply that they were conceived in falsehood. Without doubt the founding fathers of the Soviet state, certainly in the preparatory years and in the early stages of their rule, were sincere in projecting the dream of their utopian future. This is even more true of the rank-and-file of their followers. Thousands of them, it should be remembered, fought heroically and died willingly for their cause—it took more than the prospect of personal advancement to inspire them.

Human motivation is complex. The individual himself rarely knows where "idealism" ends and the lust for authority begins. The most self-centered among revolutionists rationalize the appetite for power in terms of noble goals and shining visions. It is after power is attained that its corruptions begin to blot out the memory of altruistic commitments or turn them into empty clichés.

Promises of the millennium, of course, are typical for all revolutions and for the most part believed in by those who make them. At the height of the French Terror, Robespierre was saying things like: "Our destiny, most sublime, is to found an empire of wisdom, justice and virtue." This was the mood-music as the guillotine was busily chopping off heads. This was the mood-music, no less, for the torture chambers, the slaughter of innocents, the expansion of the forced-labor population in the USSR. In the midst of the holocaust, Stalin blandly told an American visitor, Roy Howard: "We did not build this society in order to restrict personal liberty but in order that the human individual may feel really free. We built it for the sake of real personal liberty, liberty without quotation marks."

The tune has not been changed in all the years that followed. The premise of a workers' paradise in the first Party Program is repeated with only stylistic changes in the last, that of 1961: "A classless society . . . full social equality for all. . . . Socialism is the road to freedom and happiness for the people. . . . It does away with social inequality. . . . Socialism provides all peasants with land. . . ."

"Communism will bring about the fullest development of all the productive forces of society," Khrushchev declaimed in early 1956. "It will be a social system where all the fountains of social wealth will flow freely, where every individual will work with enthusiasm according to his abilities and will be compensated for his labors according to his needs." Three years later, in Albania, he called communism "the long-awaited dream of the working class, the bright future of humanity."

The flow of promissory noises never abates, never falters. The high-priests and their acolytes, at home and abroad, intone the ritual without thinking of its meaning or its absurdity in the light of events and experience. They appear to be blind to the comical aspect of explaining again and again the wonders that socialism will bring, when they have repeatedly attested that socialism has already been achieved. The repetition is not effrontery. It is habitual, automatic incantation.

Who listens? Certainly not the Soviet populace. It has become inured to the mumbo-jumbo. More than a hundred years ago, one of their great Revolutionary forebears, Alexander Herzen, wrote: "*A goal endlessly remote is not a goal, if you please, but a hoax. The goal must be nearer. The goal for each generation is itself.*" Few of the Kremlin's subjects are acquainted with this profound warning, but they know its truth in their flesh and bones. It is only in the outside world that the ritual promises still work their ancient sorcery.

The current generation in Russia, as the Soviet press no longer bothers to conceal, is bored by this stale verbiage. It scoffs at the great mirage of a socialist Elysium in their totalitarian desert; the more thoughtful resent it as an insult to their intelligence. But at least a part of the first generation found the fare thrilling. It was romantic, idyllic, above all, optimistic—a period of hardships and cruelties, and presto! the happy society in their own lifetimes.

For hordes of impatient radicals in the non-Soviet world, too, those craving instant utopia, it was all so intoxicating that the effects persisted long after the promises had been broken a thousandfold and turned into their opposites. In the long run, of course, nearly all of them were disillusioned. In the time of hangover that followed they often protested that they had been cheated, although in fact they had cheated themselves.

But they held on as long as they could. Parroting a colleague of mine in the Moscow press corps, they shrugged off every new Soviet excess with the adage that you can't make an omelet without breaking eggs. They merely failed to notice or report that the omelet was inedible and stank to high heaven.

For those who still cling to shreds of faith in Marxism, the murder of the dream of a workers' paradise, democratic and egalitarian —a dream that had warmed myriad noble hearts for a century— may well appear to be the cruelest atrocity of all in the record of Soviet communism.

Marxism was supposed to be a science, with fixed laws that took the ifs out of history. It was a guarantee of success: the advent of a viable socialism was inevitable. This was one of its great appeals in an age when a superstitious faith in science was displacing older, non-scientific faiths. The Russian years have demolished the scientific pretensions and certainties of Marx and his major disciples. The exuberance of the promises in the end made the disillusionment more dismal and frustrating.

Marxism survives as a vague pseudo-religion of many denominations, but as a "science" it is dead. A historian at the University of Michigan, Arthur P. Mendel, entitled an article in *Foreign Affairs* (October, 1966), "The Rise and Fall of 'Scientific Socialism.' " Especially inside the Soviet Union, he showed abundantly, the presumed Marxist "laws" of history and economics were being softpedaled, either ignored or pruned to match inexorable realities. Most of those, the world over, who still hold on to socialist nomenclature for its emotional and propaganda values—like the Social Democrats in Germany and the Labourites in England—have openly discarded Marx and the clutter of inevitabilities associated with his doctrines. They are no longer offered as a blueprint but, at best, as a useful hypothesis.

Costs and Continuity

An annual, or a fifty-year, report on a business enterprise which limited itself to alleged profits but slurred over the major costs would be dismissed on the face of it as falsification. This is no less true for the bookkeeping of a historical enterprise.

Defenders of Soviet communism, now as in the past, extol and magnify the credits, but disregard or dissemble the debits. At most they allude to "great sacrifices" without spelling them out fully and truthfully. They can maintain the pitch of enthusiasm only by ignoring the fearsome costs to the Russian peoples and the rest of mankind.

It is a price paid in the coin of terror, forcible collectivization, man-made famine, slave-labor camps, blood-purges, thought control, brutal exploitation of workers and farmers, persecution of religion, political oppressions, genocidal massacres, and deportations. This does not exhaust the melancholy inventory, for it must embrace other costs that cannot be reduced to figures.

There is no arithmetic to measure the wretchedness and agony of hundreds of millions of human beings, year after year, their fears and despairs and humiliations, their physical deprivations, moral degradations, and spiritual starvation. In the balance sheet there must be great spaces for maimed minds and spirits, for the silenced and intimidated, the imprisoned and undernourished, for broken families, wrecked hopes, wasted fervor, and tormented conscience. How does one calculate the price tag for denial of an inner sanctuary of retreat for religious believers, cultural isolation from civilized humanity, the intellectual trauma of coerced conformity and hypocrisy?

The price exacted from the world at large, beyond the billion human beings submerged by the communist tides, also weighs heavily in any fair accounting. The degree of the Kremlin's responsibility may be disputed, but not the fact itself that the Soviet masters were midwives to the modern scourge of totalitarianism. Professor Sidney Hook has given his opinion on this score: "There is good reason to believe that without Bolshevism and the international revolutionary strategy of the Communist International, the world would have escaped Fascism."

The Bolsheviks pioneered the basic techniques and set the pattern for fascist adaptations in Italy, Germany, and elsewhere: The one omnipotent party of blindly obedient zealots, the single-slate "elections," the gigantic concentration camps, the substitution of slogans for thought. Both in Italy and Germany, as we shall see in its proper context later, their policies directly helped open the floodgates to fascist inundations.

At the same time Moscow's obsessive drive for global hegemony sowed chaos in international relations, inspired declared and undeclared wars, provoked civil wars, imposed back-breaking burdens of armaments. Today, it continues to spread a pall of apprehension and uncertainty over the whole planet.

The magnitude of these multiple costs through half a century has been set forth in thousands of books and articles. An encyclopaedia larger than any in existence would be needed to describe and document them all. Their character and dimensions will be apparent in the body of this book, and will be summarized in the concluding chapters.

Any judgment on the communist half-century that omits or blurs the staggering toll paid by the Russian peoples and the rest of mankind, I submit, is either deliberate or unconscious falsification. What is more, the costs cannot be dismissed by reference to the milder political weather in recent years.

As Arthur M. Schlesinger, Jr. said in New Delhi in 1962: "The fact that one dictator eventually acknowledges the crimes of his predecessor is not enough to assure future justice." Neither is it enough to wash out the guilt of their regime, particularly when the crimes condoned by silence outweigh by far those confessed.

An editorial in the *New York Times* on the highly selective indictment of Stalin by his heirs declared: "The prime factor which made possible Stalin's crimes, those acknowledged and those still unavowed, was the dictatorial nature of the Soviet state and the ideological nature of the state's goals." More than ten years have passed since Khrushchev's denunciation of his departed master. Endless hymns have been sung to the Thaw and de-Stalinization. But neither the state's nature nor its goals have changed.

They cannot change, whatever marginal concessions and reforms the Kremlin may decree for tactical reasons, as long as it remains totalitarian. And it cannot cease to be totalitarian without ceasing to *be*. An end to Soviet ideology and the coming of anything like representative constitutional government would eliminate both the justification and the need for the imposed communist government. It would mean political suicide for the regime and the physical liquidation of its bosses, so that they are, in the last analysis, trapped by their history.

In any case, the hope of evolving freedom from totalitarianism is the dream-stuff of political alchemists. Suppose that Adolf Hitler had died and his successors, say Goering and Goebbels, tried to mollify a restive population by easing the terror; suppose that they, too, admitted some of Hitler's crimes and "rehabilitated" a few of his long-dead victims. Would that have altered the character of Nazism or erased its sins? Would anyone have dared to argue that we should "let bygones be bygones" and judge the Nazi oligarchy by its newly "mellowed" condition of "de-Hitlerization"?

This is the substance of the situation in the USSR. The ambivalence of world opinion on the two brands of despotism, Brown and Red, is a curious phenomenon. Although Nazism has been wiped out, mankind has neither forgotten nor forgiven its crimes. But we are importuned from some directions to forget and forgive crimes of the same order and much larger dimensions by Soviet communism—despite the fact that this tyranny is still very much alive and still engaged in the old iniquities.

The impulse of a well-intentioned and wishful-hoping world has been to exaggerate the professed "mellowing" in the Soviet empire. This has induced waves of euphoria in some quarters. There is loose talk of "liberalization," though the Kremlin mocks the word and dreads the idea. With the passing of time and changing conditions, there are inevitably modifications, adjustments, easements; but basically Soviet Russia remains a closed society, police-ridden, censor-ridden, ruled by the same Communist Party still led largely by men formed and hardened in Stalin's service. Their awesome machinery of internal espionage and terror has not been dismantled. Not a dent has been made in their monopoly of political power.

Another element is pertinent to the kind of historical assessment this book is attempting. Worried by growing popular skepticism about the essence of the matter—their right to rule—the Soviet leaders are anxiously emphasizing the *continuity* of their party.

They have no alternative, since that is the sole basis of their claims to succession. If they were to disown their past, they would in effect be declaring themselves to be usurpers.

That is why Khrushchev found it necessary to exempt large chunks of Stalinism from his revelations. That is why Brezhnev and Kosygin are cautiously but clearly restoring Stalin to respectability as a good communist, if not yet as an admirable personality. This is why, above all, Kremlin propaganda seeks to intensify the cult of Lenin—the one thread that gives the appearance of continuity. Complete rejection of Stalin—a twenty-five-year hole in Soviet history, half the life-span of the regime—would cut the thread and strip the rulers of the last semblance of legitimacy even within their own frame of reference. Already the party's credentials for ruling have been opened to so much doubt that the new bosses, as we shall see in the chapter on de-Stalinization, have all but foreclosed further criticism of Stalin and are rediscovering his "positive side."

The first Party Congress under the Brezhnev-Kosygin aegis, in March–April, 1966, did not formally "rehabilitate" the lost leader, as many top-shelf Soviet intellectuals feared would happen. But it did revive some institutions connected with Stalin's name and make clear that no additional vilification of Stalin would be sanctioned.

A quarter-century void between itself and the historic source of its authority is too dangerous for the Kremlin hierarchy. But the hierarchs cannot have it both ways. They cannot have their indispensable continuity, from Lenin to themselves, yet shrug off responsibility for Stalin's "mistakes" and for admitted mistakes since Stalin even unto Khrushchev. Our appraisal, to make logic, must take account of the entire history.

Myths and Realities

For fifty years the rulers of a great nation, with its total resources at their disposal, have operated the largest, most expertly staffed, scientifically planned, and lavishly financed propaganda machine in all history. Here was the first government on record—the only government until the birth of its fascist and Nazi counterparts—that looked upon the shaping of thought at home and its manipulation abroad as a primary function, with a prior lien on national budget, brains, and energies.

It is perhaps not too remarkable, therefore, that the Kremlin should have succeeded to an extraordinary extent in imposing on the world its own version of its own history. Yet one marvels at the scope of this propaganda achievement and the daring with which it has been managed.

The major myths of the past evolved through generations or centuries, growing as a tree grows. But the panoplied Soviet mythology has been fabricated in our own times, under our very eyes. It hasn't grown but has been deliberately constructed, wings and towers and galleries added as required and demolished when no longer useful. Events fresh in men's minds have been arbitrarily recast, words and concepts turned inside out, current biographies stood on their heads, annoying witnesses wiped out. Soviet history has been a loose-leaf record, yesterday's defeats turned into today's victories, obvious or ascertainable facts of everyday life simply denied.

An amazing aspect of this phenomenon is that the official Soviet versions find less credence inside the USSR than they do abroad.

Although dissent from the official myths is dangerous, or even punishable, within the Soviet frontiers, no intelligent citizen believes, to cite the most elementary examples, that the Bolsheviks overthrew the Russian monarchy; that they have a "classless society"; that they live better and more contentedly than people in the advanced non-Soviet countries; that the collectivization of agriculture was voluntary and has been a great success; that the Soviet system has promoted intellectual and cultural progress. Yet hordes of otherwise informed men and women in the non-Soviet world, often self-styled "intellectuals," historians, scientists, clergymen, educators, do believe such nonsense.

All nations, of course, have their cherished myths, normally rooted in their pasts. Soviet Russia is the one country in which both its history and its present conditions add up to a vast mythology. Its components are not merely untrue but often the opposite of the truth. And now, to cap the structure, we have the thriving post-Stalin legend that the society is in a process of true "liberalization," coming closer and closer to democratic standards and, in the words of a United States Senator, "definitely veering toward capitalism."

I propose to examine the more significant of the myths, separating the elements of fact from the billowing fictions. Since they are all interconnected and interdependent, a certain amount of repetition is unavoidable.

1 / Revolution

The myth that the Bolsheviks came to power
through revolution.

What transpired in the night of November 6–7, 1917, and in the
years that followed has been referred to, these fifty years, as a revolution. The proletariat, yearning for communism, rose in majestic
might and drove the bourgeois money-changers out of the temples
of labor. This is grotesque falsification. In truth, the Bolsheviks,
with no mandate except their contempt for mandates, pulled off a
coup d'état, a *putsch*, and, since it was directed against a revolution
already in full eruption, it was in essence, a *counter*revolution.

This is not semantic quibbling. It is indispensable to keeping the
Soviet half-century in focus. Long, long ago Confucius gave his
famous injunction: "See to it that things are called by their right
name." In the sense that social prophets have accepted it, revolution implies a spontaneous popular explosion—masses goaded beyond endurance revolting at last against injustice. No matter how
the definition is stretched and twisted, it does not cover the Bolshevik seizure of power. That was a deed plotted in secrecy, condemned by those in whose name it was done, denounced by many
of the Bolshevik chieftains themselves.

Lenin, Trotsky, and their cohorts did not overthrow the monarchy. They overthrew the first democratic society in Russian history, set up through a truly popular revolution in March, 1917—a
revolution that climaxed a century of struggle, education, preparation and heroism; a society Lenin himself called "the freest country
in the world." Free but weak and hungry, attempting to continue
the exhausting war with Germany—in short, easy prey for political
adventurers.

A more accurate understanding of what really happened strips the plotters of revolutionary glamour and absolves the Russian peoples of blood guilt for the disaster. The Bolsheviks did not command an uprising but engineered a conspiratorial power-grab. They did not free the people—the people freed *them*. The fall of the monarchy caught the Bolshevik leaders by surprise. Lenin and Zinoviev learned of the event from the newspapers in Switzerland, Trotsky and Bukharin from the newspapers in New York. Stalin was among the lesser figures in exile colonies within Russia.

Lenin and some thirty disciples reached Petrograd on April 16, 1917, having been conducted across Germany in a sealed train by the Kaiser's goverment—a calculated injection of poison into the already fevered Russian bloodstream. The purpose of Germany, which still had vast armies tied up on its eastern fronts, was merely to compound the chaos in Russia and drive it out of the war. Though Lenin came well supplied with German funds, he was decidedly no dupe of the Kaiser. He was calling for a proletarian overthrow of the German monarchy and of the Provisional Government in his own country with equal vehemence. Neither Wilhelm II nor his generals understood or cared what Lenin stood for.

Leon Trotsky arrived in May, others straggled in from foreign exiles and remote corners of the Russian empire. They represented the smallest of the Russian radical movements. Launched at the turn of the century as a minority faction within the Social Democratic Party, it claimed twenty-five thousand members when the Romanoff dynasty fell but probably had about fifteen thousand. Years later the estimate was upped to eighty thousand, but even that was small compared with the hundreds of thousands in the ranks of the Mensheviks and much larger memberships in the party of Social Revolutionaries, non-Marxist socialists based on the peasantry rather than the working class. In the Putilov Works in Petrograd, a stronghold of revolutionary sentiment, there were only thirty-odd Bolsheviks in mid-1917.

But theirs was a movement that scoffed at numbers and frankly mistrusted the multitudes. The workers could be educated for their role *after* the revolution; they would not be led but driven to the terrestrial heaven. Lenin always sneered at the obsession of competing socialist groups with their "mass base." "Give us an organization of professional revolutionaries," he used to say, "and we will turn Russia upside down." The differences between him and the other socialist parties were those of techniques and tempos rather than ultimate objectives.

Revolution, in his view, was not a popular surge in the romantic tradition. It was a swift, deadly blow by a small, disciplined elite, unencumbered by moral or humanitarian baggage. It was a job for full-time professionals, in Lenin's words: "a small tight kernel consisting of reliable, experienced and steeled workers . . . connected by all the rules of conspiracy."

Not an open movement but a private cabal, with the masses so much raw stuff for processing. Neither the workers nor the people at large had any inherent rights, least of all the right to choose between alternative social systems. Their hopes, greeds, and despairs were motive power to be channeled in the way an engineer channels electricity. When the advanced portion (meaning those who obeyed him) has sufficient "striking forces," Lenin explained in 1919, it must "conquer the power of the state, and then use the power of the state, that is, the dictatorship of the proletariat, as an instrument of its class in order *to gain the sympathy of the majority of the toilers.*"

Thus, in the second year of his rule, Lenin did not bother to pretend that the regime already had the sympathy of the toilers. First you hijack control, then you make them like it: except for the revolutionary jargon and the lofty goals, it was the strongarm code of gangsterdom. The Bolsheviks had left it to others to "go to the people," to organize labor unions, to stir up the sluggish peasants, and finally to topple the old order. Meanwhile Lenin perfected his conspiratorial machine to exploit an upheaval when it came.

A mass movement or a small, centrally controlled conspiracy? This was the main rock on which the Social Democratic party of Russia had split, at a "unification" congress begun in Brussels and finished in London in the summer of 1903, into groupings variously described as hards and softs, extremists and moderates, but eventually designated as Bolsheviks and Mensheviks.

There were at the start forty-odd delegates at the meeting. As the heated polemics unwound, many of these walked out to register disagreement. Their withdrawal left the group generaled by Lenin with a majority of two votes. He seized upon this accident, shrewdly, to call his faction "the majority"—*bolshinstvo* in Russian —and its members, accordingly, Bolsheviks. His opponents, though they spoke for an overwhelming majority of the socialist rank-and-file in the home country, meekly accepted the designation of Mensheviks—minority-ites—and the two false labels stuck.

The twenty-four-year-old Trotsky, wooed by both factions, took a middle ground, joining neither the Bolsheviks nor the Mensheviks, but he identified the cancer in Bolshevism with extraordinary precision. "In Lenin's scheme," he wrote in 1904, "the party takes the place of the working class. The party organization displaces the party. The Central Committee displaces the party organization, and finally, the Dictator displaces the Central Committee."

Unfortunately for himself and Russia, he disowned his own prophetic wisdom in early 1917 and joined Lenin. Perhaps the temptations of leadership and the splendors of power were too much for this ego-ridden intellectual.

Beyond a determination to capture the revolution and a Machiavellian code of conduct, the Bolsheviks who streamed into the capital had no plan. In the end the focused will of Lenin proved plan enough. He excoriated the hesitant as dolts and cowards and drove them to the *putsch*, which most of them opposed until the last hour, and many after its initial success, as an insane adventure.

The Soviets were not a Bolshevik invention. (The word means simply "councils.") During the 1905 revolution Soviets representing trade unions, peasant groups, and political organizations arose spontaneously in a number of Russian cities to direct revolutionary policy and strategy. The most important of these, in St. Petersburg, was headed by young Trotsky. They came into being again in 1917, under the imposing title of Workers', Peasants', and Soldiers' Deputies, ostensibly as a forum for discussing problems and issues, but almost at once assuming quasi-governmental authority.

With the moderate and democratic political leaders concentrating on the Provisional Government, the Soviets tended to attract the more impatient and demagogic spokesmen. The "bourgeois" elements were not excluded; they were unwelcome and stayed away.

Soviet sessions were noisy, disordered, impulsive, often in session day and night, the deputies for the most part designated in factories and military barracks, but often self-appointed. The disciplined Leninists easily infiltrated and in time had narrow majorities in the Petrograd, Moscow, and a few other Soviets; in most of the provincial Soviets they were minorities or without any representation. For the Leninists the Soviets provided a potent instrument against the hard-pressed government and they used it as a cover for their manipulations, in the way that countless communist fronts were destined to be used all over the world in the years ahead.

In raising the cry of "All power to the Soviets!" the Bolsheviks gave it a populist and even democratic ring, with no hint of the one-party monopoly to come. On the contrary, the slogan was baited with democratic pledges, couched in the vocabulary of freedom. In the preparatory months, Lenin, tongue in cheek, warned against "total power." He laughed and fumed at enemies who said he planned to abolish private ownership and impose communism. To what lengths those bourgeois gentry go in maligning the tribunes of the people! He denied angrily that his communists had communist intentions.

A more complete record of deceit can hardly be found in the annals of demagogy. The Bolsheviks lied, *had* to lie, because they knew that the population, the working class included, had no desire for expropriation and communism. The peasants, for whom the revolution meant simply personal land ownership, would have been frightened out of their wits by talk of nationalization—and they made up 85 per cent of the population. In the pre-*putsch* months every issue of *Pravda*, then edited by Molotov and Stalin, offered freedom, civil liberties, the secret ballot, a Constituent Assembly, even-handed justice, the right to strike, the right of non-Russian peoples to secede from the empire; above all, immediate peace. The Molotovs and Stalins believed in none of these things —they were promising what they knew the people wanted.

The Soviet seizure of power in Petrograd was accomplished, in Lenin's words, by "an amazingly small number." In a city of one million, the actual forces involved were less than twenty thousand, most of them newly created Red Guards. Even these contingents were pathetically duped, having not the remotest notion of the real purposes for which they were being used. They were striking out, they thought, for the multi-party Soviets, for freedom, equality, and other goals which their organizers regarded as emotional garbage.

With very little effort and few casualties, the insurgents took over the telephone and telegraph centrals, police headquarters, other public buildings, strategic points, and the main printing establishments. Only the high command of the Provisional Government, headed by Alexander Kerensky, held out late into the night in the old tsarist Winter Palace, bravely defended by a women's battalion then on duty. The last stand was of no avail. The battleship *Aurora* bombarded the headquarters from the Neva River, while the Red Guards laid siege on the ground. Kerensky and a few other leaders succeeded in escaping before the capitulation.

And so a handful of able, cynical men simply captured the revolution from its makers. Their real intentions had been carefully concealed from the Red Guards and the regular soldiers who smashed the Provisional Government, from the small left wing of Kerensky's own party, the Social Revolutionaries, who supported the *coup*, and even from the rank-and-file of the Bolshevik party.

The historic tide that swept away the throne was running wild. The more moderate socialists and democrats sought to curb the flood. Only Lenin and some of his associates—not all by any means —chose to ride the turbulence. War-weary troops were deserting the fronts and spreading like lava over the country. Peasants were seizing and dividing the land. Workers in some places were taking control of factories and mines. Along came the Bolsheviks—of whom the populace had scarcely heard—and urged them all to do what they were doing in any case.

Everybody promised peace and land. But the moderates promised it for tomorrow, when an elected parliament would lay down the rules. The Leninists outbid them. "Take what you want," they shouted, "take it now, including peace." Their membership swelled. Few of the new members had any idea of the implications of Marxism, world revolution, and the rest.

The supposed upsurge of sentiment for "proletarian dictatorship" is a subsequent invention. Earlier such things were mentioned only to be denied. That dictatorship of the proletariat turned out to be, as Trotsky and others had foreseen a dozen years before, a dictatorship *over* the proletariat, over the ruling party, and over the rest of the country.

The very idea of a Russian proletariat was a piece of duplicity. For this we have Lenin's own testimony. On December 25, 1919, when he could afford to tell some truths with impunity, he taunted some of his followers in this connection. "What is a proletariat?" he asked them. "It is a class which is occupied in big industry. But where is your industry? The industrial proletariat . . . has been dislocated, has ceased to exist as a proletariat . . . the proletariat vanished." In other words, the dictatorship of a class which was negligible when it theoretically assumed total sovereignty and was non-existent two years after the assumption!

The seizure of power for a mythical proletariat was a bluff. Nearly all of Lenin's associates were terrified by the wildness of his bluffs. They knew that his trumped-up government represented nothing and nobody, and they were frightened of the consequences. This was why so many of them urged the enlistment of partners in the game through coalition with other socialist and peasant groups. Lenin allowed negotiations with other parties to be started, but only as a tactic of deception: "a diplomatic move to divert attention from the military operations"—the awesome civil war had begun.

Only ten days after the *coup*, five members of Lenin's Central Committee resigned in protest against his high-handed methods. His "disastrous policy," their statement said, was "carried out against the will of an enormous majority of the proletariat and soldiers." They demanded a "socialist government of all parties in the Soviet," because "the alternative is a purely Bolshevik government which can maintain itself only by means of political terror." The signers included Gregory Zinoviev, who was to reign for years over the Communist International, and Alexei Rykov, who in 1924 would succeed Lenin as Premier—both of them fated to be executed by Stalin in the great blood-purges to come.

When the extent of the deception became apparent, other staunch Bolsheviks and fellow travelers—Krassin, Vorovsky, Kamenev, Maxim Gorki, Alexandra Kollontai, and others—assailed Lenin as a mad gambler and worse. Eventually all of them returned to his honeypots of power, but that could not cancel out the truth of their words.

Two weeks after the Bolshevik usurpation, Gorki, the gifted novelist of the working class, wrote in his own paper, *Novaya Zhizn:* "Blind fanatics and unscrupulous adventurers are rushing headlong toward 'social revolution'—as a matter of fact it is the road to anarchy and ruin of the proletariat and the revolution. Along this road Lenin and his aides think it is possible to commit all crimes. . . . The working class must not allow adventurers and madmen to throw upon the proletariat the responsibility for the disgraceful, senseless and bloody crimes. . . ."

Other powerful voices within the communist fold were raised. Alexandra Kollontai, later to be a famous Soviet ambassadress, charged publicly that the communist leaders, "having severed all ties with the masses, carry out their own policy . . . under cover of the party label." Another and greater woman revolutionist, Rosa Luxemburg, leader of the German communist Spartacus League, while defending the new Soviet regime in principle, denounced its totalitarian nature. "The remedy discovered by Lenin and Trotsky," she warned, "is worse than the evil it is supposed to cure."

"With repression of political life in the land as a whole, life in the Soviets must also become more and more crippled," she wrote in 1918. "Without general elections, without unrestricted freedom of press and assembly, without a free struggle of opinions, life dies out in every public institution, becomes a mere semblance of life, in which only the bureaucracy remains an active element."

Such conditions, she foresaw, "must inevitably cause a brutalization of public life." But Rosa Luxemburg was repudiated by her own Sparticists; mesmerized by Lenin's success, the German communists obeyed his orders, tried to duplicate his course—and failed dismally. She did not live to see the ugly fulfillment of her prophecies; a few months after she wrote them, she was abducted and murdered by German right-wing extremists.

Inside the bleeding Russia, protests were soon squelched, with the supression of all but the government newspapers, the expulsion of non-Bolsheviks from the Soviets, the arrests of most champions of decency, the execution of tens of thousands. In justice to these martyrs for the cause of freedom, whatever one may think of their different social theories, it should be recognized that the communist power-grab was not an expression of the dominant revolutionary trends of the preceding century but a reversal and rejection of their humanitarian essence.

Ever since December, 1825, when the "Decembrist" attack on the monarchy took place in St. Petersburg, revolutionary thought and organization in Russia had been grounded in the all-importance of the person. The great Russian philosopher, Nicholas Berdiaev, writing after the triumph of Bolshevism, emphasized that even in its most extreme manifestations, the Russian revolutionary movement still retained a religious impulse. Nechayevism, a Russian and more bloody version of Machiavellism, was the exception, untypical, and a minor ingredient. Unfortunately, with the triumph of Bolshevism, the exception prevailed.

Far from making a revolution, the Leninists strangled the revolution in its infancy. But the country did not submit meekly or forget its revolutionary heritage. Millons have paid with their liberty and their lives for a resistance, violent or passive, that began on the day the Leninists took all power and has continued to this day.

2 / The People

The myth that the masses supported the Bolshevik seizure of power.

History à la Kremlin has convinced a large part of the world that the common people in Russia, especially the workers, rallied to the defense of the Bolshevik dictatorship. The opposition, it avers, came from monarchists, capitalists, landlords, aristocrats, and other assorted "reactionaries."

To make this credible, Soviet historians have had to gloss over, with a few outrageous lies, the national elections held within eighteen days after the *coup d'état.*

The hopes of self-government unleashed by the fall of tsarism were centered on the Constituent Assembly, a democratic parliament to draw up a democratic constitution. Lenin and his followers, of course, jumped on that bandwagon, too, posing not merely as advocates of the parliament but as its only true friends. What if the voting went against them? They piously pledged themselves to abide by the popular mandate.

"As a democratic government," *Pravda* asserted on the morrow of the seizure of power, "we cannot disregard the decision of the people, even if we do not agree with it. If the peasants follow the Social Revolutionaries farther, even if they give that party a majority in the Constituent Assembly, we shall say: so be it."

In his first weeks Lenin did not yet feel himself strong enough to renege on the most conspicuous of his pledges. The balloting began on November 25, and continued until December 9. Despite the prevailing disorders and confusion, thirty-six million cast their secret ballots in parts of the country normal enough to hold elections. In most of the large centers of population, *the voting was conducted under Bolshevik auspices.*

Yet twenty-seven of the thirty-six million votes went to other parties. The peasant-oriented Social Revolutionaries received 58 per cent; Lenin's lists drew nine million, only about 25 per cent, less than half as many as the only other well-organized party. As David Shub put it in his biography of Lenin, "The Russian people, in the freest election in modern history, voted for moderate socialism and against the bourgeoisie." They voted *against* the Bolsheviks.

Lenin had no doubt that if the elected parliament survived, his imposed regime would not. He had not expected to win a majority and never had any intention of allowing such a democratic institution to sink roots. Already unsure of the allegiance of locally based troops, he had imported a division of Lettish sharpshooters as military insurance.

The assembly was scheduled to meet in the old Duma Building, the Tauride Palace, in Petrograd on the afternoon of January 18, 1918. That morning massive columns of unarmed workers and peasants marched toward the center of the city with banners hailing the parliament and proclaiming their faith in democracy. Thousands more joined up, in a jubilant spirit, as the parade proceeded. But when the procession approached Tauride Palace, its path was blocked by the sharpshooters, who opened fire without warning. About a hundred of the peaceful demonstrators were killed, hundreds were wounded, the rest fled in panic.

Despite this sanguinary prelude, the deputies from all over Russia gathered for their first—and last—meeting. Victor Chernov, of the majority Social Revolutionary party, was elected chairman. Except for the communist members, and perhaps even for many of them, it was a solemn historical moment. The Constituent Assembly was the embodiment of a vision that had been Russia's for a century. But they found the galleries and the aisles filled by noisy, drunken, jeering crowds—admission tickets had been issued solely by Lenin's soldiers.

The "guests" shouted down the delegates, intruded on the platform, and subsided only when Bolsheviks rose to speak. Others had to struggle against a raucous, whistling, foul-mouthed mob. Lenin lolled on the stairs leading to the platform, sneering and jeering and egging on his unruly bullyboys. Fighting the turbulence at every step, the democratic majority managed to debate and adopt a number of cardinal resolutions. The most important provided far-reaching agrarian reforms, under which the land would be distributed to those who worked it.

When the session adjourned toward dawn, everyone knew it would never reopen. The first and last genuine expression of the people's will after the revolution was suppressed in cynicism and violence.

The more optimistic deputies, returning to the Tauride Palace the next day, found its doors locked and sealed. The fate of the Revolution, too, was sealed. No one who respects fact could ever again claim that the regime had been approved by the masses. In an eloquent indictment of the "handful of madmen" who had murdered the elected assembly, Gorki wrote a fitting epithet:

"Yesterday the streets of Petrograd and Moscow resounded with shouts of 'Long live the Constituent Assembly!' For giving vent to these sentiments the peaceful paraders were shot down by the 'People's Government.' On January 19, the Constituent Assembly expired—until the advent of happier days—its death foreboding new sufferings for the martyred country and for the masses of the people."

The maddest of the madmen was merely amused by such rhetoric. He valued a Lettish rifleman above all the intellectual humanitarians put together. To associates who complained in the name of Russia, Lenin said: "I spit on Russia. . . . This is merely one phase through which we must pass on the way to a world revolution." Russia, in other words, was expendable, a battered beachhead in a war for world dominion.

• Red Army and Red Terror

The titanic resistance touched off by the capture of power on November 7 was raised to a pitch of frenzy by the crushing of the Constituent Assembly. But history is written by the victors. In this case their "dialectical" trick was to present the sprawling and intricate struggle of 1917–1921 as merely a two-way contest between so-called Reds and Whites, the "revolution" and the "counterrevolution."

Actually it was a bizarre complex of conflicts covering the whole political spectrum, from monarchists and national separatists to anarchists, fighting each other in shifting patterns of alliance and betrayal, with mass desertions and re-desertions. There were endless gradations of Whites, Reds, Greens, and even a Yellow-and-Blue contender. The babble of slogans for which tens of thousands died included "All power to the Constituent Assembly!" and "Soviets without communists!" Competing armies fought for the national independence of the Ukraine, with its forty million inhabitants; of Georgia in the Caucasus; of the Moslem nationalities in Central Asia.

Virtually all the clashing guerrilla formations and organized armies were anti-communist. But they were so divided by mutual hatreds that the Bolshevik forces—whipped into a Red Army by the genius of Leon Trotsky—could triumph in the end. At the lowest point in its fortunes the Soviet regime controlled only a small area around Moscow and Petrograd; many of the leaders were then packing for what they considered imminent defeat and flight abroad.

Under war cries directed against the Right, the Leninists, in fact, concentrated on demolishing the Left. With good reason, they feared opposition socialists, revolutionaries, and liberals more than all the monarchists put together. While the country was overwhelmingly hostile to the Bolsheviks, it was no less frightened of a return of landlords, aristocrats, and monarchists. For Lenin and his associates the primary dangers were the revolutionaries and democrats. Their prisons were soon crammed with men and women famous in Russian revolutionary annals. Tsarist generals willing to work for Trotsky had more chance of saving their skins than non-Bolshevik veterans of the long fight against the old order.

The civil war—one of the longest and bloodiest in modern times —was not only military. It was no less bloody on the civilian side, in peasant revolts, strikes, looting, sabotage, from one end of the empire to the other. The Red Army was the answer to the military challenge—to deal with the civilian challenge there was the Red Terror. The two, of course, were intricately interwoven.

The long reign of Bolshevism began with a decree, on November 8, abolishing capital punishment—and an orgy of executions. When Lenin, who was absent, heard of the decree he was furious. How dared they give in to what he had once called the "intelligentsia-bred prejudice" against taking life! Trotsky was to write later, "Lenin at every opportunity kept hammering into our heads that terror was unavoidable." Trotsky's own leonine head needed no hammering: he had plenty of the homicidal zest that seems to go with self-righteousness. "As for us," Trotsky declared in 1920, "we were never concerned with the Kantian-priestly and vegetarian-Quaker prattle about the 'sacredness of life' "—thus justifying in advance his own eventual murder by Stalin's killers.

In remarkably short order Lenin and the rest won a place in the select company of history's mass murderers that counts Caligula, Genghis Khan, Tamerlane, Fouquier-Tinville, and Hitler. The hostage system—the killing of innocents at random to avenge real or imagined attacks on the new rulers—was carried to extreme lengths. "One person out of ten will be shot, whether guilty or not," an early warning said. The ratio was rapidly stepped up.

Under the fanatic Pole, Felix Djerzhinski, the newly formed security organization, the Cheka (from the first letters of each word of the full Russian name: *che* and *ka*) began to carve its initials on the naked and writhing body of Russia. His "revolutionary sword" was wielded like a butcher knife.

If the Pole was the technician of Red Terror, Lenin was its theoretician. The myth has it that the Red Terror was merely the answer to its White counterpart. In fact it had been promised and justified many years in advance. "There must be submission to the armed vanguard," Lenin wrote. "During the period when the proletariat still needs the state, it does not require it in the interests of freedom but in the interests of crushing its antagonists." His terror was wreaked not only on the Whites, but also, and especially, on Reds of other persuasions.

Lenin looked down on the Reign of Terror in the French Revolution as a piffling affair. "The guillotine," he said, "only terrorized *active* resistance. . . . We have to break down passive resistance, which doubtless is the most harmful and dangerous of all." Where the French Terror was directed against real oppositionists, the Soviet Terror sought to destroy also those who *might*, because of their social origins or character, oppose the new masters in the future.

Besides prison and death, Lenin proposed calculated use of hunger and forced labor to erase actual and potential non-conformists. (Later Stalin thus showed himself to be a good Leninist.) "We shall be ruthless toward our enemies," Lenin announced, "as well as toward all hesitant and noxious elements in our midst." "All hesitant and noxious elements"—on the face of it, this was a formula that took in the whole population.

When protests against the blood madness were voiced abroad, Lenin released "an open letter to American workers." "The British bourgeoisie," he argued, "have forgotten their year 1649, the French their 1795. . . . Now the terror is criminal and cruel when the workers and poor peasants use it against the bourgeoisie."

This was Lenin at his most cynical. He knew well enough that those who shrank in revulsion from his cruelties were no less horrified by the cruelties of other dictators in other times. More important, he knew that his terror was being applied not *by* but *against* the workers and peasants.

Beyond Moscow and Petrograd, little Lenins aped the leader. In Bryansk the death penalty was decreed for drunkenness; in Vyatka for "leaving the house after 8 P.M."; in many areas for theft, anti-regime leaflets, a hundred other new-minted capital crimes. In the course of a talk to a neighborhood Soviet, Zinoviev called for the extermination of ten million: "We must win over to our side ninety of the one hundred million inhabitants of Russia under the Soviets. As for the rest, we have nothing to say to them; they must be annihilated." History proved his estimates far too modest—and he would himself be among the annihilated.

The orgy of blood-letting must be understood as a measure of the resistance met by the usurpers. Terror was no less horrifying in scale and brutality on the part of the regime's adversaries. Unspeakable atrocities were committed on all sides, and each inflamed passions and bred retaliatory savagery. Anti-Jewish pogroms unleashed by the most reactionary armies, especially in the Ukraine, added to the sum-total of death and anguish.

But between the Red and White extremes there were anti-Soviet movements which ruled out cruelty for cruelty's sake and renounced national or race hatreds. In terms of unlimited terror, Lenin and his associates must be equated with the worst, not the best, of their enemies. And only the communists added insult to injury by decking their barbarism with the raiment of a world-saving mission.

In the nature of things, the workers and peasants, being the most numerous, provided the most victims. Peasant opposition was nearly so unanimous that the government hardly bothered to conceal it. "The *kulak* cherishes a fierce hatred of the Soviet government," Lenin conceded in August, 1918. *Kulak,* Russian for "fist," was a term of contempt applied to rich peasants, particularly those engaged in usurious money-lending, but the Bolsheviks made of it a propaganda term for any peasant resisting their new order, and that was nearly all of them. "That we brought the civil war to the village," Lenin wrote in the course of a polemic with Karl Kautsky, a European socialist, "is something we hold as a merit." At least that phase of the civil strife, he thus acknowledged, was deliberately provoked—brought to the village—in line with class-struggle doctrine. But the village was 85 per cent of Russia.

Months before the White forces of tsarist restoration had become a great threat, the Bolsheviks faced a rising hostility among the very soldiers and sailors who had helped them into power. The Petrograd regiments became so restive that the government had them disarmed. The revolutionary sailors—"the beauty and the pride of the revolution," in Trotsky's words—began to pass resolutions demanding their abdication. The party shrewdly started to build up a Praetorian Guard of non-Russian mercenaries: Letts, Chinese, German and Austrian prisoners-of-war.

In April, 1918, a conference of factory workers, claiming to speak for a hundred thousand Petrograd proletarians, formally demanded the resignation of the Soviet government. The only democratic faction to back Lenin's *coup,* the left wing of the Social Revolutionaries, renounced the phony partnership and thereafter led all the rest in resistance to the dictatorship.

The blood bacchanalia shed the last margins of restraint after August 30, 1918, when a Social Revolutionary, Dora (also known as Fanya) Kaplan, shot and wounded Lenin—as "a traitor to the revolution," she let it be known. The same day a Petrograd student assassinated Uritsky, the head of the regional Cheka.

In the Bolshevik stronghold of Kronstadt, five hundred prisoners were thereupon dragged from their dungeons and mowed down by rifle fire. In Petrograd, 512 innocent hostages were shot in a few days. A Moscow telegram to all local Soviets said: "Done with weakness! Done with sentimental considerations!" A redoubtable Cheka chief, Comrade Latsis, announced: "We are exterminating the bourgeoisie as a class. Don't look for incriminating evidence." If a man's or a woman's hands were not work-worn, he said, that was evidence enough. A paranoia of power and sadistic lust turned the Cheka into scavengers of a stricken nation.

Whatever it may have been in theory, in practice Lenin's regime "evolved into a system of self-defense of a small minority against its own people—a system which has never been surpassed by any tyranny in the world's history." This was the verdict, in 1922, of Paul Miliukov, one of Russia's self-exiled democratic leaders.

• The Kronstadt Rebellion

The hundreds of large and small uprisings throughout the country are too numerous to list, let alone describe here. The most dramatic of them, in Kronstadt, epitomizes most of them. What gave it a dimension of supreme drama was the fact that the sailors of Kronstadt, an island naval fortress near Petrograd, on the Gulf of Finland, had been one of the main supports of the *putsch*. Now Kronstadt became the symbol of the bankruptcy of the Revolution. In the sycophantic writings about the glorious "new Russia," Kronstadt, if mentioned at all, is covered up with a few official lies.

The sailors on the battleships and in the naval garrisons were in the final analysis peasants and workers in uniform. Soon enough they shared the disillusionment of the country at large. It was in the local Soviet and in the Kronstadt Communist Party that the spirit of insurgence first found expression, then spread to the naval and civilian population. Kremlin history, then and since, has attempted to dismiss the rebellion as the work of monarchists and *émigré* capitalists. But it was in the first place an insurrection within the Bolshevik elite itself. Many of the victims would die shouting, "Long live the Communist International!" and "Long live the Constituent Assembly!"

The tragedy began with a mass meeting of fifteen hundred sailors and workers on March 1, 1921. Though Lenin had sent several of his best people—among them Mikhail Kalinin, well-liked because of his peasant origin and personality—to take part in the proceedings, they could not stave off a resolution condemning the regime. "The present Soviets do not express the will of the workers and peasants," it charged, and went on to ask for "new elections by secret ballot, the pre-election campaign to have full freedom of agitation." The sailors demanded freedom of speech, press, and assembly, liberation of political prisoners, restoration of the peasants' right to the products of their labor—in short, fulfillment of the Bolshevik promises.

Four days later the Kronstadt sailors formed a small committee composed chiefly of communists, which assumed control of the town, the fortress, the ships. A brutally-worded ultimatum by Trotsky as War Commissar, approved by Lenin, called for "unconditional surrender" or the "mutineers" would be shot "like partridges." When the committee refused to yield, Trotsky assigned Mikhail Tukhachevsky, the same General Tukhachevsky who was destined to be killed by Stalin, to take Kronstadt by force. Hundreds of Petrograd workers crossed the ice—the gulf is still frozen at that time of the year—to join the menaced Kronstadters.

Tukhachevsky marched on the naval town with sixty thousand picked troops. Tough Cheka forces were deployed in the rear, ready to shoot army men who might flinch from attacking the heroes of the Revolution. One regiment, in fact, did mutiny, and was whipped back into line. The siege began with an aerial bombardment at 6:45 P.M. on March 6, followed by an artillery barrage. The sailors answered with fire from the fort and from their ships. Then the Red Army advanced across the ice. At several points the ice gave way and hundreds were drowned. In the final days the town was conquered street by street.

Tukhachevsky later declared that in all his years of war and civil war, he had not witnessed carnage such as he overseered at Kronstadt. "It was not a battle," he said, "it was an inferno. . . . The sailors fought like wild beasts. I cannot understand where they found the might for such rage. Each house had to be taken by storm."

On March 17, Tukhachevsky could report to the War Commissar that the job was finished. Kronstadt was a place of death. Eighteen thousand of the rebels, it was estimated, had been killed; thousands of government troops died. Hundreds were arrested and shot in the ensuing "pacification."

The massacre of the sailors signalized the rupture of the last natural bond between the regime and the sons of the people. What remained was a thing alien and hated and cancerous. The totalitarian state had triumphed. Russia was a nation occupied by an internal enemy.

· Bloody Road to NEP

The purely military aspects of the civil war are better known in the outside world. Scholarly and voluminous studies of the subject have been published in many Western countries. Besides armies representing more or less specific political movements, there were freebooting forces under ambitious individual generals and civilian leaders. Meanwhile, until the dictated Brest-Litovsk peace in early 1918, the Germans were overrunning the Ukraine and cutting deep into the flesh of Crimea.

The most formidable and the most nearly successful of the anti-Soviet military offensives was a great peasant uprising: the Antonov Rebellion, named for its leader, a military Social Revolutionary, (also known as the Tambov Uprising, from the region where it originated). Antonov rallied the embittered peasantry, whose crops were being forcibly requisitioned. Tambov fell to him, then Riazan, Tula, Kaluga; at the peak of the drive his partisans held an area as large as France, and his armies were approaching the Moscow province. The Soviet resistance in this operation, too, was commanded by Tukhachevsky.

Superimposed on these conflicts were the several small-scale Allied interventions in the Murmansk-Archangel area on the North Sea, the Caucasus, the Siberian Far East. Then there were some forty thousand Czech prisoners of war, their ranks swelled by workers and peasants, fighting in the Urals. A *coup d'état* made in the name of peace had brought another, equally terrible and more chaotic war.

What all of the native fighting forces except the Red Army had in common was their detestation of the communist regime—although the socialist parties did, at times, side with the Bolsheviks against the other extremes. Had any substantial portion of these disparate elements been able to pool their strength under a combined command, the Soviet government would not have survived its first year. But Trotsky's armies were able to deal with them piecemeal. With both the old and the new capitals, Petrograd and Moscow, in their hands—firmly held by all-out terror—Trotsky and Lenin could throw their military strength against any point where the challenge was most urgent.

Hunger, soon to degenerate into famine, was everywhere, along with typhus, brigandage, the scourge of homeless children, *bezprizornyie*, hundreds of thousands of them roaming through the land like little wild animals. Against this background, the area of Soviet control was shrinking. In the fall of 1919, General Yudenich was advancing on Petrograd and actually penetrated its suburbs. The National Army of General Denikin had occupied most of the Ukraine. Admiral Kolchak, who styled himself Supreme Head of the anti-Soviet forces, was in control of much of Siberia. In Moscow, there was a deepening mood of panic and open talk of the inevitable defeat.

Then the tide turned. One after another the Red Army dislodged the attackers. A Polish invasion, which had cut into the Ukraine as far as Kiev, was halted and converted into a rout and a counter-invasion of Poland by the Red Army, in its turn stopped near Warsaw and sent reeling back into Russia.

As for Allied intercession, the key fact is that it was on a ludicrously small scale, lackadaisical, and wholly uncoordinated. The Allies were there primarily not to suppress the Bolsheviks, but to safeguard military supplies and weapons that might fall to the Germans, and certainly did not have their heart in the undertaking. In the aggregate fighting, the foreign share was negligible and in the overall resistance to Bolshevism it was nil. Since then Soviet mythology has magnified that episode out of all proportions to reality for propaganda purposes.

Lenin and Trotsky had achieved substantial success by the early months of 1921. It remained only to mop up the separatist movements and regimes in the Ukraine, Georgia, and other non-Russian regions; the Moslem area of Central Asia would not be conquered for several years after the main conflict had been completed. The offensive against the separatists, too, was carried out with a maximum of brutality and casualties. Stalin, in charge of destroying the moderate socialist government in his native Georgia, was so wantonly murderous that even Lenin was alarmed.

If anything is clear in this initial period, it is that the Bolshevik dictatorship did not have the consent of the Russian peoples. It was forced upon the country by unrestricted violence and deceit.

The tortured years stand as confutation of the continuing belief in some quarters that the masses submitted readily to the Bolshevik whip. The failure of their convulsive resistance should not blind us to its vast dimensions and sacrificial passion.

Meanwhile, in 1921, one of the most devastating famines in Russian history was rapidly spreading. The Soviet masters, of course, cannot be blamed for the great drought that was its basic cause. But the war "brought to the villages," Lenin's oft-repeated statement that he would never surrender to the "rural counterrevolution," had left the countryside denuded of all food reserves and seeds. Between the systematic confiscation of farm products by the regime and seizures by the many armies, the peasantry was utterly helpless against the ravages of drought and famine. American charity, administered by Herbert Hoover from 1921 to 1923, through the ARA (American Relief Administration), saved millions of lives—as acknowledged by the Kremlin. More millions perished.

In the wake of Kronstadt, with the famine deepening and communist hopes in Europe in collapse, Lenin was ready to make concessions to salvage his regime. His war communism—expressed mainly in requisitioning grain and other foodstuffs from hostile peasants—had been a ghastly failure. A New Economic Policy, better known by its initials as NEP, was announced within days after the sailors' uprising had been drowned in blood.

It should be underlined that his retreat was solely economic. The dictatorship did not relax its totalitarian grip on the political machinery. The Cheka, under the revised name of GPU, continued and expanded as a government within the government. Not one of the basic political freedoms was restored. The Red Army was enlarged through conscription and consolidated.

As the price for holding on to a political monopoly, the government gave up part of its economic monopoly. This is pertinent to an understanding of the present-day situation—of the concessions made by the regime since the passing of Stalin. Again, the "improvements" and "reforms" do not affect the monopoly of political power.

For Lenin and his associates, NEP was a bitter pill, forced down their throats by popular opposition to their instant communism. It was granted under the duress of universal resistance. Its authors looked upon the New Economic Policy as a holding operation, with full-scale socialization to be tried again when conditions for it would have matured. Meanwhile, they did not pretend that it was anything but a defeat.

NEP restored private enterprise first of all in agriculture (although legally the state still held title to all the land), then in small business both at the production and distribution ends. The government kept nationalized control of what is called the "commanding heights": big industry, communications, banking, foreign trade. With the end of the famine, this mixed economy began to flourish. Well-stocked shops blossomed on every city street. Goods that had seemed non-existent suddenly were in supply again. Small businesses and single craftsmen by the thousands competed for the trade of a population long starved for the simplest necessities. Agriculture quickly recovered momentum, its production growth beyond anything known in Russian history. By 1928, general living standards were back to 1913–1914 levels.

Despite its limited character, NEP was a victory for the people, wrenched from the dictators by main force, paid for in mountains of corpses. Politically the people were defeated, but they never surrendered. Violent opposition eased off, though it never stopped entirely; passive forms of opposition increased and have continued into our own time.

• *The Succession*

Lenin did not live long enough to see the unfolding of his resuscitated capitalism. In May, 1922, he suffered a paralytic stroke which in its later stages also wiped out his speech. Bed-ridden for twenty months, he was tortured by forebodings of future power conflicts, between the most prominent and the least prominent members of the governing Politburo, Leon Trotsky and Joseph Stalin.

In a memorandum, dictated to his wife and later celebrated as his Last Testament, Lenin urged that Stalin (born Joseph Vissarionovich Djugashvili) be removed from his post as Secretary General of the party and replaced by someone less rude, more patient and considerate. The swarthy, mustachioed Georgian, however, had used that position too shrewdly and ruthlessly to be dislodged. He had maneuvered his personal henchmen into party and government positions all over the country, so that by the time Lenin died, on January 21, 1924, Stalin was already the number-one bureaucrat.

Lenin and the country had assumed that the incandescent Jewish intellectual, Trotsky (born Bronstein, son of a middle-class farmer in the Kherson region of the Ukraine) would inherit the toga of supreme leadership. Trotsky was the Revolution's most brilliant orator and an able writer. He had been the organizer of the Red Army and its victorious strategist, his name inseparable from Lenin's.

But Stalin's genius for intrigue outweighed his adversary's brilliance and popularity. By playing off one group against the other, he succeeded in isolating Trotsky, then stripped him piecemeal of party positions. On the day after the tenth anniversary of Soviet power, Trotsky was exiled to Alma Ata in Central Asia. Before 1927 had run its course, the colorless Georgian was sole master of Russia.

About a year later Stalin drove Trotsky out of the USSR. The former war lord resided in several countries of exile, the last of them Mexico. There, in 1940, after several unsuccessful previous attempts, Stalin finally caught up with him—one of his busy assassins split the exile's skull with an alpenstock.

A serious weakness of all arbitrary dictatorships, the fact that they provide no machinery for a legal succession, was thus in evidence from the start. This lack of institutional legitimacy guarantees permanent and relentless struggles for power at the upper levels, and by reflection down the pyramid at lower levels. Designation of an heir by the incumbent dictator offers no remedy—his authority is interred with his bones. Neither Lenin nor Stalin was explicit about an heir to his mantle. Lenin, as we have noted, did rule out Stalin, who in due time assumed full power notwithstanding. It came, however, after a fierce and debilitating struggle against other contenders that kept the party and the country in a state of turbulence for nearly four years.

Since the plan of this book is not chronological, the brief tale of succession can be told here in full. There have been only three true transfers of power in fifty years—from Lenin to Stalin, to Khrushchev, to the present bosses.

Khrushchev, as a half-literate young workman, fought with the Red Army in the civil war, then joined the party. With a keen instinct for power, he attached himself at once to the bureaucratic party apparatus and rose rapidly through the patronage of Lazar

Kaganovich, whom he would ultimately demean and exile as an "anti-party" element. The charge often made abroad that Khrushchev was responsible for mass killings during the collectivization drive is unfounded. At that time he was merely a minor local official. But he would make up for it amply later as generalissimo of the no less massive purge slaughters in his native Ukraine.

While a student in a party technical school, Khrushchev caught Stalin's attention by his fervor in informing on fellow students. Thereafter his rise was meteoric. Within three years he was party boss of the Moscow region. In this strategic post for five years, he distinguished himself in the carnage of the period, personally signing the death warrants of scores of his intimate friends. In August, 1937, at Stalin's behest, he swooped down on the Ukraine. Before he was through, tens of thousands were liquidated; only two of the 102 members of the "republic's" Central Committee escaped arrest or death.

Back in Moscow, he collected his reward—full membership in the Politburo. By the time Stalin died—or was murdered by his closest comrades-in-arms—Khrushchev rated number five in the hierarchy. Georgi Malenkov, who took over the nominal leadership, held it only nine days, after which he was succeeded as First Secretary, on an interim basis, by Khrushchev. The war for Stalin's power was on in deadly earnest.

The number one menace was Lavrenty Beria, Stalin's long-time chief executioner and in command of the special security armies. In July, only four months after Stalin's funeral, Beria was lured to a meeting in the Kremlin and finished off with a bullet—by Khrushchev personally, if his boasts while in his cups are to be believed. The execution of thirty-nine alleged Beria confederates, and many others without the formality of a public announcement, made Khrushchev's ascendance secure. His status as First Secretary was made permanent. The title was not enough—in the next years he consolidated his power by ridding himself, seriatim, of all other visible contenders.

How and why he was in his turn eliminated, in the fall of 1964, is still a mystery. Surmises are many. His ill-fated Virgin Lands program and the general decline of agriculture are often cited. The growth of his power, to the point where he was turning into another Stalin, surely alarmed his associates. Most important, perhaps, his economic reorganizations were enlarging the authority of local party stalwarts at the expense of the economic elite. It is a tribute to the high art of intrigue in the Kremlin that Khrushchev apparently had no inkling of the plot to turn him into an unperson until the day it actually happened. That very morning he was still talking to astronauts in orbit, but his successors, not he, were there to greet them when they came down to earth.

For the first time, the transfer of power was without bloodletting. This is progress of a kind, but the current incumbents are hardly first-rate life-insurance risks. The top plotters, and joint successors, were Leonid Brezhnev and Alexei Kosygin, his closest and most trusted collaborators. Both of them are of the so-called post-Revolutionary generations, Kosygin having been eleven when the monarchy collapsed, Brezhnev thirteen.

Because he studied land reclamation and then, at the age of thirty-three, graduated as a metallurgical engineer, Brezhnev is reputed to be a technocrat and economic specialist. But his true career, begun as a protégé of Khrushchev in the Stalin era, has been in the party apparatus. He held a variety of posts on the regional level, was made an alternative member of the Politburo by Stalin, and became a full member after having backed Khrushchev in disposing of the so-called "anti-party" group of Molotov, Kaganovich, and Malenkov. Though he was designated "President" of the USSR, a largely honorific title, succeeding the aged Klementi Voroshilov, his real influence was exercised as Khrushchev's apparently most loyal associate.

Kosygin fought in the civil war as a teen-ager but did not join the party until 1927, on the eve of Stalin's assumption of total power. As late as 1936 he was still only a foreman in a Leningrad textile plant. But three years later he was mayor of that city and head of the whole textile industry. The one virtue of the bloody purges, from the vantage point of ambitious men who managed to stay alive, was that they cleared the path to dramatic promotions.

During the war Kosygin was made Deputy Premier, and in 1948 Stalin put him on the all-powerful Politburo. After the boss's death, he threw in his lot with Khrushchev. In 1959 he became head of Gosplan, the national planning agency, and at various times he served as Minister of Finance and Minister of Light Industry. Though so long at the center of power, Kosygin did not register on the public mind until the later Khrushchev years. Today, as Premier, he holds the top job in the government, which is a notch below the General Secretaryship of the party held by Brezhnev, who, at this writing, is gradually emerging as the real dictator.

Both leaders are colorless, unsmiling administrators, typical of the new breed of faceless men produced by an aging, sclerotic revolution. They are technicians of power, with drab biographies, little known to their countrymen. The mass of Soviet people, in fact, are remarkably disinterested in the game of succession played at the top. The elimination of Brezhnev and Kosygin, probably inevitable, will leave them as apathetic as did the exit of Khrushchev, or for that matter, the passing of one tsar and the enthronement of another "Little Father" in the past.

3 / Marxism-Leninism

The myth that Soviet communism is "Marxist" and "socialist."

A famous Russian revolutionist of the late nineteenth century, Vera Zasulich, once wrote to Karl Marx about the special problems of the transition to socialism in her country. He replied bluntly: "The inevitability of socialism is limited to the countries of Western Europe." No Russian socialist, including Bolsheviks, would have disputed that dictum before 1917.

Marx, Engels, and their followers of all shades took it for granted that socialism or communism (the terms were used interchangeably) could come only to a highly developed capitalist society. This was accepted without challenge by all of the various schools of Marxism. The attempt to bring socialism to a relatively backward country like Russia, overwhelmingly agrarian and in an early stage of capitalist development, was flagrantly anti-Marxist.

Those making the quixotic attempt were themselves deeply conscious of violating Marxist precepts. Not until some years after they acquired total authority did they begin to revise the long-held doctrine. Unable to change the facts of a premature action, they revised the theory to justify their retention of power.

The industrial revolution, or the bourgeois revolution as socialists called it, beginning in the late eighteenth century, sounded the death knell of feudalism. The introduction of socialism, in the Marxist view, could not—and should not—even begin until the industrial-bourgeois revolution was completed. Socialism was not a substitute for the bourgeois stage of history. It was the higher stage to follow.

Socialists, that is to say, *never looked upon their proposed system*

as a method of industrializing economically retarded countries.
The full development of capitalism by capitalist means, they
agreed, was a pre-condition that could not be skipped. The very
idea of "expropriating" an underdeveloped nation seemed to them
both heretical and silly, like robbing an empty till.

Their responsibility would not come into play until after the target nation had been fully industrialized. Socialism, as they saw it,
was a system for the equitable distribution of the wealth and goods
already piled up in an advanced, affluent society. The working class
would expropriate a "going concern" and administer its abundance
more justly and rationally. It would abolish private ownership of
the means of production, profits, the bourgeois market, etc., and
create an equalitarian paradise according to the formula: From
each according to his abilities, to each according to his needs.*

Neither Marx nor his disciples offered much guidance on how
the change-over from a going capitalism would be managed. Presumably the elimination of profit would automatically cancel out
avarice, crime, class conflicts, violence-breeding competition, and
even the protracted need for a law-enforcing state. The millennium
would emerge full-blown from the debris of a proletarian revolution. But what would happen if a desperately poor, largely agricultural nation, without enough to supply everyone's "needs," under-
took socialism? This question was never asked, since it ran counter
to all their theories and expectations.

By Marxist laws of "economic determinism," it was plainly un-
Marxist to provoke a socialist expropriation before the country had
matured industrially, so that it possessed a substantial middle class
and a strong proletariat. In socialist language, the modes of production "determine" the nature of the political state: politics reflect
economy, not the other way around. That a purely political event,
like the seizure of power in Russia, should "determine" the modes
of production was unthinkable. It was based on no historical law,
Marxist or any other, but on the arbitrary will of a group of politicians. It pulled the props from under the "scientific" doctrine of an
orderly and inevitable historic progression from feudalism to capitalism to socialism.

* The Stalin Constitution, still in force, emptied the formula of meaning by
changing just one word. "From each according to his abilities," it states, "to
each according to his *work.*"

The conviction that socialism would appear only in some "ripe" bourgeois society is still the essential assumption of all Marxists and near-Marxists—except the communists: a name arbitrarily assumed and now reserved exclusively for the advocates and supporters of Soviet and Chinese-type socialism. It was no less the assumption of the Leninist branch of the Russian socialist movement before 1917 and for a decade after 1917. Not one of its theorists suggested the possibility of socialism in his country before its bourgeois development had been *completed*. That it would come in Russia before it did in Germany, England, or the United States seemed as unrealistic to Lenin as to any of his Menshevik competitors.

When the Bolsheviks found themselves masters of the Russian state, they regarded it as a most un-Marxist historical accident. Accordingly they were extremely skeptical about their chances of retaining control. Most of them favored a coalition regime to supervise the fulfillment of the precondition for socialism, namely the completion of the industrial revolution. Lenin overruled them but only because he looked to a communist revolution in some advanced European nation to resolve his dilemma by providing the economic basis presupposed by Marx.

Trotsky, in 1937, wrote that Lenin's and his own calculations "were based on the hopes of an early revolution in the West." In the spring of 1918 Lenin declared frankly, "Our backwardness has thrust us forward. . . . We shall perish if we are unable to hold on until we meet with the support of other countries." On another occasion he said: "Our salvation lies in the European Revolution." American and European comrades who visited Soviet Russia in the early years were invariably reproached for the delay in salvaging the Russian Revolution by overthrowing capitalism in their countries.

Postwar chaos in Germany seemed to hold the key to that desperate hope. Even the sacrifice of his Russian regime, in Lenin's view, would have been an acceptable price for a German communist state. In April, 1919, the Sparticists established a Soviet in Munich, but it survived only until May first. Earlier a Leninist agent, Bela Kun, had captured power in Hungary and proceeded at once with the installation of socialism; despite a ferocious Red Terror, the Kun regime lasted only a few months. Moscow's hopes were then focused on Italy, where the workers were taking over factories in Milan and other cities. But the new Italian Communist party, set up under the direct tutelage of Soviet agents, merely opened a road to Mussolini and his fascists.

Another flare-up of hope in Germany came with a communist uprising in Berlin—by coincidence at the same time that Trotsky's Red Army was shooting down the Kronstadt rebels "like partridges," as promised. The dismal failure in Berlin, as much as the disorders and hunger in his own country, finally induced Lenin to adopt the compromise with capitalism called NEP; his own name for it was "state capitalism."

Even Joseph Stalin, in the initial period, recognized that communist take-overs in advanced countries were indispensable to socialism in Russia. In April, 1924, three months after the death of Lenin, he wrote that the bourgeoisie could be overthrown in Russia —they had done it—but "for the final victory of socialism, for the organization of socialist production, the efforts of one country, especially a peasant country like ours, are not enough—for this we must have the efforts of the proletarians of several countries." To spare himself embarrassment, the brochure containing this statement was withdrawn from circulation as soon as Stalin became dictator on the premise of "socialism in one country."

After the completion of his First Five-Year Plan and the forcible collectivization of agriculture, Stalin proclaimed that socialism had been achieved, and ordered the people to be happy. The Seventh Congress of the Communist International solemnly confirmed, on August 20, 1935, "the final and irrevocable triumph of socialism" in the USSR. In contradiction to all Marxist tenets about the fading out of the state after the advent of socialism, it added that "the all-sided reinforcement of the state of the proletarian dictatorship," too, had been achieved.

The claim that its domain is now socialist has not been revised or questioned by the Kremlin ever since. (In the 1950's, Molotov was lambasted by Khrushchev and his press for implying, in something he had said, that the USSR was not yet entirely socialist.) It is a claim that has been denounced by the Socialist Parties of the major nations. Some of these parties, it is true, went in for occasional "united fronts" with the communists for political expediency, but not one of them recognized the Soviet regime as the embodiment of its socialist vision.

Just before Khrushchev's visit to England in the mid-1950's, he addressed an appeal for a united front to all socialists in Europe. It was rejected at once and sharply by the Socialist International, which pointed out: "Where the communists are in power, they have distorted every freedom, every right of the workers, every political and every human value the socialists have won in a struggle lasting generations."

In 1941, Lewis Corey, formerly an active American communist, wrote: "Marxism as a progressive social force is dead." This was not exceptional but typical for socialist thinkers and leaders. The Soviet system has been an albatross around their necks. Either they had to insist that it had nothing in common with their socialism— or renounce socialism. During and after the Stalin era, the socialist movements of the world have sought to dissociate themselves from the blood-stained Muscovite aberration of their faith.

Their emphasis on freedom is not incidental but inherent in the socialist philosophy. State ownership of the means of production was to be the beginning of a process, not in itself the "triumph of socialism." True, Marx had mentioned the possibility of a transitional "dictatorship of the proletariat," but only in countries where the proletariat was a strong social force. The seminal *Communist Manifesto* had said plainly that "the rule of the working class was inconceivable until the great mass of them were united in desiring it" and "then they would be an overwhelming majority." Besides, their temporary rule would be balanced by the expected "withering of the state," a concept incommensurable with dictatorship of any kind.

• *Birth of Totalitarianism*

It was the Bolsheviks, cornered by history, who pulled the dictatorship formula out of context and made it the very foundation of their rule, emptying socialist theory of all its democratic and humanitarian content. The proposition that the so-called proletarian dictatorship would be a permanent fixture—as it has been for fifty years—of anything pretending to be socialism would have scandalized Marx, as it has in fact alienated virtually all Marxists.

The Bolsheviks at first held to this basic Marxist view. Lenin had explicitly denied that socialism could be made to jibe with long-continuing dictatorship. We have Trotsky's affirmation of this point. "Lenin, following Marx and Engels," he wrote from the vantage point of twenty years of Soviet absolutism, "saw the first distinguishing feature of the proletarian revolution in the fact that, having expropriated the exploiters, it would abolish the necessity of a bureaucratic apparatus raised above society—and above all, a police and standing army." Instead, he noted, the Soviet state "has grown into a hitherto unheard of apparatus of compulsion. The bureaucracy not only had not disappeared, yielding its place to the masses, but has turned into an uncontrolled force dominating the masses."

Lenin's excuse, as he cited it in 1921, was that "dictatorship is the state of acute war" and that they were "precisely in such a state." But forty-six years later, the dictatorship continues and is committed to continuing until "communism" is finally brought into being. The excuse has worn all too thin. Communism-to-come has merely become a transparent justification for holding on to absolute power.

It should not be forgotten that Lenin himself, in 1905, had ruled out violent assumption of such power as unacceptable to a Marxist. "He who wishes to proceed to socialism by any other path than political democracy," he said at that time, "must inevitably arrive at absurd and reactionary conclusions, both in the political and economic sense." When he did choose that path a dozen years later he was contradicting not only Marx but himself.

Rosa Luxemburg, leader of the German communist Spartacus League, only weeks after the Petrograd *putsch*, pledged that communists in her country "will never take over governmental power in any other way than through the clear, unambiguous will of the great majority of the proletarian masses in all Germany, never except by virtue of their conscious assent to the views, aims and fighting methods of the Spartacus League." In this she reflected the opinion of thousands of communists around the world who saw the seizure of power by a small and unauthorized minority as unsocialist and anti-Marxist.

This is the opinion still held, to an overwhelming extent, by socialists the world over—including, if the truth were known, more idealistic socialists inside Russia. It is not accidental that among the first to be "liquidated" wherever the communists take control are socialists and non-communist Leftist and trade-unionists. These are the people who saw Lenin's, then Stalin's, "socialism" as an outrageous distortion of the ideal, a vulgarization of their cherished purposes.

And this is how they still see it. Moderation of the terror in recent years may reconcile some foreign observers to the Soviet system. But not honest socialists. Logically they cannot accept a one-party dictatorship, which outlaws personal freedoms, scorns economic equality, and countenances forced labor, as anything but a caricature of their hoped-for system, an insult to Marxism.

Knowledgeable liberals, of course, are equally clear on this score. Arthur M. Schlesinger, Jr., for instance, said in 1962, on the basis of the Soviet experience:

> The one contribution that communism can theoretically make to economic development is ironically the very thing for which Marx condemned *laissez-faire* capitalism in the nineteenth century: that is, its capacity to accelerate development by grinding the faces of the poor. By holding down mass living standards and depriving the workers of the produce of their labor, communism can sweat investment capital, as it has done in Russia and China, out of the hides of the working class. In paradoxical fact, it is communism which has provided the best means known to history for the exploitation of the proletariat. But communism is not the best means known to history of economic development, as the record of a dozen countries proves.

The Soviet rulers, to make their grotesque distortion of socialism palatable to their own people and to supporters abroad, have resorted to an extraordinary piece of verbal jugglery. Unable to surmount physical realities, they have fallen back on new definitions —drawing a sharp line between communism and socialism.

Communism is their word for the original dream, now postponed to a far future. Socialism is their label for the existing mess of political coercion, bureaucracy, wide inequalities, thought control, and the rest in today's Russia. Socialism used to mean what they now call communism. Moscow has twisted it into a coverword for a sort of ante-chamber to communism, in which any contradiction or betrayal of Marxism passes muster.

The semantic trickery, however, doesn't fool socialists, to whom socialism still means what it has always meant. Neither does it fool honest communists, and there *are* honest communists. One of them has just given witness to this—from the grave as it were. The late Professor Eugene Vargas was for decades the most influential Soviet economist. After his death, a startling essay was found among his papers and it has been published in an underground literary-political almanac, *Phoenix 1966*, the editors of which were promptly arrested. In it Vargas declared that real communism is inconceivable without "socialist democracy and a free and independent citizenry." Unless "the serious perversions of socialist democracy" in the Soviet Union are corrected, he wrote, "this country will never achieve any communism in twenty years or even a hundred years. It is only a parody of communism that can survive in such conditions."

Paradoxically, the only people (other than the communist faithful) who unreservedly acknowledge that the existing situation in the USSR is true socialism are the implacable enemies of socialism, the defenders of free economy. They not only admit that it is the real thing, they insist on it.

Brushing aside the caveats of non-communist Marxists, they say in effect: "What we see in Russia is socialism, full-blown and undeniable. *That* is the inevitable end-product of Marxist fallacies. No matter how honestly you may disown the Soviet reality, it is inherent in a system that puts political and economic power into the same hands, that outlaws private ownership, individual initiative, and a genuinely free market." They deny, moreover, that "democratic socialism" is possible, however sincere the intentions of its advocates may be, because a state monopoly of both political and economic life could not function without dictatorial powers and the suppression of criticism.

If the society evolved in Soviet Russia is neither Marxist nor socialist, then what is it? Social scientists and laymen alike for decades have searched for a name to compass the unprecedented phenomenon. State capitalism, state socialism, the bureaucratic state? None of these makeshifts has proved adequate. In the end we have had to accept a word that, in this sense, did not exist before the rise of Soviet communism—namely *totalitarianism*.

Common usage equates it with tyranny, despotism, and other synonyms for an omnipotent state. But this is mistaken and, in addition, a lot too kind to the Soviet reality. The worst despotisms, past or present, have not necessarily been totalitarian. Tsarist absolutism, for instance, or dictatorships of the Latin American varieties, have not been total. They left areas of free decision to the individual and tolerated some institutions—economic, religious, or cultural—outside the state. Their claims on the citizen might be all-embracing in political matters, yet they exempted some elements in his private life.

Totalitarianism, in its fascist and communist variants alike, grants no such margins for private activity, dissent, or conscience. No enterprise or organization, not even a chess club or literary circle, is tolerated without state surveillance and dictation. The new kind of dictatorship compasses politics, economics, the arts, science, education, everything. It tells its subjects what they can and cannot do, say, think, feel, or believe.

Kremlin communism aspired not only to a total transformation of society but of the human being, through the "engineering" of a "new Soviet man." It thus became totalitarian, and in the process set a pattern for other ideologies seeking their own species of total transformations. Whatever the Kremlin's successes and failures in these fifty years, they tell us more about the nature of totalitarianism than the nature of Marxist socialism.

4 / Classes

The myth that Soviet Russia has become
a "classless society."

The most brazen piece of make-believe in Soviet mythology, fabricated in the middle thirties, is that the country has a "classless society." Joseph Stalin proclaimed this glorious lie—and his terror machine kept on exterminating "class enemies." When his "mistakes" were exposed by his heirs, this outrageous claim was not among them. It remains an official "fact" and a standard boast; for any party man to think aloud that there are still classes is tantamount to political suicide.

The sheer impudence of the pretense is breath-taking: the kind of falsehood only a regime safe from contradiction could hope to maintain. None of its "dialectical" word-play, however, can blur what is visible to the naked eye, which is a society of extremes in rich and poor, privilege and deprivation, strong and weak, as in all countries—only more so.

Modern apartment houses for the new middle class stand on the edges of foul slums in Soviet cities. Fine *dachas* or country vacation houses are within view of wretched peasant hovels. The collectivized peasant envies the better life of the urban worker, and both of them aspire for their children, if not themselves, the relative comforts and luxuries of middle-class officials, economic managers, and professional people.

The contrasts in living conditions for the masses and the classes are as sharp as in capitalist nations, the contrasts in power and privilege vastly sharper. A recent tourist to Russia has written: "They flash around the city in curtained, chauffeur-driven cars. They wear dresses from Paris and tailor-made suits. They eat out-of-season delicacies. 'They' are the various Soviet elites." How does one square this with a classless society? The fact that they do is proof of the magic of "dialectic" thinking, in which opposites are supposedly resolved in a new truth.

While ordinary mortals queue up for hours to obtain some of the everyday necessities, the new aristocrats shop at leisure in special stores stocked with the best the country produces and imported goods. While top officials and managers draw hundreds of rubles a month—plus an array of perquisites like chauffeured motorcars, choice apartments—millions on the nether levels struggle to survive on the legal minimum of 45 rubles a month. In factories and institutions the dining rooms are socially graded: first-rate for the important people, third-rate for the workers. Trains have three or four classes, according to ability to pay. The best hospitals are reserved for "the best people."

The upper classes have their status symbols: private suburban houses built on public land, cooperative apartments in town, cars, refrigerators, and other products in short supply, tailor-made clothes—all hopelessly beyond the great mass of the population. They take their vacations as a matter of right in elegant resorts, where a token number of skilled workers gain access only as rewards for outstanding achievement. Even enrollment in higher educational institutions is easier for the children of families with political pull or money bribes to get around academic standards for admission.

Then there are what might be called the collective status symbols of the state, in monuments and buildings unrelated to everyday needs. Soviet architecture for public buildings leans heavily to the ostentatious, the sumptuous, reflecting the grandiosity of the state, and intimidating its lowly citizens. Subways are as ornate as palaces, far beyond the call of transportation comfort. The worker goes from the luxurious marble underground station to his shoddy one-room apartment or his verminous slum. Against a background of poverty and weariness, spectacular Sputniks trumpet to the world the might and modernity of the new overlords.

To the normal mind a classless society means political, economic, and social equality. But in the USSR the very principle of equality is taboo: "a piece of petty bourgeois stupidity, worthy of a primitive sect of ascetics but not of a socialist society organized on Marxian lines." The words are Stalin's and still express official doctrine.

A minister of state in Soviet Russia earns ten to fifteen times as much as an average typist—roughly 9,000 as against 600 to 900 rubles a year. In the United States the comparable ratio is five to one. The Soviet public is not allowed to know specifically how astronomical are the economic distances between the lowest and the highest in the social structure; such things are state secrets, to hold down grumbling. But the facts, if not the exact figures, cannot be kept secret.

A British trade-unionist, George Brown, at the time a Labour Member of Parliament and now the Minister of Foreign Affairs in a Labour Government, visited Russia in 1954. "The inequalities, the unhappiness and the oppression just can't be hidden or ignored," he reported, but "there is a bureaucratic minority that is extremely comfortably off by any standards." The expensive restaurants in the bigger cities are filled with well-dressed men and women, paying prices that automatically bar the ordinary mortal, precisely as in non-communist countries: oases of abundance and swank in a desert of drabness and want.

Karl Marx once wrote that "the bureaucracy possesses the state as its private property." He was referring, of course, to the bourgeois state. But his words are far more descriptive of the Soviet Union, where the burcaucrats not only possess the state but have this private property protected by secret police, armies, censors, legions of indoctrinators. And the Soviet, unlike the bourgeois state, owns and disposes of everything.

In 1928, in the course of the struggle with Stalin, an outstanding supporter of Trotsky, Christian Rakovsky, said: "By means of demoralizing methods, which convert thinking communists into machines, destroying will, character and human dignity, the ruling circles have succeeded in converting themselves into an unremovable and inviolate oligarchy, which replaces the class and the party."

In 1933, the exiled philosopher, Nikolai Berdiaev, wrote in *The Sources and Meaning of Russian Communism*: "This new Soviet bureaucracy is stronger than the tsarist bureaucracy; it is a new privileged class which can ferociously exploit the masses. This is happening."

Trotsky himself wrote, in his exile: "In establishing and defending the advantages of a minority, it of course draws off the cream for its own use. Nobody who has wealth to distribute ever omits himself. The Soviet bureaucracy . . . is in the full sense of the word the sole privileged and commanding stratum in the Soviet society. The means of production belong to the state. But the state, so to speak, 'belongs' to the bureaucracy."

Such statements could be cited by the hundred, from as many sources. Their gist is that under communism "a new class of owners and exploiters" has emerged. It is more avaricious and self-indulgent and entrenched than such classes elsewhere, because it has also a monopoly of political and police power.

"A new class of owners and exploiters"—the description is from the classic book analyzing communist societies: *The New Class*, by Milovan Djilas. The author was confined for many years in a Yugoslav prison for this and other critiques of communism in practice. Until his disillusionment and his monumental courage in expressing it, Djilas was Vice-President of Communist Yugoslavia, and regarded as the most likely successor to Tito. No one has a moral right to prattle about the classless society, I submit, without a careful reading of his lucid book. Here we can only indicate its essence through a few quotations that no more than suggest the character of his findings.

Before the communists came to power in Russia and in his own country, Djilas declares, "it was believed that the differences between cities and the villages, between intellectual and physical labor, would slowly disappear; instead these differences have increased. . . . The greatest illusion was that industrialization and collectivization in the USSR, and destruction of capitalist ownership, would result in a classless society."

The previous exploiting classes did, indeed, cease to exist. But "a new class, previously unknown in history, has been formed. . . . The monopoly which the new class establishes in the name of the working class over the whole society is, primarily, a monopoly over the working class itself. . . . The so-called socialist ownership is a disguise for the real ownership by the political bureaucracy."

Government controls in the economy were necessary at first, Djilas believes, but it "has gradually turned into a vital personal interest on the part of the ruling bureaucrats. . . . In addition to being motivated by the historical need for rapid industrialization, the communist bureaucracy has been compelled to establish a type of economic system designed to insure perpetuation of its own power."

What distinguishes it from all previous exploiting classes, he writes, "is its collective ownership." One has to reach back to ancient despotisms like Egypt until fifteen centuries B.C. for a comparable system: "The communists did not invent collective ownership as such, but invented its all-encompassing character, more widely extended than in earlier epochs, even more extensive than in Pharaoh's Egypt."

Historically, as he sees it, Stalin, the main instrument of the new exploitation, *had* to abolish private ownership of farms, because "the new class felt itself insecure as long as there were other owners than itself." In effect he nationalized not only physical goods but the human being—the peasant through collectivization, the worker through absolute control of his job. Forced labor in camps has been merely the extreme expression of that fact. Under communism so-called free labor is also compulsory: "The worker finds himself in the position of not only having to sell his labor; he must sell it under conditions which are beyond his control, since he is unable to seek another, better employer. There is only one employer, the state. . . . Labor cannot be free in a society where all material goods are monopolized by one group. The labor force is indirectly the property of that group."

Legally, property under communism is considered national and social, "but in actuality a single group manages it in its own interests. . . . This is a class whose power over men is the most complete known in history . . . a power which unites within itself the control of ideas, authority, and ownership, a power which has become an end in itself. . . . When the new class leaves the historic scene—and this must happen—there will be less sorrow than there was for any other class before it. Smothering everything except what suited its ego, it has condemned itself to failure and shameful ruin."

• *New Classes for Old*

Certainly the ruling minority is more hated by its subjects than older types of oligarchy. This I can attest also from personal observation during six years in Soviet Russia. The absence of any countervailing social elements (church, landowners, a free intelligentsia, etc.) has denied the Soviet oligarchs the benefits of restraints on their conduct. They are in a sense victims of their unlimited authority. Self-willed dictators at the apex have bred a hierarchy of little tyrants, down to the arrogant party boss of a village, which has foreclosed a *rapprochement* between the rulers and the ruled.

In a system resting on force, it was inevitable that the squeamish, the doubters, the soul-searchers, those phychologically unable to kill and kill, should be eliminated. They were driven from, or shunned, the orbit of power. "Party members," Djilas writes, "feel that authority, that control over property, brings with it the privileges of this world. Consequently unscrupulous ambition, duplicity, toadyism, and jealousy inevitably must increase. Careerism and an ever-expanding bureaucracy are the incurable diseases of communism."

The best people, by moral criteria, are the most likely to be excluded. Those capable of applying force within stint, the fanatics and the sadists, have tended to take over. Soviet history has been a process of triumph for the most insensitive and egotistical, the connivers and bullyboys. By intellectual criteria, too, in a world where questioning and truth-seeking are crimes, the mediocre have had an advantage over the brilliant. Among the upper-echelon "establishments" of the world, the Soviet is probably the crudest. It represents the end-product of a struggle for the survival of the fittest—the fittest for a totalitarian society—and therefore the most unfit for a humane, civilized society.

The effects of almost unlimited power are corrupting even upon basically good men. Former revolutionary heroes, self-sacrificing and full of ideals, Djilas writes, "become self-centered cowards without ideas or comrades, willing to renounce everything—honor, name, truth and morals—in order to keep their place in the ruling class and the hierarchical circle." The world, he believes, "has probably never seen such characterless wretches and stupid defenders of arid formulas they become after attaining power."

Within the new class, of course, there are also wide gradations of status, power, and profit. The great majority in the bureaucracy are administrators and technical specialists: they constitute, roughly, the new middle classes. They hold their status by delegation or by the toleration of the "governing bureaucracy" in the party and government, the *apparatchiki* or managers of the power apparatus. It is this governing elite that has the largest stake in collective ownership and shows the greatest zeal in protecting it against other claimants.

In the last decade the economic managers, technocrats, engineers, and the like have been "feeling their oats," by reason of their increasing importance in modern technology. They crave more of the goods and authority inherent in their functions, and in fact need more autonomy as against the politicians for efficient production. In this they are passionately opposed by the *apparatchiki*, who are more concerned with political stability than national economic progress. Whatever the theoretical arguments advanced for limiting and postponing economic reforms and concessions in the areas of intellectual work, what is at play is the built-in conservatism of a new class unwilling, and by its conditioning unable, to share the power and proceeds with those on lower rungs.

The outrageous myth of a classless society cannot be made to jibe with the denial of democracy—not the bogus "socialist democracy" in words but the garden varieties recognized since the days of ancient Athens. Even the limited democracy inside the Communist Party of the first Lenin years has been consigned to history.

When inner-party democracy was being demanded by the Trotskyists in the 1920's, they evoked a remarkably candid warning from Leo Kamenev, one of the founding fathers. "They say today," he argued, "let us have democracy in the party; tomorrow they will say, let us have democracy in the trade unions; the day after tomorrow, workers who do not belong to the party may well say: give us democracy too . . . and surely the myriads of peasants cannot be prevented from asking for democracy."

What a horrible prospect! But obviously there was logic, the logic of totalitarianism, on Kamenev's side. Stalin won that debate and it has never been reopened. A verbal democracy, unrelated to living human beings, was his substitute. In defending his "most democratic constitution in the world," he explained on November 25, 1934: "There is no question of freedom for political parties in the Soviet Union apart from the Communist Party. We Bolsheviks consider this provision one of the merits of the constitutional project." The Moscow *Pravda* wrote rapturously: "What a delight to be able to divide the history of human civilization into two phases so clearly: Before and after the constitution bestowed upon us by the great Stalin." Nearly all the authors of the constitution, along with the editor of *Pravda*, were duly executed in its name, some of them before the document had been formally adopted.

Like any other all-powerful class, the Soviet master-elite is self-perpetuating. The sons of the influential people have the easiest access to an education and to the juiciest political and economic assignments. But even they are held back by the reluctance of those entrenched in power to surrender their jobs. The governing apparatus has been largely unchanging and therefore aging. The average age of the top four oligarchs as of 1967—Brezhnev, Kosygin, Podgorny, and Suslov—is sixty-three.

There are no signs of the "Soviet Man" who was to inhabit the classless society. Lenin's insistence that party members and high officials must not earn more than ordinary workers—a sort of "rule of poverty," as in a monastic order—was abandoned even before he died. His promise that officials could be recalled from below similarly has been forgotten; they can be recalled only from above.

Since Stalin's ukase against "rotten-liberal equality," the new class has been able, and even expected, to flaunt its economic and social superiority, just as it flaunts its medals, as visible evidence of rewards from a grateful proletariat. "Life has become beautiful and happy in our country," Stalin announced at that time, so there was no longer any reason for the elite to be self-conscious about being happy in public. One of these days everybody would live well; meanwhile the surrogates for the people would enjoy the experience, disregarding the envy and despair of lesser breeds. And that is how things have remained to the present day.

"By a revolutionary's lean and hungry standards," a *Newsweek* correspondent concluded in 1966, "the Soviet Union is now becoming bourgeois and fat. Its citizens are developing middle-class mentalities. Its law enforcement agencies are grappling with middle-class problems. Its leaders are openly catering to middle-class appetites."

The old Adam, in short, has prevailed over the new man. A new class, snobbish as well as arrogant, rules the roost, and below it are other classes, hoping and intriguing for the same comforts and advantages that have moved mortal man since the beginning of time. Only in the lowest depths, in penal camps and exile regions, among the lowest-grade *kolkhoz* workers and unskilled laborers, is there a certain equality, the kind Dostoievsky talked of through one of the characters in his novel *The Possessed:* "All are slaves and equal in their slavery. . . . Slaves are bound to be equal."

5 / Pre-1917 Economy

The myth that Russia before the Revolution
was an economic desert.

The widely accepted propaganda clichés have it that under communism, for all its wretchedness, the Russian people are better off than before 1917; that until Bolshevism came to redeem it, Russia was a primitive land of unrelieved political savagery in an economic Sahara.

To the Kremlin this legend has been tremendously valuable. On the one hand, Soviet accomplishments glow more brightly against a backdrop of "darkest Russia." On the other, it provides the Great Alibi for failures and depravities, explaining away hunger, concentrations camps, cruel officialdom, indeed everything abhorrent, by reference to tsarist legacies and conditioning.

Russian Bolsheviks don't cease to be Russians. Historic perspective is indispensable. It is important to compare the Soviet half-century with the half-century preceding—and the exercise leaves gaping holes in the communist mythology.

Not many things about Russia, or about any nation for that matter, are beyond dispute. But one of them is that life under the old dispensation, granting its hardships, was freer and more tolerable than under the new. One need only read a few of the Russian classic novels, even those bitter about the life of their time, to see this. Whatever yardstick is used—economic, political, cultural, spiritual—the pre-Bolshevik past stacks up as humanly more attractive. Given a choice based on fact rather than propaganda fable, only Russians with a relish for suffering could prefer the present system.

One of the prime Soviet victories has been its success in blackening the character of historic Russia. There was, of course, plenty of black in it, but the myth-makers have inked out significant white areas and turned all the grays into a uniform jet black. Russia *was* backward and reactionary compared to any modern democratic nation—but the comparison is with Soviet Russia.

A number of circumstances conspired to fix a distorted image of the old Russia on the mental retina of mankind. The most important of these, of course, was the large element of truth in the grim portrait of a country with low living standards, censorship, pogroms, secret police, the Siberian exile system. In addition, the West drew its limited and selective ideas about Russia from sources which, for high-minded reasons, were intent on exhibiting the country in the worst possible light.

To begin with, Russian literature was to an extraordinary degree a literature of protest, using its art to expose and indict the *status quo* and nourish a spirit of revolt. It was as if the world were to judge America solely by *Uncle Tom's Cabin, The Jungle,* and *The Grapes of Wrath.* Then there was the flaming propaganda of Russian liberals and revolutionists, at home and in the emigration, during the pre-Bolshevik half-century. Finally, there were the writings and lectures of hundreds of foreign champions of the old Russian revolutionary movements.

I do not suggest that these sources were false, but only that taken together they presented an exaggerated, one-sided picture. One does not have to perfume the past to recognize that in most things the old order was superior to the new. Its political, intellectual, moral, and spiritual climate was far more wholesome and hopeful than today's. Even in its bleakest periods, such as the reigns of Nicholas I and Alexander III, Russia was not remotely the total tyranny it became through Bolshevism. Relatively at least, the life of the mind was strong and creative, the self-respect of the individual and his rights under law better safeguarded.

There is poverty and oppression in both Russias, the old and the new, but the differences in degree tell the story. Before 1917, open dissent from the official ideology was not only possible but fashionable; social ideas were being ardently explored; cultural interchange with the outside world was wide and unbroken; simple subsistence was taken for granted by the overwhelming mass of people, especially in the villages; a vigorous opposition press and opposition parties were in being; labor unions were active and gaining strength; the frontiers were comparatively open for Russians to leave and foreigners to enter.

Merely to mention a few such facts is to point up the contrast with Soviet conditions. A Soviet citizen magically transported backward in time to 1913 or even 1900 would find personal freedoms and political liberties that are unthinkable in his present setting. He would find evils and injustices—but also that they were recognized as such and that it was possible to protest, fight, and organize for change.

It is around industrial growth, in the first place, that the communist boasts revolve. Let us therefore begin by examining that aspect.

• *Economic Upsurge*

The Kremlin has spread the legend that its industrialization began on what Stalin called a *pustoye myesto*, or empty place. It has ignored the fact that Soviet economic expansion did not improve or enrich the life of the masses but, on the contrary, made their lot more bleak and servile. It ignored the fact that as heavy industry prospered, people were denied simple necessities, including an adequate diet. But even in the dehumanized, statistical terms, the legend is warped. For it rests on a false premise about the starting point.

In truth Russian economy in its last pre-Bolshevik decades was in dramatic upsurge. While the country entered the industrial race late, it made remarkable progress, at a speed greater than that of some West European countries.

"The Russian revolution of 1917 came not at the end of a long period of stagnation and decay, but rather after more than a half-century of the most rapid and comprehensive economic progress," according to Dr. Harry Schwartz, the *New York Times* specialist on Russia. "The average annual rates of growth of industrial output in Russia between 1885 and 1889, and again between 1907 and 1913, substantially exceed the corresponding rates of growth during the same period in the United States, Great Britain, and Germany. . . . Rapid development was a characteristic feature of the whole period from 1861 to 1914."

More than four and a half million people were engaged in nonagricultural economy before World War I. Despite its technical backwardness, agricultural productivity was growing most impressively since the turn of the century. The peasants were not only feeding the nation but providing huge surpluses for export.

Ironically, it was Lenin, in his book on Russian capitalism, in 1899, who stressed the high tempo of the "technical revolution" then under way. He aligned statistics to prove that industry was expanding faster in his country than in the rest of Europe, and in some respects faster than in the United States.

In 1912, Russia was second only to the United States in total railroad mileage. General industrial output increased by 19.1 per cent in the last full pre-war year, 1912–1913—which is close to the annual rate in the First Five-Year Plan and higher than in any subsequent year. When quality factors and the dependability of statistics are taken into account, the natural industrial growth was grater than under communism. Moreover, what is important from the ordinary man's point of view, it held true not only for heavy but for light or consumer industry.

There is no reason for doubting that the same rate of acceleration would have continued without revolution, and without the extreme exploitation and mass slaughter that marked the process under the Soviets. Just before the First World War started, in 1914, one of the foremost European economists, a Frenchman, Edmond Théry, wrote his book, *Transformation of Russia*. Though he was no admirer of the country in other respects, he concluded that if Russia maintained the percentual growth it had established, it would surely outstrip all other European nations by the middle of this century. He was especially impressed by the rapid rise in farm output, "achieved without the aid of an expensive foreign labor force—as was the case, for instance, in Brazil, the United States, and even Canada."

The fact is that a normal industrial revolution had been under way for fifty years when World War I and political revolution intervened. In 1900, a Baltic German scholar, Baron Korff, wrote: "In the twenty years since I last traveled along the Volga, much has changed. Villages that then consisted of a few cabins are now towns with forty thousand inhabitants and well-paved streets. . . . The river boats are huge, with two or three decks, like Mississippi steamers. Samara, Kazan and Nijni-Novgorod resemble the port of Hamburg."

After the Second World War, in a flare-up of national patriotism, publication of a number of books on the pre-revolutionary economy was finally permitted. One of these, in 1950, was *Development of Russia in the Nineteenth and Twentieth Century*, by Professor P. Khromov. It contains tables showing impressive and steady growth from 1860 to 1917 in population, heavy industry, mining, railroads, foreign trade. These findings have been confirmed by a recent American study, *Sergei Witte and the Industrialization of Russia*, by Theodore H. von Laue, published in 1963 by the Columbia University Press.

In the nine years between the Russo-Japanese War and the outbreak of World War II, Russian industrial product doubled. It was exceeded in Europe only by Britain, Germany, and France. Many Russian products excelled their foreign equivalents and were in demand all over the world. Russian-made locomotives and railroad cars were among the world's best; high-grade automobiles, motorcycles, and bicycles were being manufactured. The Russian-American aviation pioneer, Igor Sikorsky, has attested that "aeronautical science and industry in Russia before 1914 were on a par with America in that period. Several world records were established by airplanes designed and produced in Russia at that time."

Nor were the growing ranks of industrial workers mere exploited robots, in effect helots of the state, as they are today. Labor's awareness of its rights and its power was greater than in the corresponding stage of industrialization in any other country. In her classic American analysis, *Workers Before and After Lenin*, published in 1941, Manya Gordon wrote: "Every increase in the size of the industrial plant and the number of employees registered a corresponding increase in strikes. In other words, the workers were always conscious of their right to a share of the increase in profits." In some years the number of strikers in plants employing more than a thousand people was more than twice their entire labor force; they struck, that is, more than twice a year. This is not exactly the record of the hopelessly cowed and backward proletariat pictured by a later regime which prohibits and punishes strikes.

A Russian law of June 1, 1882, forbade factories to employ children under twelve, and limited work for children of fifteen or under to eight hours a day in two four-hour shifts. In France at that time child labor of twelve hours a day was legal. While a few other countries outdistanced Russia in labor legislation by 1917, it was far more humane and progressive than under the Soviets.

But the old Russia, its present rulers argue, was heavily dependent on foreign capital and therefore "semi-colonial." This is true— but irrelevant. All young industrial societies have relied on capital and technical help from advanced countries. The United States in an equivalent stage of development also drew heavily on foreign, especially British, capital. Moreover, Lenin was no less eager than the tsars before him to lure foreign money into Soviet industry— witness his policy of "concessions" to outside entrepreneurs. Stalin, although his access to foreign capital was limited, could barely have gotten his Five-Year Plan off the ground without capitalist machinery, plans, management, and skills. Now and always, underdeveloped areas have turned to foreign investors, offering tax and other inducements to encourage them.

Russian agriculture was still burdened by remnants of feudal practices. All the same, by 1916 small-holdings of 135 acres or less comprised 71 per cent of the cultivated areas; excluding forest-holdings, the percentage rises to 80. Individual peasants owned 82 per cent of all cattle and 86 per cent of all horses. "The peasant," Sir Maurice Baring, long-time resident in and student of Russia, wrote, "not only tills the arable land but he owns the greater part of it. . . . Agricultural colleges are spreading and the number of agricultural students is every day increasing."

In one respect at least, Russian agriculture led the rest of the world, namely agrarian cooperatives of every type. By the last year of the Romanoff era, some ten million peasants belonged to cooperative credit associations, and there were over twenty thousand consumer cooperatives with over six million members. A Carnegie Foundation report in 1929, referring to the pre-Revolution period, declared: "No other country possessed cooperative organization as broad in scope and affecting the interests of so many classes of the population." The movement was especially strong in its appeal to farmers.

Without doubt the old Russia was ripe for change. Absolutism and its centralized bureaucracy hampered its economic upsurge. It was necessary to clear the road for dynamic and social forces already in existence. This was universally recognized by Russian economists and many political leaders. Instead, unhappily, the road was not cleared but demolished: the greater absolutism and more centralized bureaucracy of Bolshevism was inflicted on the nation.

Lenin, as is well known, regarded electrification as the most vital need of Russia. In 1920, his regime set up GOELRO, a planning commission for this purpose. The commission did not have to start from scratch, but admittedly based its work on existing pre-revolutionary plans that included great hydro-electric projects on the Dnieper, in the Caucasus, and other places. In transportation, too, Soviet planners started with projects worked up in the last tsarist years.

The evidence is conclusive that Russia was preparing vast industrial advances before war interrupted the process. The plain fact is that the Bolsheviks took over a young but vigorous economy, with experienced manpower, technological literacy, an industrious population, an educated class of high intellectual calibre—in a gigantic country well endowed with natural resources. To equate a primitive African or Asian country with the pre-war Russia of 1913, as communist agitators are doing, is preposterous.

We need only project the curve of progress as of 1914—in industry, agriculture, science, education—into the future for half a century to realize that the country, if it had been spared the agonies of totalitarianism, the colossal waste of collective ownership, and the paralyzing effects of rigid dogmas, would have been far ahead of the present Soviet Union. And this without such lovely "sacrifices" as millions of deaths, slave labor camps, and state-feudal serfs on the land.

Professor Hugh Seton-Watson has written: "The Soviet Union has achieved magnificent successes by virtue of the great talents of the people and the great resources of the Russian soil, *in spite of the dogma of Lenin and Stalin.*" Notwithstanding the "economic reforms" being reluctantly experimented with nowadays, that dogma and its inherent limitations have not been abandoned, for the simple reason that to do so would undermine and in the end destroy the communist regime.

The Kremlin cannot reasonably blame its economic difficulties on a low economic base, on the "dark past." The base, as we have seen, was not as low as the legend pretends. Czechoslovakia had one of the most advanced economic systems in Europe, yet when communized it quickly showed the same faults and failures—and is now in desperation resorting to the same reforms—as the USSR. The trouble quite clearly is with communist theory, wherever it is applied.

6 / Pre-1917 Politics and Culture

The myth that the old Russia was a political, cultural, and social wasteland.

Pursuing the comparison between the Russias before and after the 1917 upheaval, let us look first at the administration of justice under the tsars.

The Okhrana (security police) and Siberia were the lurid and justly detested symbols of persecution of political dissent and revolutionary opposition by the Romanoff autocracy. They have been used, for fifty years now, to explain if not to justify Soviet purges, forced labor, mass executions, and genocide.

The ratio between the old and the Soviet terrors, however, is roughly that between a pimple and a cancer. The Okhrana employed some five thousand full-time official agents and a few thousand part-time spies and informers. Its communist successors, from the Cheka and the GPU to the present organization, have had as many as two million operatives, their own uniformed secret-police armies for purely internal use and millions of hidden informers.

In extent, political persecution under the tsars was not small—it only seems strangely small today because we have become accustomed to counting political victims in millions. Statistics in this area were not concealed in the old Russia as they have been under the Soviets. The shock of surprise as one examines them is therefore a measure of the enormities of the Red Terror rather than a proof of past benevolence.

The decade of 1906–1916 was sufficiently blood-soaked for its time. Andrei Vishinsky, long Stalin's chief administrator of Soviet "justice," was not likely to underestimate anything in favor of the old regime. Yet according to his own figures there were in 1913 only 32,000 convicts at hard labor (*katorga*) in Russia, including ordinary criminals. They could all have been accommodated in one of the larger Soviet forced-labor camps; and this was at the peak of the reaction that followed the 1905 revolution. About 25,000 were sentenced to Siberia and other exile regions in the first ten years of the century and 27,000 more between 1911 and 1916.

Those who today justify tsarist political terror by reference to the Red Terror are in no better moral position than Kremlin apologists who excuse Red outrages by invoking outrages in the past. Their comparative dimensions and ruthlessness are the crux of the confrontation. Realism demands, moreover, that two vital truths be underlined.

1. With the reforms of 1864, Russia acquired a judicial system superior to most in the West, except with regard to political crimes. It had trial by jury and a bar celebrated for its elevated moral and intellectual standards. Judges were appointed for life and thereupon became independent, subject neither to removal nor transfer to other places against their will.

   So far as ordinary crimes were concerned, Russia was governed by codified laws which not even the most headstrong of the last tsars dared violate. The death penalty had been abolished as early as 1741 for all crimes except the murder or the attempted murder of the Imperial family. It was extended to cover all political assassinations only after the rise of the revolutionary terrorists and the actual murder of Alexander II.

2. The handling of political crimes, while unfair by the standards set in Russia's own practice in ordinary offenses, was incomparably milder than under the Soviets. There is really no basis for comparison, the contrast is so great. There were no juries in such cases, but only a panel of judges. Jury trials for "politicals" were abolished, it is worth noting, because the juries had proved too lenient to enemies of the monarchy.

But even political trials were public and reported accurately in the press. Evidence was examined by men who took their judicial robes very seriously. The most successful and respected lawyers did not hesitate to defend the accused, from regicides down; many of them, in fact, (among them Alexander Kerensky) built national reputations and popularity upon spirited defense of revolutionaries.

Far from confessing to lies in the Soviet manner of the future, the accused proudly admitted the truth if they were guilty and turned the courtrooms into forums to arouse the masses. Under the guise of defense arguments, their lawyers unbosomed themselves of eloquent indictments of the government and social evils—propaganda that appeared in the press as privileged matter and often was circulated in huge editions in pamphlet form.

Not one of the obscenities of judicial practice in the Soviet period—torture, the hostage system, the mock public trial, the star-chamber trial, "administrative" convictions without trial—can be equated with specifically Russian practices. Some of these methods, in fact, were common in West European states long after their eradication in Russia.

Under the law of 1864, the prosecutors not only had the right to stop a trial if they were convinced of the defendant's innocence, it was their legal duty to do so. Far from sharing the guilt of the accused as in Soviet practice, relatives could not be compelled to testify.

In the 1880's, George Kennan (great-uncle of his namesake, the former American ambassador to Moscow) made his historic investigation of the Siberian exile system, and published his findings in two fat volumes. Not only was he permitted to visit any prisons and exile places he chose but St. Petersburg gave him full cooperation. He returned to the United States to condemn what he had seen with unflagging passion. Yet he acknowledged that "the number of political offenders is much smaller than it is generally supposed to be." He estimated the yearly score of political exile, between 1879 and 1884, at 150. The totals increased rapidly after the turn of the century and in particular after 1905.

The most extreme estimates came from Prince Peter Kropotkin, the anarchist philosopher, in his efforts to awaken the conscience of mankind. Writing in London in 1909, he gave the number of all inmates in Russian prisons as 181,000 and the number of exiles as 74,000 plus some 30,000 more then believed to be in process of transportation. The totals covered offenders of all categories, with ordinary prisoners constituting a majority of convicts and "politicals" a majority of exiles.

In the entire reign of Alexander II, from 1855 to 1881, there was only one execution; a man named Karakozov was hanged for an attempt on the monarch's life. In the following twenty-seven years, which saw the emergence of the bomb as a political weapon, 114 were put to death, an average of about four a year. Not until 1906 did the annual toll of the hangman begin to run into hundreds, with a record of 1,139 in the first post-revolution year of 1906. It then fell off to 73 in 1911 and 126 in 1912. A few hundred more should probably be added for prisoners killed while "trying to escape" and not reckoned in the formal statistics.

These are the hard figures behind the impassioned protests the world over, and especially in Russia itself. This was the notorious White Terror which made the world shudder, and led Count Leo Tolstoy to write his famous *I Cannot Be Silent*. It is no slur on the noble emotions of the time to remark that the whole White Terror did not equal in sheer volume a month of the Red Terror.

The treatment of political prisoners was mild, almost idyllic, as against their fate under communism. They were rarely placed together with criminals and enjoyed an array of special privileges. For many a Russian, exile was a time of intensive reading, writing, and even revolutionary agitation. It was in Siberia that Lenin wrote his book *The Development of Capitalism in Russia*, one of a libraryful of anti-regime tracts composed by others in the enforced isolation and leisure.

The exiles were usually joined by their families and lived a relatively normal life despite harsh surroundings. They were in unlimited correspondence with friends and political comrades in Russia and abroad. Those who had money or received help from outside— committees to aid Russian political prisoners collected funds throughout the liberal world—often went in for hunting, fishing, and other sports. Lenin, Trotsky, and Stalin were all ardent huntsmen in their exile years.

Reading today the memoirs of exiles during the monarchy is an interesting experience, against the knowledge of Soviet concentration-camp purgatories. Nadezhda Krupskaya, Lenin's wife, recounting their routine in Siberia, might be talking of a middle-class winter vacation. One of her letters to a relative does have a tragic note: the maid has just walked out on her, Mrs. Lenin reports, and she has been obliged to do her own housework!

The common people in Russia never confounded political prisoners with criminals and usually held them in high esteem. Russians avoided words like "convict" in talking of political offenders, referring to them as "unfortunates" or even, among the educated, as "passion-bearers"—a term earlier applied to religious mystics who withdrew from the workaday world.

Escape was ridiculously easy. The political fugitive readily found helping hands, food, hiding places. There were no official efforts, as in the Soviet era, to smear opponents of the established order as "wreckers," "enemies of the people," and "mad dogs." Both the official and the popular attitudes scarcely fit into the picture of a benighted Asiatic despotism.

• *Labor Camps Then and Now*

Only a relative few of the "politicals" drew sentences at hard labor in prison camps (*katorga*), the nearest equivalent to the Soviet concentration camps, with their tens of millions of inmates in the aggregate. Numbers aside, how did the respective ordeals compare?

The best known description of life in *katorga* was given to the world by Dostoievsky in *Notes from the House of the Dead*, which appeared in 1862. Exactly one hundred years later, in 1962, the first description inside Russia of a Soviet forced-labor camp, by Alexander Solzhenitsyn, began serial publication in *Novy Mir*, a Moscow literary journal. It later appeared as a book entitled, *A Day in the Life of Ivan Denisovich*, in a small edition in the USSR and in large editions in translations abroad.

The two novels a hundred years apart, provide a remarkable study of similarities and differences. Dr. Mihajlo Mihajlov, the young Yugoslav professor, has analyzed these in an article published in the Zagreb *Forum* in 1964. Both authors are great artists and both wrote from long personal experiences as prisoners. "Compared with twentieth-century conditions," Mihajlov found, many aspects of " 'the worst Siberian prison camp' of the nineteenth century seem idyllic." Both books "in effect describe the attempt to turn human beings into slaves," he attests, but the brutal pressures "have been incomparably greater in the twentieth century than they were in the nineteenth."

One after another, he compares elements of *katorga* a hundred years ago—food, labor, punishments, relations with the outer world, etc.—with Soviet practices. Without exception Dostoievsky's *House of the Dead* was less horrifying than its counterpart in Stalin's years. The former camp had thirty inmates, the latter had four hundred. The tsarist camp was surrounded by a "palisade," the Soviet camp by barbed wire, searchlights mounted on watchtowers, and trained dogs. The food was bad a century ago, but the chronic hunger that figures in the Soviet novel was no part of the prison regime under the tsars. The prisoners a hundred years ago maintained contact with their families and were allowed occasional visitors. In their non-working time they could read, play games, work at hobby crafts.

Mihajlov writes about a column of convicts, in the *House of the Dead*, passing through a small Siberian town: "The prisoners talk and joke, tease one another, while passersby stop and give them alms. In Solzhenitsyn's book there is no question of giving them alms, since in the camps of Stalin's day it was generally impossible to enter into direct contact with their inmates."

In the 1860's the prisoners "did no work on Sundays, celebrated Christmas and Easter for several days on end, and those celebrating their name-day were also freed from work. The Jew, Isai Fomich, is assured by law of his right not to work on the Sabbath, a right of which he naturally makes good use. Moslems have the same privilege. The prisoners amuse themselves by rearing domestic animals—the billy-goat Vaska and geese. We further learn that the prisoners 'arrange a theater' on holidays, and occasionally were even allowed to come into contact with women."

Camp existence under communism has been a hundred times more hellish than in the Dostoievsky camp. This is apparent not only in the Soviet novel, which in general understates the hellishness, but in a score or more of the detailed accounts by ex-prisoners published abroad through the years.

Those who seek alibis for the Soviets rummage through Russian history and pick up what they need from Ivan the Terrible, Peter the Great, and Nicholas I. They normally slur over the decades immediately before the revolution. But the pre-1917 generation saw an enormous amount of political and social progress, which the communists, far from continuing, reversed and destroyed.

The 1905 uprising began with a general strike, mutinies of sailors, seizures of big estates by land-hungry peasants. It was definitely a revolution from below. The modern constitution and pledges of reform granted by the frightened dynasty were in direct response to pressures from the people. The constitution was whittled away and the pledges were in large measure repudiated in the later reaction. Had they been kept, the nation would have enjoyed political liberties not too far removed from those under other constitutional monarchies. And despite the reaction, the twelve years between the two revolutions provided a substantial base for peaceful democratic evolution.

The electoral and franchise laws were stacked in favor of the upper and propertied classes, but the democratic parties taken together held an overwhelming majority of the Duma (parliament) seats. Though its powers were continually restricted, the Duma was far from impotent. It retained enough control of the purse-strings to obtain concessions from the government and occasionally to force out unpopular ministers. And it was a powerful forum. Its debates—not merely critical of the *status quo*, but often boldly revolutionary—were published as a matter of right by the leading newspapers. Lenin in Switzerland wrote speeches delivered by his Bolshevik deputies, which then appeared in leading newspapers.

The press, to be sure, was not free in the British and American sense. But all the liberal factions had legal papers and periodicals of their own, and even the extreme parties managed to express their views in print. While most liberal papers flourished, few of their reactionary competitors could subsist without government subsidies. A number of brilliant satiric journals needled the authorities mercilessly. In 1912—called "the high point of the darkest reaction"—a Bolshevik newspaper, *Pravda,* was established in St. Petersburg, edited by Viacheslav Molotov.

By the time 1917 rolled around, the Russian people had behind them a tradition of a hundred years of revolutionary thought and action. A political institution that served as a school in self-rule was the *zemstvo* or local and provincial administration, though its democratic character has too often been exaggerated. Elected by the tax-paying population, the *zemstvos* were on the whole controlled by the propertied gentry. But they became more and more imbued with a liberal and progressive spirit, so that the central authorities came to look upon them as hotbeds of subversion. Half a century of *zemstvo* effort produced notable results in material improvements: medical aid, roads, home crafts, mutual life and fire insurance, etc. At the same time it fostered impulses to self-government and mutual help.

Another important social school was the *mir* or peasant commune, an institution of ancient Russian vintage. Although that too has been overplayed by foreign historians, it did have a good deal in common with the New England town meeting. The heads of all peasant households in a village voted and argued as equals in deciding common problems and settling local disputes.

On the economic side the *mir* was a collective enterprise; but in contrast with the socialized Marxist society, it was highly personalized, voluntary, and respectful of individual preferences. Its members had the right, usually by a two-thirds vote, to disband common cultivation of the land in favor of other systems. It was precisely this voluntary element which led Herzen, Kropotkin, and the Social Revolutionary party to reject conventional socialist doctrine in favor of agrarian socialism deriving from the *mir*.

There is a superficial resemblance, of course, between the methods of the communists and tsarist practices. But the same family resemblance holds true for all oppressive systems. Bolshevism could just as convincingly be traced as deriving from Prussian autocracy or the ancient Pharaohs. After all, the Nazi and Fascist dictatorships were close enough to the Bolshevik pattern without benefit of a tsarist background.

• *Education Under Tsarism*

For over a century before the Bolsheviks appeared on the scene, Russia was famous for its great universities, which were a match for the world's best in quality. In 1913 it had more institutions of higher learning than England, France, or Germany. "Russian scholarship before the revolution reached the very highest standard," the late Sir Bernard Pares, British historian, wrote in 1942.

Contradicting the fable that university education was only for the rich and well-born, he added that "the number of places filled by sons of the peasantry was far greater than anything that was dreamed of at Oxford or Cambridge before the present century." Under the law, in the last decades of the monarchy, 15 per cent of university students were on scholarships provided by the state; another 15 to 20 per cent were supported by private endowments.

More than a third of the student body thus comprised young men and women too poor to pay their own tuitions.

The quality of education was not only incomparably higher than under the Soviets, but higher than in most other countries. A degree from a leading Russian university was greatly respected throughout the world. Its essence was free inquiry—even in sociology, economics, and government—to the constant despair of the autocracy. None of the theories of social and political reform could be kept out of the curriculum, so that the institutions of higher learning became seedbeds of subversion and revolution. The Russian faculties were self-governing along democratic lines, and autonomous student organizations of every conceivable variety flourished despite all that a reactionary officialdom could do to frustrate them.

The Russian intelligentsia (the very word is of Russian coinage) was a unique phenomenon, a sort of intellectual aristocracy enjoying more popular respect than the aristocracy of birth. Because of the handicaps imposed by the government, mental freedom—amounting at times to license—was exercised with a peculiar zest. "This intelligentsia," Helen Iswolsky wrote in *Soul of Russia* (1943), "was something more than a culture elite: it has been compared to a religious order, in that it was austere, ascetic, and disinterested. Its representatives were not content to preach their doctrines: they sought to apply them."

Writers and thinkers, of course, had a hard time of it. But they were never frightened or silenced. What they could not say forthrightly they said elliptically, and their audiences understood them perfectly. New ideas from the outside world had free entry: the first translation of Karl Marx's *Das Kapital*, in 1872, was into Russian, fourteen years before it appeared in English, and it was freely available in Russian bookshops and libraries. Independent monthlies like *Vyestnik*, *Yevropy*, and *Russkoye Bogatstvo* were outspoken and progressive.

No, the old Russia was no more an intellectual than an economic Sahara. The best proof of this, in common sense, is in its towering achievements in letters, the arts, science. These are implicit in names that have become part of the wealth of civilized mankind—names like Pushkin, Lermontov, Goncharev, Gogol,

Turgeniev, Dostoievsky, Tolstoy, Chekhov, Merezhkovsky, Bunin, Gorki, in literature; Tchaikovsky, Glinka, Mussorgsky, Rimski-Korsakov, Scriabin, Rachmaninoff, Prokofiev, in music; Kandinsky, Repin, and Roerich, in painting; Stanislavsky and Nemirovich-Danchenko, in theater; Mendeleyev and Butlerov, in chemistry; Mechnikov, in medicine; Pavlov, in psychology; Lobachevsky, in mathematics; Tugen Barovsky, in economics; Struve, in astronomy; Herzen, Bakunin, Kropotkin, and, yes, Lenin, in social theory.

The whole world drew inspiration from Russian literature, the Moscow Art Theater, Russian ballet. A vulgar Soviet boastfulness in recent years, claiming Russian priority for all inventions, from the safety-pin to radio, has drawn the ridicule it deserves. This, however, should not obscure the truth that Russia did make vital contributions to science and invention, including early radio discoveries.

A national culture of this scope could not have come to fruition in a wasteland. Its roots are in the genius of the Russian people. That the renaissance, started in the early 1800's, could have taken place at all was proof of the psychological freedom which thrived side by side with political tyranny and, in the final analysis, overshadowed that tyranny.

Sir Maurice Baring, writing before the Revolution, could attest: "There is no country in the world where the individual enjoys so great a measure of personal liberty, where the *liberté de moeurs* is so great as in Russia; where the individual man can do as he pleases with so little interference or criticism on the part of his neighbors, where there is so little moral censorship, where liberty of abstract thought or esthetic production is so great. . . ."

The rapidity with which Russians assimilated the cultural idioms of Western Europe and reshaped them in their own image is in itself striking. The fact that the end-products were in turn absorbed by the West cancels out the exaggerations about Russia's Asiatic and Byzantine qualities. Where are the non-Russian Asiatic and Byzantine books, poems, symphonies, and scientific discoveries that fit so readily and completely into the modern mind?

One of the major communist claims for credit—and well deserved—has been the substantial elimination of illiteracy. According to some Soviet figures, only 28 per cent of the population could read and write in the last years of the monarchy. More objective statistics put it at about 40 per cent for the whole country, and much higher for European Russia. At best, however, retarded education at a mass level is a blot on the tsarist record.

The law for compulsory schooling was not promulgated until 1910; it was introduced in stages and planned to become universal by 1922. The matter, however, is not merely one of quantity. In the old Russia literacy opened up far greater horizons of enlightenment than in the Soviet era, when the printed word is a jealously guarded monopoly of the state. In any case, if the process started in 1910 had not been cut short by the war and revolution, literacy would certainly have reached the West European level in the 1920's or 1930's.

The central confusion, in appraising Russia, is the tendency to look upon a historical time-lag as if it were a quality in the nature of the people. Historical misfortunes, like the long subjection to the Mongols, are mistaken for attributes of the Russian character.

Serfdom was one of the main effects of historic backsliding and in turn the chief cause of the long retardation. It was evolved only through the sixteenth and seventeenth centuries, just when Western Europe was emerging from feudalism. But it differed from ordinary feudalism in one respect: it was never fully accepted by Russian society or the serfs themselves as a fixed and divinely sanctioned institution. Always it was regarded as something *imposed* from above by law that must eventually be repealed. Though it would last until 1861, until the day Abraham Lincoln assumed the Presidency in the United States, it was not admitted as a permanent way of life. In its heart, the nation never acknowledged serfdom as sacrosanct.

To quote Baring again, as of 1914: "The peasants never, through nearly two centuries of slavery, lost sight of the fact that this legislation was merely a temporary makeshift, a stroke of opportunism. Moreover, they kept hold of the idea that the land was theirs; that the land belonged to the people who tilled it." Pushkin, the national poet, Dostoievsky once pointed out, "was the first to understand that the Russian is no slave, in spite of century-old slavery." The communists, who rehabilitated Pushkin after a period of suppression, have reason to ponder this. The telltale fact is that the value of the person was never discounted in Russia as it was in other feudal societies. A deep respect for the individual was the common denominator of Russian moral perceptions, from Saint Sergius of Radonezh to Count Leo Tolstoy.

The glib statement that communism is a peculiarly Russian visitation rests, in the final analysis, on the accident that it first came to power in Russia. The postwar years have demonstrated that the affliction can be imposed no less successfully on Poles and Czechs, Germans and Chinese. A stronger case, indeed, can be made for the idea that Soviet communism is a negation of the Russian spirit —that Bolshevism is not a forward thrust into history but a recoil and retreat into long-outlived centuries.

In the light of his subsequent love affair with Bolshevism, it is revealing to read a comment on Russia *in 1915* by John Reed, future author of *Ten Days that Shook the World*. After a brief visit to the country during the war, he wrote: "Russian ideals are the most exhilarating, thought the freest, Russian art the most exuberant; Russian food and drink are to me the best, and the Russians themselves are, perhaps, the most interesting human beings that exist. . . . Everyone acts just as he feels like acting, and says just what he wants to."

Millions of Russians, trapped by the communists they abhor, are mortified when they hear or read about "Russian atrocities," "Russian communism," "Russian attacks on Europe," and the like, when the reference is to Soviet and communist behavior. For they look upon Marxism, communism, and their derivatives as an international infection, originated in Western Europe. They reject the assumption that Bolshevism is a purely Russian disease.

7 / Resistance

The myth that the Soviet people love
the communist system.

"There is perfect harmony between the rulers and the ruled. Russians may grumble—don't we all?—but they support their government the way we do ours. They are intensely loyal. The people have been taught to love their chains."

These reassurances are culled from actual reports by Western tourists returning from Russia. In the 1960's, just as in the bigger tourist invasion of Stalinland in the early 1930's, the typical short-term visitor is impressed by the surface calm, the holiday parades, the declarations of loyalty by a few "ordinary Russians" he may have questioned through an interpreter-guide. He sees no barricades, hears no exploding bombs, and naïvely assumes that the "monolithic unity" advertised by the regime is a fact.

Even if this were true, a spell of sightseeing is scarcely enough to confirm it. The relations between a totalitarian police-state and its citizenry are never so casually appraised. Opinion-sampling, after all, is a monopoly of secret police operatives, who employ informers and truncheons instead of questionnaires. And "ordinary Russians," who hesitate to express their true sentiments in the bosom of their families, would hardly confide to a stranger and a foreigner.

"The system of serving foreign tourists in the USSR has been carefully planned," according to a recent Soviet refugee familiar with the techniques, Yury Krotkov, in his book *The Angry Exile*. "Routes, hotels, transportation, interpreters, the whole organization is devoted to one aim—the effective presentation of the achievements and triumphs of the socialist system. . . . As a rule all activities are prepared and rehearsed in advance, at times so skillfully that it can seem to the tourist as if he were exercising his own free will."

Certainly the Soviet leaders, judging by their conduct rather than their words, do not share the complacent tourist view. Why, otherwise, would they maintain a political-police establishment unprecedented for size and ruthlessness? Why would they surround their country with barbed-wire and death decrees to keep the "intensely loyal" citizens from running away? Why would they deploy veritable armies of trained "agitators" to "sell" communism to the people, if they were already sold on it? Why would they jam foriegn broadcasts and lie to the country about how the people live in the West?

Common sense should tell us that no regime lavishes huge slices of its budget, brains, energy, and manpower on internal security unless it feels itself insecure. The Kremlin has better sources of information than any visitor to its domain. Its own estimate of the love and loyalty of the people has been spelled out, decade after decade, in terror, periodic purges, frantic warnings against enemies within, draconic laws against dissent.

"Communist regimes," Milovan Djilas wrote in *The New Class*, "are a form of latent civil war between the government and the people." In the USSR it has been more actual than latent. A great gulf of mutual distrust yawns between the government and the people. By this I do not mean that all the people or even a majority of them are awarely "opposed" to the system. I mean only that most Russians, and this includes rank-and-file communists, are not consciously or ardently "for" the *status quo* in the way Americans or Britons are automatically for their respective societies.

Psychologically they have never given their consent and imprimatur to the Soviet way of life. In most other countries, people identify themselves with their government, whether they like it or not. Even in pre-war Russia, they were wont to say, "*We* have sent an ultimatum to the Kaiser. . . . *We* have liberated the serfs." Soviet citizens, however, refer to the regime in the third person: "*They* have done thus-and-so. . . . *They* have built some more apartments." And the pronoun packs as much contempt as the speaker dares to reveal.

• *Permanent Civil War*

Even the most sadistic police-state does not engage in large-scale liquidations and brainwashing just for the fun of it, or prescribe capital punishment for "crimes" which in other civilized countries are unknown as such, or treated as misdemeanors. These are measures of self-protection against real or potential dangers. The extent of the peoples' distaste for their Soviet fate can be deduced from the magnitude, the ferocity, and the persistence of the Kremlin's counter-measures.

No ruling group in the annals of man has diverted so much of its wealth and thought to its own defense against the population. After half a century of limitless power, it is still promoting what in normal nations is taken for granted: loyalty to the existing order. The communists have failed to win what social scientists call *legitimacy*, the assumption of the citizen that his country and its government are indivisible. (This central failure became especially conspicuous in June, 1941, when the country was invaded—but the lessons of the Russo-German war are so crucial for our balance sheet that a separate section will be devoted to it.)

From the day the Bolsheviks seized control of a weakened and chaotic nation, there has been in effect a continuous civil war between the dictators and those to whom they dictate. In the first years, as we have seen, the contest was open and military. Since then it has been largely concealed and political, yet quite obvious to those who watched with unblurred eyes; and even bloodier than the military phase. Once we grasp this concept of permanent internal conflict, much about Soviet Russia that seems enigmatic and baffling begins to make sense.

The many millions who have perished in the struggle, whether finished off in police dungeons and slave-labor centers, or starved in punitive man-made famine, are the casualties in that war.

The hordes of inmates of isolators, prison camps, penal colonies, are its prisoners-of-war.

The special KGB army, with its own air force, tanks, artillery, and communications system—an elite soldiery better paid and fed than the regular armed forces—represents the regime's shock troops in that war.

The perennial *chistkas* or purges, the extermination of this or that layer of the population "as a class," the dispersal of entire "republics" and "autonomous regions" are battles in that war. The more spectacular events, such as the forced collectivization of farmers, the blood-purges of the late thirties, and the postwar purges of returning troops, are major campaigns in that war.

The incessant propaganda—exhortations to sacrifice, threats against enemies at home and alarums about foreign enemies—is the psychological offensive that has become an element in all modern warfare.

Yes, permanent civil war—that is the reality under the outward calm, the key to the whole Soviet scene. On their side of the invisible barricades, the unarmed masses have responded with every species of open and passive resistance. Necessarily, they have resorted to guerrilla methods: sniping, sapping, sabotaging. Vast numbers of Soviet functionaries, police officials, local communist "activists," "Stakhanovite" pacesetters in industry have been waylaid and murdered through the years. In every town and village communists feel themselves engulfed in suspicion and hatred: they are the satraps of an internal force of occupation and the symbol of their authority is not a title but the ubiquitous revolver.

Though there has not been a year without episodes of violent resistance to the regime, they are rarely mentioned in the Soviet press. When they are of a major character, with heavy casualties, officials may allude to them vaguely as "irregularities" or "disorders" in some area. Occasionally a brief press report about the trial and conviction of people involved in some riot confirms the whispered rumors about the occurrence. Sometimes the news of shocking events even reaches the press abroad, usually with a long delay. There have been major strikes despite laws against it. There have been anti-government demonstrations amounting to uprisings, crushed as brutally as the revolt in Hungary was crushed.

On July 12, 1941, only a few weeks after war started, workers in Shakhty, in the Don coal-mining area, were joined by the local Red Army garrison in an armed uprising. They proclaimed an independent Cossack republic. After several days of spirited fighting, the rebels were annihilated. The following year, from August 3 into September, over 15,000 Kuban Cossack troops of the Red Army mutinied, killing the political commissars. They were defeated by the forces of the secret police.

Large-scale slave revolts broke out, from 1952 to 1956, in the concentration camps of Vorkuta, Karaganda, Norilsk, Kungur, Karabash, Tayshet, etc., and as far away as Sakhalin Island. They were as desperate, as hopeless, as the Spartacus slave revolts in ancient Rome, and similarly drowned in blood, with hundreds, perhaps thousands, shot down. Much has been written about these events but the gory details are still a state secret. It is fair to surmise that the beginnings of camp uprisings played a role in the Kremlin's decision, while Stalin was still alive, to dismantle the forced-labor network in part and improve conditions in what remained.

Bloody riots are known to have erupted at Temir-Tau in the Karaganda region in 1959; at Novocherkassk in the Rostov area in 1962; at Pskov in 1963. In Tiflis, the capital of Soviet Georgia, in March, 1956, there were huge demonstrations, in which thousands, mostly young people, fought from behind barricades. The government threw tanks and heavy artillery against them; estimates of the dead ran as high as seven hundred.

The Novocherkassk tragedy is worth recounting because, after years of rumor and guesswork, the facts were brought out and made public by eye-witnesses who escaped to the West. In June, 1962, demonstrations against the government were touched off in a number of areas by the announcement of higher prices for meat and dairy products. Apparently the bloodiest struggle occurred in Novocherkassk, a city of 100,000 about sixty miles from Rostov.

It began on June 1 as a peaceable student demonstration. Workers left their benches to join them. By next day some 20,000 were in the streets. The local militia proved inadequate and uncooperative against the demonstrators. The first regular soldiers brought into the city refused to shoot into the crowds. Moscow then rushed in motorized units of KGB troops which did the job of "pacification." An eye-witness, writing in *Nashi Dni*, an *émigré* magazine in Germany, said that he counted more than two hundred dead in the central square and that the toll was heavy in other districts.

After the bloodbath, two Kremlin leaders, Mikoyan and Poliansky, flew to Novocherkassk with promises and soothing words. The city was quarantined for six weeks: nobody could leave or enter without a KGB pass. Not a word appeared in the press, of course, but soon the story was being talked about in whispers throughout the country. The "Budapest of Russia," some called the city. Novocherkassk is the kind of explosion that, given foul political weather, could start a landslide and bury the dictatorship.

We have a right to surmise, on the basis of past experience, that for every strike or riot that becomes known in the outside world, scores have taken place. One of the best-informed American students of Russia, William Henry Chamberlin, in a book he wrote in the war years, said that in Russia, historically, periods of seeming quiet "are broken by episodes of fierce revolt that reveal another aspect of the Russian character: the aspect of the eternal rebel." Under communism the periods of apparent stability have been few and far between. Only the rigid censorship has hidden this truth.

· Passive Resistance

Far more extensive and persistent has been the passive resistence: work slow-downs, wastage and diversion of public property, universal law-breaking. More than any scholarly theories, it helps explain the low productivity and low quality on farms and in factories.

The tactics of non-cooperation come as naturally to most Russians as they did to the masses in India when they were opposing British colonialism. The refusal of the peasants in the collectivization years ago to sow beyond their own immediate needs—for which they paid with millions of lives in 1932–1933—exceeded in scope anything that India had experienced. Their half-hearted work on the collectives ever since, in contrast with the zeal they bring to the tiny plots they have been permitted to farm privately, is a continuation of those tactics. In the factories, slow-downs on the job ("Italian strikes," in Russian slang) and spoilage of goods persist in the face of incredibly harsh laws intended to stop it.

The worker and the peasant alike helps himself to products and small tools as if they were his by right. Embezzlement of state funds, pilfering of state products, falsification of state accounts are as common in Red Russia as drinking was during Prohibition in the United States. It has become a way of life. Doubtless pervasive poverty is the main cause, but it also has overtones of defiance through acts of protest against an odious existence. No sense of moral wrong-doing attaches to cheating the government.

The Soviet newspapers are candid in exposing the unpleasant facts, obviously because they are too widespread to be hidden, and sometimes dare hint at the more unpleasant political implications.

Thus *Sovietskaya Rossia* writes (June 26, 1966) that "the dragging off from the factory, office, construction site, etc., of anything you can lay hands on has become deeply rooted among ordinary Soviet citizens." Then it adds: "Whereas it is very easy to get help from the public to catch a person who has committed some petty theft of private property, it is almost impossible to catch such a person who has stolen a factory bus or lorry." The public, that is to say, will not help apprehend those who rob their common foe, the state!

Exasperated references to an extraordinary variety of frauds are standard in Soviet speeches and editorials. Dozens of pages in an historic address by Georgi Malenkov at the Nineteenth Party Congress were devoted to inveighing against thievery, neglect of duty, illicit trade, criminal bookkeeping, and the rest of the familiar communist corruptions. The litany of complaint on this score was kept up by Khrushchev and is now intoned by his successors.

According to the Moscow *Party Life* in 1964, the number of "volunteer guards" of divers types had reached six million—probably a boastful exaggeration. These are a post-Stalin species of neighborhood vigilantes (*Druzhiny*, or state guards, seems to be the generic term for them) under names like People's Voluntary Militia, Comrades' Courts, Daily Life Brigades, organized at the government's behest to watch and, if necessary, "discipline" their blocks and districts.

But these millions have been unable to cope with the groundswell of "hooliganism," alcoholism, and thievery. The incidence of vandalism, rape, and murder is chronically on the rise. The problems of juvenile delinquency are standard fare in the press, especially in youth papers like *Komsomolskaya Pravda*. In 1965, Moscow and other cities imposed a 10:00 P.M. curfew for children under sixteen not accompanied by adults. Indicative of the worsening situation is a government program for "Preservation of Public Order" promulgated in July, 1966, enlarging the authority of the police, setting more drastic penalties for a long inventory of common crimes and enjoining the courts against leniency.

Old-style banditry exists on a scale unknown in pre-revolutionary times, though in communist theory such evils were to fade out once private enterprise had been socialized. Since "politicals" have been confined with ordinary convicts—an insult that had been abandoned by the monarchy in its last century—much has become known about the criminal elements. The *blatnoi*, as they are called, live either in the forests or in the largest cities, concealment being easier in both places.

A number of these gangs are the demoralized remnants of wartime bands which fought the Soviet government in the Carpathians, the Baltics, the Caucasian mountains—in effect fugitives from the law. But uniquely in the modern world of crime, some of the gangs pretend to have a Robin Hood flavor, robbing the rich and helping the poor. The best-known of these calls itself Black Cats. No doubt the public, which believes their pretensions, spreads a good deal of romantic nonsense about them. But this much seems true: the banditry is directed against government property and officialdom rather than private people and their possessions.

There are strong political overtones, no less, to the highly ramified illegal "free economy" flourishing on an immense scale in the folds and interstices of the socialized society. I shall have more to say about it in the section on the planned economy.

And there are endless acts of pure malice against the authorities, the Soviet press now and then reveals, in which loot plays no part. Let no one supppose that there is no fire under the smoke of the Kremlin's continuous outcries against "wreckers" and saboteurs. The sand in the gears may be an accident—or it may not. The line between natural inefficiency and purposeful vandalism, between apathetic neglect and deliberate damage, is not always easy to draw. The high incidence of broken-down machines, flooded mines, disrupted assembly lines, inexplicable explosions that have figured in Soviet purges reflect a fundamental lack of interest, even where there is no forthright sabotage.

The nerves of the Soviet oligarchs and their privileged entourage are consequently strained to the limit. Their souls are guilt-ridden; the fearful contrasts between idealistic professions and gory official crimes have set up intense inner tensions. A besieged minority in a conquered nation, they see a threat in every frown, menace in the most innocent criticism, hostile design in every failure of its complicated politico-economic machinery.

Romain Rolland, in defending the Soviets, once said that "the proletariat must be led to their happiness against their own will." He did not reckon with the consequences of such fanatic arrogance. He could not know the old Russian proverb: "One is not driven into heaven with a club."

Henry Yagoda, who headed up the GPU in the 1930's, until he was himself arrested and shot, told an American correspondent, William Reswick of the Associated Press: "We are a minority in a vast country. Abolish the GPU and we are through." An article smuggled out of Russia, signed only "X," in the June, 1965 issue of a Russian-language magazine in New York, *Novy Zhurnal*, said approximately the same thing: "The overwhelming mass of the population . . . would, of course, sweep it all away in a single day if they were free to do so. The Soviet rulers are perfectly aware of this, so the guiding principle of their government is to see to it that the population is not allowed freedom."

No one who has lived in the USSR could be ignorant of the fact that concealment of the facts, suppressed or doctored statistics, and overt lying are important elements in Kremlin internal strategy. "From top to bottom," the anonymous writer declared, "the regime is permeated with lies. . . . They fill their ideology, the newspapers, the magazines, the public statements of government officials, economic reports, everything." A recent article by an American analyst, Leon M. Herman, dealt with the fog of evasion and distortion around official Soviet economic data. "In order to preserve its grip on the government," he concluded, "it must deprive the citizens not only of the means to change the leadership, but also of any facts that may prompt them to question the authority of the rulers."

All the news fit to print in *Izvestia*, and all other Soviet newspapers, doesn't include even terrible accidents and catastrophes. In the Urals, in 1958, an atomic reactor exploded killing many thousands. In the Moscow area, in the summer of 1962, a series of train wrecks claimed hundreds of lives. Almost two hundred persons were killed when an experiment went wrong in Podlipki, also near Moscow, where research on missiles is conducted underground. A good many Soviet astronauts, as American and other intelligence agencies know, have perished—some in the air after launchings, others on the ground during simulated tests. But from their press and radio, Russians would never have known about the disasters. They did know, because such things are spread, perhaps even exaggerated, by word of mouth.

By and large, therefore, they put little faith in newspapers, radio, and official rhetoric. Many of the more egregious official lies are recognized as such, sooner or later, by the better-informed minority, further undermining the credibility of their political betters.

A book titled *Political Map of the World*, put out in Moscow in 1958 declared: "The main burden and the principal victories in defeating the Fascist Germans, and later the Japanese imperialists, fell to the Soviet Union." At another point it said that in the 1956 Suez crisis, "England, France, and Israel, with the help of the United States, unloosed a military adventure in Egypt." Surely some of the readers must have remembered that the United States had joined the USSR *against* that undertaking, and that Japan had been beaten before Russia entered the war.

A tenth-grade history textbook contains no references to the Soviet-Nazi pact of 1939, no mention of the Soviet-Finnish war or of the Baltic and East Polish annexations. But tenth-graders do grow up, eventually learn the truth, and are forever bitter about having been lied to. The state's power over the people's minds is thus steadily narrowed through what has been called the "erosion by skepticism."

No one can measure the effects upon the Russian people of half a century of pitiless propaganda and indoctrination, never challenged and never refuted. It has amounted to mental and psychological terror. The phenomenal fact, however, is that it has not always or necessarily "worked," and at times has even backfired against the regime. It happened that I was living in Moscow during the worst years of the Great Depression in the United States. The Soviet press, of course, was filled with accounts of its horrors. Yet I found myself obliged to convince Soviet friends that there really *was* a depression. Because their press and radio were concentrating on it, they assumed it was untrue or exaggerated.

American visitors to the USSR have often commented, in pleased astonishment, on the contrast between the frantic official anti-American campaigns and the friendliness, even affection, they were shown by individual Russians. Erwin C. Canham, editor of the *Christian Science Monitor*, for instance, on returning from the USSR in 1959, wrote: "Forty-two years of bitter propaganda poured into the minds of the Soviet people have not produced hatred or malice against the United States or the West generally."

Adlai Stevenson declared himself "baffled" by the fervent demonstrations of friendship with which his party was greeted wherever it went in Soviet Russia. They were clearly spontaneous. The Stevenson tour coincided with the landing of U.S. forces in Lebanon and the normal anti-American propaganda was at a pitch of frenzy. Moscow just then had more reason to stir up hostility toward prominent Americans than the outbursts of affection they actually witnessed.

The visit to the USSR by Richard M. Nixon as Vice-President, similarly, produced an unscheduled pro-American demonstration, in Novosibirsk, where his party drew tremendous and ethusiastic crowds. Again, it was unplanned, unexpected, and embarrassing to Khrushchev, who had been unfriendly, even rude, to Nixon. Had the authorities wished to stage a warm, popular demonstration, they would have done so in Moscow or Leningrad, not in Siberia.

It has usually been said that the Soviet people were eager to show their friendly sentiments for Americans *despite* their government's anti-American tirades. More likely it was *because* of it. Was it perhaps a safe and convenient occasion to indicate contempt for the anti-American rantings and a vague but abiding sense of America as a symbol of freedom? In any event, the Kremlin's anti-American propaganda obviously has been far from successful. In the face of failure in this conspicuous area, it would be illogical to assume that internal propaganda has been any more successful with respect to other issues.

• Voting with Their Feet

Those who profess to see unity between the Red dictatorships and their citizenry cannot evade the obligation to account for the constant streams of fugitives from communist countries. It has been and remains a one-way flow: in Europe from the communist East to the free West; in Asia from the Chinese mainland to Hong Kong, Taiwan, Macao; from North Korea to the south, from North Vietnam (when it was still possible) to South Vietnam.

Several million Russians fled in the first Soviet years—to Europe, China, Iran, Turkey. After World War II, millions of Soviet citizens fought (often in the literal physical sense) against repatriation to their victorious homeland, and about half a million succeeded in remaining as displaced persons. In all there are today more than seven million fugitives from communism in Europe. Following the Korean armistice, 24,440 Chinese "volunteers" in prisoner-of-war camps had a free choice of returning to their country and families or remaining as emigrants. More than half of them, 14,200, chose not to return. J. Edgar Hoover, head of the FBI, in a book published in 1962, said of the communist bloc: "From 1945 until 1962 some ten million persons, denied a meaningful ballot, voted in the only possible way—with their feet—and fled." Other estimates are close to fifteen million. The figure would have been many times greater if the opportunities for escape had been greater.

The monstrous Berlin Wall, raised by Khrushchev and Ulbricht to stem the flood of East Germans fleeing westward, stands as the repulsive symbol of the anxiety of people under communism to throw off its yoke. In August, 1966, the East German bosses had the effrontery to "celebrate" the fifth anniversary of the wall. They didn't say that during those years 3,510 of their subjects managed, notwithstanding, to climb or crash or dig under the wall to freedom; 69 others were known to have died in the attempt.

Since the Soviet Union captured East Europe, melodramatic escapes from the Sovietized nations have become a familiar ingredient in the daily news. Fugitives have come by truck, by purloined planes and trains and boats; they have swum across rivers and tunneled under mined frontiers. The world has heard only of the more daring *successful* escapes; it could only guess about how many failed in their bid for freedom and paid for it with imprisonment or their lives.

A substantial number of the Soviet and East European participants in the Olympics in Australia chose not to return to their homelands. Sportsmen from communist countries taking part in contests in non-communist cities regularly seek asylum in the West. In late March, 1967 nearly 100 fans who had come from Soviet-bloc nations for hockey championship games in Vienna—100 out of the 600 who had wangled permission for the trip—defected. The flights to freedom among actors, ballet dancers, and other members of Soviet-bloc cultural missions abroad have become almost routine. By now, it takes a defection as conspicuous as that of Stalin's only surviving child, his daughter Svetlana Alliluyeva, to make big headlines.

Wherever the communists take over, people try to run away.

More than 300,000 Cubans have abandoned their homes and possessions to escape communism since Fidel Castro came to power;
hundreds more perished in the attempt, but the desperate flights
have not ceased. Soviet escapees and non-returners are among us in
every country of the non-communist world, and their numbers
keep growing. We hear less about escapes from the USSR only
because they are more difficult—the Soviets have a much longer
experience in policing frontiers. If the Iron Curtain around Soviet
Russia were lifted, we would see an exodus that would make the
Biblical flight of the Israelites from Egypt look trivial by comparison.

Tensions, deep-running grievances and hatreds, open and secret
resistance to the regime, have been the hallmarks of the fifty Soviet
years. Communists on the lower levels, being closer to people, are
overwhelmingly among the discontented. A study of Soviet attitudes, based on systematic interviews with hundreds of defectors
and written by Dr. A. Inkeles, was published in London in 1959 as
The Soviet Citizen. It divides the population, as reflected in the
judgment of those questioned, into believers and non-believers. "It
is striking," Dr. Inkeles noted, "that the great majority of party
members are seen as non-believers. A frequently quoted estimate
was that only 10 per cent . . . believed in the party ideology."
Even after discounts are made for the likely bias of escaped men
and women, the basic picture remains credible and significant.

• *"Disorder and Panic"*

No one is more sharply conscious of the great gulf separating them
from the people and from the ordinary communists than the rulers
themselves. This is implicit, where it is not explicit, in everything
they say or do. When Hitler struck at their country, an offensive
against the "inner enemy" had the priority in the Kremlin reaction
over the offensive against the invaders—and with good reason, as
we shall see. At no time, however, was this chronic fear more vividly
dramatized than in the first week of March, 1953, when Stalin died.

The official myth had been that the populace loved the dictator
and was loyal to his works. But his associates and heirs were too
frightened to hide their fears. From the first bulletin reporting
Stalin's brain hemorrhage to the orations from the Lenin mauso-
leum in Red Square, their pronouncements were all filled with un-

abashed exhortations for "unity" and "vigilance" in the face of "internal enemies" and frenzied appeals to the nation to "rally around the party."

The Romanoff autocracy, upon the death of a tsar, had never felt it necessary to beg for loyalty to his successor; that was something which, perhaps mistakenly, it took for granted. But the Kremlin made no such assumptions. Its announcements in connection with Stalin's illness and demise will one day be recognized as among the most amazing state papers extant. The most powerful governing clique on earth, in its hour of presumptive heartbreak, could not afford to restrict itself to weeping over and eulogizing the lost leader, but felt itself compelled to load medical bulletins with propaganda urging popular backing, as if it were a fledgling government scared of being booted out.

The very first announcement, along with the report of the stroke, called on party members and the masses to "display the greatest unity and cohesion, stanchness of spirit and vigilance." Vigilance against whom, against what? The Soviet public would know, even if some foreign reporters on the scene didn't.

One expected the death bulletin, at least, to be a solemn and sorrowful statement of fact without political commercials. Instead, it not only hammered away at the theme of "monolithic unity"—protesting too much—but explained *why* the people should trust and follow the surviving bosses. It was "sales copy" in support of the "tested leadership," braced with promises of "further improvement" to meet "the material and cultural needs" of all sections of the populace. Not in all history has there been such a fantastic death notice.

Far from concealing its apprehensions, the ruling coterie explained that the speed in setting up a succession government within twenty-four hours was aimed to prevent *"razbrod i panika"*—disorder and panic. The phrase was not tossed off casually, being repeated pointedly in the editorials in the following days. What kind of "disorder and panic" were they so anxious to head off? Why the eagerness to show at once a united front at the top against any challenge? Who was being warned not to take advantage of confusion and rivalry? With millions of agents spying on everybody everywhere, the Kremlin surely had its finger on the pulse of national sentiment. It would hardly have made such a spectacle of trepidations before the world and its own country unless it thought them well founded.

"The word 'panic' escaping the lips of the rulers of the world's most powerful government," Bertram D. Wolfe would comment, "betrays a fear that is ineradicably in their hearts: they fear the prostrate people over whom they rule, they fear the outside world which they plan to conquer, and they fear each other. . . . The first words of the orphaned heirs on the death of the dictator are not human words of sorrow but ominous words about 'disorder and panic' and vigilance and uncompromising struggle 'against the inner and outer foe.'"

There we had the essence of the missing legitimacy—a virtual admission that their rule was still tentative, without roots in popular acceptance, threatened and on the defensive. The Bolshevik masters have often and rightly been described as "the frightened men in the Kremlin." Apparently the passing of Stalin raised the chronic fear to panic dimensions.

Nothing since 1953 suggests any moderation of these feelings. Their fears are manifold. Besides those common to all tyrants, they labor under dreads unique to new, revolutionary ruling groups. They know that their authority has no sanction in tradition or long-time convention, none of the aura of legitimacy that sustains the inner assurance of hereditary monarchs, for instance. Themselves masters of the *coup d'état*, the stab in the back, they cannot for a moment escape the shadow of such threats to their own survival.

As individuals, Soviet leaders live in a climate of intrigue and duplicity. They dread the frown of more powerful colleagues. They are nervously alert to shifts in the unstable balance of competing egos. Without exception they have climbed to the heights over too many corpses of friends and allies to trust anyone or to sleep peacefully. And collectively they dread the vengeance of the amorphous masses upon whom they have inflicted hurts and woes. The stench of festering resentment and hatred is ever in their nostrils, no matter how many guards they set to guard other guards in an endless progression.

• *The Mood of Defiance*

Khrushchev turned on the departed master whom he had served so diligently, not because of a change of heart, but because of pressures from below, both in the party and in the populace. What became even more evident, however, was that the people could not be reconciled with the regime. They refused to be bought off. The so-called de-Stalinization, partial and ambiguous though it was, was welcome, but generally accepted as a sign of weakening at the top. More significant than the "improvements" exacted from the Kremlin has been the new boldness, the new mood of defiance, generated in all sectors of Soviet society.

The sum-total of fears is constant, but a new balance has been established. The people used to be more afraid of the *vlast*, or power—now the *vlast* is more afraid of the people. Force, it would seem, has lost its old efficacy, certainly among young people without a personal memory of the Stalin era. The whole population is slowly, fumblingly, learning the most difficult of human arts: not to be afraid.

Khrushchev, at a writers' conference in 1957, threatens to shoot literary trouble-makers, but they continue to make trouble. In 1962 he fumes against "decadent" art, poetry, movies; for a while apprehensive artists and writers lie low, and a few confess their sins; but before long, they are again writing and painting as they prefer.

The defiance spreads. Young economists ask publicly for access to all vital statistics. Leading jurists press for more independence in the courts and curbs on the police and prosecutors to assure fair trials. A Professor Strogovich defends the Western principle that a man is innocent until proven guilty. A rash of non-Marxist ideas breaks out on the face of the technical and even the general press: biologists, sociologists, political scientists demand more leeway in their various disciplines. Long-ignored or forbidden philosophers, Russian and Western, are "rediscovered" and quoted respectfully. Writers ask publicly for an end to literary censorship.

All of it is cautious, wrapped in the cellophane of party language, but portentious in reflecting a new almost forgotten courage. Physicists and chemists, among them Nobel Prize winners, speak up in defense of persecuted artists; artists join in appeals for more autonomous scientific research. On the eve of the Party Congress, in the spring of 1966, a petition signed by many leaders in Soviet science and culture warns Brezhnev and Kosygin against the feared "rehabilitation" of Stalin.

Other petitions, in the same period, from groups of writers and individual literary celebrities, protest the trial and severe sentences meted out to two of their colleagues, Andrei Sinyavsky and Yuri Daniel. A round-robin, signed by sixty-two Moscow and Leningrad writers, urges the party to obtain the release of the convicted men and offers to stand surety for their good behavior. At the same time, eighteen members of the philosophical faculty of Moscow University protest the dismissal from his teaching post of one of the witnesses in the defense of the two writers. A professor at the same university who testified against Sinyavsky and Daniel, is asked by his students whether he did so voluntarily; when he admits that he did, the entire class walks out.

The trial of these two authors, in February, 1966, in itself offers significantly novel features: The defendants plead innocent and prominent citizens appear to defend them. Students try to picket the court; about two hundred young people gather in a public square to demonstrate against the prosecution, and are dispersed of course. Everyone understands that far more than the fate of two erring authors is involved; that the case is being used to impress the Kremlin with the sentiment for freedom of the word and greater legal protection for the individual. Then, despite the rising toll of arrest and cautions from high quarters, the "literary underground" swings into action. Key documents in the case—excerpts from the court proceedings, copies of various petitions and open letters denied legal publication—are circulated in the country in an illicit "white book" and it is also smuggled out to the West.

Meanwhile, nonconformist novels, poems, plays continue to appear. A few are suppressed, numerous arrests are made, but the dictators dare not crack down on the defiant writers and distributors in any decisive manner. The feeling grows that the masters are uncertain of their ability to enforce their will, hesitant about testing their strength at this point.

Precisely as in the old pre-Bolshevik Russia, the intelligentsia takes the lead, expressing aloud what the masses feel or say in private. Small discussion circles, *kruzhki*, multiply not only in the capital cities but in the provinces—all reminiscent of the romantic *kruzhki* that flourished under the tsars. Highly secret, camouflaged as poetry readings or social gatherings, moving from one apartment to another, they are hotbeds of political freethinking. For every "circle" that is raided, its leaders shipped to Siberia, a dozen others spring up.

Clandestine little magazine and news bulletins, usually crude mimeographed affairs, appear on the college and university campuses. Illegal copies of prohibited Russian or foreign books, handwritten or multigraphed, pass from hand to hand. Few self-respecting, educated Russians would admit that they have not read Boris Pasternak's *Doctor Zhivago*, though it is still among the forbidden works. New works even by well-known and officially tolerated writers, after having been barred by the government, soon mysteriously begin to circulate.

Party-line lecturers in schools and workers' clubs are heckled and sometimes jeered. Students walk out on party-line teachers. In the bigger universities, discussion sessions, organized by students under innocent-sounding titles, turn into excited debates that alarm the authorities. Frequently the press, by way of intimidating rebellious elements, carries reports of trials in which instigators of secret literary, political, or religious organizations have been given stiff sentences.

The restiveness, as is to be expected, is especially evident among the young. Their alienation from communist society takes the form, at one extreme, of what the Russians call "hooliganism," juvenile delinquency, alcholism, a passion for Western rock-and-roll and exotic clothing. At the other extreme it is manifest in open contempt for regime spokesmen, the study of forbidden literature, demonstrations of sympathy for persecuted writers and editors, myriad other signs of intellectual liberation. The youth press and politicians constantly complain that students boycott the Marxist-Leninist courses, or attend classes only enough to get passing marks.

At a congress of the Komsomol (Communist Youth) League in May, 1966, party stalwarts demanded firm measures against young people who ignore and defy Marxist-Leninist "ideals." Brezhnev himself, in a message to the delegates, charged that too many youngsters hold "parasitic and undisciplined views" and have "a weakly developed sense of public duty." He called for their re-education. To divert blame from themselves, speakers blamed the West. Its propagandists, the head of the Komsomol organization charged, seek to promote an "ideological degeneration of our young people, undermining their faith in communist ideals." The admission that such "degeneration" was gaining ground was clearly implied in the charge. At the following congress, a year later, the same kind of complaints, warnings, demands for re-education were repeated. The regime's alarm over the alienation of younger citizens today echoes through virtually all party invocations. It has become standard procedure.

The intensified anti-God campaigns in recent years are a direct reaction to the growth of religious faith. Tourists routinely report that "only the old" crowd the churches, which is not true. Besides, they should stop to think that in the fiftieth year of Soviet power even the old believers have been raised in an atheist society, educated in atheist schools, subjected all their lives to atheist propaganda and social pressures. Their attendance at religious services, perhaps even more than the presence of younger people, gives testimony to the long-term failure of the anti-religious drives.

The defiance spreads. The discontent and soul-searching is not new. It has existed throughout the Soviet half-century. What is new is its growing assertion in public. The permanent civil war assuredly is entering a new phase, in which overt opposition begins to outweigh the convert variety. The confrontation between *They* and *We*, between the older conformist generation and its sons and daughters, is increasingly in the open. However it may end, talk of perfect harmony between the rulers and their subjects is so much gibberish.

8 / World War II

The myth that in World War II the people fought
to defend the communist regime.

From the first hour of the invasion the situation was catastrophic.
Along a fifteen-hundred-mile front from the White to the Black
Seas the Germans were pushing forward at *blitz* speed. Soviet armies were melting away, running off in chaotic spills of retreat
eastward and surrender westward.

The Germans could not build barbed-wire enclosures fast enough
to contain the millions of prisoners and deserters—it was hard to
tell them apart, because the defense was so half-hearted, the line
between voluntary and involuntary submission so nebulous. The
invaders took close to four million prisoners in the first four months
—on a scale, that is, suggesting that the Red forces were not
really fighting back. Before the Nazi tide of victory was stopped, it
had engulfed a third of the Soviet population in a territory several
times as large as France. Not since the Mongol invasion in 1236–
1240 had Russian armies been so decisively defeated.

The Kremlin had not been caught off guard. It had long been
aware of the German plan to conquer Russia. A large-scale Red
mobilization in Soviet frontier regions had been under way for
many months under the guise of maneuvers.

Nor were the Soviet forces inferior to Hitler's. In his postwar
book, *The Generals Talk,* the British military expert, Lidell Hart,
attested: "Hitler embarked on the invasion of Russia in the face of
knowledge that his forces would be fewer than those opposing him
at the outset, and were bound to be increasingly outnumbered if
the campaign were to be prolonged." The 121 divisions Germany

could muster, he knew, would face 155 divisions in Western Russia. And the German military men did not underrate the fighting qualities of Russian soldiers.

How, then, explain the great Soviet debacle? The answer is to be found in the reluctance of the population and its armies to defend an unpopular political and social system; in their burgeoning dream of *freedom through defeat*. Hitler, by quickly puncturing that dream, saved Stalin. Once the Russian peoples were convinced that the Germans had not come to liberate them from Bolshevism but to enslave them to Nazism, the fate of the invaders was fixed. Blindly, drunkenly, stupidly, the Hitlerites drove the Soviet masses to rally in despair around their hated masters.

For nearly a quarter of a century the Soviet dictatorship had been rearing a new generation in its own grim image. It was a gigantic enterprise in "human engineering," as the communists called it, with a "new Soviet man" as its end-product. As a vital part of this job, the Russian past had been distorted and ridiculed, its religion especially condemned and persecuted. Then, on the morning of June 22, 1941, came the first great test of this portentous handiwork. The Nazis crashed into Russia. And at once the regime confessed that its engineering had been a grisly failure.

In the hour of crisis, it could be expected, the Kremlin would summon the country to a crusade in defense of communist society, the collectivized farms, and socialized industry. It did nothing of the sort. That faceless, godless robot, the new Soviet man, might never have been. Instead, the dictators appealed to the insulted past. They barely mentioned the Soviet years. The very words "socialism" and "communism" were all but expunged from the propaganda lexicon. The memory of Russian heroes out of the past, great tsars and generals, was invoked, the names of Marx and Lenin were rarely alluded to.

It was a humiliating retreat from the official ideology, a restoration of old-fashioned national patriotism. It was to endure for years, until the time when victory seemed assured and reconciliation with the masses no longer urgent. With every month Moscow was to become more forthright in reviving old Russian values—old values in the Ukraine and other non-Russian areas as well—and brushing aside Soviet values. The nation was assured continually that it was fighting a Great Patriotic War, the Fatherland War, not a communist war.

The people were frightened, bewildered, but also, as self-exiled Soviet nationals eventually could attest, curiously exhilarated and hopeful. Could it be that liberation from communism, like its imposition, was coming through war?

• *Hitler's Biggest Blunder*

Not until July 3, 1941, twelve days after the start of the invasion, did Joseph Stalin, chief architect of the shattered Moscow-Berlin Pact, address the country. As most people understood, the delay meant that their hierarchs were assessing the state of mind of the populace. His radio address was like an echo from the far-off outlawed past. "A great danger hangs over our fatherland," Stalin said tremulously, in his thick Georgian accent. "Our war for the freedom of our fatherland will merge with the struggles of the peoples of Europe and America for their independence, for democratic freedoms. . . . Comrades, citizens, brothers and sisters! I address myself to you, my friends."

Brothers and sisters—never before had a Soviet leader used that old-world form of address. Democratic freedoms—he was uttering in earnest words that until then had been heard only in derision. Stalin expressed gratitude to the U.S. government and Winston Churchill, the top villains in the preceding twenty-two months of alliance with Nazi Germany. Again, as in the glorious resistance to Napoleon in 1812, Stalin pleaded, the people must fight "a fatherland war of liberation."

The note of deep patriotic tradition set the tone for all that followed. The Soviet slogans were swept out of sight. Traditional military formations, the elite Guards units, were restored, and shoulder boards, a very symbol of the *ancien régime*, blossomed on officers' uniforms. The system of political commissars attached to, and thoroughly resented by, officers was suspended.

Most indicative of all, as the war progressed religion was made not merely legal, but respectable; crusading against God was forbidden; church bells, silent nearly ten years, rang out again, even on the radio. Before long, the Communist International was formally dissolved—a move, it was generally interpreted, to placate the democratic allies, but also useful as an indication to the masses that messianic communism was a thing of the past. Under the impact of the invasion, in short, the Kremlin substantially disowned Bolshevism.

It had to disown, too, nearly two years of zealous partnership with the Nazis. Even the thick-skinned Georgian, one supposes, was embarrassed by the need to turn yesterday's ally into today's fascist beast, and yesterday's capitalist imperialists into today's stalwart companions on the road to common freedom. Moscow, under the pact, had delivered to Germany millions of tons of foodstuffs, metals, oil, cotton, and other products essential to the war effort. More important, it had swung the support of the world-wide communist apparatus to Hitler's side. In the Balkans, the Communist Parties were under instructions to help the Germans take over their own countries.

When the Russians finally began to stand up to the invaders, the West talked glibly of their "loyalty to the Soviets" and to Stalin personally. Inside the USSR that delusion was shared neither by the government nor the governed. Again and again Stalin explained to foreign guests like Harry Hopkins and Joseph E. Davies that his people were not fighting for communism but for their fatherland.

Ever since the terrible blood-purges and the imbecile Moscow trials in 1936–1938, a shocked world had been told that the carnage was necessary to destroy the enemy within, in preparation for possible war. Yet the Kremlin now declared itself deeply alarmed by swarms of traitors, saboteurs, and other species of internal foes. The "fifth columns," it warned, were everywhere. From the outset, the Soviets fought a war on two fronts: against the foreign enemy and against "dangerous elements" at home.

Priority was given to the domestic menace. Long blacklists had been prepared in advance by the NKVD (successor to the GPU). Hundreds of thousands were taken into custody at once. In every city, town, and neighborhood, special "military tribunals" were set up to identify and extirpate anyone suspected of, or denounced for, anti-regime sentiments. They had the power to sentence to death. At the same time, thousands in prisons and concentration camps— especially political and military personalities who might provide leadership in case of revolution—were summarily shot. As one wartime defector put it: "Our rulers behaved like a frightened wolf-pack."

To protect the government against subversive broadcasts, all private radio receivers were simply confiscated. The Volga German Republic was abolished, on the theory that even after the lapse of centuries, its citizens might still be sympathetic to Germans; the entire population, about 400,000 men, women, and children, was exiled and dispersed. Later other "republics" and "autonomous regions," in particular Moslems in the Caucasus and Crimea, were awarded the same fate.

To a government with multitudinous eyes and ears, it had been no secret that thousands had been praying for war as the best chance to throw off their shackles. The communists themselves had provided the precedents: during the First World War, they had urged not only Russians but all belligerent peoples to turn their national wars into civil wars. The lack of legitimacy, the Kremlin's dread of the people under war conditions, had in large measure motivated Stalin's alliance with Hitler. The reality surpassed his worst forebodings.

The Red forces were fighting on their own soil against an unprovoked invader, normally a guarantee of keen battle morale. They were on flat terrain wide open to rapid retreat. Can there be any doubt that the millions taken by the Germans had not resisted resolutely? Certainly Stalin had no such doubts. That was why he issued his notorious edict, unprecedented in modern history, that all Soviet captives were to be considered deserters and their families stripped of support. That was why special divisions were deployed *behind* the fronts to block retreat, by force if necessary. But who was to block the blockers? Besides, millions were retreating forward, in waves of real desertion.

A German journalist who has written extensively about the Eastern campaigns, Jurgen Thornwald, refers to "the real joy with which the population everywhere received the advancing German soldiers; the words of greeting, first church services in twenty years." In town and village alike the inhabitants turned out with bread and salt, the ancient Slavic ceremonial of welcome. Civilians by the tens of thousand flocked to volunteer for non-combatant services to the Germans. They enlisted willingly, in this honeymoon phase, for transport to Germany in labor contingents. In many cities the people made gay bonfires of books by Lenin, Stalin, Marx. Communist "activists" tried to run away, as much out of fear of their next-door neighbors as of the foreign forces.

A top-secret report from occupied Russia to his political superior in Berlin, dated October 24, 1942, signed by Dr. Otto Braeutigam, a German specialist on Russian affairs long stationed in Moscow as a diplomat, is available in the Nuremberg trial records. It says in part:

Were the war being conducted only for the smashing of Bolshevism, then it could have been decided long ago in our favor, for, as all experiences of this war have confirmed, Bolshevism is hated by the Eastern peoples, above all by the great mass of peasants. . . . In the Soviet Union we found on our arrival a population weary of Bolshevism, which waited longingly for new slogans holding out the promise of a better future for them. It was Germany's duty to find such slogans but they remained unuttered. The population greeted us with joy as liberators and placed themselves at our disposal willingly and freely with body and life.

Another German officer who had served in Russia for years before the conflict, Harwith von Bittenfeld, would testify: "With an intelligent political policy, we could have won the war in the East simply because the Russian people themselves would have overthrown the regime."

But Hitler's policy, instead, was arrogant and deeply insulting. He did not seek affection in Russia but blind obedience based on animal fears. All Slavs were openly treated as *Untermenschen* suited only for future colonial exploitation. Prisoners-of-war were massed in the open in sub-zero weather, neglected, underfed, and maltreated, so that hundreds of thousands perished miserably. Enough of them made their way back to Russia, however, to spread the news of Nazi racist contempt and inhumanity. Volunteer enlistments dried up, after which hundreds of thousands—ultimately millions—were forcibly deported from occupied Russia for labor in Germany.

The famous General Koestring, when he fell into American hands in the last stage of the war, said bitterly: "We Germans, through ignorance, greed, and inefficiency, squandered out great capital in the struggle against Bolshevism." He identified that "capital" as the peoples' hatred of the Soviet regime and their yearning for justice.

Hitler was committing his greatest and in the end fatal blunder. Quickly enough the real nature of the conqueror was manifest: his racist insanities, his cruelty, his plans for permanent occupation and dismemberment of Russia. He accomplished what Stalin could not: the creation of a genuine fighting spirit in an old-style patriotic dedication. The *Führer*, a Soviet escapee said later, "played his greatest trump, the peoples' trust, into Stalin's hands."

• *Patriots in Enemy Uniforms*

In a fine recent novel, *Parallax*, by Vladimir Yurasov, a Russian *émigré* who had fought as an officer in the Red Army against the Germans, there is a memorable scene. An American official is interrogating the hero, a Soviet officer seeking asylum. "Why did men like you—Red soldiers—put up such a heroic fight for the regime?" he asks. The Russian replies: "All I can say is that we fought for our homes and our homeland, and not for the Soviet regime."

But a million Soviet soldiers and officers, possibly more, chose to fight for home and homeland in another way—by donning German uniforms in the hope of overthrowing the communist regime. Their intentions were patriotic, but the consequences for themselves were tragic.

Defeatism is in the Russian revolutionary tradition. In the First World War, the Bolsheviks in particular cheered every defeat of their own country as another opportunity for rebellion. The Nazis had few illusions about the Soviet military volunteers: these were not their friends but merely the enemies of their common enemy.

Soviet Russia was the only participant in the great war which supplied substantial fighting forces to the enemy. The largest and best known formation (except in the USSR, where it has been smeared out of recognition) was the Russian Army of Liberation (ROA by its Russian initials), better known as the Vlasov movement. General Andrei A. Vlasov, chief of the ROA, had been an authentic Soviet hero, decorated personally by Stalin for his successful defense of Moscow, and a member of the Central Committee of the ruling party. But when captured by the Germans, he readily agreed to organize, from among Soviet war prisoners, forces to fight communism, with a constitutional democracy as his professed goal.

The Hitlerites reneged on all their promises to Vlasov and his staff. Not until the final months of war did they allow the ROA to engage the Red armies, which was the original purpose. The truth is that Berlin did not trust any patriotic Russians, even in German uniforms, fearing that they might one day interfere with Nazi plans for their country. Not until its final agony did Germany unleash its Russian contingents against the communists, but it was too late to affect the outcome. Until then they had been used, under protest, on other fronts. Toward the end of the war the Vlasov movement was credited with nearly a million men. Only a small fraction of them, however, was actually in ROA. There were other groups, particularly national-independence formations of Ukrainians, Cossacks, Georgians, and Turkomens.

After the German collapse, Vlasov and his main associates surrendered to the Allies—and were promptly turned over to Stalin for execution. Tens of thousands of their followers, similarly, were handed over to Moscow for imprisonment and mass extermination. It was not an episode in which the Western statesmen involved could take any pride, the only excuse being that they knew not what they were doing. Vlasovites were just a small part of the Soviet citizens driven with Allied bayonets and truncheons into east-bound transport trains for delivery to Kremlin vengeance.

At the war's end an estimated six million Soviet men, women, and children—the imported slave laborers and liberated war prisoners—were stranded beyond their native frontiers, mostly in areas under Allied occupation. Several million of them refused to return to the USSR. They knew full well the hardships and humiliations that awaited them as unwanted displaced persons in alien lands, but anything seemed to them better than resuming life under communism.

Never before in history had so many nationals of a victorious country, including uniformed men who had helped win the victory, repudiated the government and social system of their homeland. They represented a true cross-section of the Soviet population —peasants, workers, intellectuals—so that there is some justice in the claim that it amounted to a limited "plebiscite" on communism.

To placate the Soviet dictator, the United States and its Allies, alas, used force to repatriate his runaway subjects. One of the American prosecutors at Nuremberg, Thomas J. Dodd, later U.S. Senator from Connecticut, said subsequently:

> During my participation in the Nuremberg war crimes trials, in the postwar period, I learned something of the desperation and hatred and terror of the hundreds of thousands of Russian war prisoners and slave laborers held by the Nazis, whom we, through incredible ignorance, returned against their will to the Soviet authorities. My soul is still tormented by the nightmarish accounts of mass suicides, in which men slashed their wrists with tin cans and women jumped with their children from upper story windows rather than face return to Soviet Russia.

While we were driving them into trucks and trains, a Soviet Repatriation Commission was engaged in a fantastic man-hunt wherever their terrified countrymen might be hiding. On November 6, 1946—ironically on the eve of another happy Soviet birthday—Andrei Vishinsky told a United Nations committee that his country, as of right, demanded the surrender of "more than 1,200,000 refugees and displaced persons." Evidently the Moscow Marxists were not giving up private property rights in human beings.

In the end all but half a million, the so-called non-returners, were herded back to Russia. There they were treated as deserters. Even loyal demobilized Red troops who had fought outside the USSR were subjected to purges. Because they had had a glimpse of life without benefit of communism, they were considered unreliable and, at best, a source of infection. Relatively few were permitted to return to their families and previous homes; the rest were dispersed to other areas, where their influence on local opinion would be reduced.

The alliance between regime and people for struggle against a foreign aggressor was never complete. As victory became more assured, the old civil conflict was resumed. By the time hostilities with Germany ended, hostilities between the Kremlin and the populace were again in full swing.

Through the war years wishful hoping had foreseen great and

happy changes in the Soviet system as the reward for heroism and sacrifice. Without making promises, the regime subtly encouraged the people to believe that the nightmare past was ended and an era of comparative freedom ahead. The moratorium on communist slogans, the new rights of worship, the leaders' guarded allusions to democracy—all seemed a tacit agreement for a new start.

The Kremlin's acceptance of the Atlantic Charter and Mr. Roosevelt's "Four Freedoms" seemed to the ordinary Soviet citizen at least an omen of reform in the right direction. The very experience of cooperation with Western democracies, he thought, would promote wholesome changes. He knew that the United States had contributed to the Soviet effort more than eleven billion dollars in military supplies and food, including entire American-made and -equipped factories. At one point, though not without needling by the U.S. Ambassador, Stalin stated publicly what everyone knew privately: that Soviet Russia could not have won the war without American help.

William Henry Chamberlin wrote during the war: "It seems almost incredible that the Soviet dictatorship, strong as it is, will not be influenced and modified in many ways by this tremendous ordeal of the Russian people. The dictatorship may well be loosened."

But the incredible came to pass. The dictatorship was not loosened but grimly tightened. The old terror was back in full swing, along with the old slogans, compulsions, attacks on religion, and ferocious crack-down on writers and the arts. Yesterday's gallant allies were once again "imperialist" enemies, with implications that Stalin single-handedly had won the war—even against Japan! Every department of Soviet life was purged and re-purged, and the camp population swelled.

A revised history of Soviet Russia, prepared under Stalin's personal supervision, contained a passage about Russia's war with Napoleon:

The general upsurge of popular patriotism in Russia was the decisive factor in the triumph of the Russian Army. Frightened, not only by Napoleon but first of all by their own peasants and serfs, the feudal lords appraised the victory as a triumph of the autocracy and serfdom. They asserted with satisfaction that the simple people had never displayed such loyalty as in 1812. Others went to the extreme of insisting that for the Russian the word liberty had no meaning; that obedience had become a habit with him.

This is an almost perfect summation of what happened in World War II. Again the rulers, like the feudal lords in 1812, frightened by their own subjects, hastened to rob them of their victory. But in 1812 Russia did not forget the peace its people had lost. Thirteen years later came the Decembrist uprising, harbinger of the revolutionary surge that could no longer be repressed. We may be sure that in 1945, similarly, the lost peace was not forgotten by the victims. The story of the war has been told; its aftermath is very much an unfinished story.

An able American journalist thoroughly familiar with Russia through long residence there, John Scott of *Time-Life*, wrote in October, 1959, that he had seen a process of political disillusionment during his visit to the USSR that year: "It has already brought the Soviet Union to a position where, in my opinion, in the event of a war or civil strife which forced a choice upon them, most Soviet citizens would reject the Soviet government and communism, unless a foreign invader unified them, as did Hitler, with the threat of an even more cruel dictatorship if he won."

9 / First Five-Year Plan

The myth that the First Five-Year Plan was a triumphant success.

To the victor belong the spoils. Having defeated and banished Trotsky in early 1928, Joseph Stalin proceeded to confiscate his ideas. The Left or Trotskyite Opposition had been demanding curbs on the *kulaks* or better-to-do peasants and a faster pace in building industry. Stalin took over both policies and carried them, Stalin-like, to irrational and heartless extremes.

The Soviet economy had been restored roughly to its pre-war condition during the NEP years. Industrial production was on the rise, but Stalin chose to end NEP—all economic life, down to the lowliest pushcart trade, again reverted to state monopoly. Then he announced a Five-Year Plan for super-industrialization and collectivization of agriculture, so immoderate that his associates were shocked and the country frightened. Nikolai Bukharin, the leading communist theoretician after Lenin, publicly denounced this new course as "feudal exploitation" and privately as "idiotic illiteracy." (He was executed, of course, in the purges some years later.)

The plan was launched like a war of conquest directed against the whole population. It was Stalin's Great Leap Forward. The goals set were wildly unrealistic, with little relation to available technical brains and capital but with an abundance of exuberant slogans.

In a mystic transport of "historic mission," the regime doomed millions to extinction, tens of millions to thinly disguised slavery, the whole nation to incredible suffering. Upon the alleged "completion" and "fulfillment" of the plan, half the country was caught in a fearful famine, the other half was on short rations, agriculture was wrecked, the forced-labor population in camps was nearing the ten-million mark. Along the western frontiers of the country additional guards and bloodhounds were massed to stop the desperate scramble of frightened peasant families into Rumania, Poland, the Baltic states, and Finland.

Amazingly, this saturnalia of death, hunger, and unexampled exploitation has gone down in history as a fabulous "success"!

A realistic examination of Stalin's first *Piatiletka* or Five-Year Plan, 1928–1932, is indispensable to a meaningful assessment of the Soviet half-century for at least two important reasons.

First, the belief that communism, whatever its faults and crimes in other respects, is a virtual guarantee of rapid economic progress for underdeveloped nations derives primarily from the delusion that this plan was fabulously successful. That stubborn belief has colored and distorted world opinion on communism in practice.

Second, it was in connection with this plan, in the first half of the 1930's, that the non-Soviet world fell into the habit of swallowing Kremlin economic boasts almost uncritically, and in particular without reference to their human costs and content.

No other economic enterprise in all history has been so vastly publicized, glamorized, misrepresented, and misjudged. Everywhere except in Russia itself, where its malignant features were too apparent, its announced goals and results were accepted not only willingly but eagerly. The explanation for this phenomenon is not far to seek. It can be found in the psychological timing.

The *Piatiletka* had been under way for a year when a great depression hit the advanced industrial countries. Millions of bewildered and frightened people, especially intellectuals, wanted to believe that someone somewhere had an answer to their ordeal; the redoubtable Russians seemed to offer one. They were determined to credit in full every Muscovite propaganda tale and shout down anyone who raised doubts about what seemed the one bright spot in a dark world.

Over in Russia new plants were going up, at a time when their own were closing down. The symbolism of this contrast blinded them to the violence, death, starvation and mass enslavement that went with the plan. And when it was supposedly "completed"—in only four and one-third years—few bothered to question or test the

Kremlin's extravagant claims and plainly falsified statistics. In its craving for a miracle, the world settled for a counterfeit.

As originally charted, the plan covered every department of the nation's life, promising great advances in light or consumer industries, food production, housing, schooling, nearly everything. Meticulously the planning agency, Gosplan, detailed higher living standards. The purchasing power of Soviet currency would rise by 20 per cent, "real wages" by 66 per cent; the cost of living would be lowered by 14 per cent.

But these promises were lost in the shuffle, sharpening the cutting edge of disillusionment. In whatever affected the individual directly, conditions deteriorated quickly. Agriculture, the principle industry, was wrecked and driven to famine: the first great famine in Russian history caused, not by natural, but by political disasters.

Had the whole blueprint been taken into account, in presenting the balance sheet of the "completed" plan, gains would have been more accurately offset by failures and immense losses in light industry, in living levels, unit productivity, and other factors. Taken together, the purported statistical triumph—even without counting the cost in life and the rise of slave labor—would have appeared in its true colors as a substantial failure.

A speech by Stalin, made public in July, 1931, added up to a devastating indictment of the economic situation at that point. In most enterprises, he complained, the turnover of labor was "at least 30 to 40 per cent . . . during half a year or even a quarter of a year." The majority of workers were deserting their jobs "to seek fortune" elsewhere. "Rationalization of industry," he said, had "long gone out of style." Many plans presumably fulfilled or over-fulfilled, were just "on paper," and more of the same. This was the picture, with only one more year to go. Yet when the final year was finished, he did not hesitate to claim magnificent victory.

At the end of 1932, when the masses were ordered to celebrate the success of the plan, the famine was at its worst. Each morning wagons were collecting the night's dead in Ukrainian and Caucasian towns; corpses lined the roads, like so many logs, in Central Asia. A work-book system that in effect tied every worker to his job had just been promulgated. The last sparks of freedom and human dignity had been quenched.

In 1937, the government would carry out a national census. But the loss in population it revealed was so catastrophic that the results were suppressed and the statisticians punished. But Western demographers, analysts of vital statistics, have since then calculated the extent of the catastrophe. The population growth rate fell from 2.51 per cent in 1929 to 1.5 per cent in 1932. In the two years 1933–1934, the population, already decimated in the preceding four years, fell by 6.4 million in absolute figures; taking into consideration the sharply lowered birth-rate, the demographic loss in life came to about nine million.

Against this backdrop of great wretchedness and new extremes in political tyranny, the joyous clanging of cymbals for the "success" of the *Piatiletka* made tragic irony. The operation had been successful but the patient was nearly dead. The country had been transformed into a crucible in which men and metals were being melted down and reshaped in a cruel heat, without a touch of compassion for the human slag.

If industrialization were an end in itself, unrelated to human purposes, the USSR had an imposing amount of physical property to exhibit. Scores of new factories and industrial "complexes" were erected. A quarter of a million slaves—more slaves than Peter the Great mobilized to build a new capital on the Neva swamps—hacked a canal between the White and the Baltic Seas. The country possessed forty-one blast furnaces and seventy-one open hearth furnaces (about one-quarter of them truly new, the rest old plants reconstructed); twice as many oil pipe lines as in 1928; a network of power stations with a capacity four times greater than pre-war Russia had. Two-thirds of the peasantry and four-fifths of the plowed acreage were "socialized"—that is, owned and exploited by the state-employer just as it owned and exploited factories and workers.

Measured for bulk alone, the plan achieved much—but only in heavy industry, and even there it fell far short of the original goals. With all the other phases of the blueprint forgotten, to talk of fulfillment is to mock common sense.

On the qualitative side, even in heavy industry, the picture was dismal. Capital costs were far greater all down the line than planned—all construction, for instance, allowed 50 per cent for overhead, compared with 12 per cent in the United States at that time. Error and spoilage and waste of raw materials surpassed the worst fears of the planners. A sour witticism of those years was that the plan for *brak*, spoiled goods, was being over-fulfilled. Reckoned in any terms, the costs of the plan were brutally exorbitant—and paid for in starvation, terror, privation, epidemic diseases, and many varieties of forced labor.

Stalin—and that was the heart of the matter—looked upon human beings as the most expendable of his resources. He was not interested in enriching the country or improving the lot of its people, but only in strengthening the power base for the dictatorship.

• *Statistical Magic*

Speaking at a party conference in January, 1933, Stalin announced a quantitative fulfillment of 93.7 per cent of the Five-Year Plan. The figure, close enough to 100 for practical purposes, has remained the Kremlin's formal estimate of the result. It referred only to "census industry," disregarded segments even in that group, and made no discounts for atrocious quality, investments of capital and manpower far beyond Gosplan intentions, runaway inflation. Moreover, his bookkeepers had reached his figure by *averaging* extremes of over- and under-fulfillment, which made hash of the vaunted success. For it guaranteed a lopsided economy. Under the semblance of planning, there was in fact confusion and chaos.

As the plan developed, it took curious turns. Its most conspicuous accomplishments and failures alike had been largely unexpected and certainly unplanned. The goals for agrarian collectivization stood formally fulfilled in two years, seemingly the greatest victory of all—but more than half the nation's livestock had been slaughtered in the process and food shortage was universal. Conscript labor and prison-camp labor, never mentioned in the plan, had become its distinctive feature. Railroad mileage was added—but transportation was tied in hopeless knots.

Many of the government's interim claims were so outrageous, even comical, that only a totalitarian regime would have dared to advance them. It boasted that tens of millions more workers had been drawn into industry than expected, thereby "liquidating unemployment." The low productivity of labor was thus passed off as an over-fulfillment of the plan! The immensely larger amounts of capital used up, reflecting inefficiency and runaway inflation, were similarly acclaimed as over-fulfillment. Because one breadwinner could no longer hope to feed a family, additional millions of women flocked to heavy work normally reserved for men, in construction, coal-mining, road-building, etc.—and this was played up as proof of the growing equality of the sexes. Such optical illusions and propaganda magic, though recognized as lies at home, were treated solemnly as facts outside.

Now let us look at the basic figure on which the legend of success rests: Stalin's 93.7 per cent, leaving a margin of only 6.3 per cent of non-fulfillment.

At the beginning of the final year, 1932, it was officially declared that the plan would be carried out fully if a growth of production by 37 per cent were attained. In point of fact, as Molotov subsequently stated, the growth that year was only 8½ per cent. Simple arithmetic shows that when it takes 37 per cent to finish a job and only 8½ per cent is accomplished, the job is no more than 79 per cent complete—*prima facie* evidence that Stalin's percentage was spurious.

The whole statistical method under the official claims is open to challenge. It assumed that the plan started from scratch and reached 93.7 per cent of what it aimed at. Actually there was production of 15.7 billion rubles in the year preceding the launching of the plan. The target for 1932 was 34.3 billion, in the ruble values of 1926–1927, which meant an increase of 20.9 billion that year over the last pre-plan year. If, as claimed, the increase came to 18.6 billion, the margin of failure was 11 per cent, not 6.3 per cent as represented by Stalin.

The statistical jugglery was so deft that not many foreign economists saw through it. The Kremlin simply compared *total results* with the *totals planned*, instead of comparing the *actual increase* with the *planned increase*. A consideration of its summary for the steel industry, for instance, will illustrate this difference.

Steel output in 1928 was 4.2 million tons. The plan foresaw an increase of 6.1 millions, for a total of 10.3 millions. Actual production in the final year was 5.9 millions; this meant a growth of 1.7 millions over 1928, or 28 per cent of the planned expansion. The Kremlin, however, said in effect: "We aimed at 10.3 and got 5.9, therefore our plan was fulfilled by 57 per cent." On this basis, if production had not increased by a single ton, if it had remained at

4.2 millions, the plan would have been carried out by 42 per cent—extraordinary progress while standing still!

When this piece of sleight-of-mind is uncovered, many of the Kremlin's boasts are strangely deflated. Steel output instead of growing by 57 per cent—in itself a sad failure in view of the huge investments—fades down to 28 per cent. New housing, with an official credit of 84 per cent, in fact increased only by 44 per cent (while the need for housing grew by several hundred per cent because of the influx of urban workers). The mileage of railroads in operation, instead of the 89 per cent increase claimed, in truth grew by only 44 per cent.

A few branches exceeded the quantitative totals called for—petroleum output, manufacture of steam turbines, etc.—provided we go along with a method of computation that assumes zero as its starting point. The margins of failure in most other important branches may be judged from the following percentages of increase compared with the 100 per cent planned: tractors, 28 per cent; automobiles, 13 per cent; brick, 28 per cent; cement, 37 per cent; lumber, 40 per cent; electrification, 77 per cent. The failures in steel, cement, lumber, and brick are significant. Obviously new construction, the essential factor in the whole plan, could not go beyond the construction materials available. The Stalin claim of 93.7 per cent fulfillment is patently "doctored" when the increases in the building materials available for that fulfillment range between 28 and 40 per cent.

The disastrous operational conditions in transportation were not denied by Kremlin spokesmen. Yet that was the funnel through which the entire industrial program must of necessity flow, in a nation of continental size. Transportation was not only badly planned but even those defective plans were not carried out. The *Piatiletka* called for 17,000 kilometers of new railway; only 6,500 kilometers were completed. In the ten preceding years, despite the dislocations of civil war and without ballyhoo, 18,500 kilometers, or nearly three times as much as during the plan, were completed.

Some of the statistical trickery in the plan can be traced to manipulation of the value of the ruble. Gosplan calculated production in 1928 at 8.1 billion *pre-war* rubles. The equivalent in 1926–1927 rubles it gave as 15.7 billion rubles. The government thus identified the 1926–1927 rubles at about half their value before the war. The plan as officially published set production for the final year at 21 billion *pre-war* rubles, which would be about 42 billion in 1926–1927 rubles. Strangely enough, however, the planned production for 1932 was set at 36.6 billion in 1926–1927 values, or some five billion less than called for by its own two-to-one ratio.

Reducing the whole business to pre-war rubles, as did the original plan, the actual claimed increase of 18.6 billion in 1926–1927 rubles amounts to 9.3 billion in pre-war rubles, which comes to 72 per cent of the planned growth, not Stalin's 93.7 per cent. Economic specialists, both American and Russian, with whom I discussed the problem in Moscow, believed that the plan, at a conservative estimate, had been only *half*-fulfilled. Vast areas of the economy were in worse condition than in the pre-plan period.

In agriculture, the Kremlin's own figures tell the grim story. They show 699 million centners of grain in 1932, the final plan year, as against 801 million in 1913, and 733 in 1928, and 1,058 million set as the goal—this despite an enlarged area under cultivation. (One centner equals 110 pounds.) The harvest per hectare declined from 8.4 centners in 1913 to 7 in 1932. The disastrous failure in the domain of livestock—which can be translated as food, leather, draught power, etc.—was too evident to be juggled arithmetically; it reached only 50 per cent of the plan. Instead, the unauthorized slaughter of a horse or a pig was made a crime punishable by death. In terms of the plan, beet sugar stood at 32 per cent, wool at 34 per cent, cotton at 58 per cent.

Agriculture, consumer industries, housing facilities, living standards, the currency were as much a part of the *Piatiletka* as heavy industry. When these are included in the final reckoning, when the price in life and agony and greater political oppression is added, the plan turns out to be a great failure. Parrotwise the world repeated propaganda formulas about "decades of industrial progress crowded into a few years"—a cruel hoax on those who today are tempted by communism as an instrument of economic progress.

I have been reluctant to impose statistics on the reader, but they are pertinent to the present claims for Soviet industry, and to the hopes of new nations flirting with communism. The techniques of falsification developed by Stalin have in essence been applied in the years that followed.

• *The Rise of a Police-State*

The First Five-Year Plan, conceived and commanded by Stalin, laid the foundations for subsequent economic growth. That is the only justification for its enormities that can be, or has been, advanced. In the nature of the case, no one can prove beyond cavil that equivalent industrialization could not have taken place in a comparatively democratic Russia, just as it *had* taken place in other countries, without the pressure-cooker methods of a total state. But anyone can prove that such development, perhaps at a somewhat slower pace, would have resulted in a more balanced economy, a more rational relation between its parts, a more solid basis for further natural growth—and a happier population.

The plan also laid the foundation for the most thorough-going police-state in modern times. Nearly all of the evil techniques and institutions now identified as "Stalinism" were brought to their perfection of ugliness not only during but *for* the plan. It touched off a delirium of violence, fear, and sadism. In cold truth, the main "achievement" of the *Piatiletka*, the only one beyond doubt, was the full development of communist totalitarianism.

The industrialization cannot, therefore, and should not be considered other than in the context of its sinister political consequences. The burden of proof is upon those who still believe that economic progress at a forced communist tempo is possible without its accompanying horrors.

Concentration camps for foes and doubters, of course, were started in Lenin's time. One of the worst of these, in Solovki, has produced a number of blood-chilling books by former inmates. But the system on a prodigious scale, as a vital adjunct of the economy and with its special dimensions of depravity, came to its full flowering during the *Piatiletka*.

References to camp inmates as "slaves" enrages Soviet officialdom and its foreign admirers. But the label, in actuality, *understates* the obscenity. Ordinary slaves, whether in ancient Rome or the American Southland, had a cash value and were maintained by their owners as they did other livestock. They were fed, clothed, protected against extremes of weather. Besides, even as slaves, they lived in the same world as free men; usually they raised families. The Soviet forced laborers were both slaves and convicts, shipped in cattle cars from their normal world to the harshest regions, worked far beyond the limits of human endurance, subjected to chronic hunger, freezing, and disease. They were, in short, expendable—it was cheaper for their masters to replace them with fresh victims than to keep them alive.

It was in these five years—probably the most celebrated such time-span in history—that labor unions lost their last remnants of influence and the "proletariat" was reduced to indentured servitude. All the devices for getting more work for less wages known to capitalism in its most primitive stages were introduced: piecework, widely differentiated wages, work quotas set by pacesetters, "socialist" competition among workers, and drastic penalties for lateness and absenteeism.

As for farming, surely no one in his right mind would recommend the Soviet reality to his own countrymen. At least five million peasants were driven from their land, most of the rest herded by unlimited force into misnamed "collectives." The locust plague of *bezprizornyie*, homeless children, had for the most part been brought under control by 1928. Now it was raging again, as additional hundreds of thousands of boys and girls, their homes broken by arrests and deportations, roamed the country.

Despotic economic methods made more despotic social and political drives inevitable. Persecution of religion, "the war on superstition," was intensified, in particular in the countryside, where the Orthodox Church still retained large influence. The Godless Society solemnly launched a "five-year plan for the liquidation of religion." Thousands of churches were closed, church bells were melted down for scrap metal, icons were burned in public; priests, mullahs, and rabbis filled every slave camp.

The same stepped-up "Bolshevik firmness" made a hell of life in every other corner of normal existence. Under NEP, certain private enterprise had been legal; now it was turned *post-factum* into a crime. All those who had engaged in it—hundreds of thousands of small shopkeepers, artisans employing a few helpers, petty traders and entrepreneurs—were deprived of all possessions and expelled from their homes. "Nepman" became a sobriquet more insulting than capitalist or merchant.

This new species of criminals-by-decree was added to the already existing *byvshiye*, "former people," treated as enemies of the state. Millions in the aggregate, the pariahs included even children born and raised since the revolution if their parents had been "formers." They were stripped of the right to vote, becoming disfranchised or *lishentsy*, in effect outlaws—denied food rations and the right to schooling, driven from their homes, employed only as unskilled or "black" labor, or simply left to beg and starve and die.

Purges were ordered in all offices and institutions, to "expose" and punish *byvshiye* who might be "hiding" in respectable jobs. Failure to denounce any of these hapless souls, if one knew they were concealed "formers," was a punishable crime. Social origin—who were your parents?—became the first test for employment, party membership, entrance to schools, and indeed survival. Even good communists were purged solely on the ground that a parent or grandparent had been a merchant or landlord. A great majority of the three million Jews in Russia automatically fell into the outlaw category, since most of their families had been petty shopkeepers or craftsmen with a few employes and apprentices—few other callings were open to them under the monarchy.

Although the state was in desperate need of brains and industrial skills, it unleashed a merciless drive against the so-called "old intelligentsia." With the revolution only eleven or twelve years old, there obviously could be no "new" intelligentsia. All educated men and women were thus suspect and arrested in droves, rarely apprised of the nature of their "crimes." Engineers, technicians, chemists, etc., were especially vulnerable on the theory that they might be more expert at sabotage. At the same time culture came under heavy fire. There was a systematic crackdown on writers, artists, educators, historians, through more thorough censorships and continuous purges of cultural organizations and institutions.

Apologists for the Kremlin later would explain the general inefficiency by the dearth of specialized skills, forgetting to note that the old elites had been deliberately killed off or put to cutting trees and digging canals as prisoners. One is reminded of the old story about the man who had murdered his father, then pleaded for mercy as an orphan.

• *Anything for Valuta*

To meet the shortage of technological skills, the Kremlin imported tens of thousands of Western specialists, down to the foreman level, together with Western machinery and blueprints. The largest contingents were American; an English-language daily was published for them in Moscow. In many of the most publicized of Stalin's industrialized "miracles," such as Dneiptostroi, the Stalingrad tractor complex, and the Gorki automobile factory, the planning, the technical direction, nearly everything was American or German or French—only the slave labor and the capital were provided by the Soviets.

Russia was able to buy experience and machinery that other countries had attained in slow and costly trial and error. In comparing the percentual growths of Soviet industry and industry in other countries, this factor is too often overlooked. Had the capitalist West refused to collaborate with the USSR, the Five-Year Plan would have died aborning.

To pay for foreign brains and equipment, the Kremlin quickly used up its gold and foreign currency reserves, then set out to raise more by open and devious means. Great works of art were sold to foreign museums. The Orthodox churches were stripped of their historic treasures. In the merciless push for *valuta*, hard currency, a system of ransom was instituted—in effect, the export of human beings—under which friends and relatives abroad could arrange for the release of a Soviet citizen from Stalin's utopia by paying large amounts in hard foreign currency. Special shops, Torgsin, were opened in all large cities where food and other deficit goods could be bought only for gold, silver, jewels, and foreign money. In the midst of deepening hunger, the government did not scruple to export food to pay for machines and foreign engineers.

More barbarous means of pressing the last ounce of *valuta* out of the Soviet people were developed. There was the instrument which I have called "gold-mining in torture chambers." Tens of thousands of people suspected of possessing valuables were rounded up by the GPU and tortured—I use the word advisedly, in its most literal sense—until they "voluntarily" surrendered their hidden gold pieces, dollars, silver spoons, or a piece of jewelry. The GPU made no class distinctions in crowding its torture pavilions: servant

girls, professors, factory workers were sweated and frozen and terrorized for weeks indiscriminately. Thousands were "processed"
over and over again; the fact that they had handed over valuables
implied that they might have more to hand over. People known to
have well-to-do relatives in America or Europe were forced to write
begging letters for money, which the authorities confiscated when
it arrived. Every GPU center had a quota to fulfill.

One of the most distressing aspects of the search for hard currency, especially for an American residing there at the time, was
the influx of veritable armies of tourists. Avid for dollars, Stalin
opened the gates of his hermit empire to anyone who had the
price. Advanced divisions of the great invasion—then and thereafter mostly Americans—poured into Moscow in the summer of
1929. The flood swelled with every year, until the gates were
slammed shut so that Stalin could concentrate on his new blood-
purges in the later 1930's.

Starry-eyed and reverent and drunk on propaganda juices they
came. Flocks of amateur sociologists, bubbly school teachers, liberal clergymen, socialites keen on kicks, men and women convinced (mistakenly) that sex had been socialized, miscellaneous
neurotics—all eager to see with half-closed eyes and proclaim with
wide-open mouths the glories of the *Piatiletka*.

They picnicked happily in the graveyards of a stricken nation,
were herded from museum to factory, from theater to workers'
club, from model prison to model collective farm. They took notes,
snapped pictures, stuffed themselves with caviar in the midst of
famine, and stoutly "denied" that there were concentration camps,
lishentsy, homeless children. They gushed with enthusiasm and resisted unpleasant truth as if it were a personal insult. In the day-
long and nightlong food queues, in the hordes of hungry peasants
jammed in and around railway stations, they discerned wonderful
"discipline" and dedicated "sacrifices." Without question they
swallowed official statistics, official alibis for miseries that could not
be concealed.

Then they went home and, on the basis of a ten-day or two-week
tour, reported as accredited experts that the regime was making
"terrific progress" and that the people simply adored Comrade Stalin. The nice girl-guides, mostly "formers" who hated the Soviets
and hated their jobs as licensed liars, privately laughed or cried over

the gullibility of their well-fed charges. A few talked too much and ended up in Siberia.

All other resident foreigners were as disgusted as I was. A British correspondent then in Moscow, Malcolm Muggeridge, who characteristically reacted in satire rather than sorrow, wrote subsequently of the hilarious spectacle offered by famous Western intellectuals viewing the Soviet shambles and "displaying toward it an imbecile credulity which an African witch-doctor would have found enviable." But the depression was still raging in their homelands, and facts had become a bourgeois prejudice.

As conditions deteriorated and hatred of the authorities deepened, the Kremlin needed more and more scapegoats. All its failures were blamed on saboteurs and "wreckers." To prove it, melodramatic "demonstration trials" were staged, forerunners of the infamous Moscow blood-purge trials of 1936–1938, complete with fake confessions. Mobs inside and outside the improvised courts were instigated to howl for the blood of the accused, and always got it in full measure.

Space limitations do not permit the more detailed depiction that these and a hundred other monstrous practices deserve. Suffice that the GPU, ruthless and reckless, its lusts for victims inflamed by indulgence, became a government above the government. It was the largest employer of labor, not only in camps and on its own industrial projects (canals, railroads, mining, and forestry in inhospitable areas) but by contracting out prisoners to so-called free projects. There was not a large Plan enterprise in the whole great land without its quota of shabby, emaciated prisoners—their wages going to the GPU—who were marched back to their camps or prisons when other workers returned to their families.

This was the macabre reality behind the *Piatiletka* boasts and statistics. In a 648-page book I published in 1937, *Assignment in Utopia*, devoted largely to this period, I wrote at one point: "In my heart of hearts, I have always felt the futility and the ghoulish cynicism of reducing these years of travail to arithmetic." If the Five-Year Plan had met and exceeded its every industrial goal it would still have been a hideous failure, as long as men sanely value life above steel and petroleum.

Was the Five-Year Plan a "success"? Certainly not for the peasantry, living under the new state-feudalism. Certainly not for the individual worker, bound to his bench like a galley slave, underfed, underpaid, overworked—under the lash of managers, the police, and his own trade-union officials. Certainly not for the socialist dream, which precisely in these years was purged of its last vestiges of idealism, melted down to a dehumanized formula for a totalitarian superstate exploiting helpless serfs. Least of all for the human spirit, outraged by sadistic cruelties on a scale new in modern history.

10 / Industrialization

The myth that communism is a rational short-cut
to modern industrialization.

The world prestige of Soviet Russia as a great industrial power
reached a peak in the late 1950's that carried over into the early
1960's. In the West, and in the United States especially, it became
the fashion, not without a touch of hysteria, to speak of the coming supremacy of Soviet economy and military potential. The myth
that communism offers the shortest road to viable industrialization
gained new credence.

For years official Soviet production figures had been accepted
and publicized by influential quarters abroad not only uncritically,
at face value, but with deliberate emphasis on positive aspects of
the data. Scholarly studies questioning the veracity of Moscow
claims and exposing weak sectors covered by juggled statistics were
brushed aside as dog-in-the-manger barking. The dominant opinion
seemed determined to paint a picture of a dynamic Russia inexor-
ably catching up with a static America.

The launching of the Sputnik in the fall of 1957, followed by
other Soviet "firsts" in space, seemed to justify the bias that had
eagerly magnified Soviet economic prowess. Western self-confidence
was shaken. At the same time the jitters in the United States over
an alleged "missile gap" in Russia's favor added to the sense of
capitalist decline and doom.

The mood of the moment in America, at the more pessimistic
end of the opinion spectrum, was mirrored by Walter Lippmann's
declaration that "as compared with our great rival and adversary,
we are at this time in a decline" which, he thought, called for noth-

ing less than "a reappraisal in depth of our cultural values and of our policies."

Central to this state of mind in the West was a claimed annual growth of the GNP (Gross National Product) in the USSR, from 1955 to 1960, sharply above the American growth rate. It appeared to support Khrushchev's flamboyant boasts that the Soviet economy, or at least its industry, was narrowing the distance between the two giants and must in due course overtake the most advanced capitalist nation.

Two close students of the Soviet economy, both eminent economists, Professor G. Warren Nutter in America and Dr. Colin Clark in England, for years challenged the accuracy of Moscow's figures on growth. "Both of us," Dr. Clark wrote in 1962, "reached the conclusion that the true rate of growth of productivity in the Soviet Union was in fact lower than in the United States; therefore, far from overtaking the United States, the Soviet Union was indeed falling gradually further behind." But few would listen.

Then, around 1961–1962, deflation of the myth of exceptional Soviet tempos of growth set in. When the Kremlin, with unconcealed alarm, began admitting a sharply slowed-down rate, and openly considering economic reforms with free-market overtones, world opinion shifted. A number of other reputable economists, including Dr. Naum Jasny and Dr. Abram Bergson, published books in which—though by different analytical roads—they reached substantially the same conclusions as Nutter and Clark.

After 1960, the Soviet Russian rate of growth began to decline. On this, there is no disagreement among the experts, inside or outside the country, although there are considerable differences in estimates of the precise degree of the drop. Gradually, and in some cases reluctantly, authoritative opinion, both official and private, edged away from the former exaggerations toward a more sober view of the Soviet economy.

According to an evaluation by the economic staff of the CIA, made public at the beginning of 1964, overall Soviet growth in the preceding two years was less than 2.5 per cent annually, well below that of the United States. Estimates from other sources credited the USSR with higher percentages; all of them attested, however, that the country had ceased to be a world pacemaker, its growth rate having been exceeded in those years by every major nation.

From the vantage point of Moscow statisticians the picture looked better than in Western analyses, but even there the direction was plainly downward—from a claimed growth rate of 11 per cent in 1959 to 7.5 per cent in 1964, the lowest level since World War II. Referring to these figures, Dr. Boris Meissner, in the quarterly *Modern Age* (Winter, 1966–1967), wrote: "The actual growth was approximately 5 per cent, a rate lower than that of the United States or of the German Federal Republic. . . . Light industry fell from 8 per cent to 2 per cent."

A study made for the Joint Economic Committee of the U.S. Congress, released in mid-1966, showed that the Soviet GNP, as compared with that of the United States in the same years, rose from 32.1 per cent in 1950, to 44.2 per cent in 1958—an impressive narrowing of the gap by 1.5 per cent annually. Then the Soviet pace began to slow down, to 46.7 per cent in 1964, an average "gap-narrowing" by only 0.4 per cent a year. An updating of the figures for 1965 placed the Soviet GNP at 44.7 per cent of the American—no longer a reduction, but a *widening* of the gap by 2 per cent.

The pace in 1966 and early 1967—in Moscow figures which may or may not survive objective analysis—again showed conspicuous increases. The claimed expansion for the first six months of 1967 was 10.6 per cent from the corresponding half year in 1966; by coincidence the percentage is exactly the same as in the United States for the same months.

At best, however, the gross Soviet product stands at about 45 per cent of the American—in absolute values, 333 billion dollars as against 739 billion in the United States: an immense gulf between the "second industrial nation in the world" and the first. If the gross economy totals are measured on a *per capita* basis, production per inhabitant, the USSR drops back to fifth place, behind the United States, France, Germany, and the United Kingdom.

The showing for the Soviet Union is a lot worse when calculations are made for national *income* per inhabitant. The Soviets' own figures then put the country in eighth place. Adjusting those figures to dollar values, on the basis of the official Soviet exchange rate, it slides down to thirteenth position. In a number of individual consumption indices significant for industrial expansion—coal, petroleum, gas, and electricity—the USSR in 1966 ranked tenth, the American superiority being almost threefold. Even in the postwar years of most rapid growth, 1950–1958, the rate of accretion was matched or exceeded by a lot of countries, among them Japan, Germany, Austria, Greece, Turkey, and even Israel, Jamaica, Burma, Venezuela, and Rhodesia. The postwar Japanese rate of growth was 12 per cent.

Allowing for variations in methods of statistical reckoning, the fact beyond doubt, which is all that concerns us here, is that the claimed dramatic tempo of growth which scared the West has been reversed to an admitted sluggishness that alarms the Kremlin.

The high percentages of increase in the postwar years, moreover, have been more generally recognized as a phenomenon to be expected after a destructive war. They were related to the natural impetus of recovery in a badly shattered economy and did not reflect the true Soviet capacities. It was the same phenomenon operative in other war-torn countries, such as Germany, France, and Japan.

These three nations, it may be objected, received large injections of American capital. But the score is more than balanced by the Soviet seizure of reparations, authorized and unauthorized—twenty billion dollars in 1960 values, at a conservative estimate—in Central and Eastern Europe, Finland, Italy, and Manchuria. This "foreign aid," in addition, accrued to the Soviet Union mostly in processed forms, ready for use: mountains of industrial goods, machines, entire production units, among them Germany's most advanced precision equipment and research installations. The famous Zeiss factory, for example, was transferred *in toto* to Soviet Russia —not only the plant and its contents, down to the stores of sand, but all the workers and managers who could be located and kidnapped.

The famous "missile gap," it was discovered, was pure war-of-nerves fiction. It did not and never had existed. And the United States, once it tackled the job, quickly matched and eventually surpassed the Soviet space spectaculars. The USSR had orbited a satellite earlier, it became apparent, not because of technological superiority, but because of a *political* decision geared to propaganda objectives.

Russia has been chary with information on the subject. It is believed that its own scientists and its huge contingent of German specialists made some vital engineering developments, related, in the first place, to greater engine thrust. But they discovered no new breakthrough principles not known to the West, merely applying the common stock of space knowledge a few years sooner. Some of this knowledge had been acquired by the Soviets through long years of massive espionage in the United States, Canada, and Great Britain. Subsequent American achievements leave little room for doubt that, had the United States started as early as the USSR, it could have had a Sputnik in orbit at about the same time.

The truth is that an authoritarian state, answerable to no one but itself, can obtain striking results by a "crash program" on limited goals. It can commandeer the best brains, materials, and manpower for the favored target and back it with unlimited financing. This is the kind of thing other nations, temporarily near-authoritarian in wartime, have also done: witness the American "Manhattan Project" that netted the first atomic bombs. Sputniks and other such special projects are no more proof of overall economic superiority than were the Great Pyramids in ancient Egypt.

The most telling blow to the legend of Soviet Russia's impending victory over the United States in the economic race was delivered by another major crisis in agriculture. It recalled the world to the elementary but somehow neglected reality that heavy industry is only one facet of a nation's progress; that its farming, the living conditions of its people, reserves of raw materials, quality levels, and other factors cannot be disregarded without falsifying the picture.

In October, 1961, Khrushchev announced that very soon his country "will occupy such a position in the international grain market that the imperialist gentlemen will begin to feel how our agriculture is expanding." Instead, less than two years later, he was importuning those imperialist gentlemen to sell him their capitalist grain, and depleting the Soviet gold reserves to pay for it. Canada, Australia, and the United States, from their surpluses, did sell enough to prevent hunger and possibly a famine. Despite a bumper crop in 1966, the USSR is committed to huge purchases of cereals at least through 1968. It is compelled by more open discontent to give the people a better diet. Specialists on the international food market believe that Russia, once a major exporter, will for a long time to come figure as a grain-importing nation.

Under Khrushchev's successors, the Kremlin has retreated from his more exaggerated pretensions. Their current Five-Year Plan (1966–1970), unveiled in April, 1966, is more moderate and more candid about mounting difficulties. The targets set by Khrushchev for 1970 have been trimmed down as much as 68 per cent in a number of sectors; some of the consumer goals for 1970 are the same as those prescribed for 1965, and even lower. This time the familiar incantations about overtaking and outdistancing the United States were conspicuously missing.

In *Prospects for Soviet Society*, soon to be published by the Council on Foreign Relations, the keynote contribution is by Professor Cyril E. Black of Princeton. Titled "Soviet Society: A Comparative View," it provides a wholesome corrective on runaway enthusiasm about Soviet achievements. Professor Black widens the focus of analysis to take in all indices of national life, not only production and consumption, but wages, social services, and all other measurable elements, and relates the composite findings to the rest of the world.

One conclusion that can be drawn [he writes] is that on a *per capita* basis, the USSR ranks in measurable economic and social indices about twentieth among the 130 or more countries for which accurate information is available . . .

In the perspective of fifty years, the comparative ranking of the USSR in composite economic and social indices *per capita* has not changed significantly. So far as the rather limited available evidence permits a judgment, the USSR has not overtaken any country or surpassed any country since 1917, with the possible exception of Italy, and the nineteen or twenty countries that rank higher than Russia today in this regard also ranked higher in 1900 or 1917.

The overall picture is thus startlingly unlike the one based on gross product alone. And Professor Black adds that "other countries at a similar or more advanced level have achieved an equivalent or better record of development at a significantly lower cost in human lives and hardship."

· The Bogus Miracles

Short-term fluctuations in world opinion on the Soviet economy, however, are less significant than its permanent characteristics. Russia since 1917 has been transformed into a powerful industrial nation. Industrialization, it has been demonstrated, *can* be achieved by an authoritarian state. The real issues are those of effectiveness, as compared with industrialization by conventional processes: its relative cost in material, political, and human values; its ability to absorb rapid change in technology; the kind of society it provides for the population.

Living conditions in all other industrial societies have kept pace with industrial expansion. Not so in the USSR, where consumption per person in its fiftieth year is less than 30 per cent of what it is in the United States and also sharply lower than in any major European nation or Japan. Overall production, that is, continues to rise at a fast rate while individual consumption and well-being remain stagnant.

The usual pattern in free-market economies in this century has been an increase in agricultural productivity greater than that of the economy as a whole; in the USSR the reverse has been the case. Communist-type industrialization, it is thus quite clear, takes place at the expense of the consumer and agriculture. It can force the rate of industrial growth by heavy "inputs," in the economists' term, of capital and manpower, but only by holding down wages and farm prices at murderously low levels over several generations.

"The example of Russia, and later China," Dr. Ernest Conine wrote in the *Harvard Business Review* (May-June, 1965), "offers convincing proof that a backward country can industrialize with impressive speed, if it will force its citizens to do what no people have ever done voluntarily: endure grinding poverty and regimentation in order to maintain a high investment rate."

Other industrial societies have been built without penalizing the people as outrageously as in the Soviet Union. The only merit claimed for the communist alternative therefore appears to be its speed of development: the belief that it is a "short-cut" to industrialization. But that, too, does not stand up in the tests of historical comparisons. Other nations have industrialized as fast or faster, without excruciating communist methods.

Feudal Japan, to cite the most obvious example, reached first rank more swiftly than the USSR, beginning in the 1890's and from a less promising base than Lenin inherited, in a country with more limited population and natural wealth than Russia had. But the most significant comparison is provided by the very United

States which the Kremlin hopes, with diminishing confidence, to catch up with.

It is scarcely significant to compare *current* tempos of expansion in Russia and the United States. A nation already full-grown neither needs nor can absorb the tempos of growth of a nation in a relatively early stage of industrialization; in fact, excessive growth in an advanced country—an "over-heated" economy—is sometimes considered dangerous. For a fair comparison of the two economic systems, the Soviet period should be matched against an equivalent period in American development.

The Bolsheviks took over an economy roughly equivalent to that of the United States in 1875. To discount the stagnant Russian years of war and revolution, we may date the Soviets' "1875" as 1928, when the 1913 Russian level was reached again. The USSR from 1928 to 1966 would thus correspond to the United States from 1875 to 1913. A number of eminent Western economists, notably Professor Nutter, have shown in statistical graphs, that overall American industrial expension in those thirty-eight years was as large as, and in many departments larger than, in the USSR. And, what is most important, the American economy grew in ordered freedom, at high levels of living and without the terror that marked the Soviet growth.

While the Soviet tempo of industrialization and construction has been impressive, it is thus not remotely the "miracle" being acclaimed. The average annual growth rate in its most productive periods, say 1950 to 1958, as Professor Black points out, has been "exceeded over long periods" by the United States and Australia in the nineteenth century, and by Japan in the twentieth. The rate of growth both in absolute and *per capita* figures has been higher in South Africa, Japan, and other countries.

Russia would assuredly have developed as fast, or faster, under any system. Besides, the Soviets had the enormous advantage of access to the accumulated technological wealth and experience of the West. The USSR in 1928 did not, like the United States in 1875, start technologically from scratch.

"What made it possible to establish gigantic factories of the most modern types in the space of a few years" in the Soviet Union, Leon Trotsky pointed out in 1937, was, among other things, "the existence in the West of a high capitalist technique." In a sense, Soviet industrialization has been parasitic, drawing on the colossal progress in the most advanced countries. In 1944, Stalin told an American guest, Eric Johnston, that "about two-thirds of all the large industrial enterprises in the USSR had been built with U.S. material or technical assistance."

The Soviet economy "works" after its fashion. As Professor Milton Friedman of the University of Chicago wrote in this connection, "A horse-and-buggy works as a means of transportation, but it is far less efficient than an automobile. . . . If one goes back to the nineteenth century," he continued, "what were the great success stories of economic development? Britain, the United States, Western Europe, Japan. Each of these succeeded in achieving a dramatic increase in economic output and equally in the standard of life of its ordinary citizens. In none of them was there anything approaching a controlled society."

• *Failures in Quality*

Whatever the tempos and the gross bulk of Soviet industrialization, the crucial question is indeed how effectively the resultant economy "works" as compared with non-communist economies. A large industry that limps and falters may be less desirable than a smaller one that walks steadily and meets the needs of the people. How efficient is it, in terms of the quality and durability of its product; the output by one man in an hour; the ability to absorb the latest techniques and tools?

Answers to such questions can be dredged from the general technical Soviet press, which is carefully monitored and analyzed by many Western experts. They have also been coming more copiously and more candidly from Soviet sources in connection with their current discussion of "economic reforms." These are not exercises in theory, but have been forced upon the regime by breakdowns, dwindling resources, alarming declines in quality, lack of communications between the state as manufacturer and the state as consumer. The story the answers tell is one of shoddy goods, low output per worker, high mortality of machinery and plant, startling lack of balance between different branches of the economy, bureaucratic resistance to change.

The picture of Soviet industrialization painted by propaganda is based entirely on *quantity*. It begins to fall apart as soon as one examines *quality*, in the end-product and in the labor that goes into it. It takes two to three Soviet workers, and in isolated cases as many as eight, to match the production of one worker in the United States or Western Europe or Japan. Soviet manufactured goods, with negligible exceptions, cannot meet Western competition except in the poorest countries. "Many countries, including socialist countries, do not want to buy our finished products because of their poor quality," a prominent Soviet economist, Abel G. Aganbegyan, has stated. Nations receiving Soviet products under foreign-aid agreements have repeatedly rejected them as unusable.

A detailed study of the Soviet quality factor was made for a U.S. Congressional committee in 1964 by Joseph A. Gwyer of the U.S. Library of Congress, one of the most respected American specialists on Soviet economy. Based almost entirely on published Soviet sources, it leaves little margin for doubt that inferior goods are endemic under communism and that the production totals in Kremlin statistics should therefore be heavily discounted. Mr. Gwyer writes at one point:

> Khrushchev complained, on April 24, 1963, that his country spends annually more than seven billion rubles on repairs of capital equipment, that this job keeps over two million workers and 800,000 metal-cutting machine tools constantly busy. . . . It appears that the figure of seven billion rubles was quite a conservative estimate in the light of recent revelations by A. N. Demyanovich, currently the Deputy Director of the Committee of Coordination of Scientific Research, who stated that the current annual repair bill caused by faulty production runs at about fifteen billion rubles.

A few highlights should suffice to show the general condition— one doesn't have to eat a whole potful of soup to know that it is putrid.

Soviet statistics indicate that they are producing more machine tools than the United States—as is to be expected, American industry having reached a saturation point on such equipment. But Moscow's figures do not reveal what can be learned from its press, namely, "how many failed to operate either at the end of the assembly line or weeks later, after costly and labor-consuming installation at the place of consignment." Repairs on existing machine tools occupy 3.5 times as many workers as are engaged in manufacturing new units. One-third of machine tools in operation are kept busy on repair work. Electrical motors, during their first year of life, spend 30 to 40 per cent of total working time undergoing repairs. In any given time, 30 to 40 per cent of all vehicles are idle, awaiting repairs or spare parts. Every Soviet tractor, Mr. Gwyer shows, undergoes repairs each year at a cost of one-third or more of the original costs; total expenditures on spare parts for farm tractors in a typical year, 1962, exceed the outlay for new procurement that year.

More up-to-the-minute Moscow reports confirm that these conditions have gotten worse in the last four or five years. The *Kommunist* (1967, No. 2) complains that the repair industry now "occupies almost two and a half million workers and over a million metal-cutting lathes, which is equal to 40 per cent of the machine tools in the country and more than there are in the basic plants of the metal industry. And the lathes used in repair services are of more recent vintage than those used in the machine-building industry."

An interesting side-light on the quality factor—even in weaponry, to which Moscow assigns its best brains and resources—has been provided in the Vietnam war. The Soviet surface-to-air missiles (SAM-2's) in North Vietnam have, at this writing, a batting average of 20 per cent: about 300 hits in 1,500 fired. The U.S. military will not pass this missile with batting averages under 66 per cent under rigorous simulated battle conditions.

Consider the automotive industry, so basic that it is almost the test of the vitality of a modern industrial society. Its output in the Soviet Union in 1967 is at the rate reached by Americans in 1910. The introduction of the industry in the USSR began in the 1930's with the purchase of a complete Ford factory from Detroit, installed, equipped, and for some years run by Americans. Thirty years later, the current Five-Year Plan sets annual output of 800,-000 cars, trucks, and buses as its goal for 1970—and may actually reach 460,000 that year, according to a U.S. intelligence study. But the USSR admits that it is unable, after thirty years in the business and in possession of heavy industry, second only to the American, to equip a modern automobile plant!

Instead Moscow has turned to Fiat in Italy (the United States probably providing three-fourths of the machinery and financing) to design and build plants with an ultimate capacity of several hundred thousand cars a year and is negotiating with motor companies in Japan and France for the balance. If and when a high figure is reached in 1970, communists will acclaim yet another Soviet "achievement" though nearly all of it will be Soviet only in the sense that it is on Russian soil and paid for with more "sacrifices" by the Russian peoples.

The same condition holds true for other Soviet industries. The introduction of plastics, synthetic fibers, and other products of the new chemistry has been made possible to a large extent by equipment and whole factories bought in foreign countries. One of the main justifications for the punishing rate and costs of industrialization was the attainment of independence from the outside world. Actually the USSR is almost as dependent on the West as it was during the war, when American tools and weapons to the tune of nine billion dollars (and two billion more in foodstuffs) probably prevented a Soviet industrial bogdown or defeat.

The Soviets have dropped behind the world parade in the new industrial techniques. They need synthetics and plastics in the petro-chemical field; light-weight, high-strength metals; improved electronic computers; advanced miniaturization and automation equipment. Were the great Western producers to deny these and other essentials to Moscow, along with the scientific information for their use, the whole myth of a great self-sustained Soviet industrial power would collapse.

The Kremlin should thank its stars (and perhaps does) that its prophesied "doom" of capitalism has not come true. There is nothing essential the Soviets have that the West needs—no inventions, machines, techniques—but the USSR is in dire need of practically everything in these catagories that the West possesses.

• The Plague of Shortages

Back in 1932, Molotov, annoyed by complaints about living conditions, said: "It is necessary to oppose vigorously the idea that socialism means production for use." Marx must have turned once more in his grave. But the Molotov brand of socialism lived up to his prescription. Scarcity is the special mark of Soviet life. Scores of observers have remarked (and it is true notwithstanding) that a Woolworth store or an American mail-order catalog, by dramatizing the abundance, diversity, and cheapness of goods under other systems, could cancel out decades of Soviet propaganda.

Pharmacies in Moscow, for a long time, dispensed medicines in bottles without stoppers, and essential medicines are themselves chronically in short supply. The citizen must often wait a year for lenses for eye-glasses. For months at a time, often for years, such staples as razor blades, safety-pins, paper and paper products (including toilet tissues), kitchenware, sheets and pillows, electric bulbs of desired wattage, cannot be found, even in Moscow and Leningrad. When missing items finally appear, they are quickly snapped up and another hiatus follows. Though they risk severe punishment, youngsters constantly waylay foreign tourists, begging to buy a shirt or a pair of pants, fountain-pens or watches, at almost any price in rubles.

An American journalist, John Scott, attending a concert in the magnificent new Palace of Congresses on the Kremlin grounds, asked why there were no programs. Because of a paper shortage, he was informed. His comment, in a report to his editors: "What an anomaly! A theater which makes Lincoln Center seem modest, a performance unmatched anywhere—in a country of huge forests—and no paper for programs." (I am reminded of the magazine *Nashe Dostizheniye—Our Achievements—*started in the early thirties and abruptly discontinued. The reason, Muscovites said with a discreet wink, was the lack of paper.)

When available, consumer goods tend to be, if anything, lower in quality than large industrial items. Famished as they may be for nearly everything from footwear to television sets, more and more consumers are in open revolt against extremes of shoddiness. As a result, warehouses are increasingly loaded with unwanted goods. The public clamors, for example, for shoes, whatever the price. Yet the Soviet economic press reveals that 1.5 billion rubles in shoes are stacked up, unsalable, because they are too heavy and ugly.

A startling statement on the dimensions of this inventory of unsalable goods has come from an unimpeachable Soviet source. The journal, *Voprosy Ekonomiki* (1963, No. 1) reported: "Poor quality of products, commodities not in demand by the population, still appear in stores. . . . Commodity stocks in the country are growing rapidly. During the period 1959–1961 their rate of growth was almost three times greater than the increase in retail trade turnover. *These stocks have now reached an enormous sum—almost 27 billion rubles.*"

The best way to judge how an advanced economy "works," Gwyer points out, is by evaluating "the quality and reliability of the goods this technological society manufactures. . . . Judging from information coming from the Soviet Union, the Soviets are very unhappy with the quality of their own goods. Soviet industry employs more than one million inspectors. Despite all possible efforts to limit the output of defectives, the losses directly attributable to the output of defectives are constantly growing."

If private industry had to operate under such conditions, it would quickly go into bankruptcy. In a totalitarian state, the losses are taken out of the stomachs and the hides of the population.

"Subject only to minor fluctuations," Colin Clark has written, "the United States, ever since the 1890's, has maintained a steady rate of growth of real product per man-hour of 2.3 per cent per year." This is about one-third higher than the Soviet man-hour growth rate, which has also been surpassed in varying degrees in nearly all other free-economy nations. Kosygin, at a Party Plenum in September, 1965, conceded that "the rate of growth in labor productivity in industry . . . has slowed down somewhat in recent years." This despite more machinery and increased capital investments. In the same years, labor productivity was rising steadily in most West European countries. In 1966, Soviet productivity showed some improvement, but not enough to affect the overall picture.

Probably the most telltale example of economic disequilibrium is to be found in Soviet transportation—in its primitive road system, for example. The USSR, with an area about two and a half times as large, has a road network only 5 per cent of the American network. Of this total, only about one-quarter is hard-surfaced, as against nearly three-quarters in the United States. "In spring and autumn, when the Soviet Union's unpaved roads turn into puddles of slush," Dr. Albert Feller said in a bulletin of the Institute for Study of the USSR, "thousands and thousands of vehicles are brought to a stop." Vast areas of the country are inaccessible for the duration. This in the second largest industrial country in the world.

One of the chronic bottlenecks is an acute lack of engineers and technicians, nothwithstanding the great numbers turned out by Soviet schools. One reason is that a large part of this personnel is siphoned off by the bureaucracy for purely administrative and inspection chores. Another is that trained technicians serve as foremen and supervisors, because the country still does not possess enough skilled practical men for such jobs. Some years ago, *Pravda* complained that in the fishing industry there was one "technical man" for every 1.8 workers; at a metal plant there was one engineer to five workers. These of course, were horrible examples—presumably there would not be enough people to go around if the condition prevailed everywhere—but they point up another acute industrial problem.

The judgment of the communist leaders themselves, in dealing with deficiencies they are eager to correct, is as harsh as that of foreign students. Kosygin and Brezhnev, like Khrushchev before them, have attacked the backwardness of their economic functionaries in the introduction of new machines and new methods. In late 1965, Kosygin pointed to examples of available technical progress being ignored and asserted that "mechanization and automation are being put into effect far too slowly." Because of delays, he charged, "the installed equipment becomes obsolete even before it is put into operation." Some of these delays, he said, run to four years and more in the chemical industry, in iron and steel and an array of other branches.

More than a hundred thousand construction projects, some of them initiated five to ten years ago, stand unfinished. This means not only serious obsolescence before completion but immense capital outlays frozen unproductively. A Moscw dispatch to the *New York Times,* based on published Soviet information as of early 1967, reported that "about 30 billion rubles are presently tied up in construction projects throughout the Soviet Union." It quoted disclosures by an *Izvestia* staff economist, Otto Latsis, that the building of a metallurgical plant in western Siberia was dragged out for eight years; that new mining complexes in the Rostov region were put into operation five to ten years behind schedule.

Adjustment to technological advances is not easy under any system. Obviously it becomes infinitely more difficult under conditions where the incentives of personal profit and commercial competition are almost totally absent.

· Truths That Will Out

The harm worked by defects in a national economy are not merely cumulative, not a matter of simple addition. They multiply geometrically, each failure breeding new and larger failures. It is this process that finally compelled the Soviet dictatorship to seek correctives. Its economists and other specialists have not merely been allowed but encouraged to examine and criticize the functioning of the economy—*but not the state monopoly, national planning, or socialism as such.*

Within these limitations, they have made, in the last few years, truly startling revelations. Taken together, the picture they present is blacker than any painted by the most critical foreign economists writing on the subject.

Consider, for example, the lecture given at a seminar in the Moscow University in the summer of 1965. The lecturer was the eminent Soviet-Armenian scholar Professor Abel G. Aganbegyan, then head of an Institute of Economic-Mathematical Studies in Siberia and, at thirty-three, one of the youngest corresponding-members of the Soviet Academy of Science. What he said has not been published in the USSR; conceivably he meant it to be "off record." But a text was soon being circulated in manuscript throughout the country and a few copies reached the outside world. A translation in full was run by the Italian socialist journal *Bandiera Rossa (Red Banner)* in July, 1965. Excerpts, some garbled, have seen print in many other countries.

Professor Aganbegyan's description of the economy was so gloomy that its dissemination abroad apparently distressed the powers that be. His was the familiar dilemma of scholars in a police-state when their candor exceeds their political prudence. Whether on his own or under official orders, the young professor eventually granted an interview to Theodore Shabad, a correspondent of the *New York Times*, published under a Novosibirsk dateline on November 21, 1965. But it did nothing to discredit the document, if that was his intention.

The scientist implied that some of his words had been misinterpreted and tried to whittle down the measure of his personal responsibility for some statements. They reflected, he said, "generally recognized truths about the economy. . . . I never expressed them as my personal opinions." Understandably, he stressed that he was not "a rebel against existing institutions who viewed the Soviet culture in a pessimistic light." Perhaps, he said, he had expressed himself in "too sweeping" terms.

However, he did not explicitly disown the text published abroad, as he could have done, or declare it a falsification. In substance his interview therefore confirmed the authenticity of the document. What follows are some highlights from the lecture, as published in *Bandiera Rossa*; if they represent "generally recognized truths" rather than his personal opinions, their significance is that much greater:

During the past six years the rate of development of our economy has decreased by two-thirds or so. The rate of development of our agriculture has decreased by about nine-tenths (from 8 per cent per year to 0.8 per cent). During the same period the rate of increase in goods in circulation has decreased by three-fourths. There was also a large drop in the rate of increase of the population's real income. . . . In certain cases instead of an increase there has even been a decrease since 1958. . . . The Seven-Year Plan has failed. Not only that, but with the end of the first ten-year part of our twenty-year plan none of the quotas has been attained. . . .

During these years we have experienced a decrease in effective productive accumulation and the rates of development of industrial production are continuously decreasing. There is an increased gap between the possibilities offered by technological progress and the actual achievement of these possibilities. We have the worst and the most backward productive structure among all the industrially developed countries. Our productive capacity, which to tell the truth isn't really so good, is not utilized to any more than 70 per cent of capacity.

The chief sector of our heavy industry, the machine tool industry, has made two million machines available to our economy. The number of machine tools we have is equal to the number in the United States but only half of ours produce effectively, while the others either are not used or are being repaired. We employ more workers to do repair work than to produce new machines. . . .

At present the employment problem (spoken of in the West as the unemployment problem) is very strongly felt here. Jobs must be created for ten million young people in the next five years. At the same time one finds that there has been an increase in the number of persons without work in the past two years. This phenomenon occurs above all in the small and medium-sized cities. On an average 25 to 30 per cent of the population able to work fails to find employment in these cities. In the large cities the figure covering this phenomenon is 8 per cent. . . .

With respect to the increase in living standards, things are going badly. Here there is a very large gap with respect to planned quotas. There has not, in fact, been any rise in the standard of living during recent years. Ten million people have suffered a decrease in their living standards. . . .

Everything that has been said is highly alarming because it is not just a question of the situation existing in our economy today, but one of the existing trend and this is very, very much worse. . . .

We spend a great deal for defense and we have much difficulty in competing with the United States in this field because we must spend almost as much as they do while our economic potential is only about half theirs. . . .

The principal causes [of the poor economy] are domestic. First of all there is the mistaken direction of economic development in which our country is headed. Second, all of the systems of planning, incentives and management of the Soviet economy do not correspond to the real requirements placed upon us. We have been holding doggedly to the line of ultra-industrialization for many years; even in recent years when there was no longer any necessity to do so. . . .

Calculations which have been made have shown that in the present situation the average collective farmer can earn 1.50 rubles per day on the collective farms and 3.50 rubles on his own private piece of land. Is it worth his while then to work on the collective farm? Obviously no! Under existing conditions if the people were allowed to leave the countryside hardly anyone would remain behind. . . .

Building and housing plans are never fulfilled in the USSR. Housing authorities as a rule do not utilize the credits made available to them. . . . Our prices and our monetary value relationships serve no purpose at all. . . . Our system of economic levers has nothing in common with the plan and goes against the interests of the economy. It creates, in fact, contradictions between the interests of the state and those of the enterprise. . . .

We have an absolute lack of information. The figures published by the Central Statistical Office (ZSU) are blown up. Thus we are planning and managing the economy when we do not have any real information about the actual situation. . . . Among other things, the argumentation against the statistics of the [United States] CIA put forth in our magazines by the ZSU is absurd; the Americans are closer to knowing the truth of our statistics. . . ." [The sentence is uncompleted in the original, but its meaning is clear enough.]

The academician's references to growing unemployment—ranging from 8 to 30 per cent in urban areas—have amazed those who follow such things. One of the standard boasts of the USSR, as of Nazi Germany in its time, has been that it abolished unemployment. A *Dictionary of Political Economy* published in Moscow in 1964 still says: "The socialist economy liquidates unemployment, finally and forever." Because of this premise of socialist planning, the Soviet state provided for no employment agencies, no labor exchanges, no unemployment insurance. Whether the professor's estimates are accurate or not, the existence of the problem is conceded by the authorities. Erudite papers on the subject have appeared in the technical press, and it was on the agenda of the last Party Congress.*

Vermont Royster, editor of the *Wall Street Journal*, traveled eight thousand miles in the USSR in 1962, studying its economy against his rich background of economic expertise. "The Soviet Union is a feudal society" he wrote on his return. "In the true sense of the word, and measured against any of the advanced nations of the West, it is a backward country, whether the test be industry, agriculture, technology, labor skills, or the standard of living of the people. . . . It has an economic system . . . which 'works' but which does so mainly by brute force and awkwardness and therefore by its inefficiencies constitutes a drag on the nation's progress." The country is advanced, he conceded, compared to India, Burma, or many parts of Latin America, "but compared with the great industrial nations of the West, the only honest word is 'backward.' "

---

* Since 1966, labor exchanges (called "commissions for job placement") have gradually been introduced in difficult areas, and the Soviet press is discussing the need for unemployment doles. The Moscow *Trud* (March 26, 1967) published startling data on lack of jobs for graduates of secondary schools. The official assumption that these unemployed young people would be absorbed in agriculture has been defeated by their refusal to face life in the villages.

The communist "short-cut" to industrialization leads into a morass of disequilibrium, waste, and want. Sheer growth in heavy industry, having been made a political fetish, has operated to distort natural development by creating wild disproportions between industry and agriculture, between heavy and light industry, between production and transportation, between production and consumption, between quantity and quality.

The profound crisis in Soviet agriculture is too conspicuous to be disputed by anyone. The crisis in industry is amply mirrored in the fumbling attempts somehow to build a few free-market methods into the elephantine and inflexible state monopoly. The Kremlin no longer denies that the gap between its own and the American economies is widening. There is a crisis, acknowledged and openly bewailed, in the productivity of labor. Depletion of gold reserves is evident, among other things, in the restoration about three years ago of Stalin's notorious *valuta* shops, where food and other deficit goods can be bought only with foreign currency. The Soviet ruble, its value arbitrarily set at $1.11, is still not convertible into foreign exchanges—its export and import strictly forbidden—and still grotesquely irrelevant to real purchasing power; a black market in money flourishes as always under such conditions.

There we have in capsule form the reality of Soviet industrialization, so imposing when reported only in quantitative totals garnished with exclamation marks. Unquestionably the USSR has emerged among the leading industrial nations, but it is structurally the weakest among them, the only one muscle-bound by dogma and deprived of the vitamins of individual ambition and ingenuity. Professor Abram Bergson remarked sagely in a 1964 book, "If socialism were an especially productive system, one might think that by now this fact would have been manifest."

An American official described as "a government authority on Soviet affairs" was quoted by the *U.S. News & World Report* (March 13, 1967) as follows:

It is becoming more apparent that communism is a failure as a way to run a modern economic society. It can't compete with the free market system. . . . The Soviets have cheated on agriculture and housing in their heavy-industry phase. They have a soggy, no-incentive system. They haven't been able to bring themselves to end collectivization in agriculture, they have an inhibition against making consumer goods the center of the economic-growth process. This could mean the loss of control over their system—and so far, preservation of the communist regime has come first.

The statistics presented in this chapter may be contradictory at points, or even marginally in error. In reading the Russian and non-Russian literature on the Soviet economy, one confronts wide differences in the findings. The student in this area must be a combination of puzzle expert and economic detective to reach any conclusions he can credit with confidence. But the variations, though important to specialists, are not particularly relevant for this book. Our concern here is with the larger picture, with the society as a whole, which obviously is not affected by a few percentages of leeway in one direction of another.

Whatever its size and tempo—and this is the crux of the matter —industrialization is not an end in itself. Unless it enriches life, attends to the basic needs of the people, sustains a more just and moral society, it is a sad failure no matter what the statistics may show.

In Soviet Russia industry has expanded but life in fundamental terms has diminished. The vaunted "short cut" to industrial supremacy is neither short nor logical nor supported by the historic experience of mankind. Where it has had its largest and most thorough test, it has led a great nation and a great people into quagmires of want, confusion, and relentless exploitation.

11 / Planning

The myth that centralized national planning is a magic
formula for growth and prosperity.

One of the major industries in a planned economy is the planning
industry. Itself in essence immune to planning, it lives parasitically
on the whole economy, developing vested interests of its own, as
shown by the resistance of the planning bureaucracy to economic
reforms that cut into its prerogatives.

It is glandular in growth, this planning industry, out-running all
others in rate of expansion by wide margins. The disease has been
reduced to an arithmetical formula by a well known mathemati-
cian, Professor V. M. Glushkov, vice-president of the Ukrainian
Academy of Science—a formula that, significantly, is very widely
quoted in the USSR in these worrisome times. If unchecked, he
calculated, the volume of planning tends to increase at least as the
square of national output, so that by 1980 it would have grown 36-
fold, requiring the services of the whole population!

The prospect is intriguing: a society in which everybody plans
for nobody. Already there is an element of truth in the fantasy—so
many of the planners are engaged in useless motion. The system
generates armies of clerks, accountants, controllers, all splashing
about in a paper ocean; armies of bureaucrats raveling and unravel-
ing red tape.

Official statistics show administrative personnel of 1,300,000 in
the central planning apparatus and its direct agencies, but there are
hundreds of republic, regional, and local committees, bureaus,
party commissions involved in the planning process. Western specialists place the aggregate planning bureaucracy at between seven
and ten million. Some Soviet experts go even higher—N. P. Fedo-

renko, head of the Central Institute of Mathematical Economics, estimated about twelve million persons in "the sphere of administration" related to planning. But additional millions in all enterprises, down to the lowest, must give part or all of their time to keeping up with the vagaries of the plan.

Every private business director knows how much time and money goes into formulating even short-range planning and budgeting for a single firm. It is an obligation inherent in ownership.

But the USSR is history's most colossal super-monopoly, the single owner and manager of everything, attempting to prescribe for and synchronize the whole economic universe of a big nation. Here, too, it is an obligation deriving from ownership. Total state ownership was not instituted to make possible total planning, but the other way around: a single plan was needed to serve and fortify a single state-owner. Under communism, *political* planning, as Djilas has made clear, takes precedence over *economic* planning.

The same handful of men at the apex responsible for the economy, it should be borne in mind, must also manage the multitudinous activities of the ruling party and government, education, the armed forces and oversized police establishments, foreign affairs and (insofar as it can) the world communist movement. Each of these in itself calls for planning and for coordination with one another and with the economy.

How can they possibly carry out such a gargantuan task? The answer is that they can't and don't. At most they try to plan the small part of the economic iceberg above water. The rest unavoidably is left to its own devices, theoretically in harmony with plan guidelines, in practice distorting and nullifying much of what is planned. All the same, the dimensions of the job keep growing until, as now, they threaten to choke the economy.

Those abroad passionately sold on planning (there are few in the Soviet Union) take a naïvely superficial view of it all. Instead of leaving things to the "anarchy" of a free market, directives are issued from on high, and millions of enterprises carry them out. What could be simpler?

The reality is more complicated. The relations between resources and supply allocations, between specialized skills available and production targets, between consumer needs and producer capacity, the fixing of prices on an infinite number of commodities and services—in a free-market economy these and myriad other inter-relations are adjusted almost automatically. In a planned economy they represent monumental problems which the fifty-year Soviet test has shown to be insoluble.

Ever since Stalin made it famous, from 1928 forward, intellectuals in the advanced West and in backward areas alike have been dazzled by planning as an idea. It was "the mystique of planning," more than Marxism as such, that gripped their imaginations. It seemed to promise "order" in place of a free-wheeling economy marked by inequality of income and occasional recessions and depressions. Theory was de-emphasized in their thinking in favor of the supposedly "practical" side: a command economy under a Supreme Bookkeeper. Like all converts to a new belief, they closed their eyes to its shortcomings.

In late 1932, an eminent American economist, Stuart Chase, published a book, *A New Deal*, which ended with these amazing words: "Why should the Russians have all the fun of remaking a world?" From the context it was clear that he was referring, in the first place, to planned economy. The lucky Russians were then "having fun" in extraordinary ways: dying by the million in a man-made famine, crowding into hideous slave-camps, queueing up for hours in all weathers for their meager rations. I was among them as a reporter and didn't find the amusements too hilarious.

At a later time, when he was moved to deplore certain Soviet atrocities, the celebrated French writer, Jean-Paul Sartre, was careful to reaffirm his faith in planning. Even if there is "absolute horror" in Russia, he declaimed, "we shall not condemn them while they continue to assure access to Reason in the conduct of economy."

These are just two samples of irrational confidence in the magic of planning. "It is an extraordinary testament," one analyst sadly concludes, "to the power of words over facts, of ideas over evidence, that these views should be so strongly held." Dr. Colin Clark has written: "It took people a long time to understand that the word 'plan' in Soviet Russian did not mean what we call a plan at all, but meant a sort of manifesto, designed primarily to provide a political stimulus, but bearing little relation to the ascertained facts of the situation, or to any prospects which might intelligently be expected." And he, too, wondered why it "aroused such uncritical enthusiasm among Soviet well-wishers in the Western countries."

In the more rational mood of recent Soviet years, forced upon the regime by its economic troubles, the costlier defects and contradictions of the system have been up for public examination. No matter how painstakingly various adaptations of elementary capitalist techniques are trimmed with "socialist" labels, every uttered criticism casts doubt on the basic principles of total planning and is another nail in its coffin. But the funeral is still far off. No one in the USSR proposes, no one dares propose, as long as Marxism-Leninism is official state dogma, that the whole business be properly buried.

• Built-in Fallacies

There are, in the Soviet Union, according to the official journal *Planned Economy*, close to two million enterprises. The top 200,-000, classed as census industry, produce about twenty million separate items. The central planning apparatus, Gosplan, works up annual and long-term directives for only 18,000 commodities, less than one-tenth of one per cent of the total.

The rest are fitted into the overall plan, in theory at least, at lower levels—countrywide, regional, local—through species and sub-species of trusts, commissions, committees, bureaus, comprising what one American economist calls "a crazy-quilt of subordinate and supplementary planning agencies several layers thick." Egregious failures in gathering and processing information, often falsified at its source through fear or greed, lead to unrealistic targets. In the nature of a process so complex and overlapping, error, self-serving distortion, and duplication breed inefficiency and at points full chaos.

But the figures cited above do not compass the entirety of a huge nation's economy. In the London *Survey* of April, 1956, Dr. Leon Smolinski explores the all but incalculable number of economic activities that lie outside the patterns of planning—compensating in some measure (at shocking cost) for its inadequacies.

First, there is the universal practice by factory managements of fabricating their own secondary supplies, because they dare not trust other sources to make deliveries at the proper time or of the proper kinds. To fulfill plans, "Soviet factories tend to grow into highly integrated empires which, instead of getting their semi-manufactured products, such as castings, forgings, spare parts, from large-scale, efficient, specialized outside suppliers, produce them in their own plants, on an uneconomically small scale . . . at a prohibitive cost."

Every factory thus is likely to maintain a series of auxiliaries. It costs ten to twenty times as much, for example, to produce screws and nuts on a tiny scale than in big specialized plants. But what is cost when the plan itself is at stake? Practically all machine tool factories have their own forge shops, whereas in the United States only fourteen in a thousand have them.

Second, along with the industrial "giants" there are large numbers of small, outmoded units. In the Russian republic alone, supplementing the dozens of huge modern rolling mills, there are in operation eighty small ones, dating from the nineteenth and even the eighteenth century. Their productivity per worker is fantastically low, but in its anxiety for plan fulfillment, the trust dares not close down even the smallest and most inefficient operations under its control.

The same holds true for other trusts. In the electric industry, the planners focused on large district stations and their output has steadily increased. At the same time there are 53,000 pygmy stations with average capacity of 50 kilowatts, maintained and added to despite the fact that their power costs ten to twenty times more.

"Eighteenth-century steel mills and 50-kilowatt stations," Dr. Smolinski attests, "continued to crowd the path of Soviet industralization and lower the overall efficiency with which Soviet industry operates." He does not add, because it is implicit, that in a competitive economy, the uneconomical antiques would have been driven out of existence.

Even in the most modern undertakings, as Soviet economists constantly point out, auxiliary functions—shipping, office work, repair facilities, etc.—are often as primitive and costly as in the distant past. The abacus, a medieval wooden calculating frame, can be found in many an industrial "giant." In some offices, Professor A. L. Liusternik has written bitterly, the main change since Peter the Great's time is that pens are used instead of quills.

Inflation is "the syphilis of a planned economy," Trotsky once warned, because money values "express the will of bureaucracy and not the amount of socially necessary labor expanded." And inflation has been a constant, ever worsening, in the Soviet Union. Soviet planners fix as many as eight million prices (seven hundred for cherry preserves alone, *Pravda* reported). But the prices are arbitrary and useless to management, since they do not reflect true costs. A French economist and socialist, André Philip, was astonished to learn during a Soviet visit in 1956 that prices for various commodities were often decided by consulting foreign mail-order catalogs.

It was possible to pretend that overall planning made logic in an earlier stage, when quantity was the only criterion of accomplishment. Rewards and punishments (including the death penalty) could be distributed by merely weighing and measuring. Obviously, the more primitive an economy, the more easily it lends itself to central direction. But as the economy grows larger and more complex, more and more concerned with quality, precision, diversity, synchronization of its parts, planning becomes more difficult— until it approaches impossibility.

A cartoon in an East European communist country has a child saying, "Mom, I want to read a fairy tale," and Mom replies, "Then read your daddy's plan fulfillment reports." The temptation to fill out with doctored bookkeeping the margins of failures in actual output is too strong for thousands of managers.

Stalin set the style when his *Izvestia* said, in November, 1929, "Let us put statistics on socialist rails in order that they shall not be detached from the class struggle." This meant lying in figures to confound the enemy and the public. It is the economic counterpart of "socialist realism" in literature, depicting Soviet life as it should be, not as it is, and it plays havoc with a plan. Finally, the Kremlin, while holding to this rule in literature, has disowned it in economics and is now engaged in a campaign against "successes" on paper that mask failures in reality.

It is a matter of official record that for decades factories have exaggerated their needs, then hoarded the materials, equipment, and spare parts as insurance against shortages in the future. Many plants have stockpiles sufficient for two or three years of future production. Mountains of capital goods are thus tied up unproductively.

At the same time management of enterprises has underestimated capacity. The lower it can keep the planned goals, the more easily it can over-fulfill them to win praise and bonuses. It has steered clear of innovations, since re-tooling is time-consuming and temporarily at least retards output. In general, initiatives are risky—there is always the chance of failure that might be called sabotage—and industry directors prudently avoid them.

Enterprises skimp on variety in commodities, holding sizes, shapes, and colors down to a minimum. The smallest possible assortment makes for larger bulk production.

Above all, they give quantity the priority over quality. Better quality can be commanded and exhorted, but it cannot be minutely planned for millions of products. Under true market conditions the customer is the judge: if he cannot obtain what he wants from one supplier, he turns to another. There is no such natural selection of the best in a monopoly economy.

Without the balance wheel of demand and supply, the state swings between deficit and excess. Some years ago, for instance, the government took note of grumbling about the lack of simple sewing machines, and orders went out for their production. In due time so many flooded the country that they are still being bought up to use as small tables, of which there is a great shortage.

The difficulties of national planning have been mirrored in unceasing revisions of its structure and apparatus. It has shifted repeatedly from centralization to de-centralization and back again. In the quarter century from the start of the First Five-Year Plan, six different men held the top planning post, that of chairman of Gosplan USSR. Of these, four were executed and a fifth, Kuibishev, died under unexplained circumstances while he was under investigation. Under Khrushchev and his heirs, the planning chiefs, in theory seeing far ahead for a great nation, have held their posts for *an average of only eighteen months.*

• A Self-Perpetuating Moloch

Can these and endless other inherent ills of planning be cured without killing the patient? Today, that is the heart of the Kremlin's economic dilemma.

Examples of the chronic ailments and the proliferating bureaucracy have filled the Soviet press and official lectures year after year, without the slightest effect. Western analysts with access to the communist press have no dearth of authentic data in this area. Professor Albert Parry of Colgate University, in his book *The New Class Divided*, published in 1966, could write:

The Plan loomed up as a self-perpetuating Moloch, an unwieldy monster demanding sacrifices instead of being there to serve. . . . So all-embracing was its mode of supervision that the construction of a new steel mill was spelled out down to the location of each nail, in 91 volumes totaling 70,000 pages. The Plan's committees and councils multiplied so prolifically that one factory received seventy different ukases from fifteen government bodies, every one of which had authority to issue such instructions. Another plant was showered with 111 instructions from nine planning committees, and the bulk of these contradicted each other. A Regional Council of People's Economy submitted its plan and in due time received it back approved, but in the next six months there came 137 supplements and orders changing the plan out of recognition.

This kind of thing is not exceptional but fairly standard. According to the Soviet *Economic Gazette* (November 17, 1962), construction plans for one region were changed five hundred times in a single year. The Ministry of Lumber asked its client enterprises to fill out 118 different forms, containing 400,000 indices. The Moscow Likhachev auto plant, in order to obtain its annual supply of ball bearings from the GPZ factory next door, had to furnish four hundred pounds of supporting evidence. About 100,000 tons of metal are shipped out of the Leningrad region and about half of it is then re-imported for local uses.

No one, from the highest to the lowest, makes the slightest decision without piling up documents to prove that it had been authorized by the proper instances. Should things go wrong, you must be in a position to disown responsibility. If you can possibly avoid decisions entirely, by passing the buck to a higher planning level, so much the better. "Moscow doesn't believe in tears," an old Russian saying has it.

The result is self-protective paper work and perpetual meetings —a Soviet director spends from half to two-thirds of his working time outside his factory "conferring," though he knows from experience that the conference will yield only more resolutions agreeing to do better. Documents on the distribution of tires go through thirty-two separate units; and with every change in plans this whole road of thirty-two stations has to be traveled again.

Speaking at a meeting of workers from industry and construction, on April 24, 1963, an official declared: "Many important affairs continue to flounder in a pile of paper. In the first quarter of the current year, the *Sovnarkhoz* [Council of National Economy] of the RSFSR, for example, sent off to the *oblast* and *krai* [smaller political regions] more than 120,000 letters, resolutions and directives; that is, daily out of the Council came 1,600 documents."

The authoritative journal *Planned Economy* attested in 1962: "There are so many corrections made that the plan as it was drawn up by the planning organ and approved by others no longer exists." *Pravda*, on July 25, 1963, confirmed this chaos: "In 1962 alone, Gosplan RSFSR changed the gross output plan of the Leningrad *Sovnarkhoz* 32 times, made 65 changes in its commodity production plan and 52 in its cost-of-production plan. We are still feeling this year the repercussions of such planning." *Izvestia* reported on April 6, 1961: "The issue of a new model of footwear or clothing has to be sanctioned by the Artistic Council, the Commerce Ministry, the Bureau of Prices of the Gosplan, the Institute of Scientific Research."

One textile plant received plan orders and counter-orders forty times in a single year. A factory making parts for tractors was rewarded for over-fulfillment of its target figures, then punished when it was discovered that it had done so by cutting the useful life of its products by half. Workers in the ZIL auto plant in Moscow were commended for reducing the weight of the car by one hundred kilograms, then had their wages clipped because the planned goals were set up in tons.

In some machine-building factories, the plans have included as many as 40,000 "indicators," requiring three months of effort by large staffs to process—after which revisions begin pouring in from various planning groups. In the end, many industrial specialists complain, the plan ceases to make much sense and the director does the best he can, ignoring some directives and interpreting others to his own purposes.

Technological ignorance, compounded by hectoring pressures from many uncoordinated offices, muddles everything. Inadequate and insufficient transportation, recognized by the government as one of the weakest links in the economic chain, often pulls the very foundation from under planned activities. Mining enterprises have been caught adding rock to ore in order to meet their quotas for output. The famous Magnitogorsk steel complex, "The Pittsburgh of Soviet Russia," receives its coal from sources two thousand kilometers away. Mines of enormous potential have been put out of use through the exploitation of easily accessible areas in such a way that access to the rest was blocked. The White Sea Canal, "the longest canal in the world," constructed with slave labor at a cost of tens of thousands of lives, still has pathetically little traffic.

While lowlier activities, say those of window-cleaners and charwomen, are not planned at all, most aspects of national life are hopelessly over-planned. Even the work of research laboratories, in most cases, is still blueprinted to the last detail. A scientist or technologist who stumbles on a new idea has to cut his way through forests of red tape before he is allowed, if ever, to deviate from the plan to pursue it. One can understand why, as the Moscow *Voprosy Ekonomiki* revealed in 1963: ". . . from the time of a scientific discovery to the time of its industrial acceptance takes about eight or nine years." This is at least twice the lead-time in advanced non-planned countries.

The ever-proliferating bureaucratic machinery produces such a nightmarish maze that one wonders, in reading about it, how anything gets done. In the system of distribution, the intermediary organizations run literally into thousands. In a single year (according to *Planned Economy*, 1963) the Chief Supply Directorate of the USSR added 229 new units: "The number of supply and sales organizations in separate districts, territories and economic regions is reaching astounding proportions. For example, as of October 1, 1962, there were 669 supply and sales organizations employing 11,600 workers in the Rostov area, and in the Don district, 523 of these organizations employing 16,000 workers."

No one item of red tape, disbalance, delay, confusion, excess and shortage, loss in capital and in raw stuffs, may mean much in a gigantic economy. But thousands of them taken together, manifest in every branch of economic endeavor, make a tragic joke of the extravagant claims for centralized planning.

• *Fighting the Infection*

Every infection or bodily disorder, we are told, tends to produce antibodies to fight its ravages. Soviet agriculture has been saved from complete debacle by a tiny private sector—about three per cent of the nation's cultivated acreage. Planned industry, too, has its antibodies, in part tolerated but mostly illegal. They take up some of the slack in the planned economy. They provide an outlet for enough individual initiative to cushion the impact of socialist failure and scarcity, some means for "getting around" the road-blocks and absurdities of planning.

At least four of the antibodies are perfectly familiar to every Soviet citizen. They are the *tolkach, blat, vzyatka,* and most important, the "underground capitalist," or black-market economy. These are all interrelated, one shading into the other.

Tolkach means a "pusher," but in the Soviet setting may be more accurately described as a "fixer." Every payroll large enough to accommodate some extra employees has one or a few fixers. Sometimes they are paid by one enterprise but assigned to work at another, or to maintain helpful liaison with many outfits in another city. At other times they are headquartered in the employing organization and available for trouble-shooting wherever it may be needed.

This ubiquitous and invaluable *tolkach* enables producing or distributing units to deal directly with one another, bypassing the slow-moving bureaucracy of planned state channels. He scrounges for deficit parts, materials, tools, when the authorized sources do not have them or are too immobilized by red tape to make deliveries. He unclogs bottlenecks. He makes sure that supplies for his factory are not diverted to another, or conversely, diverts products earmarked for someone else to his own employer.

The value of the *tolkach* (who often manages to draw several salaries and expense money to match) depends on his skill as a manipulator, his wide acquaintance among key officials and managers in his field of operation; on competence, contacts, charm, and an easy conscience. While the fixers from time to time get lambasted in the official rhetoric, they are not illegal. In any case, the *tolkach* is far too useful in keeping an unwieldy machine running to be repressed. Nobody can know how many of them there are, but hundreds of thousands is a safe guess. In the city of Dniepro-petrovsk, the metallurgical complex employs four thousand, the machinery industry, three thousand.

Blat, in its Soviet usage, is a catch-all word that covers infinite varieties of influence and "pull" to get things done. Friendly mutual help on a *quid pro quo* basis is part of it: the manager of a plant, for instance, exchanges nails of which he has a surplus for glass from a manager who needs nails. Whom you know counts for more than cash in the pocket in circumventing the road-blocks of bureaucracy, obtaining permissions, documents, admission to special schools, a hundred other favors. At the time I resided in Russia, a popular synonym for *blat* was *bukva* Z: the "letter Z" standing for *znakomstvo*, "acquaintances."

Vzyatka means simply bribery. Illegal in any form, it is tolerated at the lower financial levels. A few rubles slipped to the clerk will speed up the issuance of a document—nothing is done in the USSR without some official piece of paper. When a railway or airplane ticket is not available, twenty or thirty rubles to an intermediary quickly produces one. Well-heeled parents of scholastically backward children can get them into college notwithstanding; the payoffs, if the Soviet press is to be believed, have run into many thousands of rubles.

There is hardly anything, in the words of *Krokodil*, a Moscow satire journal, "that the bribers do not make into a business proposition. They accept money for everything: for a petty little service and for their friendly attentions, for a ray of hope and for a lost conscience. . . . You want to work in a beauty parlor—you pay. You want to get a diploma for so-called courses for raising qualifications—again, you pay. You want to insure yourself against being dismissed—pay over and over again."

All of it is outside the bounds of the state plans, of course, yet saves the planned society from utter paralysis. So while it is unlawful, it is permitted up to a point. But large-scale or persistent bribery is another matter. Always subject to heavy punishment, a decree issued in April, 1962 made it a capital crime "under particularly aggravated circumstances." The system thrives despite death penalties, as Soviet press reports make quite apparent, and the guilty include highly-placed party and government officials, prosecutors and court functionaries.

Finally there is that nether world of private enterprise. Beneath the planned surface, a runaway Soviet diplomat wrote, "there are immense processes that defy the Marxist theories—processes to which the Soviet leaders, like it or not, have to accommodate themselves." That this anti-regime phenomenon has become wider and more daring in the intervening period has been sufficiently evidenced, in the last decade, by decrees making some of this private zeal punishable by death.

A thick book chronicling the ingenious and frequently prodigious schemes for self-enrichment could be drawn from the Soviet press, though it reports only the worst cases. Red China has had a field day in its anti-Kremlin propaganda by simply disseminating such proofs of capitalist tendencies picked from Soviet sources. Groups of artisans, supplied with materials and machinery by conniving functionaries who share in the profits, make and sell every conceivable consumer product that happens to be in special demand. Factories divert substantial portions of their output to the black market, with the help of conniving accountants. There have been instances of private trade in horses, grain, and especially building materials now that the state permits the construction of small country houses for personal use.

In one case in the Kirghiz Republic, leading officials condemned to death had stolen "state and social property to the value of more than thirty million rubles" (three million in the devalued ruble) and disposed of it through underground channels. Firewood and lumber are sold privately by groups set up like conventional capitalist companies, and they do a business to the tune of hundreds of thousands of rubles a year. "In the building trades," a report by the Institute for Study of the USSR, based on Soviet sources, has stated, "shady deals are on such a scale, that whole towns have been built from stolen materials, originally intended for the construction of state-owned housing." References to "underground millionaires" in the press tell the story.

In hoodwinking and defrauding the state the sky is the limit. Most of the esoteric private economic schemes could never be launched and maintained without the help of influential officials and inspectors. Frequently the public prosecutors are themselves deeply involved. Corruption in government is no novelty under any system of life. But in a country where everything from a newsstand to the largest industrial trust is "government," and where the economy is planned, corruption has deeper implications. In a crude fashion, it represents the supply generated by demand, where the plan does not do the job. The basic motivation, of course, is personal aggrandizement and the moral fiber of the nation is obviously weakened. But the inner justification is that the state is the enemy and "people must live."

Perhaps the most significant fact, sociologically, is that a state can plan the economy, but not the response of human beings. A Norwegian scholar, Professor T. Frederick Barth of the University of Bergen, speaking in Pittsburgh recently, said, "No matter how detailed central planning may be, at one point local individuals take over and try to mold the system to their needs." He was not referring specifically to Soviet Russia, but there his words are exemplified every day and in every place.

The vast majority of the Soviet citizenry have been born and raised under Soviet communism, taught from the kindergarten up to despise private trading, yet the instincts for personal gain are as strong as in any other part of the world, perhaps stronger because of the universal poverty. Even young children, *Komsomolskaya Pravda* complained, seem to develop a merchandising impulse. They start innocently by collecting and swapping postage stamps, for instance, then begin to trade rare specimens for cash and accumulate the proceeds with adult passion. The Kremlin blames its indoctrinators, foreign broadcasts, leftovers from the past, but maybe the biggest leftover is human nature.

· Electrons to the Rescue

To avoid being swamped by the sheer volume of planning imposed by the size and growing technological nature of the economy, some Soviet economists and scientists look hopefully to electronic computers, whole battalions of them. Notes of desperation run through their proposals and conjectures. In the background is recent Soviet experience with automation, and it hardly sustains optimism. The same sloppiness of state operation that generally affects production takes its toll from automated branches. Breakdowns are, if anything, more frequent, due to unclean lubricants and general inefficiency in maintenance.

Besides, the very magnitude of the task defeats the hope. All the world's computer manufacturers combined could not fully meet Soviet needs, even if the country could afford the costs and provide the trained personnel. A Western student of the problem, Jan S. Prybyla, has said:

> If computers are to be applied to the planning machinery in its present shape, the Soviets will need (and this is a Soviet estimate) something like one million computers working day and night at the rate of thirty thousand operations per second. . . . The net result may well be quicker bad planning. This is because computers have to be fed information, and it really does not make much sense to process more rapidly the present avalanche of trivia.

Of course, limited areas of planning could, in theory, be assigned to computers. Again, effectiveness would depend on the accuracy and pertinence of the inflow of information, which, however, has been notoriously inaccurate, frequently tainted by misrepresentation at its source, and further tampered with on its long and circuitous journey to the top. One Soviet professor has declared that to play a meaningful role computer output would have to be increased thirty-six-fold—but its reliability would have to be increased a thousand-fold.

A top cybernetics specialist, writing in *Izvestia* (July 11, 1966), complained about "the low reliability of computers and ancillary devices, and the sub-standard quality of magnetic tapes." The best Soviet-made computers, he said, "operate only a few hundred hours between failures, while ancillary devices break down practically daily, and the information stored on tape cannot be stored without some loss for more than a month." It is easy to understand why the Kremlin is so eager to import Western and Japanese equipment in this field. By its own admission, the Soviet Union has not yet learned to make dependable electronic tubes.

The dream of an electronic Leviathan to pull them out of the swamps of planning is a symptom of the spreading panic, as skepticism about the whole system grows. While wonder machines might accelerate the tempo of an economic procedure, they cannot overcome the inherent fallacies. The computer is a tool, not a substitute for economic reason.

Meanwhile, obsolescence of plants and equipment and the slowness of the processes of replacement further confuse the planning. At some point, in a normal economy, the construction of new productive capacity, which accounts for so much of Soviet statistical "triumphs," must be slowed down in the interests of consumption. That point apparently has not been reached in the USSR. It had been expected, from Stalin's initial plan forward, that construction of heavy and intermediate industry would, in proper time, automatically start a flow of consumer products. The expectation has not been realized. It is as if the big industry were cannibalizing itself—construction for construction's sake. There is, so to speak, no end-product.

On the Soviets' fiftieth birthday, with nearly forty years of planning to look back upon, the belief seems unanimous in the country that it is not functioning well, and, in many respects, growing more unwieldy. The differences of opinion are those of degree.

The responsible leaders can no longer hide the paradox of huge stocks of unsalable goods along with chronic shortages; mountains of equipment being outdated while awaiting installation; unfinished construction deteriorating as bureaucrats try to remember what it was intended for; surging technological change in the outside world which the Soviet system, frozen by bureaucratic habit and indifference, can absorb tardily, if at all; transportation snags of every variety. Among the more knowledgeable citizens allusions to the magic of planning is good for a laugh.

One need not preclude the theoretical possibility that some nation somewhere may one day apply successfully some of the basic principles of planning. It is being done on a reduced scale, through money controls and other devices, in the mixed economies of certain capitalist countries—how effectively is a subject of serious debate in every one of those countries. But all-out central planning, nationwide and monolithic, has proved itself, after four decades, as essentially impractical and inoperative.

On the frozen swamplands of Siberia close to the Arctic Circle, swept by cruel blizzards, there is a ghost railroad—some 550 miles of rusted rails, caved-in stations, bridges and barracks, a few derelict locomotives and cars. The Dead Road, *Izvestia* called it on July 14, 1960, and this is the title of an article in the magazine *Novy*

Mir in 1964 by A. Probozhin, an engineer-surveyor who worked on the project.

The railroad, abandoned and decayed, is of no earthly economic use. It was built entirely by slave labor, from early 1949 until Stalin's death four years later, in temperatures of 60°F. below zero under conditions of horrifying hardship. Every stick of wood and pound of metal had to be hauled across thousands of miles of almost impassable terrain and through waterways that are ice-free only for a few months in the year. The slaves died like flies, but new contingents were brought in from the huge Arctic prison camps to take up their futile and murderous task.

How did this man-killing monstrosity come to be?

Stalin, with some fatuous notion that a railroad paralleling the Arctic seas would support his Far North maritime trade, where the waters are open only about two months a year, had ordered the construction. No one dared question his wisdom and the job went on, year after year, almost forgotten in Moscow, taking its brutal toll in death and suffering.

Today the Dead Road stands as a sinister symbol of the inhumanity, the wastefulness, and the essential imbecility of industrial activity under totalitarianism—of the arbitrary decisions by "infallible leaders" that pass for centralized planning. Neither *Izvestia* nor *Novy Mir* spelled out these lessons, but their readers, we may be sure, drew the proper moral from the fantastic story. Its publication was intended as an example of Stalin's "mistakes," but it is no less an example of the dangers of economic enterprise without natural market controls.

12 / Economic Reforms

The myth that the "economic reforms" foreshadow
a return to the free market.

At the half-century point, Soviet communism is wracked by a great debate on economic reform that exposes its most sacred dogmas to profane probing and tinkering. The built-in fallacies of the command economy have always been known to regime insiders. Now the secret is out. The Kremlin is openly seeking remedies for admitted ailments—remedies that will not undermine the authority of the ruling party and the privileges of the New Class.

The Soviet public, its cynicism honed by long experience, takes it for granted that every official admission of a pimple hides a boil, every admission of a boil hides a cancer. This instinct is probably sound—the managers of the communist economy are far more likely to understate than to overstate its difficulties.

Heretical words like *profit, interest, rent, market prices* run through the press and speeches, not in derision as in the past but in respectful earnest. They do not and cannot mean the same thing in a totalitarian economy that they do in a free economy. All the same, it is galling to communists to have to give even the appearance of trafficking with capitalist ideas. The fact that they do so notwithstanding is proof enough of the gravity of those ailments.

Try as they will to present them as socialist discoveries, the projected remedies come out as adaptations of capitalist practices. Profit incentives, demand and supply, money leverages, rational pricing, autonomy for individual enterprises—all had been rejected by Marx and his inheritors. Their adoption, even their consideration by the USSR, has encouraged assumptions, but only abroad, that Soviet Russia is edging toward capitalism. The Kremlin, annoyed alike by the cheers of capitalist foes and the jeers of ex-comrades in Peking, makes angry denials.

All the "reformers" of necessity devote a lot of mental energy to proving that their ideas conform with Marxism-Leninism. Whether or not they believe this, it is the condition of their being allowed to write and speak. No debate under communist aegis can be free. Several East European economists, similarly projecting reform in their respective countries, have told Westerners privately that "the plan must go." Without doubt some of their Soviet counterparts feel the same way, but they would be silenced if they tried to say so. Their job is to salvage the system, not to discredit it—and in a way that saves face for the enthroned ideology.

In 1966 the Moscow *Kommunist* denounced infidel delusions: "Bourgeois ideologists are not only showing their malicious intentions but also their crass ignorance in trying to see a departure from socialism in the introduction of market values in our economy." Earlier, *Pravda* hit the same note. "The Soviet people," it declaimed, "indignantly reject the wilfully slanderous statement by bourgeois ideologists" that the reforms under study "would allegedly lead to reintroduction of capitalist conditions." On the contrary, the paper insisted, the reform program "strengthens the centralized planning and administration of the national wealth."

This, in theory at least, is true. If the reforms already undertaken and those under discussion succeed in bringing some order into the confusions of central command, the result would be a more effective socialist economy, not a pale imitation of capitalism. The innovations are strictly within the bounds of total state ownership and control, not intended to displace planning but to make it more effective.

By the time a free-market concept is fitted into the strait jacket of a monolithic economy, it bears little resemblance to the capitalist original anyhow. Applying free-market principles to an unfree economic system calls for squaring the circle. Because of the compulsion to reconcile it with state monopoly, every reform has in it the seed of its own defeat. The widespread belief among non-communists that the USSR—and the East European dictatorships, which are engaged in equivalent experiments—are moving toward capitalism is therefore mostly wishful thinking and semantic confusion. Though the reforms are couched in the vocabulary of rational economy (profit, interest, etc.) they leave the totalitarian substance untouched.

Perhaps the most useful by-product of the search for remedies is that it is enabling the Soviet people and the world to see more clearly some of the facts of Soviet economic life. The Kremlin was compelled by its growing difficulties to permit public and critical examination of the economic configuration. Its discomfiture has been well summed up by an American economist, Dr. Rush V. Greenslade. In his contribution to a study of *New Directions in the Soviet Economy*, prepared for the Joint Economic Committee of the U.S. Congress and published in July, 1966. Having dealt with slowed-up Soviet productivity, he wrote:

"More chilling to party hopes than these economic developments is an apparent loss of faith in the economic system itself. In 1961, the system of central administrative direction of the economy under the tight rein and driving whip of the Communist Party was unquestioned—at least publicly. Since then, first the academicians, then the economic administrators and now the highest party leaders have openly acknowledged the grave deficiencies of the command economy."

In the beginning the leaders stood aside, merely allowing the critics to present and argue their views in the press and at academic conferences. Then, in 1964, they proceeded with a very modest test of the new ideas by instructing a number of textile and other consumer goods plants to make direct contracts with retailers and put their accounting on a profit-and-loss basis.

At the aforementioned Party Plenum in September, 1965, called especially "for the reform of Soviet industry," Premier Alexei Kosygin in essence confirmed the diagnosis of the reformers. "The forms of industrial management, planning and incentives now in effect," he declared, "no longer conform to present-day technical-economic conditions." He went on to assert that only "the supreme criteria of economic activity—profit and profitability" could "reflect the real level of work of an enterprise." In the recent past men would have found themselves in Siberia for voicing such heresies.

Not one of the proposed innovations, it should be noted, has been originated by the party bosses or their Marxist theoreticians. The initiatives have been taken by professors and industry officials who all, while giving ardent lip-service to Marxism-Leninism, by-pass its supposed "laws." The ruling shifts would prefer the existing procedures, in which they make all the decisions, except for its one disadvantage: that it doesn't work.

• *Physicians and Witch-Doctors*

The regime, of course, did not succumb to a sudden attack of common sense. It has been driven by the cumulative economic costs of total planning to try to hold them within more tolerable bounds. Basically, the limited reforms in question aim to decentralize some decision-making and encourage individual enterprises to operate "profitably." Within the bounds of state targets and priorities, they would have more autonomy to organize production, and to supply specific "customers" instead of turning all their output over to the state. They would be expected to build their own investment funds, borrowing from the government when necessary and paying interest on the loans.

Actually, the changes authorized thus far are disappointing to the reformers. Between his speech at the Party Plenum and the opening of the Twenty-third Party Congress six months later, Kosygin evidently had been under pressure from the party bureaucracy to go slow. The current Five-Year Plan, as outlined at the congress, prescribes greater authority for management in a small minority of enterprises, sales and profit guides instead of quantity control, direct deals between factories and retailers, and a few other retreats from decision-making at the center.

These the innovators consider too few, too limited, and too slow to overcome the acknowledged defects. In general, the Party Congress went only an inch on the road of "market socialism" where it has been expected to travel many miles. The extreme caution suggests that the inner party struggle on the reform issues has not yet been resolved. Brezhnev emphasized that "much has to be done before the new system of planning and economic incentives can be fully implemented."

In particular, there was a thundering silence at the congress on the thorny problems of a more rational price system, widely recognized as the key to economic reform. The unreality of existing conditions may be judged from new wholesale prices in heavy industry that took effect in July, 1967. They will double the prices of crude oil, raise coal prices by 75 per cent, and metals from 35 to 40 per cent. The steep increases amount to acknowledgment that the book-keeping in all basic enterprises has been false, resting on artificial values. It reduces to a shambles all the calculations, during decades of allegedly pragmatic planning. But the stepped-up prices are of necessity arbitrary too. They represent the best judgments of bureaucrats, not the operation of competitive processes. Assuming, for argument's sake, that they are correct now, how long will they remain valid?

By the end of 1966 only some 700 enterprises had been brought under the reforms. As of mid-1967, by Moscow's count, 3,600 plants, involving about one-quarter of planned industry, were applying some elements of the reform principles. But already there are loud complaints from management and economists of constant interference from central officials. The habits of bureaucratic command are deep-rooted.

The dilemma of the leadership is excruciating. While admitting that planning is in a dead-end street, it dreads changes so radical that they might downgrade the role of the party and its bureaucratic elites. The loudest opposition to change comes, not from top economists, but from leading political conservatives, fearful that relaxation in planning might weaken the grip of the dictatorship on the country.

Their fears are certainly not unreasonable. Having retreated in as vital an area as the nation's economy, the party opens itself to bolder challenge politically. In a dispatch in the *New York Times* in January, 1965, Max Frankel quoted an unnamed Czech economist as saying: "I do not think that our politicians realize as yet that the reform they have reluctantly accepted can succeed only if it turns into a revolution that will sweep away the faiths of a lifetime." Obviously the Soviet politicians *do* realize this.

That is why the same Party Congress that decreed a few approaches to "market socialism" acted to reinforce orthodoxy, to tighten and stabilize the party and bar the way to outside claimants to authority. More forceful measures against restive intellectuals were foreshadowed. The more liberal rules for admission to party membership introduced by Khrushchev were nullified. Apparently distrustful of impetuous youth, the congress raised the age for joining the party from twenty-one to twenty-four. Right down the line the Brezhnev-Kosygin team sought to reassure its New Class that economic changes will be balanced by stringent defense of its privileged position.

The picture that comes to mind, as one follows the debate, is of a bevy of eminent physicians gathered around a sickbed. The patient is planned economy. The doctors are famous economists, mathematicians, cyberneticists, directors of industry. And hovering on the edges, making them nervous and afraid, are Marxist-Leninist witch-doctors sneering at the bourgeois therapies being argued, and holding tight to their ideological voodoo.

The Soviet regime is caught between the new medicine and the old witchcraft. Everyone is agreed on the seriousness of the patient's condition. The momentum of production keeps falling, despite a stable rate of investment. The chief planning official, N. K. Baibakov, attested that "gross production per ruble of fixed productive capital has declined, in industry as well as in agriculture." The good life for the masses to which the dictatorship is committed seems as remote as ever. The disproportions between different branches of the economy become increasingly pronounced. The economy is too inflexible to absorb new technological developments.

But the proposed cures, from the vantage point of the New Class, appear as frightening as the disease. The real issue in the USSR today is no longer whether decentralization and greater initiatives at local levels are needed. It is, rather, how much reform the regime can grant without eroding its power monopoly. Speaker after speaker, at the Party Congress, emphasized the primacy of politics over economics. A new Politburo member, A. Pelshe, spoke for them all when he complained that "sometimes ideology has been supplanted by industrial training" and called for more ideological vigilance.

If anything is clear, it is that the communist oligarchy has no intention of weakening its own position, whatever the cost in economic waste and dislocation. It will try to combine a minimum of economic liberalism with a maximum of political orthodoxy. It will concede as little as it must, and as slowly as it can, to the demands of economic reason.

In communist East Europe economic reform is similarly blocked by the vested interests of the political bureaucracy. On returning from an extensive tour of the region in late 1966, Paul Underwood of the Cincinnati, Ohio, *Enquirer* wrote with some enthusiasm of the great changes under way. Yet he concluded his dispatch by stating: "One is inclined to say there is not much hope for effective internal change until all the various party bureaucrats are forced to relinquish their monopoly of political and economic power." Which is another way of saying: until communist dictatorship goes out of existence. Without political monopoly the regimes would be doomed.

In Czechoslovakia, where the debate is considerably more candid than in the Soviet Union, the contradictions between economic reason and political dogma have been expressed sharply by leading advocates of reform. One of the boldest is Eügen Loebel, manager of a state bank. Writing recently in *Kulturny Zivot* (January 20, 1967), he complained that "the micro-economy is still ruled by the macro-economy," which is to say domination of individual enterprises by the center.

By way of example he cited cases: prosperous enterprises being taxed to subsidize backward competitors; wage levels set by national organs that cancel out the effectiveness of incentive plans locally; managers appointed by headquarters whose technical expertise is not equal to their political influence. Loebel doubts that economic reform can be useful under these restrictive conditions. What he asks for is a genuine consumer's market, truly competitive, for all Czechoslovakia. But this is precisely what the party and economic elites fear and fight.

And this holds true, in far more acute forms, in Soviet Russia. All of them struggle with the impossible problem of reconciling relative economic permissiveness with continuing political dictatorship. From Brezhnev and Kosygin down, everyone appears to understand that to be effective the reforms must go farther and deeper. But they are prisoners of their power structure; they can hardly renounce the ideology which is their only excuse for self-perpetuating rule. In the words of Dr. Greenslade, they face "the danger that a true transformation might disrupt the whole intricate web of centralized control levers that makes up the authoritarian system."

Lenin faced the same dilemma after the civil war, the Kronstadt Rebellion, and the famine. He chose to gamble on the New Economic Policy (NEP), which restored private enterprise except at the so-called "economic heights." He was paying with economic freedoms for the retention of political dictatorship. He could risk it because the people were then drained of all energy and the bureaucracy was not yet strong enough to rebel against withdrawal of its new privileges.

The leaders today are extremely unlikely to take such drastic steps. Unlike Lenin, they have to take account of the New Class, perhaps powerful enough to resist its own liquidation. Agriculture, which needs reform most, is getting the least of it. In that department, the only true reform would be the restoration of private farming. Unlike Tito in Yugoslavia and Gomulka in Poland, who allowed peasants to leave the collectives if they wished (which the overwhelming majority promptly did), the Kremlin hierarchs are paralyzed by the knowledge that Soviet collectivization took a gruesome toll in life. They find it hard and dangerous to admit that it was all a blunder.

We may expect that the reforms already adopted will be extended. Probably the process has passed the point of no return. But it will not be the kind of bold, across-the-board action the more optimistic advocates of "market socialism" are recommending. The leadership will temporize, make piecemeal revisions, in the hope of muddling through with the help of Western trade—today its most urgent need—and the sorcery of "cybernetization and computerization" to take over some of the planning burdens.

• Return to Free Market?

Can partial, timid reforms solve Moscow's economic crisis? Neither the Soviet economists behind the campaign nor Western analysts believe they can. Indeed, it is a wide-open question whether the mechanisms of a free market can be successfully superimposed on a planned economy anywhere. In Yugoslavia, where this has had the most extensive test, it is far from successful. After more than fifteen years, the country is still harassed by chaotic prices, inflation, monopoly profits in some areas and heavy state subsidies in others, unemployment, and deadly inner-party struggles.

Management may be ordered to go all-out for profit. But how can it obey when the costs and availability of raw materials, retail prices, and other such factors are manipulated by an all-powerful state? The true meaning of profit as a reward to owners and investors is lost. It becomes just a way of measuring the difference between the value of inputs and outputs—in effect merely a revised bookkeeping procedure. Despite some incentive bonuses (in effect even before the reforms), 60 per cent or more of the profits go to the state. Interest and rent, in the same way, are accounting chips, shuffled from one state pocket into another.

"As long as the workers are not free to bargain through organizations independent of the state over what proportion of the 'surplus value' produced is to go to them in the form of wages and bonuses," Professor Sidney Hook argued (*Problems of Communism,* March-April, 1967), "so long as the industries are not given sufficient autonomy to make the basic decisions depending upon the consumers' wishes but receive their directives from a central planning source, the economy of the Soviet Union remains essentially unaltered."

To give autonomy to some plants and not to others, to some industries and not to others, seems a prescription for additional chaos. The logic of the reforms, if followed, would extend the autonomy to virtually the whole economy, except for military and a few other priorities, and that would be the end of planned economy. A limited "market socialism" bids fair to prove itself a fatal contradiction.

Direct links between producers and consumers normally make sense. But a national economy is so interdependent that the links would have to be forged in all directions, with the supplier of raw stuffs, with the producer of machines, intermediary semi-finished goods, spare parts. "Islands of rationality" would tend to be drowned in an ocean of command bureaucracy. Prices, unless they develop in substantial independence on a demand-and-supply basis, reflect only some central planner's preferences and make hash of individual profit-planning. Dr. Greenslade has written:

Economic institutions are like teeth. If the teeth get worn, loose, and decayed, they can be replaced by a shiny new functional set. But the new ones can't go in until the old ones come out. Similarly, two different institutions cannot simultaneously produce a mix of output that the market wants and the one the planners want.

In the concrete reality of the Soviet system, the salutary, or even cosmetic, effect of a patina of market trading is unlikely to be realized. To be beneficial, markets require flexible prices, an overall reduction of excess demand, and alternative sources of supply. . . . The economic effect of the reforms can be forecast in advance. Because the reforms are so circumscribed, their net effect cannot be large, either for good or bad, but their nature is such that there are likely to be both kinds of effects.

On the one hand, the positive incentives if they begin to be effective may lead to improved efficiency at some enterprises, and direct contracting may result in smaller stocks of unsold consumer goods and to that extent greater consumer satisfaction. On the other hand, the same incentives if they begin to be effective may lead to output mixes counter to the plan, reshuffling of supplies as between enterprises, refusal to accept unwanted equipment, layoffs of workers, and unemployed capacity. . . . It can be assumed that bureaucratic interference to counteract these symptoms will appear almost as soon as the symptoms. In short, the new system cannot operate as long as the old is on the job in full strength.

Besides, he points out, there are the political factors: "It is difficult to picture the party and the planners presiding over the dissolution of planning. . . . Neither the economic bureaucracy nor the local party apparatus is likely to accede gracefully to its own withering away."

The evidence, as of early 1967, supports Dr. Greenslade's prognosis. Basing himself on an analysis of the Soviet economic press, made for the Institute of Studies of the USSR and published in April, 1967, I. W. Majstrenko concluded:

With the reform now in its second year, experience shows convincingly that two factors—the centralized control of industry and the enhanced initiative of the enterprises—contradict one another. . . . Centralization is incompatible with the operation of industry on a profit-making basis and a market founded on supply and demand. The successful realization of the reform is conceivable only under a market economy, a fact which is well appreciated by all those Soviet specialists and enterprise managers who have gained experience during the first phase of the reform.

Political conservatives in the USSR warn that to give up central control of price determination is to sound the death-knell of planned economy—surrender of the country to "the anarchy of the market place," then capitalism and the end of the regime. Yet without free or relatively free pricing, most of the other reforms lose their vitality.

At best, the reforms if carried a lot further are a guarantee of tensions between natural market pressures and the Kremlin's commitments to political objectives. Behind every factory or trust director stands a party functionary or apparatus. Is there any doubt how they will resolve a conflict between production for the consumer market and production for the state? As long as the state is the sole owner, economic operations will remain primarily politically-motivated rather than profit-motivated.

This contradiction is dealt with in a book smuggled out of Poland and published in its original language in Paris in 1966 under the title *Poland Little Known*. The internal evidence is that the secret author, who used the pen name George J. Flemming, is close to his country's affairs, presumably of the communist elite. He expresses contempt for foreigners who take the economic-reform excitement too seriously. As long as a regime remains communist, he says, "they are only churning in the same vicious circle." Whether in Poland or Hungary or Soviet Russia, he believes, "there are none and there cannot be any basic changes beneficial to the economy without a change in the political system. Anything else is not even a half-measure."

What happens, then, if it becomes apparent in a few years that the marginal piecemeal reforms have proved ineffective, and that a new NEP or a fundamental revision along Titoist lines is blocked by the party and economic bureaucracies? No one can know the answer. By that time the economic troubles assuredly will have multiplied in number and dimension, piled as it were on the present troubles. The resultant crisis is likely to be deeper and more dangerous to the dictatorship than it is today.

According to a familiar fable, especially popular in the mid-thirties, the Soviets would move gradually to "the Right," the capitalist world to "the Left," and one day they would meet in the center and live happily ever after. The fantasy flourished when Stalin, having pushed through his Five-Year Plan, seemed to be moderating his ferocity at home and seeking united-front friends abroad. Then it faded out in the blood-purges, the pact with Hitler, and intensified Soviet subversion in a renewed mood of militancy.

In the last few years the fable has been revived, in large part because of the Soviet talk and some experimentation with free-market devices to overcome the mischief wrought by total planning. Again we hear theories about the USSR going more capitalistic as the non-communist nations become less so, and the two systems "converging" at the center. And again it is pure fantasy.

If the current economic tinkering in Soviet Russia presages a return to capitalism, the one certainty is that it will not come gradually and peacefully as the myth-makers think. The communist masters are so deeply entrenched that they could not, even if they wished to do so, relinquish their monopoly of power—and that includes domination of the economy. Should capitalism or some approximation of it be restored in the Soviet Union, it will not be through step-by-step evolution but through some type of military or popular revolution.

Meanwhile, from their own angle of vision, the quandary of the leaders holds a certain ironic pathos. It took their regime fifty years of incalculable travail, only to return part-way to the starting point of market principles and middle-class objectives. The plight of foreign communists is even more ironic, obliged loyally to applaud attempted revival of the free-enterprise assumptions they excoriate at home, and to profess delight over the erosion and cutting back of communism.

13 / Collectivization

The myth that collectivized farming is the answer
for hungry nations.

Karl Marx's fantasy of a happy communist future was centered on
the urban working class, the proletariat. There was in it little room
for the tiller of the soil, short of his transformation into a landless
wage-earner. Socialist theorists since Marx—denizens of cities like
himself, far removed from the life-giving earth—have been unable
to fit the property-minded peasant into their Utopian schemes, and
inclined to despise him as inherently *petit bourgeois.*

By the irony of history, however, communism in this century has
been imposed on predominantly agrarian countries. In every one of
them, exactly as the theorists had feared, the farmers have fought
against socialist regimentation. When driven into collectives by
force, they have performed listlessly, often to the point of sabotage.
In the two instances when a communist regime was obliged to give
them the right to leave collectives—Yugoslavia in 1952 and Poland
in 1956—the exodus was instant, joyous, and almost unanimous,
and foodstuffs at once became more abundant.

Soviet Russia's agrarian failure, tragic for the peasants and disastrous for the country, has been too great to be papered over with
managed statistics. In the fiftieth year of its dictatorship, after
thirty-eight years of collectivization, communism is still unable to
feed the nation out of its own production. Output on the farms is
one of the lowest per man-hour and per acre among the major
countries. From one of the world's prime exporters of grain, Russia
has become a grain importer.

In the first years of collectivization the government said that as
soon as Soviet agriculture had one hundred thousand tractors, the

superiority of socialized farming would become apparent. By 1965 there were more than one and a half million tractors and millions of other farm machines, along with half a million trained agronomists, livestock experts, and other agricultural specialists. But only the inherent inferiority of the system has become increasingly apparent.

"The present situation in agriculture causes serious alarm," said a speaker at the most recent Party Congress, in March, 1966. Alarm has been the keynote word on Soviet agriculture through the decades. And the sorry record has been duplicated wherever the Red flag flies. One after another, self-sufficient or food-exporting nations have seen their agriculture blighted by Marxism-Leninism. From Eastern Europe to Asia and the Caribbean, the hallmarks of communist rule have been rationing, food queues, acute shortage, occasional food riots, and in both Russia and China, hideous famine.

Eastern Europe before the Second World War was among the world's reliable breadbaskets. The Danubian countries were famous for lush farms and lush cereal exports. In Poland, food was plentiful and cheap. What is now East Germany fed most of all Germany. Since the advent of communism, the baskets have been emptied, invariably because of measures to socialize the land and its farmers. The once rich agricultural nations now all have to buy some food abroad, and without exception they have imposed rationing at one time or another.

East Germany is the most fully collectivized of the Soviet-captive nations—and the hungriest. Its main staple is potatoes, but the potato crop fell by 43 per cent after the "successful" collectivization of 1961–1962. In Czechoslovakia, where farming had been up to West European standards, *per capita* production is today below pre-war levels. In Hungary, early in 1966, after steep rises in retail prices on meats and dairy products had been announced, riots broke out in and near Budapest.

Like Lenin in Russia, Mao Tse-tung rode to power in China by exploiting the land hunger of the peasants. They were incited to murder millions of landlords (most of them poor by Western yardsticks) and divide the land. Then, in due time, the land was taken away from them by the super-landlord, the state. Beginning in 1958, the Peking bosses herded the peasants into so-called communes that were in effect dehumanized slave camps. Production thereupon all but collapsed and the livestock population dropped by 40 per cent.

The grim harvest was a succession of hunger years and the epidemics of undernourishment, climaxed by famine in 1961–1962, in which the death toll has been estimated as high as twenty-five million. Mao was obliged to scrap the communes in their original forms and the peasants returned to the lesser evil of collectives, or to private plots. Red China continues to spend its limited hard currency reserves on buying food in the world of private farming. The blood-chilling fact is that the nation, with perhaps one hundred million more mouths to feed, now raises less food than before the coming of communism.

A striking contrast in agricultures was provided, in the late 1950's and early 1960's, by North and South Vietnam. The North had been on pitiful rations from the inception of its communist existence, and in 1961–1962 suffered near-famine. Every available piece of ground around public buildings, schools, factories has been sown to sweet potatoes, gourds, and other quick growing vegetables. But South Vietnam, though already harassed by Viet Cong guerrillas in those years, had adequate crops. The land distribution undertaken by President Diem was beginning to show good results —it was in part to disrupt that process that Hanoi moved to escalate its guerrilla offensive.

Although Cuba before it fell to the communists was a poor country, its living standards were among the highest in Latin America. Farm production made up a third of the national income, and it supported exports, aside from sugar, of rice, meat, cattle, eggs, and dairy products. Soon after the victory of Fidel Castro, however, the rice harvests sank sickeningly, from 6,750,000 quintals in 1957 to less than a million in 1962–1963. Eggs suddenly became a luxury. Staple foods were put on a ration basis; at this writing the quota is three pounds of meat and three pounds of rice per month.

While mainland China was starving, Taiwan offshore became a substantial food exporter. While Eastern Europe was struggling to maintain its pre-communist diet, Western Europe saw a 25 per cent growth in farm produce. Meanwhile the most effective programs of land reform were introduced in Japan and Taiwan, both on a private basis and both without violence.

Communism, in sum, has failed dismally in the basic human enterprise of feeding the people. With the possible exception of Red China, for which reliable information is scant, the worst showing has been made by Soviet Russia. For all the grave shortcomings of Soviet industry, it is a glowing success compared with Soviet agriculture.

A few years ago the then Premier Khrushchev concluded a eulogy to Major Yuri Gagarin, the first man to orbit our planet, with an impassioned appeal for better farm production. He called upon the peasants to match the astronaut's feat in the skies with feats of diligence on the earth. Unwittingly, he thus pointed up a deeprunning paradox of communism in practice. A system able to produce Sputniks and Luniks in the newest area of human endeavor was bogged down in farming, the oldest area.

• Peasant Non-Cooperation

In 1965, Soviet Russia farmed 75 per cent more crop land than the United States, using four times as many farm workers, and produced less than half as much grain, for a population nearly 20 per cent larger. More than 35 per cent of the labor force of the USSR is on the land, compared with about 7 per cent in the United States, but the Soviet problems are those of deficits, the American those of surpluses. Grain production in Soviet Russia *per inhabitant* is at about the 1910–1914 average.

An American specialist who has studied the problem on the spot in the USSR, John Strohm, wrote in 1964: "A good Illinois farmer can work ten times the acreage, feed twenty times as many hogs, take care of thirty times as many chickens as Russian collective farmers. One U.S. farmer feeds himself and twenty-seven others with a high protein diet; one Soviet farmer feeds only himself and four others with a 75 per cent starchy diet. This low productivity in Russia is approximately what prevailed in the United States around 1870. Soviet agriculture is thus nearly a century behind America."

This decidedly does not imply that Russians are hopelessly inferior farmers. Before the revolution, scratching the soil with primitive plows, they were able to feed their country and generate huge exports. Now, despite considerable mechanization, they do neither. Yet they have not lost their ancient skills: on their small private plots, as we shall see, they are diligent and productive. The difference is not in the peasant but in the collectivization. His work on the socialized fields is at best indifferent, at worst deliberately harmful. The general apathy, amounting to passive resistance, is not always conscious, but the effects are as devastating as if it were knowing sabotage.

Farming is a creative process, calling for deep interest and loving care. But the peasants have never resigned themselves to their communized fate. They work for the state as little and as indifferently as they can get away with, dreaming of a family farm of their own.

The press perpetually inveighs against sloppiness and delay in harvesting, in transporting crops to collection points, in maintenance of equipment. Weeds choke growing crops. Soviet agronomists have estimated that 25 per cent of fertilizers, which are in short supply, never reaches the fields; much of it remains near the railroads where it is dumped, congealing to the hardness of stone. State elevators receive what Khrushchev once described as "mud, ice, snow, and unthreshed stalks." Year after year, city "volunteers" must be rushed to the farmlands to help salvage crops, but vast amounts of produce always remain on the ground to rot and freeze notwithstanding.

All the ills of bureaucracy and central planning known to industry afflict agriculture as well, often in worse forms. The ratios between the administrative-managerial personnel and the productive farmer are shocking to Western farm experts. Falsified bookkeeping by collectives is universal. Farm officials have been known to buy tons of butter and milk through distributing agencies and pass them off as their own production.

At the same time theft on state and collective farms is of epidemic dimensions. At a plenary session in 1961 Khrushchev charged angrily that in his native Ukraine "half of the cultivated corn was pilfered and plundered as it stood." In most villages party officials have to mobilize "activists" to guard the fields day and night, and in some places peasants are searched as they leave for home.

A few years ago the Soviet economic journal, *Voprosy Ekonomiki*, calculated an annual loss of 250 million man-hours through absenteeism by some 700,000 collective farmers. It is disclosed that in the Russian Republic and four others, sheer neglect caused the death of nine million sheep and millions of cattle. In 1964, as reported by *Pravda*, the chairman of the Union Agricultural Technical Facilities complained that labor is done manually "while at some warehouses the most valuable machinery and equipment, particularly milking machines, corn harvesting combines, cotton harvesting machines and others have been piling up for a long period." A year earlier the *Economic Gazette* reported that "at the beginning of 1962 more than 100,000 tractors and about 30,000 harvest-threshers could not be used because of lack of spare parts," and added blandly, as if it were a familiar fact of life, "no improvement is expected this year."

The Kremlin makes little effort to hide this passive resistance. It lives with the knowledge of peasant hostility. Scolding the farmers for their *petit bourgeois* nature is a staple of the official oratory. Long ago feudal lords learned that serf labor is grudging at best, and the Soviet lords are in no better case.

Lenin had referred to the "diabolic" side of the peasant. Nearly two generations later, speaking in Rumania in June, 1962, Khrushchev declared: "There will always be a psychological problem in the peasant's soul: no one is born a communist. In the Soviet Union, farmers keep looking into the barn for their horses, even after they have given them to the collective." He did not add that the problem could readily be solved by returning the expropriated horses and land to their owners. On May 22, 1963, the Moscow *Komsomolskaya Pravda* wrote, in connection with farm troubles: "It is easier to wipe out the malaria-bearing mosquito than the virus of individualism, the irrepressible cult of property." To the peasant, "revolution" has always meant a farm of his own—and he feels that he has been cheated.

But beyond that, communism has built-in deterrents to good farming. It may be possible to run a factory or mine with regimented labor, but not a farm. There are far too many on-the-spot decisions to be made that cannot be foreseen by planners. A true farmer has a feel for the land and an instinct about animals that the communist directives cannot possibly substitute. Even when local people are authorized to use their own judgment, the habit of obedience to the center is too ingrained to overcome. Ideas inherently good, like the emphasis on corn after Khrushchev's visit to the United States, are fouled up by indiscriminate imposition on the whole country.

An unusually good harvest, as in 1966, does not mean that the basic agricultural system has suddenly improved. It reflects primarily exceptionally favorable weather. The official claim of 170.8 million tons of grain in 1966 refers to "weight in the field." On the basis of long experience with Soviet figures, the U. S. Department of Agriculture, after discounting excess moisture and foreign matter in the field count and crops that will not be fully harvested, has adjusted the estimate to 135 million tons. Other crops important to the individual consumer appear to have done less well than grain. The potato crop, second only to bread in the national diet, was below the previous year. The livestock industry, too, has not matched the record in cereals; the growth in cattle numbers was only about one-third of what it was in the preceding year and the number of pigs has declined by 3 per cent.

For propaganda reasons related to the impending golden anniversary, Soviet spokesmen have made the most of the good grain harvest in 1966. Yet they have not gone so far as to suggest that the chronic ills of collectivized farming have been cured. That this restraint was wise became plain quickly in strong indications that the "jubilee year" is not likely to match the 1966 record. As of mid-January, the portents for grain in 1967 were discouraging. "Preliminary evaluations" of winter grains, which account for a large part the bread crops, were pessimistic. Apparently in order to prepare the public for bad news, the Central Statistical Administration reported retarded sowing and acutely inadequate moisture (40 to 70 per cent of normal) in the principal growing regions.

Nature is not overly friendly to agriculture in Russia. Only 10 per cent of the cultivated land, it has been estimated, is truly arable. The rest calls for exceptional energy and care. Great expanses are too cold, too arid, too shallow. For that very reason Russian farming, in particular, demands the wholehearted attention, high incentives, flexibility to operation that only a devoted individual farmer can provide—the kind that he does provide on the thin margins he is permitted to work as he pleases.

• *The Private Sector*

Stalin, having conquered the peasantry and instituted new versions of the serfdom abolished by Alexander II, made one concession fortunate for the country. He gave the socialized peasant the right to cultivate a minuscule plot—averaging two-thirds of an acre—around his own hut on a private basis, to own a cow and a few animals, and to sell his produce in the open market at free prices. Intended as a temporary sop, it proved so dramatically productive that it has remained to this day.

Unwittingly, the regime has thus provided a sort of laboratory test of the vitality of private as against public farm work. This private sector, as it is called, is lowest on priorities for equipment, fertilizers, and insecticides. Denied modern machinery, it must rely almost entirely on hand labor. It has been taxed and until recently was forced to deliver set portions of its production to the state at fixed prices. Nevertheless, it has outproduced the collective fields on a spectacular scale. The peasant who performs wretchedly on the public land performs amazingly well on his own plot, and he derives more income from it than he earns on the state's farms.

According to the government's own figures (*Voprosy Ekonomiki*, 1966), private plots with a mere 3 per cent of the nation's sown acreage accounted for 30 per cent of the gross harvest, other than grains; 40 per cent of all cattle-breeding, 60 per cent of the country's potato crops, 40 per cent of all vegetables and milk, 68 per cent of all meat products. Their fruit yields, according to another official source, are double those of state orchards for equivalent areas, its potato harvest per hectare two-thirds higher than on collective farms. Even in grain, which is a very minor element in the private sector, it produces one-third more per sown unit than an average socialized farm.

Except for bread, the same magazine cited above shows that the peasant family draws its food—90 per cent of its potatoes, 80 per cent of its vegetables, almost all of its milk, eggs, and meat—not from the socialized farms but from its own plot. Had it not been for the despised and deprived private sector, most of the farm population would have died of hunger long ago.

Any inclination to blame the failures of Soviet farming on the laziness or inefficiency of the peasant is thus negated. When his self-interest is engaged, he shows himself to be both competent and hard-working. His entire family puts all its free time—and some stolen from the collective—into its own plot. This 3 per cent of private enterprise supplies most of the non-cereal needs of a hundred million people in the countryside and in large measure supplies the urban population, especially in small and middle-sized towns. For more than thirty-five years now it has been responsible for staving off hunger in its more extreme forms.

In the early 1930's a political anecdote went the rounds. A large airplane building program having been announced, people asked, "Why do we need so many planes?" The cynical answer was: "So we can fly anywhere in the country where there is something to eat." Thirty years later, the sour joke has in a measure come true. Private growers in the Caucasus or Crimea regularly fill a few suitcases with oranges, lemons, cauliflower, spinach, or some other product and fly to Kharkov or Moscow, at times when these items are in great demand. They earn enough on the private sale of their cargo to pay for the round trip and leave a profit.

The contrast between the two modes of farming is visible to the naked eye. Professor Ellsworth Raymond of New York University has visited Russia several times to observe the agrarian economy. Reporting on one of the trips, he wrote:

Traveling across Soviet Russia, I saw stretching for miles around each village the weedy, parched, sparse collective fields. But around every hut was a lush little garden, bursting with greenery. These are the tiny private plots which the regime allows the peasants to work as they please. To use every inch of the soil, even the front lawn is planted with vegetables. The ground between plants is as clean as if a housewife swept it with a broom. These cases of devoted care are the last remnant of private farming in the USSR. Their produce, sold at open city markets for whatever price the traffic will bear, gives the peasants more income than their collective farm wages. Without these small gardens, the USSR would starve.

The same story has been told about other communist countries. In every East European nation, the peasant dawdles on the state's fields, but works with zest on his own. Whether in Russia or Bulgaria, in China or Cuba, the indisputable record by this time is that communism and effective farming do not go together.

• *Hell in 70,000 Villages*

To gauge the magnitude of the agrarian tragedy, we must look again at the monstrous costs of collectivization. Of all Soviet innovations, this is the one for which the people paid most and received least.

Stalin told Churchill that collectivization took more Soviet lives than the war. Compulsive killers boast of their scores: he was exaggerating, but not by much. His decision to turn the peasants into state-controlled proletarians, too, touched off a fearsome war, a war of aggression against a population larger than Germany's. The defenders were unarmed and unorganized, so that their defeat was a foregone conclusion. Yet they never wholly capitulated. Moscow treated them as an "internal colony" to be mercilessly exploited to provide "primitive capital accumulation" for industrialization, and their attitude to this day remains that of colonial subjects who hate their foreign masters.

The word collectivization has a harmless, technical ring, giving no inkling of the monstrousness it covers. In the twelve years before 1929, under constant official cajoling, less than 2 per cent of peasant families entered any type of commune voluntarily. This is the measure of the duress that was needed to stampede them into joining. The first draft of the Five-Year-Plan set 10 per cent as the portion to be collectivized. In the intoxication of the all-out drive the sights were raised to 50 per cent, and in the main grain-growing regions to 100 per cent.

On December 29, 1929, Stalin issued the slogan of "liquidation of the *kulaks* as a class." *Kulak* originally meant an affluent peasant, with overtones of usury. Now the term was redefined to fit anyone who owned more than two cows or the equivalent. Average peasant holdings were then about fifteen acres, and the upper five per cent of the "rich" *kulaks* averaged only about thirty acres. But in practice the *kulak* label was stretched to cover any peasant who insisted on holding on to his own parcel of land.

The slogan was an imperious command to smash and disperse between twenty and thirty million men, women, and children as quickly and rapaciously as possible, in order to make the others see the virtue of sinking their farms, animals, and equipment into collective estates called *kolkhozes*. Sixty-five days later, on March 2,

1930, the slogan was revoked, damping down the madness it had ignited. Actually the ruthless campaign had been going on before December and was to continue for years after March, but the brutalities reached their peak in those nine weeks.

Raw force had rarely been applied so massively in such a brief period. Hell broke loose in seventy thousand villages. At least a million families, which means five million people, were deprived of everything, even their clothes and household utensils, and carted off into harshest exile. They were herded at gunpoint into cattle cars and dumped weeks later in the lumber regions of the frozen north, the deserts of Central Asia.

Tens of thousands died of exposure, starvation, and disease in transport, and no one dared guess the death-rate in the wilderness where this humanity was scattered. Some of the human wreckage was merely flung beyond the limits of their native villages. Hordes of little children, with the help of their parents, escaped to shift for themselves. Great numbers of the panic-stricken victims, to evade deportation, left their goods and homes to seek refuge in the cities, where they were once more corralled, stuffed into disease-ridden cars, and hauled away to the dumps. For those of us who saw the "liquidation" at close range, the experience is freighted with horror.

The outside world seemed barely aware of the catastrophe. It was a time of know-nothing Stalin-worship, particularly among Western intellectuals. The British Fabians, Sidney and Beatrice Webb, who had never met a real Russian peasant, in their two-volume glorification of Soviet communism expressed frank abhorrence for the creature. They wrote of the Russian villagers with their "characteristic peasant vices of greed and cunning, varied by outbursts of drunkenness and recurrent periods of sloth"—"stubborn" and "formerly servile" but "now becoming rebellious." With that purblind appraisal established in Volume I, they could accept complacently the crimes of forced collectivization in Volume II.

Let no one underestimate the fury of the "rebellious" peasants. Collectivization officials were afraid to venture out in the dark, and for all their caution hundreds were murdered. Men and women slated for exile managed to set fire to their own homes and barns. Brigades arriving to remove church bells and icons sometimes found believers armed with sticks and pitchforks to prevent the sacrilege. Fruit farmers uprooted their trees. Red Army and GPU troops were ever on the move putting down uprisings; resisting villages were surrounded and literally shot into the blessed new collective life.

The most startling act of sabotage and the most hurtful to the national economy was the frantic slaughter of millions of animals by their owners. By 1929 the losses of the civil war had been made up; there was more livestock than in 1916. Now the peasants hastened to kill their animals rather than relinquish them to the state. The death penalty was decreed to halt the thing: one human life for the life of a pig or goat.

By the end of the Five-Year Plan the country had lost half of its cattle and horses, two-thirds of its sheep and goats, two-fifths of its hogs. Much of the food difficulties from that day to this can be traced in part to that gesture of defiance. When Khrushchev, in September, 1953, bewailed the fact that there were eight to nine million fewer cows in the USSR than at the beginning of 1928—before the First Five-Year Plan, that is—he was attesting to continuing effects of the peasant resistance twenty-five years later.

When the pressure was eased, more than half the families that had "voluntarily" joined collectives resigned. But at a somewhat slower pace the coercion continued and by 1932 close to 80 per cent of the national acreage had been feudalized. And in the autumn that year came the second great famine in the Soviet epoch, concealed at the time but since then officially admitted.

What makes this famine unique in history is that it was manmade, deliberately allowed to take its course in order to chastise and humble forty or fifty million citizens. Having put on the harness of collectivization, the peasants proceeded to sabotage the new system by planting and harvesting only enough for themselves. It was the most extensive example of mass non-cooperation in all history. But they underrated the savagery of the enemy.

The Kremlin saw what was coming. Grain was then cheap in the world market and a few million dollars diverted from foreign purchases of machinery might have prevented the calamity. Stalin instead decided to seize the whole harvest from the recalcitrant peasants by force, leaving them to starve. Every bloated baby belly, every cadaver that cluttered the country roads, was his purposeful doing. It was an act of war as surely as if he had killed those millions by gunfire or poison gas. In the most stricken regions cannibalism spread.

• Communism Breeds Hunger

What did Soviet Russia get in return for this inhumanity? A farming system that has never worked. By 1939, agrarian production was from 5 to 8 per cent lower than in 1928, although more and more land had been brought under cultivation. The country was strictly rationed until 1935, and on a miserably low diet thereafter. When war came, hunger might have proved Hitler's best ally, had not the United States funneled in millions of tons of foodstuffs (part of a total of eleven billion dollars in lend-lease that Moscow still refuses to repay).

When Stalin passed to his reward, his heirs hastened to disown what one writer called "the awkward legacy of unharvested crops" —wild exaggerations of production claimed by Stalin's coerced statisticians. His lying totals during two decades, Khrushchev disclosed, had exceeded reality by 50 per cent. In Stalin's last year of life, 1952, for instance, grain production came to 80 million tons, not the 120 million he reported.

Once in power, however, Khrushchev was soon engaging in falsification on his own account. The U.S. Department of Agriculture figured that over-estimates on grain from 1956 to 1962 added up to 137 million tons. In the bad harvests that followed, those full granaries to which Khrushchev had alluded turned out to be empty.

The USSR has had good crop years and bad ones, but it has never attained true self-sufficiency. Its emergence as the second largest industrial nation is made meaningless, in human terms, by the fact that it ranks low among the world's economies in the output of farm products per inhabitant. Let them eat industrial statistics, the leaders might say if they dared. Even in the best harvest years long and sullen food queues are part of the human landscape in some regions. Prices (except for bread, which is subsidized) are so high and earnings so low that three or four times more of the average family budget goes into food than in advanced Western countries.

A correspondent for *Newsweek* reported in May, 1966, that

"rural Russia, which begins only a few miles outside Moscow, seems at first glance scarcely changed from the Russia Tolstoy wrote about." At the first touch of spring, roads become rivers of sticky mud; thousands of more distant villages are virtually cut off by mud. The living standards of the 108 million people in the rural areas, he went on, are far below those in the cities, which in turn are dismally low. In the villages, "more often than not, fields are worked by one wheezing tractor and phalanxes of stoop-shouldered women. Running water, gas, plumbing, or more than one paved street in a farm village is the exception rather than the rule. Western experts estimate that a third to half of the USSR's farms are still without permanent electricity."

The Party Congress in 1966 projected a number of measures to fortify the nation's agriculture. Larger capital will be put into it. The collective farmer's monthly income, now at around 30 rubles, it was promised, will be raised by 1970, on a guaranteed basis, to 60 rubles. Not many believe that this can be done: the additional payments would take more billions than the total military budget. But if all the measures were successfully carried out, Soviet farming would still be the least productive among the major nations. The most that can be hoped for is some marginal improvement that leaves the underlying maladies untouched, since they all derive from the sacrosanct collective system.

Proposed remedies, along with assertions that the patient is recovering anyhow, have marked the whole career of socialized farming. Announcements that the grain problem had been "solved" were made by Molotov at the Seventeenth Party Congress, by Stalin at the Eighteenth, by Malenkov at the Nineteenth. "The grain problem, formerly considered the most acute and serious problem," Malenkov said in 1952, "has been solved, solved definitely and finally in the Soviet Union." The transcript notes "prolonged and stormy applause."

Khrushchev began his reign in 1953 with the glad tidings that the country had already become self-sufficient in grain resources. Six years later he had to correct himself: the 1953 results had been about the same as in 1913—now with 55 million more mouths to feed.

The record of proposals that would "definitely and finally," a favorite official cover-phrase, restore agriculture to health and vitality is grim and gloomy. There was the plan for *agrogorods,* agrarian towns, announced with great hoopla by Khrushchev in the Stalin time. The idea was to uproot the peasants from their villages, settle them in town-like barracks, and thus bring them closer to working-class psychology. The program never got off the ground, but it made good, self-deluding conversation for the harried upper classes.

An array of new laws expected to win the loyalty of the collective farmers was promulgated after the passing of Stalin. That they failed of their objective was evident in the new schemes advanced year after year. The most spectacular was Khrushchev's so-called Virgin Lands program, to bring huge sub-standard areas under forced cultivation. More than eleven million new acres were plowed up in two years, mostly in Kazakhstan. Hundreds of thousands of young people were badgered into moving to the Virgin Lands, where they lived under wretched conditions, mostly in dug-outs, some in tents, summer and winter. There was a bumper crop in the new lands in 1956, a good crop in 1958, after which erosion and other chronic defects of the terrain began to show up—as they had in tsarist times, when similar experiments were undertaken. The hopes for the program withered along with the crops, leaving many dust-bowls in their wake.

A Polish journalist who visited Kazakhstan reported in the Cracow *Zycie Literackie* (November, 1965): "The whole idea proved a great and painful fiasco. The epic adventure fell flat on its face. Its result was not only a deficit of grain but also a deficit of faith, which cannot be imported." Among the young people driven from their homes and schools to the primitive Virgin Lands, he said, the disappointment is expressed in one bitter sentence: "They have fooled us again."

As the program of reclaimed land fizzled, Khrushchev in the early sixties unveiled a new savior of agriculture: plans for gigantic immediate expansion of fertilizer production. "This is the end of our economic backwardness," he declaimed in anticipation of the miracle. But again little came of it. The chemical industry was and remains in bad shape, and little is heard any more of the ambitious program. The farm economy, indeed, would have been unable to use effectively the fertilizer planned—it was wasting the limited tonnage already available.

"A panacea per plenum" someone has called the continuing attempts to make the unworkable collective system work. The fever chart shows occasional improvement, especially when the weather is kind, only to sink again. The crisis appears to be permanent. The only feasible solution, as the leaders know full well, would be to return to some form of private farming. This they will not, because they dare not, undertake. Totalitarian industry and political life, they have ample reason to believe, could not survive side by side with a free agriculture.

Virtually all foreign visitors to the Soviet countryside have remarked on the startling preponderance of middle-aged and old people, especially old women, on the farms. Younger people are conspicuously few in number. The flight of youth to the cities is a universal fact everywhere in the modern world, but in the Soviet Union it has assumed alarming and in some regions catastrophic proportions. In other industrially developed lands, though this exodus may rate as a problem, full mechanization and high output per farm worker make up for the loss of manpower. In Russia, where 35 per cent of the work force is still in agriculture and modernization of farming is inadequate, the effects are infinitely more damaging.

Under the law farmers are tied to the land by the simple device of denying them a passport, without which one cannot live or work in industrial communities. But young people get around it in a variety of ways. Children under sixteen can get work and residence passports in towns on demand; having finished elementary school, they rush to some urban area before the deadline. Within one year after completing their four years of military service, also after graduating from intermediate schools, colleges, and universities, the rules permit young people to decide to settle where they please—most of them do not return to the unappetizing villages. Even without passports, too many millions are deserting the impoverished, drab, and painfully boring rural life to be driven back even by a police-state.

The gravity of the problem was recently emphasized by a study in what is obviously one of the hardest-hit areas, the Smolensk province. The study was conducted by the Laboratory of Labor Reserves of Moscow University and published in two articles in *Literaturnaya Gazeta* in July, 1966. The findings begin by pointing to the low productivity per hectare—one-fifth of what is produced on the same kind of soil in Western Europe—then ascribes it primarily to shortage of farm-hands, especially young farm laborers.

The whole Smolensk region, it appears, has been steadily losing population but the decline in its rural areas is especially sharp: from 1.62 million before the war to 0.65 million now. That much of this is due to the flight of the young is clearly indicated by the falling membership in the *Komsomol* or Communist Youth organizations. In 1960, there were still 33,700 Young Communists on the Smolensk *kolkhozes* and *sovkhozes* (farms operated directly by the state, like factories); by 1965 their number had dwindled to 10,000. In some villages, the study shows, young people of working age have practically disappeared. The last wedding in the village of Pomogailova took place in 1961, the last birth was registered in 1963. There are villages, if the researchers are to be believed, in which the voices of young children have not been heard for years.

The natural growth of the rural population in Smolensk—surplus of births over deaths—has dropped to less than 6 per cent of what it was in 1950. "The members of the village Soviet of Kardimovsk," a plaintive statement reads, "affirm that in their bailiwick it had never happened that the passport regulations in force had prevented a young person from leaving the village." Among those graduating intermediary schools and not continuing further education, only 4 per cent of rural Smolenskers return to their home villages. Already there is not enough farm labor to bring in the flax and potato crops and to maintain the herds of cattle and pigs.

Obviously Smolensk is an extreme case; presumably that is why it was selected for the inquiry. Elsewhere, especially in Central Asia, the population is growing, though the increase is nowhere as big proportionately in the farm districts as it is in industrial regions. Smolensk is not typical, yet in magnified terms it describes a nationwide situation, reflecting the low living and working conditions for peasants.

A careful analysis of the speeches and decisions on food and farm affairs at the last Party Congress was made by experts of Radio Free Europe. "The long catalog of shortcomings, losses and failures in the government operation and performance of Soviet agriculture is all too familiar," it concluded. "The Soviet system of socialist agriculture is the antithesis of a model of abundance and efficient, let alone equitable, agrarian order *for the developing nations to follow.*"

Unfortunately it is precisely in the underdeveloped areas, in the hungry nations, that the myth of communist agrarian magic appears to exert its strongest appeal. This is surpassingly strange, now that the collective system and its realities of dire want and chronic crisis are so clearly on view. A conference with a few typical Soviet *kolkhoz* farmers, under conditions that guaranteed their safety and candor, would soon enough erase the delusions held so grimly by certain leaders and opinion-makers in the backward areas.

Asia, Africa, Latin Americans—and some North Americans, too —might look with profit on the experience, nearly 350 years ago, in another underdeveloped area: the Plymouth colony on the shores of what was to be New England. The settlers had paid heavily in life for several disastrous crop years under a communal system of farming. But the turning point came after the 1623 harvest. What had happened is set forth in the memoirs of Governor William Bradford. After much debate and searching of conscience, the colonists went over to private farming. The Governor ordered "that they should set corne every man for his owne particular, and in that regard trust to themselves." It was a panacea that worked.

Communism breeds hunger. This is the plain truth that must be brought home to new or old nations flirting with the idea as a road to agricultural reform.

14 / Living Standards

The myth that communism provides abundance for the ordinary citizen.

One of those Soviet political anecdotes that throw a revealing light on realities:

A party agitator, addressing a factory meeting of workers, holds forth on the country's glorious achievements. For an hour he piles up statistics on growth in steel, petroleum, coal, new housing units, railroads. Then he wipes his brow and invites questions from the audience. "Don't be shy, comrades," he urges, "what would you like to know?"

Finally a shabby little man in the back row stands up. "I have only one question, comrade," he says meekly. "If everything is so good, why is everything so bad?"

The great gulf between industrial expansion and the squalid living conditions of the masses has been an unchanging feature of the Soviet economic landscape. Heavy industry has held undisputed priority, whatever the cost in retarded consumer industries and depressed living standards. Among the leading industrialized nations, the Soviet Union presents the unique paradox of a country in the front ranks in gross production, second only to the United States, but in the rearmost ranks—twentieth according to most Western calculations—in consumption per inhabitant.

Not until the mid-fifties did real wages, in true purchasing power surpass those of 1928, the last NEP year, which in turn had only reached the 1913 levels. Since then, improvement has been too thin to affect the character of life. Government statistics emphasize the great rise in ruble incomes since 1913, but critics readily demonstrate that prices have risen at roughly the same rate. As of 1964,

Mihajlo Mihajlov (imprisoned by Tito for his candor) attested in his now celebrated report on his summer in the USSR, that Soviet living standards were "about 40 per cent lower than in Yugoslavia," which itself is no workers' paradise. More than one-third of the national consumer product goes to the 30 million people at the top of the social pyramid, the other 190 million share the remaining two-thirds.

Consumption of goods per person in 1950–1960 was about one-quarter of the United States, 40 to 60 per cent of West European nations. "The distribution of income within the Soviet society," Professor Cyril E. Black of Princeton University attested, "has also been significantly more unequal than in countries of a comparable level of development, and lower income groups are taxed more heavily." He was referring, of course, to income taxes which are quite low for those in the higher earning brackets, compared to such taxes in America or England, but relatively higher for people in the low earning categories. The high costs of growth, he added, "are borne primarily by the lower income groups, in contrast with an elite that lives comfortably and free from progressive taxes."

Soviet statistics on living norms have always been cagey, ambiguous, with large areas blacked out altogether. Analysts abroad have to be economic detectives, making deductions from available data in other Soviet areas, to reach approximate judgments about incomes, personal budgets, and living conditions. In an article on the subject, "Figures Unfit to Print," in *Problems of Communism*, Leon M. Herman traced the deepening secrecy since 1927.

"The first indicators to be suppressed," he showed, "were those relating to the living standards of the population." For instance, "the Soviet government discontinued the release of statistics concerning public health. This step was taken shortly after the trade-union press reported that the rate of industrial accidents increased alarmingly as a result of higher work norms imposed on newly recruited, inexperienced workers." Within a few years the blackout spread to the cost-of-living index, real wages, adjusted for price inflation, family budgets.

The obvious purpose of the secrecy on matters until then published in the USSR, and routinely published in all other countries, was to hide from the masses and the outside world the calamitous decline of life standards.

Prices, rather than wages, determine living conditions—and the government, setting both arbitrarily, can juggle figures to confuse and conceal as it pleases. The ruble, pegged today in theory at $1.11, is entirely artificial; it cannot be exchanged for any other currency at home or abroad. (In the black market an American dollar brings as much as twenty-five rubles.) Besides, the chronic shortages in consumer goods and their incredibly low quality make comparisons with other countries all but meaningless. Since Soviet and non-Soviet estimates alike rarely take such elements into consideration, the picture they project tends to be a lot rosier than the reality.

Average earnings for factory and office workers in 1965–1966 have been estimated at 95 rubles a month, about $26 a week.* If the current Five-Year Plan is fully carried out—a big "if"—the figure by 1970 should be 114 rubles monthly, about $32 a week. Existence for the ordinary citizen in 1970 will consequently remain as cramped and penurious as it has always been. The aristocrats of the labor force, steelworkers, average $41 a week—this according to Meyer Bernstein, head of the United Steelworkers of America's International Affairs Department, who visited the USSR and its steel mills in late 1966; the average is based on weekly earnings-plus-bonuses of $68.50 by the most skilled down to $13.50 at the lowest levels. Consumer prices, whether figured in money or in man-hours of labor, are steeply higher than in Westen Europe or the United States.

"We priced various articles at the Gum and Zum stores in Moscow," Mr. Bernstein reported. A few of the prices he gathered translated into dollars: a suit of clothes, $191.40; women's shoes, $44; a small stereo radio, $247.50; a small tape recorder, $198. The same items, if and when in stock, can be bought at more reasonable figures, of course, in less swanky shops. When matched against the average income of $26 a week, however, it helps point up the plight of the ordinary consumer.

But averages are misleading. Tens of millions must subsist on the legal *minimum* wage, which is now between 40 and 45 rubles a

* This figure is considered excessive by some non-Soviet specialists. Thus two economists in Paris, M. Petrovich Kolojarski in *Russkaya Misl*, in January, 1966, and Lucien Laurat, in *Est-Ouest* in May the same year, both calculated the real monthly average in 1964 to be only 65 rubles. The facts are sufficiently bleak in any case. I have adhered to the official statistics.

month, and which under the plan would reach 60 rubles by 1970. The monthly income of the largest single group of wage-earners, the collectivized peasants, counting both cash and farm produce, is below the industrial minimum; the range, official figures show, is between 614 rubles a year for specialists such as tractor drivers to 172 rubles at the other extreme for simple farmers. In parts of Central Asia and remoter Siberian aeas, even the legal minimum is enjoyed only by the luckier minority of wage-earners. A requiem for the pledged communist abundance!

According to Marxist theory, the abolition of private ownership and profit in the means of production should have redounded in higher living standards for the workers. When this miracle did not transpire, the regime resorted increasingly to daring lies. "For two or three years now," Stalin declared in December 1, 1935, "we no longer have any poor, unemployment has ceased, undernourishment has disappeared and we have firmly entered the path to prosperity." At about the same time he announced that there were "no more slums" in his country.

Food queues, unhappily, were universal at that time, the housing situation was disastrous, the ruble was selling in the black market at 4 or 5 per cent of its supposed valuation. And slums in Russian towns and cities were then, and have remained, among the foulest in Europe.

In 1964, for the first time in thirty years, the *Statistical Yearbook of the USSR* finally lifted secrecy from the earnings of wage and salary groups. This called for some political courage, since the data confirmed what everyone knew from personal experience: that the levels of living were extremely low. The income of the working population (aside from farmers), the *Yearbook* showed, was less than one-quarter of corresponding incomes in the United States. Economists abroad, making conservative discounts for purchasing power, quality, and other distorting factors, placed actual wages in the USSR at five to six times lower than in the United States, three to four times lower than in Western Europe.

To put a better gloss on the general poverty, Soviet statisticians invariably add what they call indirect "social wages" to the direct earnings. This refers to services and benefits dispensed by the government, such as education, paid vacations, old-age and veterans' pensions, maternity leaves, medical care, children's creches, institutions for the aged and disabled. It even included the generic category of "culture and enlightenment," meaning that the boring propaganda with which the people are deluged is charged to wage earners as extra income.

A recent Soviet analysis asserts that these "fringe benefits" of Soviet citizenship add about 35 per cent to the average wage, more modest earlier estimates put them around 25 per cent. Without doubt they are vital to the recipient, especially the low rents and bread prices. The government it should be remembered, is at the same time employer, storekeeper, and landlord, like the corporation in an American "company town" early in this century. It exploits the worker, both at the wage and the price ends of the economy, and exacts not only income taxes, but "voluntary" contributions to various civic organizations, along with dues to the state-controlled trade unions; until 1958 it also forced everyone to purchase "voluntarily" government bonds to the tune of one month's wages.

The much propagandized benefits merely return to the employee a small part of what has been taken from him. If he received more wages and paid less for his purchases, he would have no need for so many "free" services from the state. Moreover, those celebrated benefits are not uniquely communist. Basically they are the kind nearly all modern societies provide, not alone through government, but through trade-union contracts and private philanthropy. Neither in the USSR nor in capitalist countries does the beneficiary get something for nothing; he pays indirectly instead of directly.

The average American, Frenchman, or West German, too, receives free education, medical clinics, pensions, day nurseries, unemployment insurance, vacations with pay, etc. He, too, shares in free "culture and enlightenment" (museums, libraries, parks, etc.) as fulsomely as a Soviet citizen. If these "social wages" were added to his direct wages, the comparable average income would appear, if anything, less flattering to the Soviets than the contrasting direct incomes.

In available health services per inhabitant, according to Professor Black, the USSR ranks below nearly all of the major nations. In the number of hospital beds—one for every 140 people—it was surpassed by twenty-five countries, including all the English-speaking nations. Infant deaths for one thousand live births in 1960 came to thirty-five in Soviet Russia, which was higher than in nineteen other countries; the Netherlands was in first place with 16.5 infant deaths per thousand, the United States in-between with 26.4.

• *"Living Space"*

In Soviet Russia, as everywhere, housing is a crucial test of living conditions. It has been pathetically inadequate throughout the Soviet half-century, with the prospects of meaningful improvement in the immediate years ahead extremely dubious. The 1919 Party Program declared that solution of this problem was "a most important task." Forty-two years later, in the 1961 Program, it was still rated "a most acute problem." A formal decision in 1957 ordered the "liquidation" of the housing shortage. Ten years have passed but nothing has changed. Most basements and cellars, even in the biggest cities, are occupied by as many families as can be pressed into them. Hundreds of thousands of workers, to put it conservatively, still live near their industrial sites in crowded, vermin-ridden barracks.

Although it does not phrase it this way, the Kremlin does not deny that the ordinary wage-earner has a smaller area of housing than a convict in an enlightened Western prison system. The "living space" per person set by law in the leading Soviet cities is nine square meters, or about 97 square feet: a room less than 10 by 10 feet, which happens to be the allotment per inmate in the better American prisons. Not one of the 27 largest cities, however, comes close to providing this legal minimum; half of them average out at less than six square meters; only Moscow, Kiev, and a very few others can provide more than six.

In 1960 *per capita* living space for the whole country, the government figures showed, had risen to 5.26 square meters. In the first six months of 1961 the Soviets claimed construction of 15 million square meters of housing—only one million more than West Germany, with one-quarter as many inhabitants, built in the same months. John Scott of *Time-Life*, returning to Leningrad after an absence of three years, reported: "New housing has been put up in several areas around the city, but officials admitted that the legal sanitary minimum has not been achieved, in spite of rigorous restrictions against any outsider moving into Leningrad."

At the beginning of the 1960's most of the new housing still provided one room per family, with a common kitchen for three families. By now, the standard, for a family of four or more, is the two-room apartment, but with only marginal improvement in the living space per person. In Moscow and other primary cities, the waiting period for a new apartment, unless the family can swing heavy political influence or a hefty bribe, is at least five years. There is thus unwitting pathos in an article by an American communist in the *Worker* (December 5, 1966) on the wonderful progress in the USSR. In an inventory of the splendid advantages of the Soviet over the American worker, he lists "a right . . . to be in line for a new apartment."

Figures do not begin to convey the torments involved in the housing shortages. Families are forced to double up. People intrigue and quarrel and go to court over a few feet of space. Neighbors are denounced to the police in the hope that, if deported, their "living space" will become available. On bulletin boards one finds notices of "a corner" being wanted or being offered for rent—and it refers quite literally to a corner in an occupied room. Disputes in common kitchens and washrooms and inside corridors embitter daily existence.

Divorced couples are frequently obliged to continue living in the same room, with a curtain to separate them. The divorced couples sometimes bring new partners to their respective sides of the curtain. A satirical writer, Mikhail Zoshchenko, once wrote a tongue-in-cheek story on how Soviet conditions sustain the institution of marriage. Husbands and wives, he explained, unable to divorce because they cannot find separate quarters, eventually make up and live happily together.

The quality of new housing, as of so much else of the new, is abominable. A Soviet witticism refers to it as "instant antiquity." Repeatedly the press has disclosed in futile anger that walls and ceilings crack and the plumbing goes *kaput* even before the new apartment houses are occupied. Some of these structures in Moscow itself until recently were festooned with nets to catch falling bricks and pediments.

The findings of the United Steelworkers Union, quoted earlier, indicate that the American trade-unionists did not see the interiors of working-class housing. But "from the outside the workmanship appeared to be poor. We observed similar poor workmanship on the interior of the hotels and enterprise buildings. Loose door hinges, wobbling door handles, loose-fitting windows, rusting bath water, missing sink stoppers, poor electric lighting, badly placed switches, all of this and much more was typical of the buildings we entered." It is a fair assumption that the condition of ordinary apartments would be no better, more likely worse, than in hotels and factories.

Yet the Russians must have been competent builders in the past, as witnessed by solid structures dating back to the last century and obviously destined to outlive the Soviet buildings. The most desirable dwelling places in the Soviet Union, even in small towns and villages, are those of pre-revolutionary vintage.

For intimate and vivid accounts of the squalid and harried everyday life of ordinary people, I recommend *The Angry Exile*, by Yury Krotkov, published in England in 1967. The author, a successful Soviet writer, defected in London while with a group of tourists. His living quarters, in one of the solidly built pre-revolution houses, were "better than normal by Moscow standards." He was one of nineteen occupants who averaged almost ten square meters per person—"and this for Moscow, at the present time, is luxury:"

Our apartment contained eleven rooms. It had one kitchen with eight gas-rings, three bells (one general and two individual), a telephone in the corridor which was in constant use, a bath, and a lavatory, which only the fastest were able to get to in the morning (the others stopped in the public lavatories on their way to work). There were eighteen people in the apartment, besides myself.

Seven families, seven meters for electricity, seven tables and cupboards in the kitchen, and seven launderings a month, since none of my neighbors used state laundries. This was not because they did not like them, but because they were economizing. There was not a single washing-machine in the apartment; we had never even heard of a clothes-drier. But there were three television sets and two radios. Furthermore, all eighteen people ate at home. They never went to even the cheapest cafeteria, much less a restaurant. Again it was because of the expense. . . . My apartment was somewhat typical. But at the same time we were exceptional, in that each resident could say with satisfaction: "It's crowded, but the people, thank the Lord, are decent. They don't spit in their neighbor's soup, as they do in Apartment 5."

• *Making Ends Meet*

How do Soviet workers and peasants manage to live on their meagre wages? The answer is that there are many ways, legal and otherwise, to add to family income. The peasants, of course, have their tiny plots and gardens. Most important, the vast majority of women, and nearly all grown-up children not in school are employed so that few families have less than two wage-earners. Besides, man is a resourceful animal. Millions do a bit of black-marketing and engage in private "moonlighting" such as repair jobs for neighbors, all of it necessarily with materials and tools stolen from government supplies.

Working-class families, even on the outskirts of capital cities, often keep a cow, goat, or pig, or they may have a small backyard vegetable garden and a couple of fruit trees to help fill out their needs. Many of them even produce surpluses which they sell privately. Denounced as "speculators" (although derogatory labels no longer deter Soviet citizens), they are barred from the public markets to which collectivized peasants bring their products. In January, 1967, the Moscow trade-union paper, *Trud*, proposed that the stigma of "speculation" be removed from this type of transaction and special shops be opened as legal outlets for the produce of marginal urban gardens and orchards. The paper did not conceal that its proposal was prompted by the chronic shortages of fruits and vegetables in the existing state shops.

A few words are in order about the living conditions of Soviet women, whose supposed new "equality" is always touted in communist propaganda. Actually they have no more privileges, in law or in the economy, than their sisters in the West—unless employment on hard and dangerous jobs normally reserved for men can be rated as a privilege. Back in 1931, I remember, the young Jack Howard, now head of the Scripps-Howard Newspapers, wrote a series of articles after a visit to Soviet Russia. The first of them (I quote from memory) began something like this: "No sooner had I crossed the border than I saw Russian women enjoying their new equality—they were carrying logs."

Thirty-six years later, they are still carrying logs, digging ditches, sweeping streets, laying bricks, carrying hods, scrubbing the decks of ships, tending furnaces in steel mills and doing other "men's work." The employment of women in coal-mining was prohibited in England in 1842; a century and more later the Soviet press was boasting of the high output by women's brigades in coal pits.

Nearly 50 per cent of wage-earners in the USSR are women, compared with less than 25 per cent in the United States. The principal reason for this, of course, is that the male head of a family rarely can support it by his own labor. The pretense that women prefer outside work to what Lenin once called "the primitive and deadening tasks of the household" is largely a propaganda fable.

The truth is that working-class women have no choice. Though they work in a factory or office, they still carry their responsibilities as wives and mothers, doing the cooking and washing and house-cleaning at home. They still must combine care of their children with the outside employment. Those who have an old mother or mother-in-law living with them and helping with the chores are the lucky ones. Soviet men have no more appetite or talent for household tasks than men elsewhere.

Western scholars have always been hampered by the lack of reliable Soviet data on the family budget. Only in the late 1950's did the authorities begin to disclose such information, and that in forms obviously intended to veil the low standards—with statistics based, for instance, on relatively high-earning families of skilled workers.

According to official figures, 54 per cent of the family income goes for the purchase of foodstuffs in state shops. Since everybody also buys some of the higher-priced products in the peasant free market, it would be fair to raise the expenditure for food to 60 per cent. This, according to United Nations figures, compares with food budgets ranging from 35 per cent of income in Austria down to 19 per cent in the United States. The Soviet worker has a balance of only 40 per cent of his earnings—about 30 rubles a month, or eight dollars a week—for clothing and all other non-food necessities.

There is one grim item of living expense that appears in no official or foreign budget studies. It has to be deduced from information in other areas. Yet it has a serious and painful impact on the family budget. I refer to the high incidence and high costs of alcoholism.

The regime cannot conceal the immense scale of the consumption of hard spirits or the economic and social problems that it creates. The nation was faced, *Komsomolskaya Pravda* acknowledged on July 31, 1954, with "abysmal drunkenness and abysmal boredom." The continuing preoccupation of the press, books, the theater, with the scourge of alcoholism indicates that there has surely been no improvement since then. A study of one thousand divorce cases recently made in Leningrad, showed that the largest single cause of the break-up, cited by nearly 30 per cent of the wives, was drunkenness.

De-drunking clinics are standard in all population centers and never sufficient to care for all those rounded up by the militia in a night. The growth of crime, from hoodlumism to sordid murders, has been blamed by the government upon excessive drinking. A recent defector, interviewed in Germany, in describing life in Sverdlovsk in 1966, said at one point: "There are drunkards living in over half the apartments. Unless seen with one's own eyes, it seems incredible. . . . They do it, first, out of sorrow, and then out of habit. It is disgusting and depressing."

The plague of alcoholism is far beyond anything known in the old Russia, although it also had a reputation for hard drinking. Most social psychologists, including some in the USSR, agree that it is a fair measure of the drabness and oppressive boredom of life, an escape from unpleasant reality. The cold figures are astounding. In 1962, a typical year, the population spent over 12.5 billion rubles on hard spirits—as much as it did for all meat and fish products, canned goods and fats! That it works havoc with the family budget is obvious enough. Sale of alcoholic beverages in 1963 was 2.6 times greater than in the last decade of the monarchy; after making adjustments for a one-third growth in population, it still indicates a shocking rise in alcohol consumption.

From Soviet statistics on the pertinent industries, Western students have calculated that to the 60 per cent of its aggregate income that a family spends for food, about 15 per cent should be added for average expenditures on alcohol and tobacco, since both these items are ignored in Soviet budgetary statistics. If this is true, the margin remaining for non-food necessities, including clothing, averages about 25 per cent—25 rubles a month, that is, or six dollars a week.

Foreign tourists who see the major cities and the Black Sea rivieras briefly can have no real idea of the gray, impoverished lives led by the overwhelming mass of the population. Beyond a few pampered cities, conditions are in most respects as primitive as they were fifty years ago. Edwin C. Canham, editor of the *Christian Science Monitor*, having alluded to the evidence of industrial growth, added: "Off the beaten track it is a different story. Slums, even in Moscow, are pervasive and dreadful. Elsewhere, one can step into the Middle Ages." He was there in the late 1950's, but nothing substantial has changed in this respect in the intervening years—nothing in Russia *can* change basically so fast. Ask a Soviet person how he is, and he is likely to answer, "*Luchi chom zavtra*" —"better than tomorrow."

No nation, however potentially rich, can afford history's most gigantic bureaucracy and internal security establishment, the costs of propaganda and censorship on an unprecedented scale, the inherent waste in centralized planning, the fantastic Soviet mismanagement, plus a tremendous military set-up, space spectaculars and its Soviet bloc at this writing supply about 80 per cent of the military-economic aid to North Vietnam and its Viet Cong for the war on South Vietnam and its allies. With an economy about half the size, the USSR maintains a military establishment as large as that of the United States, an anti-missile missile program far greater than America's, and space operations at least as vast. The Soviet military budget for 1967 was raised by 8½ per cent, and it is no secret that additional high-priced military projects are concealed in the civilian budget.

Someone must pay this staggering bill, and in the last analysis it is paid by the people in the coin of atrocious living conditions. The poverty is so all-embracing that there probably is no other country where the sense of private property is so abnormally developed, the value attached to the simplest material possessions so high. Every scrap and tag-end in the garbage-heap of living is preserved, fought over, traded. Every building, store, bakery, farm, and pile of building material is guarded by armed men and women.

True, more vacuum cleaners, refrigerators, washing machines, television sets are being produced. But they are wholly inadequate for the vast population and accessible only to those in middle-class economic brackets. Spare parts and repair facilities are scant. Unless the family has a member who is mechanically apt, there is almost no point in acquiring such luxuries.

A medium-sized refrigerator costs about 400 rubles, representing four months of average income. To obtain one the customer pays in advance, gets on a waiting-list, and if lucky will receive it in a year. Then, according to the Soviet press, his chances are no better than fifty-fifty that it will still be operating a year later. A family-sized Volga, the standard car, costs 5,600 rubles, the equivalent of three years' wages for the best-paid middle-class employee. Again it must be paid for in advance and the waiting period may run to five years. In 1966, there were over 150,000 hopeful car buyers on waiting lists throughout the country.

• Goulash Socialism

The sovereign worker, in whose name the whole communist enterprise was undertaken, must devote much of his spare time to scrounging for food and other products in short supply. The distribution system is so inefficient, standing in line for deficit goods so unavoidable, that some member of the family must devote many hours a day to shopping. The shopper often carries a "perhaps bag" —for items that perhaps may show up unexpectedly; one buys anything available as a hedge against future shortages. Purchases are weighed out into the buyer's bag or into old newspapers; modern wrapping and packaging has not yet reached the second largest industrial power on earth.

The customer is always wrong—he is cheated, short-weighted, and pushed around. Breakdowns in everyday equipment are as frequent as in industry. Carl T. Rowan, former head of the USIA, after a recent visit to Soviet Russia, reported stalled elevators everywhere. He quoted a Russian as saying: "They can get to the moon but they can't get me to the fifth floor." The "they" is characteristic; always Soviet citizens speak of the rulers in the third person.

The Soviet worker, so heroic on postage stamps and posters, in real life is poor and harried, bedeviled by propaganda and vigilante attentions. The atmosphere in the celebrated free clinics is familiar to anyone who knows charity wards in other countries; they are likely to be shabby, overcrowded, and little concerned about the sensitivities of their anonymous clients. The Soviet day nurseries and boarding schools have been widely acclaimed, yet they can care for only about 10 per cent of the children under fifteen. This poses problems in households where both father and mother must work to make ends meet.

Naïve enthusiasts who have been spared the ordeal of continual living under Soviet communism may think of the USSR as a sort of superior welfare state. Unfortunately it is closer to an immense poorhouse. Communism, before it was tried on the scale of a great nation, was geared to high human purposes, to happiness, economic justice, and equality. These were to be the criteria of success. The sad part of the story is that the vision, sincerely held by most of the early Bolsheviks, was blotted out by purely materialist criteria—blast furnaces, airplanes, sputniks, the desperate struggle for sheer subsistence.

Khrushchev may be remembered in history for reducing the whole purport of Marxism to a pot of stew. What all communist regimes are after, he said during a visit to his fiefs in Eastern Europe, was more goulash. But if goulash is the decisive test of the good society, the major capitalist nations have already achieved it— why experiment with new cookery and cooks? Indeed, Hungary and its neighbors, and Russia itself, had a lot more goulash—or *borshch*—before the communists took over the kitchens.

The irony of the business is that communists who deplore and deride materialist criteria in their own affluent homelands do handsprings of enthusiasm over progress toward goulash socialism in Russia. If and when the ordinary Soviet citizen has a refrigerator, a telephone, and a car, we can expect foreign enthusiasts to hail it as an exciting achievement and an argument in favor of communism. The fact that the American citizen already has these things, however, is no argument in favor of capitalism but only a symptom of gross materialism.

The tragedy, as some of us see it, is not only in the failure of communism to provide enough goulash but in the fact that its humanist values have been displaced in a sort of *reductio ad absurdum* of stomach goals. Should those goals be reached in Soviet Russia, which now seems decidedly unlikely for a long, long time to come, the larger tragedy will remain—a well-fed prison is still a prison.

For fifty years the justification offered for the incalculable sacrifices in death and suffering and indignity visited on the Soviet people has been that they were an investment for the future—if not for themselves, then for their children. But time has run out. The *grand*children are now on the scene, insistent on collecting the interest on the long and grim investments.

"Governed by fanatical materialists," Joseph A. Gwyer wrote, "the Russian people have been called upon to sacrifice their liberties, their national traditions and their religion for the sake of material progress; and all that they have received in return is a rate of material progress far below that of most other countries. The poor and uninformed peoples of Asia, Africa, and Latin America are persistently being told by communists, by fellow travelers and by just plain muddleheads that communism, while it may have certain drawbacks, is nevertheless the key to material advancement. It should be made clear how very mediocre the economic results of communism have, in fact, been."

The perceptive Yugoslav, Mihajlo Mihajlov, in touching on the low living standards in Soviet Russia, declared: "Yet it is a fact, no matter how paradoxical, that the common Russian people do not consider material poverty the greatest misfortune." What they crave even more, he wrote, was freedom; what they most miss is "spiritual sustenance." They would not, we may be sure, condone the kind of glorification of their communist system that ignores spiritual deficits on the mistaken assumption that they are compensated by material abundance.

Only the physical aspects of living conditions, in any country, can be reduced to economic statistics. There is no arithmetic to measure social degradations and spiritual hungers. Day after day the Soviet citizen contends with the nuisances of police surveillance, red tape, documents, passports. He spends a large part of his time in long queues or in the dreary waiting rooms of bored and arrogant little officials—for permissions, purchases, the everlasting pieces of paper that regulate his day-to-day existence. At frequent intervals his right to his cramped "living space" is checked to make sure he isn't occupying a few square feet more than his legal due.

No matter how clear his political conscience, how carefully he avoids "dangerous" ideas, malice or error may bring the dreaded call to headquarters for "a little talk." Unless he has official permission, he cannot visit another town for more than seventy-two hours, and his host, too, faces punishment if he fails to inform the police of his illegal presence beyond that limit.

Where, in an account of living standards, do we fit in the grandmother who secretly, over the heads of more prudent parents, talks to the children about God? Or the man who comes into possession of an illicit leaflet, reads it greedily behind the locked door of the lavatory, then flushes it down the bowl? Or the parents who baptize their child in secret, fearful that someone may tell and endanger their jobs? The plight of an open believer in the USSR is like that of the village atheist in a God-fearing American community—it's legal but extremely uncomfortable.

But why catalog the endless fears and hardships? The world by this time should know what life is like under a totalitarian dispensation. Stalin's only surviving child, Svetlana Alliluyeva, on defecting to the free world, said that she objected to being treated as a piece of "state property." Perhaps she summed up the quintessential ordeal and humiliation of all Soviet citizens.

15 / De-Stalinization

The myth that the Soviet Union has become "liberal" and is evolving toward democracy.

In February, 1956 Nikita Khrushchev made his celebrated "secret speech" denouncing the homicidal proclivities of Joseph Stalin. Barely a year later, at a Soviet Writers Union conference, he was threatening to shoot writers who might start trouble like their colleagues in Hungary. If the Budapest rulers had shot the literary ringleaders, he said, the recent unpleasantness in their country would have been averted. Should any Soviet writers misbehave, he went on grimly, "My hand will not tremble."

His audience could not doubt the seriousness of his warning. Only several months before he had proved his iron nerves by sending hundreds of tanks into Hungary to crush the revolt; then his KGB had kidnapped tens of thousands of young Freedom Fighters and hauled them to Soviet concentration camps—where many of them still languish.

In December, 1958 the Soviet government promulgated a law prescribing the death penalty for a long array of offenses, some of them barely more than misdemeanors in other lands: anti-Soviet agitation and propaganda, private trade and other economic crimes, attempting to escape from the country. The law was broadened on May 5, 1961 to punish by death "acts of aggression against the administration" in penal institutions, evidently to counter continuing resistance and disorders in prisons and exile camps.

Since none of the capital offenses already on the statute books had been removed, Soviet Russia today applies the death penalty "legally" to more real and pseudo-crimes than in Stalin times. (Ordinary non-political murder is not on the list—a hangover from judicial practice under the monarchy.) Announcements of executions are so frequent that they have ceased to attract attention, and the public realizes that for every killing made public, dozens and scores go unrecorded.

A decree against "parasitic elements" legalized the deportation of those so defined by administrative police action, that is without resort to courts. While the parasites listed in the law are alcoholics, hoodlums, the wilfully idle, etc., the definition is broad enough to give the authorities a handy "legal" device for disposing of anyone they please. The parasite decree was used, for example, to imprison a recalcitrant poet, Joseph Brodsky, though clamorous protests abroad and by some daring Soviet writers in time obtained his release.

Millions of young people in a variety of vigilante formations have been invested with quasi-police and quasi-judicial rights, as a civic duty, to spy on their neighbors, "try" and punish the immoral and the "loud-mouths" (meaning grumblers) and other assorted miscreants. In the city of Odessa, according to the Kiev *Pravda Ukrainy* (June 10, 1962), there were 610 "comrades courts," one of the standard vigilante activities. Multiply the figure by all the cities and towns in the country, and the other varieties of vigilantism and you begin to see the vastness of these extra-governmental operations.

Children, the Soviet press proudly reports, are being taken from their parents in "unhealthy" homes—usually a euphemism for religious homes. In general, Western analysts of the Soviet press agree, there has been an actual increase of interference in the private life of the ordinary citizen in the last dozen years.

Two prominent writers, Andrei Sinyavsky and Yuli Daniel, have been publicly tried and sentenced to long camp terms for allowing their works, unpublishable at home, to be published abroad under pseudonyms. Dozens of others have been jailed for allegedly anti-Soviet writings without benefit of public proceedings. Immediately after the death of Boris Pasternak, author of *Doctor Zhivago* (still forbidden publication in the USSR), his friend and secretary, Olga Ivinskaya, and her daughter were imprisoned on trumped-up currency charges—a powerful state wreaking vengeance on two helpless women.

Adapting a trick first used by Tsar Nicholas I, the Kremlin has had many of its critics—writers, students, scientists—certified as "mad" and confined in lunatic asylums. *Ward Seven,* a novel by one of these politically "insane," Valeri Tarsis, describing the ordeal of the victims, has been published in Europe and the United States.

The persecution of religion has been intensified since the passing of Stalin, particularly in the 1960's. Churches, monasteries, mosques, and other places of worship have been closed on a variety of pretexts—their number was reduced by half between 1958 and 1964. Where there were eight Orthodox seminaries, there are now only three. The provisions against religious teaching to children are being more stringently enforced. Priests, rabbis, and others officiating at baptisms, weddings, religious services for the dead are required to register those requesting such rites by name—making economic reprisals easier.

An American Baptist journal, *The Watchman-Examiner,* in its January, 1967 issue, carried a report out of Soviet Russia, understandably anonymous. It dealt primarily with the half-million or so Baptists, but the information applies no less to the Russian Orthodox and other faiths.

"The anti-religious campaign which began quietly in the late fifties grew like wildfire in the sixties," the report said, "disrupting the relatively cordial relations between church and state which had been the postwar norm. By 1964, all religious groups had suffered crippling loss of parishes closed by fiat. People found it increasingly difficult to lead a normal religious life, both in society, as pressures initiated by the state multiplied, and within the churches, as state limitations and controls increased to a level reminiscent of the early Stalin period."

Both among priests in the Russian Orthodox ranks and ministers in the "sects," as the Russians call the Baptists and other such denominations, there have been in the last two years open movements of protest against the submission of their respective hierarchies to government domination. A number of the documents, usually in the form of "open letters," have reached the outside world. It is known that several of the leaders of these movements are under arrest; the extent of repressive measures against their followers can only be surmised.

These are random facts from life and politics *since the inception of so-called de-Stalinization*. But they have not made a dent in the thriving illusion in some foreign circles that the Soviet Union is going "liberal" and edging toward democracy!

In some ways this most recent of the myths about Soviet communism is the most mischievous. Moscow itself, which detests the word and the concept, has not claimed the degree of "liberalization" credited to it in the outside world. The strange anxiety to believe in the miracle of a totalitarian system evolving into its opposite is the source of the mischief. For it generates wishful-hopeful fantasies about the "convergence" of the two worlds and the imminence of a genuine detente between the communist and democratic worlds.

Even the reckless conduct of the USSR in foreign affairs has failed to scotch the legend of a meaningful evolution toward an open society. A partial inventory of highlights from the record suffices to show that in the international arena, Stalin has been out-Stalined by his successors.

There was the bloody suppression by the Red Army of popular uprisings in East Germany in 1953 and Hungary in 1956. At the very time Khrushchev was posturing as an angel of peace at the Geneva Summit Conference in the summer of 1955, his agents were arranging an arms deal with Egypt's Nasser that has kept the Middle East in bloody turmoil ever since. There was the erection of the Berlin Wall; the secret installation of Soviet nuclear missiles in Cuba aimed at the United States, a gambit that brought the world to the brink of nuclear war; the dispatch of Soviet arms to the primitive Simba rebels in the Congo, resulting in the massacre of hundreds of whites and thousands of blacks; the massive equipment of North Vietnam with Soviet planes and weapons for use against South Vietnam and its allies—by 1967, some 80 per cent of the military and economic aid to Hanoi was coming from the Soviet bloc.

All of this and more under the resuscitated Stalin slogan of "peaceful coexistence!" The Western will to believe in a new, more moderate and cooperative Kremlin appeared robust enough to survive such blows to credulity. Even Senator Robert F. Kennedy, who surely is no hard-liner on relations with the USSR, felt it necessary to remind his audience, in the course of a speech on

China in early February, 1967, that "It was not Stalin, but Khrushchev, who in the fortieth year of the Russian Revolution, crushed Hungary and six years later came to the brink of nuclear war in his Cuban adventure."

• *The Limits on Change*

Since Stalin's death in March, 1953, his self-appointed heirs have sought to disown some of his murderous excesses and to obscure their own complicity in his crimes. They have labored, in particular, to clear the communist system and its ruling party of the stigma by blaming certain past horrors and present troubles upon the blunders and aberrations of one man. In the hope of containing the general discontent, they have in effect provided scapegoats—not only Stalin but his police chiefs, Yezhov and Beria, and some of his surviving henchmen, Molotov, Malenkov, and Kaganovich.

Their belated concern for "legality" of course did not signalize a change of heart but only a calculated change of tactics. Khrushchev and Anastas Mikoyan, the first to outline the de-Stalinization gambit, had been the dead dictator's most zealous comrades in crime and his loudest sycophants. "It is not good will, still less humanity," Milovan Djilas has written, "which prompted Stalin's associates to perceive the harmfulness of Stalin's methods. It was urgent necessity that prompted the ruling class to become more 'understanding.' "

Every "concession" was aimed to batten down some area of restiveness. Slave labor on the Stalinist scale, an important element in the economy in an earlier period, had become more and more of an economic drain. The costs of administration were higher than the value of the unpaid labor extracted; with industry growing more complex the need for sheer muscle power had receded. Besides, the economy was so close to paralysis that some leeway had to be provided for mental initiative and talent, throttled by dread of purge.

The measures of moderation taken, far fewer and more limited than the world was led to believe, thus had no relation to considerations of justice. They were intended to shore up the foundations of the Soviet system and head off possible overt opposition. Nothing whatsoever has been done to identify those guilty of the worst crimes, the torturers and mass killers, and not one of them has been punished. Many of them still hold posts of great power, at or near the top of the oligarchy. The revelations, moreover, were made in a way to preserve Stalin's operational methods.

Without doubt existence has become more tolerable for the Soviet citizen. The terror and its apparatus have not been dispensed with, but they have been moderated in scope and their operations are now more discreet. A latitude of opinion and expression in many fields is permitted that would have been unthinkable twenty or thirty years ago. Official controls on literary and other cultural activities have been eased.

It is only by contrast with the most malignant periods in the Stalin epoch, however, that the new Soviet atmosphere seems almost benign. By comparison with conditions under Franco in Spain or Tito in Yugoslavia, let alone democratic societies, life in Soviet Russia is still bleakly tyrannical. Robert Conquest, a British poet who is also a specialist on Russia, writing in the U.S. journal, *Problems of Communism*, in 1962, put the issue in focus: "If Khrushchev's Russia were judged by any standards operating before the rise of Hitler and Stalin, it would be thought a revoltingly oppressive dictatorship."

Any abatement of the terror is welcome, especially to those bearing its weight. But in truth nothing *fundamental* has changed. Soviet Russia remains what it was: a rigidly totalitarian state. Its power structure, its morality and ideology—the things, that is, which made Stalinism possible—are intact. The dictatorship still has absolute control of the world's largest police system; of the press, schools, employment, virtually everything else. The internal passport system remains in undiminished force. Foreign travel is not a right but a high privilege reserved for the elites; it is organized in group tours under police monitors, but there have been numerous defections notwithstanding. The misnamed trade unions still have no voice on wages, hours, and most working conditions; their chief purpose, specified in their constitutions, is still "to mobilize all the workers for the fulfillment and over-fulfillment of the state production plan."

The supposed new freedoms and reforms all stop safely beyond the line where they might impinge on the power monopoly and its key institutions. Thus physical and social scientists may now explore and criticize everything—except the eternal rightness of the regime and its politico-economic theology. Creative men and women may stray from the dogma of "socialist realism"—provided they do not attack the dictatorship and its infallibility. Economic theorists in their discussions and writings may bypass Marxism-Leninism—provided they give lip-service to it.

In practice, the new freedom of expression is an elaborate game of double-think and double-speak. The regime is untouchable, its ideological underpinnings are sacrosanct. The rules of the game are constantly revised to protect the oligarchy against the doubts of freethinkers. Some subject areas are off bounds. It will be time enough to suspect outcroppings of liberalism in the system, if and when the authorities allow publication of an honest defense of religion or capitalism; if and when Soviet citizens may with impunity criticize the Kremlin's policy on Vietnam, or expose the sins, not of the past, but of the present leaders.

In brief, what was before 1955 an absolute despotism, has become, very relatively, an enlightened despotism. The leash has been lengthened, but the collar has not been removed. None of the new rights has been confirmed and made permanent by law; they are arbitrary gifts that can be arbitrarily withdrawn by the givers, as in fact happens in many cases. The people and the rank-and-file communists have no more voice in shaping their own fate and national policy than they did under Stalin. Decision-making belongs to the power monopoly.

All the heights of authority in cultural and scientific organizations, in the newspapers and magazines and in educational institutions, are manned by totally obedient servants of the Kremlin. Should they manifest any non-conformist tendency, unless it is with the consent of the bosses for tactical reasons, their jobs and sometimes their liberty are forfeit. The "cult of personality" may be assailed as an abstraction, but without mention of specific crimes and faults beyond those already mentioned by the anointed leaders.

That de-Stalinization has changed nothing essential was attested by the late Eugene Varga, perhaps the foremost Soviet economist, an Academician, and during most of his life close to the Kremlin leadership. He died in Moscow in October, 1964. A long essay of his, unpublished and quite obviously unpublishable in the USSR, has appeared posthumously in an illegal magazine, *Phoenix 1966*, about which I shall have more to say later. Dealing with the changes since the passing of Stalin, Professor Varga asserted that they have not altered the pattern of Soviet life and rule. He wrote:

As before, power in the state belongs to the party and the bureaucratic elite; as before, the economic processes and the political relationships remain concealed from the working masses. Neither the trade unions nor any other groups of citizens has anything to do with the management of industry. As before, workers vote mechanically in the elections for the pre-elected deputies to the Soviets, and as before, the ministers, the presidents of the executive committees, the secretaries of the provincial and district committees appointed by the party Central Committee continue to rule in the name of these Soviets. As before, the contrast is drastic between the luxuries enjoyed by the ruling elite and the exceedingly low wages of the great majority of workers, employees, and collective farm laborers. As before, all this gives rise to innumerable crimes. As before, social consciousness is dominated by the official ideology inculcated from above as infallible dogma. And all of this, as before, breeds social immorality.

• The "Liberalization" That Isn't

The "secret speech" at the Twentieth Party Congress in 1956 that initiated de-Stalinization is still secret in the Soviet Union. Only party insiders were allowed to read it. The full text was released by the U.S. State Department and has been widely published and annotated in the free world. Its general purport and some of the specific charges have percolated down to the average citizen in the USSR. Why, then, is the whole document being denied to the populace most directly concerned?

The probable answer is that the Kremlin does not want its subjects to know and ponder what Khrushchev did *not* say. The outside world has read far more into the speech than it contained. Evidently the regime prefers that the Soviet masses, too, should believe vaguely that *all* of Stalin's iniquities were confessed and repudiated. In truth the accusations and revelations dealt only with narrow segments of the Stalinist reality.

By silence, the "secret speech" and de-Stalinization have condoned the worst of the dead leader's depredations. His high-handed brutality against prominent party and military men and a few intellectuals was castigated, but not forcible collectivization, not the millionfold arrests, deportations and executions, not the man-made famine of 1932–1933 and the other major crimes and atrocities in which the whole population, rather than the elites, were victimized. Khrushchev said that "thousands of absolutely innocent people perished," though he knew there were millions; his personal contribution to the total ran into hundreds of thousands.

Indeed, he and other speakers on the historic occasion at the Twentieth Party Congress balanced excoriation with praise of Stalin. Specifically he was praised for having crushed Trotskyites, Bukharinites, and "bourgeois nationalists"; neither then nor since has the Kremlin denounced the Moscow blood-purge trials. Far from ruling out state violence, Khrushchev defended "necessary terrorism" against internal enemies, complaining only about its use against "good communists."

The much-advertised "rehabilitation" of Stalin's victims followed the same selective pattern. Khrushchev said that 7,679 had been rehabilitated and presumably several thousand more were added to the ghostly company before the process was tacitly halted. But this is a drop in the ocean of tens of millions of innocents. Only some of the well-known were exonerated and restored to posthumous respectability, not the myriad simple Ivans and Marias. Enough was admitted to encourage a new "image" but nothing basic was disowned.

By their silence, also, the de-Stalinizers accepted all of Stalin's most flagrant lies: that full socialism has been achieved; that collectivization was voluntary; that the First Five-Year Plan was a roaring success; that the East European satellites had freely chosen communism; that the three Baltic republics had "voted" to enter the Soviet Union; that the massacre of some fourteen thousand Polish officers at Katyn Forest during the war was a German, not a Soviet atrocity; that the USSR almost single-handedly defeated Germany and Japan. Neither the Stalin-Hitler pact, nor the invasion of Finland was mentioned. The whole Soviet mythology has been carefully preserved and reinforced.

Above all, the anti-Stalin campaign, in its inception and thereafter, did not surrender an iota of the arbitrary power used by Stalin, but merely made an implicit promise that his methods would not be employed so rashly against party leaders and activists. Having finally consolidated his supreme power by early 1955—a process he began when he and Malenkov murdered Beria and thirty-nine of his subordinates—Khrushchev was telling his associates that they need no longer fear sudden death. It was not a liberal explosion but a power play.

In effect the whole enterprise offered reassurance to the uppermost classes, not to the average citizen. As a Russian scholar in Germany, Dr. Herman Achminow, summed it up: "The Soviet party leaders decided to sacrifice Stalin in order to save Stalinism." Stalin had become the focus and symbol of universal fears and hatred: the symbol was removed in a sacrificial rite, without affecting the substance.

At best de-Stalinization promised a return to what its authors called "Leninist norms," to the policies and methods of the Lenin years. That was scarcely a prospect to warm the hearts of liberals. Had those in the non-Soviet world who have hailed the new moderation done their homework on the Lenin period and Lenin's code of conduct, they would have found little, if anything, to support their optimism. An impression has been deliberately fabricated that at last "the truth" is being told; it is an extremely restricted truth, however, larded with the same old lies.

Not until five years later, at the Twenty-second Party Congress, after a lot of zigging and zagging on the subject, did Khrushchev and his chief spokesman at that gathering, Alexander Shelepin, return to the assault on Stalin. This time, their purpose was all too clear. It was to smear Molotov, Kaganovich, and others of the anti-Khrushchev leaders—the so-called anti-party group—with the Stalinist brush.

And even on this occasion, Stalin was commended for his communist faith and his firmness in destroying enemies. "We shall punish mercilessly all the enemies of our people," Shelepin warned. And Khrushchev in substance promised that he would be as good a communist as Stalin, but without his unfortunate faults.

The rock-bottom reality, in the words of Boris Souvarine, is that "the system functions as in the past, the single party remains omniscient and omnipotent, the secret police operates in silence, the dreary press remains as it was, the strict discipline imposed on intellectuals keeps the official dogma intact."

The decisive institutions created by Stalin, such as collectivized farming, "corrective labor" exile, central planning, have not been changed. Information is still rationed through multiple censorships. Foreign newspapers and magazines are not available to the public; even technical publications from abroad are extensively scissored to remove "dangerous" thoughts before being released to scholars and researchers. Foreign correspondents are more stringently spied upon and restricted in their movements than in the 1930's. Most non-diplomatic aliens residing in Moscow live in special buildings, watched day and night by police guards who make a record of Soviet callers and whom they are visiting—a procedure that was never that open in Stalin's time.

Foreign tourists are more carefully watched than ever in the past, and more often subjected to interrogation and arrest. In August, 1966, the Supreme Soviet decreed rigid limitations on their movements and this was backed up with press warnings to Soviet citizens against contact with foreigners; no prudent Russian dares invite visitors from "the other world" to his home. Official anti-Semitism, expressed in Jewish quotas in higher education, exclusion of Jews from diplomatic and other sensitive posts, etc., has gone beyond Stalinist practices.

Anyone who equates such things with trends toward liberalization and democracy obviously has a shockingly low opinion of those noble concepts. This thought apparently prompted Edmund Stillman and William Paff to remark, in their recent book, *Power and Impotence:* "Only a calamitous insensitivity to the depth and meaning of the free political culture of the West could produce the notion that the 'normalization' and moderation of Soviet society that has taken place since Stalin makes Russia today—or very soon—'like us.' "

• *The Levels of Terror*

It is with regard to the terror, legal and extra-legal, that the most farfetched and inaccurate assumptions have been made by the half-informed. The secret police are still ubiquitous, arrests continue on a scale that would shock any country without memory of even larger repressions in the recent past.

The government, despite its revelations about that blood-chilling past, has gone out of its way to keep the picture of its security forces untarnished. In the very speech that initiated de-Stalinization, Khrushchev warned explicitly that "distrust of the state security organs" was "incorrect and harmful." On the contrary, he said, it was essential to strengthen them in every way. He returned to the theme at the following Party Congress in 1959, denouncing as "stupid and criminal" any suggestion that the secret police be weakened.

Since Khrushchev's forced retirement, the new leaders have staged various celebrations of historic dates in the annals of the secret police, to remind the citizenry of their debt to "our glorious Chekists"—and, more to the point, to apprise them that the Chekists were still very much around. The prestige of the huge security apparatus is continually guarded and burnished: conspicuous evidence that the regime is keeping its powder dry. KBG troops and tanks have gone into action repeatedly in recent times to crush riots, runaway strikes, and other manifestations too big for the ordinary police.

In a study of terror since Stalin, published in *Problems of Communism* in 1962, Professor Jeremy Azrael of the University of Chicago denied that "coercion is withering away" in the USSR. While "the level of coercion has dropped," he underlined "the need to discount the more sanguine claims and predictions now being aired." The regime, he made clear, "still attempts to imbue the population with the conviction that nothing of political significance escapes the secret police." In Orwellian terms, Big Brother is watching!

Another scholar, Paul Barton, an exiled Czech sociologist, writing in the same magazine that year, cited evidence from official Soviet sources indicating an increase of repressive measures in the past ten years. "These developments," he summed up, "belie any claim that the Soviet system since the death of Stalin has moved in a straight line toward eliminating coercion and replacing it with persuasion. . . . Indeed, a system of totalitarian one-party rule could not survive if it did not retain the power to enforce its will, however much it might ration and combine coercion with other methods of government."

"If it becomes necessary we will restore the old methods," the Assistant Prosecutor General, P. I. Kudriavtsev, assured an American interviewer, Prof. Harold J. Berman of Yale. The same threat is implied, where it is not spelled out, in all the internal propaganda. Whatever the non-Soviet world may be induced to believe, no one inside the USSR believes that the terror has been abolished. Its cruder forms are less in evidence, but the basic system continues on a scale without match in any civilized country. The Brezhnev-Kosygin team especially has not disguised its purpose of re-imposing "discipline" over the intellectual and social forces set into motion by the two anti-Stalin waves, in 1956 and 1961.

Millions of camp inmates have been released since 1953. Some have been transferred to the less onerous "corrective labor *colonies*," others forced to settle in the same inhospitable areas as free workers. Presumably many of the camps have been dismantled; the rest have been renamed "colonies." The electrified barbed-wire and the police dogs, one guesses, have been removed from around the verminous barracks and living conditions for the prisoners have been ameliorated. The improvement began, in fact, in the last year of Stalin's life.

The Kremlin remains as always tight-lipped about this ghastly skeleton in its closet. Analysts, on the basis of reports by ex-prisoners now abroad, chiefly repatriated foreigners, are unable to estimate the size of the prison population in the 1960's, but they have no doubts that the forced-labor system remains in massive operation. If both camps and colonies are counted, the figure at the least exceeds a million. In 1957, Assistant Prosecutor General Kudriavtsev indicated that only eight to nine hundred thousand were still left, but his official job, after all, was to minimize the reality.

A painstaking study by B. A. Yakovlev, published in Munich in 1965, was based on interviews with returned non-Russian slave laborers: Poles, Germans, Hungarians, and others. From their personal knowledge he was able to compile a list of 225 old-style concentration camps still extant in the late fifties and early sixties, several of them holding as many as five to eight thousand prisoners. Since these were primarily camps for foreigners, they represent only a small fraction of the aggregate institution.

Fresh light on the continuance of forced-labor camps was thrown very recently by a foreign prisoner released only in January, 1967, after serving two years in a Soviet prison and three years in a concentration camp. Alexander Dinces, a veteran of the Polish wartime resistance, came to the United States in 1948. In 1961, he was unwise enough to step on Soviet soil on a transit visa from Scandinavia to Poland. He was arrested and drew a five-year sentence. After his release and return to America, he recounted his ordeal in the Polish-language émigré press and in broadcasts for Radio Free Europe.

Mr. Dinces had found himself, he wrote, in a complex of fourteen labor camps, three of them for women, called "Dubrovlag," near Potma, 250 miles east of Moscow. (From other sources we know that the Potma operation actually embraces thirty-six camps, with a total of over seventy thousand prisoners.) His own camp, for foreigners and stateless convicts, held about fifteen hundred men. Others such complexes, he learned from inmates through the years, exist in all parts of the country. The conditions he described —overwork, undernourishment, lack of medical attention, prevalence of scurvy, ulcers, and other diseases, inhuman punishments, and the shocking death rate—suggest that little genuine improvement has been made in these penal institutions. In the last months of 1966, Mr. Dinces reported, there was a large influx of new political prisoners, evidently as a result of the harsher law against "anti-Soviet elements" decreed in July and in September, 1966.

The oft-repeated Soviet assertion that there are "no more political prisoners" in the USSR is ludicrous on the face of it. The ever greater number of "crimes against the state" defined in recent decrees obviously produce contingents of political prisoners. What the claim means is merely that people condemned for political activities are classed as ordinary criminals.

It is revealing of the Kremlin's ambivalence on the whole subject that, in all the to-do about de-Stalinization, it has never given a factual accounting of the forced-labor system, its magnitude and its methods. Only glimpses of the obscenity have been provided in the Aesopian language of fiction—by the famous novel *A Day in the Life of Ivan Denisovich* and a very few other literary works. After the second attack on Stalin in 1961, Soviet publishing houses were quickly deluged with personal stories on camp horrors—ten thousand manuscripts was Khrushchev's estimate when he ordered that the theme be dropped.

The few published were in limited editions. Even the *Denisovich* novel by Solzhenitsyn, which could have sold into the millions, was limited to one hundred thousand copies. Circulation in the USSR is not determined by demand but fixed by the thought-control managers. The dimensions and depravities of the slave system have always been known to the people, yet the authorities do not permit a forthright exposure of the facts or offer one themselves.

Besides, as an active process de-Stalinization is dead. It has been curbed to a degree where it could fairly be called *re*-Stalinization. The brakes were put on quite early, as a matter of fact, under the shattering impact of the Polish and Hungarian uprisings and the reaction of Soviet students to those events. On December 30, 1956, *Pravda* was already instructing its readers: " 'Stalinism' above all means communism and Marxism-Leninism. We believe that when Stalin's mistakes are weighed against his achievements it will be seen that his mistakes were secondary."

By 1963, this paper, main mouthpiece of the party, was all but restoring him to respectability: "The party fully acknowledges Stalin's services to the party and the communist movement. We now believe that Stalin was devoted to communism and that he was a Marxist; it is neither possible nor necessary to deny it."

More and more often the Kremlin has found or made opportunities to emphasize the "positive side." There was not a word about Stalin's misdeeds in the latest Party Program, adopted in 1961. His leadership in the war effort is again being lauded. During a visit to Stalin's native Georgia in October, 1966, Leonid Brezhnev paid tribute to him for great revolutionary services.

On the eve of the Twenty-third Party Congress, a group of top-shelf Soviet intellectuals, including communists, appealed to Kosygin and Brezhnev against the rehabilitation of Stalin, which was then widely rumored. "It is difficult to doubt," their letter said at one point, "that a large part of striking, truly horrifying facts about Stalin's crimes has not yet been made public." They obviously were hinting that more revelations, rather than a whitewash, were needed to reassure the country. The Party Congress did not in so many words restore Stalin to glory but it restored some political institutions associated with his name and carefully avoided any further criticism of him. The leadership clearly hopes that this chapter of unsavory history can be closed.

• *Orgies of Optimism*

It has been argued that, minuscule as the liberalization may be, it shows evolution "in the right direction." The fact, however, is that the regime has not moved in a straight line in any direction. It has fluctuated between permissiveness and crackdowns. The so-called "thaw" reached its softest point in 1954–1956 and the trend since then, in its zigzag course, has been toward a deepening freeze intellectually and politically to offset the greater frankness in the sciences and economic reforms. In culture, the pendulum between official moderation and harshness is at this writing visibly swinging toward harshness. Khrushchev's heirs are making manifest their intention to tighten "discipline" and enforce authority.

The idea that a totalitarian society can evolve toward democracy is at bottom naïve, a product of the ingrained optimism of free men. In theory it may be argued that the autocrats, in some dim future, may choose to dilute and to share their power. As a practical matter such a development is too remote to be treated seriously now or in the near future.

Had anyone suggested that Hitler's Nazism could gradually evolve into an open society tolerant of political dissent, he would rightly have been hooted down. It seemed clear that the Nazi creed could not to any meaningful degree change its essential nature. The situation is exactly parallel in the case of Soviet communism. The difference is in the fact that Western man, from the beginning, has been obsessed by the hope that Bolshevism would just go away, and the hope persists.

When Lenin introduced NEP, restoring free enterprise and private farming, the world heaved a sigh of relief. Another wave of hope was generated by Stalin's victory over Trotsky, the apostle of "permanent revolution," and the new slogan of "socialism in one country." That was eagerly accepted as a species of Soviet isolationism, the end of "world revolution." The West rallied with trade and technological aid to help Stalin industrialize. A more affluent Russia, it was argued, would inevitably become more conservative and normal: fat communists would be less dangerous than lean ones.

The wildest orgy of wishful nonsense, however, was touched off by Stalin's own "thaw" in the mid-thirties. Suddenly he was kissing babies and milkmaids for the cameras, drafting "the world's most democratic constitution," and above all seeking popular-fronts and united-fronts with anyone accessible to his charms, including the beast of prey on Wall Street. At that time the initiatives for what is today called "bridge-building" between the two worlds came from Moscow, not Washington.

Many reputable experts excitedly announced that Russia, for all its faults, was evolving in the right direction. Political pundits rushed into print with books about the emerging new Russia, communist but democratic. The record for self-delusion was established by a prominent pro-Soviet journalist who brought glad tidings in the September, 1935 issue of *Current History*. "The Bolshevik revolution," he attested, "is slowly, almost imperceptibly, abdicating. When the change to democracy is completed, the world will wonder how it happened."

The world, alas, has no chance to wonder—except about how it could have yielded so readily to the euphoria. The whole fantasy of evolution was soon enough washed out in the blood-purges and the pact of friendship with Hitler.

Yet another bout of optimism came when Nazi Germany, in contempt of the pact with Stalin, invaded Russia, driving the USSR, willy-nilly, into the democratic camp during the war. Stalin, now a certified freedom-loving ally, grateful for the unstinting American aid, surely could not revert to his totalitarian past. The "Grand Alliance" and "One World" promised a new, hopeful start with the USSR as a loyal partner in the United Nations.

But revert he did, even before the fighting was finished. Renewed euphoria had to wait for his demise and the effulgence of the "thaw" that followed, then the Spirit of Geneva and out of its ashes the Spirit of Camp David, with the wonders of de-Stalinization as climax. In every case the optimistic slogan was of Moscow coinage, worked to the limit to tranquilize and exact concessions from the world of freedom. Many of the very pro-Soviet people who had defended and glorified Stalin—and denied his excesses and crimes—now hailed his degradation and its portents for democracy.

For those tempted by the myth of liberalization, Robert Conquest, in an article in *Problems of Communism* (November–December, 1962), provided a useful check-list of ten areas in which the unchanged and unchanging nature of Stalinism is on view:

1. Most important, a self-perpetuating party bureaucracy remains completely in charge. No sharing whatever of its power with any other part of the population has taken place.
2. The peasant, in spite of minor improvements in terms of tenure, continues to be a collectivized serf.
3. The trade unions remain, in practice, simply adjuncts of the party and governmental machine. Wage decisions are still imposed on the worker.
4. The consumer, though to a lesser degree than formerly, still has to put up with low standards because of a channeling into capital goods and defense products of a proportion of the national income far higher than he would freely grant.
5. "Socialist realism" remains the official law of the arts. Truly heterodox work is still banned.
6. Control of all organs of information remains strictly a party monopoly. Foreign broadcasts are jammed. And even foreign books are admitted only as selected by cultural bureaucrats.
7. The minority nationalities continue to live under strictly centralized control from Moscow. Great purges, carried out in reprisal against an extremely mild degree of nationalism, have lately swept away the party leadership of republics from Latvia to Azerbaijan and Central Asia; the influx of Russians has led to the virtual partition of Kazakhstan.
8. Travel abroad is permitted only to a limited number of citizens.
9. The labor camp network, though much shrunken since Stalin's time, continues to function. The laws against political opposition remain draconic. . . .
10. Soviet political history, including the record of collectivization and the purges, is still taught in an entirely false and misleading fashion. So is foreign history.

The list could readily be extended. True, some of the old Stalinism is being applied less brutally, to avoid exacerbating popular and even inner-party discontents. The most significant development in post-Stalin Russia, as mentioned earlier in the chapter on Resistance, is not in the feeble ameliorations. It is in the new courage and self-respect manifest in the population, especially among youth and the intelligentsia.

The old fears and threats seem to have lost some of their power to intimidate. The regime no longer inspires as much awe as it used to. Its mystique has worn thin. Literary men and scientists write open letters of protest to the party leaders on acute issues. They dare come to the defense of persecuted colleagues, as they did in defending Sinyavsky and Daniel and in urging their release subsequently; or when the celebrated physicist Piotr Kapitza demanded that the *avant-garde* painter Alexei Anikeyenok be allowed to exhibit his works.

The college and university campuses are increasingly vibrant with daring discussion of tabooed subjects. The soul-searching under way, the hero worship of young poets who voice popular aspirations—all of it is reminiscent of generations of rebellious students in tsarist times. Fewer writers make groveling confessions of guilt when officially reprimanded. They write and occasionally succeed in publishing poems and stories and novels far outside the limits of the permissible fixed by the hierarchs. The Soviet press is deluged with letters from readers, some of them boldly signed, asking questions and making complaints.

This new mood was no part of the intentions of the regime in moderating the terror and partially disowning Stalin. The evolution it indicates is not within but *outside* the communist system, *against* the system. It is therefore more *re*volutionary than evolutionary. What is apparently "thawing" is not the regime but the self-respect and self-confidence of a new generation and a new intelligentsia, reflecting now as throughout Russian history the deepest sentiments and intuitions of the masses. The fact that the Soviet Union even today has more political prisoners than the whole non-communist world put together, underscores the political ruthlessness of the dictatorship—but also the obduracy of its subjects in fighting the ruthlessness.

Soviet communism at its half-century point is being challenged by its subjects. What this portends, as the Kremlin surely knows and fears, is not an evolutionary process but a potential of revolution. For the regime the area of maneuver and compromise is strictly limited. It cannot dilute its power monopoly without risking expulsion and extinction. And apparently it dares not use raw force again—not because it rejects all-out terror on principle but because it is uncertain of its efficacy under the new psychological conditions.

No one can guess how this historical dilemma, pregnant with destiny for Russia and the world, will be resolved. The one fixed element in the equation of forces has been well identified by Djilas: "Ideas, philosophical principles and moral considerations, the nation and the people, their history, in part even ownership—all can be changed and sacrificed. But not power. Because this would signify communism's renunciation of itself, of its own essence. Individuals can do this. But the class, the party, the oligarchy cannot. This is the purpose and meaning of its existence."

16 / Imperialism

The myth that Soviet Russia is anti-imperialist and anti-colonial.

In January, 1966, a so-called Tricontinental Solidarity Conference of Latin American, African, and Asian communists took place in Havana, Cuba, with seventy-nine Communist Parties and "liberation fronts" represented. It was largely financed by Moscow and the forty-man Soviet delegation dominated the proceedings. A message of greeting from Brezhnev for the ruling party in the USSR set the tone and the theme. "Today," it said, "Havana attracts the attention of all fighters against the forces of imperialist aggression and colonialism and for the national and social liberation of peoples. . . . The U.S. imperialists are challenging all progressive forces."

The Havana meeting was called to plan communist seizures of power in Central and South America. It produced blueprints for organization, strategy, and tactics—resting primarily on systematic terror—to achieve this purpose in a number of specified Latin American countries and one "colony": Puerto Rico. The groundwork was laid for an intensified campaign of Red imperialist aggression; a Military Directorate was set up to synchronize the offensive. And all of it was conducted under the banners of struggle against imperialism!

The sheer audacity of the show was breath-taking. Another expansionist adventure by the only active imperialism extant, disguised as "progressive" anti-imperialism! But it conformed to the propaganda pattern in international affairs laid out by the Leninists from the outset and followed by communists ever since. Its essence has been to attack the declining Western imperialism—by now more history than functioning reality—as a cover for the new, dynamic communist imperialism, the most ambitious in all history, aiming at nothing less than One Communist World—the ancient "Stop-thief!" trick on a global scale.

Communists, in speech or print, never mention the West and the United States in particular without the qualifying word "imperialist." The device is undoubtedly effective. The repetition year after year, day after day, of the same formula and its variations— "imperialist West. . . American imperialism. . . the colonial powers"—has stamped the desired stereotype on millions of minds, especially in areas where memories of colonial subjection are deep and painful.

Because it refers to an outlived era, irrelevant to the present, the stereotype is fraudulent. But it accomplishes its purpose, which is to obscure the new varieties of imperialism promoted by Moscow, Peking, and Havana. The West itself, through a sense of guilt for its past colonialism, tends to go along with the communist distortions. Thus the United States and other democratic powers supported a communist-inspired United Nations resolution demanding immediate and unconditional independence for all colonies— so formulated that it exempted communist colonies!

Great Britain, France, Holland, Belgium, Spain have dismantled their empires, retaining at most a few meaningless shreds. In some cases, indeed, they are open to blame for imposing independence prematurely on unprepared peoples. In Africa, only Portugal still clings to its ancient colonies. Dozens of new, self-ruling countries have been born. The United States has divested itself of the Philippines, and Puerto Rico has been given the right to independence for the asking.

No supremely strong nation in history has rejected the temptations of territorial aggrandizement as resolutely as the United States, or has been so slow and reluctant in assuming the obligations of world power. It has acted, perhaps too vigorously, to accelerate the dissolution of the empires of other nations, notably in India and Indonesia. Having come through two world wars as the leading military nation on earth, it hastened to demobilize and disperse its strength. That this was unwise after the second of the wars, when only communism was prepared and eager to fill the vacuums left by the collapse of fascism and Japanese empire, became apparent quickly enough.

In this context, the communist insistence that the United States and the West generally are engaged in building empires is a blatant propaganda hoax, among the biggest of the Big Lies in our lie-soaked age. The only formidable and expanding imperialism on this planet today is centered in Moscow. Some of its acquisitions, annexed by force and marked by genocidal atrocities, have been cemented into the Soviet Union. Others are mislabeled "peoples' democracies" and remain separate nations *in form*, but they are as subservient to the new imperial master, and as unconscionably exploited in his own interests, as old-style colonies.

The fact that a number of them are apparently straining at the leash (to an extent grossly exaggerated in world opinion) does not alter the colonial relationship. Colonies have strained at the leash under any type of imperial organization; proconsuls and puppets, being human, have always pressed for a little more autonomy in their sphere of rule. Even Vidkun Quisling, Hitler's creature in Norway, pressed Berlin for more autonomy. Symptoms of resistance to the Kremlin behind the Iron Curtain should not be permitted to blur the rock-bottom facts of the situation:

1. Every one of the East-Central European communist regimes has been imposed by Soviet force or threat of force, and not one of them has risked the test of free election. Though manned by local citizens, it is an instrument of colonial occupation.
2. These regimes have been kept in power solely by Moscow's military might—hurled against the people of East Germany in 1953 and Hungary in 1956, and poised for instant action elsewhere if necessary.
3. Not one of these regimes could conceivably survive without that alien might to guarantee its life.

The peoples behind the Iron Curtain have learned the sad way that they cannot count on help from the West in an attempt to throw off the Russian yoke; their rulers have learned that they *can* count on Soviet support against the people. This, on the one hand, has reduced the potential for open revolt. On the other, it has dramatized for the satellite governments *their life-and-death dependence on the power which created and installed them.* Their puppethood is therefore more complete than ever. Were they to show genuine resistance, the Soviets could bring them to heel by threatening to set them adrift to face their restive subjects alone.

No marginal improvement of conditions in a satellite country can alter these quintessential facts of dependence and subservience. Any "mellowing" in Czechoslovakia or Hungary, as in the USSR itself, does not touch the substance of the communist system. It is calculated to contain discontents, relax tensions dangerous to the rulers and offset damage done by central planning. The monopolies of political power, again as in Soviet Russia, are not affected.

Nor do conflicts of national interest among the satellites, say between Rumania and Czechoslovakia, affect their dependence on the master-state. The supposition that the puppet nations are "no longer a monolith" misstates the case. They never *were* a monolith. Domination by the USSR did not automatically wipe out either old or new ethnic, frontier, and economic quarrels, any more than membership in the British empire ruled out conflict and competition among some of the members. Imperialist powers even exploit such tensions to fortify their control, on the divide-and-rule principle. The whole "monolith" argument has been stood on its head by those seeking consolation from quarrels among the East European regimes. These would represent a greater menace to their common Soviet overlords if they *were* united.

Internally, at this writing, the processes of moderation are barely discernible in East Germany, Rumania, and Bulgaria, and making a belated appearance in Czechoslovakia. In Poland the movement is steadily in the direction of more repressions; Gomulka has been chipping away at the cultural, political, and religious concessions wrested from the dictatorship by the people through the Posnan uprising and its aftermath. Hungary, too, after a period of relative restraint, now appears to be on a more repressive course—new restrictions have been decreed; waves of arrests developed in 1965–1967; new concentration camps have been set up.

Notwithstanding the plethora of articles abroad to the contrary, the satellites remain totalitarian police-states, with swollen secret-police establishments at home and reinforcements on tap in the

USSR. The masses have not been granted the slightest participation in political life, no voice in legislation or policy-making. The press and publishing generally are state monopolies policed by censors, and religion continues to be persecuted. Citizens still stake their lives on daring attempts to escape to freedom, or use legal trips abroad as an opportunity for defection.

The masses accept such favors as the bosses dispense, press for more, and now as always look upon the communists as quislings. No matter how he may bribe them with "improvements," the Hungarian people never forget that Janos Kadar rode to power on Soviet tanks, just as the Polish people never forget that Gomulka has canceled out most of the new freedoms and all of the new hopes they won in 1956. In a book smuggled out of the country and published in Paris in 1967, the perspicacious Pole hidden under the pen name of George J. Flemming put the reality bluntly: "Poland's thirty-two million people are condemned to live with the party and the regime, but most live despite them and against them." This holds true for the great majority of the nearly one hundred million in Moscow's East European empire.

The Russian presence in the satellites is today less obtrusive, to avoid inflaming anti-Russian feelings, but it is no less real. Soviet occupation troops in both Hungary and Poland are stationed at some distance from the capitals and other large cities. But *the deepest, most pervasive presence, alien and hated, is communism itself, imposed on unwilling populations and maintained by force.*

• *Illusions of Independence*

In a recent book surveying Eastern Europe, one of the authors, Dr. Andrew Gyorgy, declares hopefully that each of the communist-captive nations "is bound eventually to turn against Russian control and shake off this latterday imperial domination as it did the Austro-Hungarian or Turkish overlordships." When we recall how long those overlordships lasted, how many wars were fought to overthrow them, the historical analogy is scarcely consoling.

But it is only a partial analogy in any event. For the peoples involved, the problem is not merely to shake off Russia, but to shake off communism. They want to be rid not only of the Russian yoke, but also of the communist harness. As the politically conscious opponents of the regimes see it, certainly, the primary advantage of national freedom is that it would enable them to drive out communism. The Soviet-installed rulers know this only too well. No matter how nationalist they pretend to be—as a device for currying favor with their subjects—sheer self-preservation compels them to stop short of actual independence. They have no impulse to suicide.

Seeming gestures of disagreement with Moscow, often made with its consent and in some cases at its instigation, have been magnified in world opinion. They generate illusions in the West (which may be their purpose)—illusions translated into more of the trade, credits, and technical aid desperately needed in the Soviet empire. At the bargain price of an occasional token disagreement with the USSR, more semblance than reality, the satellites are drawing from the West the kind of economic and political cooperation that in the aggregate fortifies the entire bloc.

There is, to put the matter mildly, room for suspicion that some of the symptoms of "independence" are in fact stratagems to beguile and disorient the non-communist world. Is Rumania's Nicolae Ceausescu, in suggesting that both the Warsaw Pact and NATO be dissolved, really "defying Moscow"? Is it not more likely that he is doing a diplomatic chore for Moscow? The end of NATO and the withdrawal of American troops from Europe have always been prime objectives of the Kremlin, which has no need for a formal Warsaw Pact to exercise control over the communist-bloc military forces.

The Western hope of weaning East Europe away from the USSR—known in its American version as "bridge-building" to the East—derives from a self-induced conviction that momentous changes are under way in the Soviet world. Curiously, that hope overlooks the one pertinent case history on record, namely American aid to Red Poland for more than a decade now. That particular bridge was built before the metaphor was adopted, according to the very blueprints now being laid out for the other Red nations, and under conditions more favorable than any that exist today in the other communist societies. The traffic on the Polish-American bridge has been strictly one-way, the American taxpayer giving and the Polish dictatorship receiving, without the courtesy of a thank-you or a diminution in hate-America propaganda.

Yet Warsaw in this period has become not less but more servile to the Kremlin and the internal "liberalization" touched off by the 1956 uprising has gone into reverse. U.S. Ambassador Jacob Beam, on leaving Warsaw in 1964, said bluntly: "The American policy of helping the Gomulka regime surmount its economic difficulties has not led to the more liberalizing evolution in Poland which could have been expected." And since 1964, the regime has become ever more repressive as against the intellectuals, youth, and the church. In short, the bridge has accomplished none of the things Washington now hopes to achieve elsewhere by the very same methods.

In the book, *Power and Impotence*, by Edmund Stillman and William Paff, the authors remark about Poland: "Indeed, one might argue that American economic aid since 1956 has had the effect of stabilizing an unpopular regime's power and slowing up the process of domestic reforms." They put their fingers on the central fallacy of the bridge-building doctrine.

The political engineers seem to be under the misapprehension that the Soviet dependencies, and the USSR itself, are panting to liberalize their national life; that our good-will and economic generosity will encourage and speed up the process. In fact the communist rulers have allowed some relaxation and undertaken some limited economic revisions with the greatest reluctance and only under the pressures of crises and discontents. They would prefer to keep things as they are. In the measure that access to free-world machinery, credits, and expertise operates to remove those pressures, it takes the heat off and strengthens the hands of party hard-liners. The effect in general is to *slow up* the change we intended to accelerate.

The West has persuaded itself, in the words of one of the main persuaders, Walter Lippmann, that the Soviet Union today is "simply another great power." The cold war, it insists, is ended or about to expire. All the evidence, however, is that the Kremlin has not retreated from its global ambitions. If anything, it is giving them renewed emphasis, with the accent on wars of liberation. Anti-Western and anti-American invective is as violent as ever. The schools for revolution in Moscow, Prague, Havana, and other Red cities are training more terrorists and guerrilla experts than ever before. Talk in official Washington of détente and accommodation have been brushed aside by Brezhnev as "a strange and persistent delusion."

To square all this with the assumption that the USSR is just another great power is a feat of mental acrobatics. What conventional national interests are served in continuing support, as a cost of billions of rubles, of far-off Cuba and of insurrectionary movements in Central and South America? Why would a normal world power invest more capital and manpower than the rest of the world combined, in radio and other species of global propaganda?

Soviet communism has relinquished none of its long-time ambitions. It fights resolutely for authority over Communist parties, undergrounds, and paramilitary formations in the entire non-communist world and—because of political turbulence within Red China—appears to have won it. There is no precedent in history of a garden-variety great power with such instrumentalities inside eighty or more other nations.

The oversized Soviet diplomatic and trade delegations in the outside world are notoriously busier with intelligence and espionage than with diplomacy and trade. On the basis of information he garnered in Paris, C. L. Sulzberger of the *New York Times* reported on June 19, 1966: "Almost half of Russia's 75 envoys to non-communist countries are affiliated with KGB or GRU [espionage services]. The present Soviet ambassador to Havana, who uses the name Alekseyev, is actually a full colonel in the KGB, named Shitov, originally sent to Cuba to organize clandestine security. Four out of five Soviet diplomats in Cameroon are intelligence agents, thirteen out of sixteen in Ethiopia, seven out of eight in Senegal." The significant fact about "Moscow policy," he added, "is that it is conceived by the Communist Party, not the Soviet government, and is largely applied by the KGB."

In the Soviet empire, East Germany's Ulbricht is a cringing puppet and Poland's Gomulka is a close second in this respect. Satellite leaders incessantly pledge and repledge their allegiance to the USSR. At a party meeting in Sofia in early 1966, virtually every speaker intoned the same formula: "The cornerstone of Bulgarian foreign policy is fraternal friendship and collaboration with the Soviet Union." Janos Kadar, the man hand-picked by the Kremlin to help crush the Hungarian revolt, at the Twenty-third Party Congress in Moscow spoke for all satellite satraps when he ridiculed those who doubted the "eternal and historically determined" unity between Hungary and the USSR, and unreservedly endorsed all

Soviet policies. His speech could not have been any stronger in its acceptance of Soviet tutelage if his Moscow superiors had written it, as perhaps they did.

• *Colonialism, Soviet Style*

Soviet imperialism, of course, departs in some ways from the older historical patterns, but hardly to the advantage of the colonial peoples. The two main differences are these:

1. Though it still maintains large Red Army forces in Poland and Hungary and could bring overwhelming force to bear on all the satellites instantly, it does not govern directly but through local communists. To that extent the colonial status is camouflaged, even as the Nazi conquest of Norway was partly camouflaged by setting up Quisling and his fifth-column government.
2. A Western imperialist power of the past was normally content to collect taxes and enforce the law, without disturbing local traditions, religion, and ways of life. But the Soviets, having taken over another nation, at once compel it to accept their communism and power structure, their ideology and rule by terror. They suppress the victim people's national traditions, culture, and preferred way of life. Domination under the new imperialism is thus more thorough and more onerous than in old-style colonies.

Communism before the war, it should be recalled, was weaker in Eastern than in Western Europe. Countries neighboring on the USSR knew more about unpleasant truths about life under communism and were less vulnerable to Red propaganda. How, for example, could they ever forget the tides of runaway Soviet peasants that spilled over their Soviet frontiers during Stalin's collectivization? In all of Estonia there were no more than three hundred communists. In Poland the communists were a small underground party. In Rumania there was one communist for every 21,000 in the population—fewer percentually than in the United States today.

The most hateful aspect of colonial captivity, for the people, was therefore the imposition of communism. They would have been more content had they been obliged to pay tribute to the conqueror (as Finland did, to escape the fate of puppethood), as under old-style imperialism.

In every one of the victim countries, communism brought economic deterioration along with its political and spiritual oppressions. The workers despise their phony labor unions. The peasants abhor socialized farming. Everywhere productivity is low and scarcity of consumer products chronic. The built-in restraints on production and efficiency have been even more apparent and harmful in relatively advanced countries than in the more primitive areas.

Before the Second World War, what is now communist East Germany produced one-third of all German motor vehicles; by now this branch of industry has been reduced to insignificance. Czechoslovakia, where the communists took over a prospering modern industrial society, withered in the new political-economic climate faster and more obviously than, let us say, Bulgaria—if only because there was so much more to wither. As socialist laboratories, the East and Central European nations have been a conspicuous loss.

Punished by the inherent faults of communism, the captive states were further penalized by the exactions of Soviet need and greed. An exiled Estonian economist, Dr. Alexander Kutt, in an analysis published in 1966 by the Assembly of Captive European Nations, showed that these countries in the ten years of 1955–1964 were forced to contribute 12.8 billion dollars to the Soviet economy. Most of this total represented Soviet overcharges on its exports, the rest underpayments for imports. This extortion, moreover, has been on a mounting scale, from 503 million dollars in 1955 to over 2.2 billion dollars in 1964.

There were of course comparable siphonings of wealth by the master-nation before the decade covered by Dr. Kutt and there have been since 1964. A few available figures for 1965 leave no margins for doubt on this score. The USSR still exacts more for crude oil exports to the satellites than it charges West European buyers; the price to Czechoslovakia, for example, was two and a half times higher than to Italy.

Some of the Kremlin's techniques of exploitation were noted by the Spanish philosopher, Salvador de Madariaga, in his book, *The Blowing Up of the Parthenon* (1960): "The Soviet Union has set up a thoroughly organized system of jointly owned firms, treaties of commerce, arbitrary price-fixing, currency manipulation and other devices whereby it is sucking the blood of the Eastern European nations as no colonial empire ever dared to do in the past." The system of joint companies, with 50 per cent of the ownership and profits assigned to the USSR, comes remarkably close to what American gangsters call "muscling in."

A ghastly light was cast on the blood-sucking operation by the recent suicide of Erich Apel, chairman of East Germany's Planning Commission and a notable figure in the communist hierarchy. Through Apel's diary, which he had sent to friends in the West page by page for two years, it was confirmed that he had fought to tamp the excessive flow of his country's economic life-blood to the Soviets. The climax came in negotiations of a 15-billion-dollar five-year trade agreement between East Germany and the USSR. "This is no trade treaty," he insisted, "but an instrument of colonial oppression."

Frustrated by his failure to limit Moscow's rapacity, Erich Apel shot himself on the day the treaty was signed. This, be it noted, was in December, 1965, when a self-hypnotized world was talking cheerfully about the "loosening of the bonds" and the impending dissolution of the Red empire.

These, we may surmise, were some of the things the Foreign Minister of Thailand, Thant Khoman, had in mind when, speaking of communism on June 14, 1966, in South Korea, he said: "The new form of colonialism is the most frightful and odious scourge of our time." He knew the realities behind the "anti-imperialist leagues" set up by Moscow through the decades, behind the endless "anti-colonial" twaddle from all communist sources.

No one doubts the earnestness of Soviet opposition to what remains of Western colonial systems. It is sparked, however, not by sympathy for the "exploited slaves" but by Moscow's determination to spread its own colonial network. Political altruism is no part of its nature. Red "anti-imperialism" has been, from Lenin's day to this, a strategic instrument, designed to undercut capitalist world stability and to clear the road for communist conquest.

• Dishonored Slogans

The appearance of Bolshevism on the world stage in 1917 was made with a dramatic flourish of anti-imperialist rhetoric and gestures. "Peace without annexations and indemnities" was the Leninist peace-cry as the First World War ground to a close. The new Soviet government loudly renounced the inheritance of the tsars' imperial loot, in foreign real estate or special rights. Non-Russian nationalities within the Russian empire were solemnly assured of the right to secede, which was written into the Soviet constitution.

In the perspective of fifty years of Bolshevik conduct, these early professions seem archaic and incredible. Very quickly the USSR reasserted all the prerogatives of empire, reclaimed every "historic right" of the old Russia, even if centuries old, and enforced Russian supremacy over the non-Russian nationalities in the Soviet Union with unlimited ferocity.

At the end of the Second World War, Soviet Russia was the only victor nation to impose large-scale annexations and indemnities, not alone on defeated enemies but on Poland, which was an ally. Moscow took over the Baltic republics (Lithuania, Latvia, and Estonia), thick slices of Polish, German, and Rumanian territory, some Finnish soil, the Carpatho-Ukrainian areas; it indemnified itself not only with some twenty billion dollars in reparations, but with hundreds of thousands of human beings carted off for slave labor in the USSR; and it extended its empire of captive peoples deep into Germany. The United States and a number of other countries have not yet recognized the absorption of the three Baltic states.

In a letter to Karl Kautsky, the Austrian socialist thinker, Friedrich Engels wrote in 1882: "The victorious proletariat can force no blessings of any kind upon any foreign nation without undermining its own victory by so doing." Soviet respect for sacred Marxist texts, however, is entirely selective. The blessings were visited on nearly a hundred million unwilling foreigners, during and after the war. The heroic resistance of Finland defeated the Soviet invaders but the peace settlement did transfer some Finnish territory to the aggressor.

The melancholy history of the immediate postwar years is too generally familiar to require detailed repetition here. Soviet duplicity and threats, compounded by Allied timidity and psychological fatigue, turned one country after another—Bulgaria, Poland, Rumania, Yugoslavia—over to Muscovite captivity. Massed Red forces on the frontiers toppled the coalition government in Czechoslovakia, adding another to the dishonor roll of captive nations. In a few, bold, carefully spaced strokes, three- and four-power occupation authority was displaced by all-Soviet domination in the eastern third of Germany and half of Berlin.

As for renunciation of tsarist conquests, it was forgotten almost as soon as it was uttered. Though the USSR had just signed the American-sponsored Kellogg Pact outlawing war, its Red Army in 1929 invaded Manchuria to nail down extraterritorial rights in the Chinese Eastern railway exacted by the monarchy. That brief but sanguinary war on China was strangely ignored by the rest of the world.

Previous servitude in the Russian empire was the Kremlin's political excuse for annexing Bessarabia, eastern Polish provinces, the Baltic countries, and various cities and territories in the Far East. It was the alibi for unsuccessful Soviet attempts to seize Armenian provinces from Turkey and special rights in northern Iran. Amid the thunder of communist "anti-imperialist" propaganda, Moscow was restoring and enlarging the old Russian empire. It has not willingly relinquished an inch of foreign soil ever held or claimed by the Romanoff dynasty.

Its spokesmen by this time dispense with ideological trimmings in a forthright old-fashioned defense of "historic Russian rights." Nikolai V. Podgorny, President of the USSR, was speaking in Khabarovsk, a city only a few miles from the Soviet-Chinese border, on June 1, 1966. "The soldiers of the Far East military district," he said, "the sailors of the Pacific fleet and our militant border guards are faithfully guarding this dynamic region, created by the hands of our forefathers and covered with the sweat and blood of our people." It might have been a minister from the Court of Nicholas II talking.

The long civil war following the Bolshevik seizure of power was in largest part a struggle to reimpose Russian dominion over the non-Russian parts of the old empire. The far-left socialist regime in Georgia (Gruzia) was crushed by the Red Army as bloodily as the reactionary far-right government in the Ukraine. In Central Asia several of the principalities held onto independence for some years after Soviet rule had been consolidated in European Russia, but were beaten down by military might in the end. The right to secede remained where it had been filed away, in the constitution.

Any reference to it today, inside the USSR, is the shortest and most certain road to a slave colony.

In the Communist Party Program of 1919, the emphasis was still on the dangers of "Russian great-nation chauvinism." In the latest version, as of 1961, it is on "bourgeois nationalism," a crime of which, as a practical matter, only non-Russian citizens can be guilty. Ukrainians, Belorussians, Azerbaijans, Kazakhs, any of the scores of non-Russian nationals seeking more rights for their local "republics" or "autonomous regions," objecting to the grosser forms of Russification, attempting to salvage a little of their own culture, have been ruthlessly silenced, purged, and murdered ever since the early 1920's.

Communists suspected or guilty of "bourgeois nationalist" agitation or sentiments, meaning a warm spot in their hearts for their own nations and histories, have been annihilated even more swiftly than non-communists. The blood-purges of the late thirties wiped out virtually all the top-echelon communists in the non-Russian areas. Similar purges on a more limited scale have been carried out, without benefit of publicity, in recent years. Whatever the fluctuations in political climate, from harsh to mellow and back, absolute control of the empire from Moscow has been undeviating.

The "equality" vouchsafed to all peoples in the USSR—to the entire "fraternal Soviet family," in the official cant phrase—is so much crass hypocrisy. In practice it has come down to rule by Kremlin appointees of their own race or nationality, and the use of their own language to propagate ideas prescribed by Moscow. Not only religious faiths but national traditions, heroes, self-esteems have been violated by the Soviet regime far more brutally than by the tsars. The monarchy had been interested primarily in exploiting these peoples, whereas the communists in addition seek to convert them.

All nations in the Soviet Union, in George Orwell's inspired formula in *Animal Farm*, are equal but the Russians are more equal. A Soviet Russian may be, indeed must be, a Russian patriot as well as a Soviet patriot, but a non-Russian citizen will be denounced and punished as a "bourgeois nationalist" if his Soviet patriotism shows too many traces of his own native patriotism. Anything in his culture that does not fit into the dominant Soviet and Russian ideologies is by definition "reactionary" and treasonable. He is expected to join enthusiastically in glorifying the entire Russian heritage and to show gratitude for the boundless blessings of Russian big-brother leadership, protection, and culture—not only in the Soviet era but from the day his people were lucky enough to have been conquered and annexed.

"Great and versatile are the merits of the Russian nation," one S. Koralev exclaimed in a Soviet magazine in 1950, "not only in respect to the other nations in the USSR, but also in regard to all mankind." "The leading place within the family of equal nations of the USSR belongs to the great Russian nation," M. P. Kareva wrote in 1952. Such random samples are typical of an ardent Russian patriotism, reconciled "dialectically" with Soviet patriotism. But it is a mix forbidden to Ukrainians, Lithuanians, Central Asians, or other national patriots. These must even condemn revered heroes of their own peoples who opposed subjugation of their respective countries by tsarist Russia, whether a hundred or three hundred years ago.

The non-Russian nationalities, in short, must pay tribute to what is always called "the first" among the "equal" tenants of the Soviet prison-house. Their communist and cultural leaders as a matter of course, as simple self-protection, acknowledge the primacy of the Russian republic and abjure any special sentiment for their own land or people. "Our elder brother, the great Russian nation"—this is the standard obeisance in all their documents and speeches and editorials.

After citing a number of humiliating examples of this kowtowing, Dr. W. W. Kulski comments: "The very fact that such acts of abjuration were deemed necessary points to the vitality of national feeling among the non-Russian nationalities." The clinching proof is in the fact that the Kremlin, even in this its fiftieth year, never desists from harping on the "dangers of bourgeois nationalism."

• *Fate of Russia's Jews*

Unique and far more tragic is the plight of the one minority without a fixed territory in the Soviet empire: the three million Jews, a race that has lived in Russia almost as many centuries as the Slavs. A moving book about their ordeal was published in the United States at the end of 1966: *The Jews of Silence*, by a young Israeli writer, Elie Wiesel, based on his visit to the USSR during the Jewish High Holy Days in 1965. He has both a keen eye and a passionate heart.

Their religion is hounded with even more zeal than the Christian and Islamic faiths. In the whole of European Russia, where most of the Jewish population is concentrated, there are only three rabbis (one each in Moscow, Leningrad, and Odessa), according to a delegation of American clergymen who visited the country in the spring of 1967. Their ancient Hebrew language proscribed, the Yiddish press and theaters that still existed in the 1930's reduced almost to nil, these millions, Wiesel found, will survive physically but are menaced by extinction as a separate people and culture. "Cry out, cry out until you have no more strength to cry," is his summary of what Soviet Jews begged him to tell the world. "You must enlist public opinion, you must turn to those with influence, you must involve the governments—the hour is late."

Under the tsars the Jews were third-rate citizens confined to The Pale, delimited zones in western Russia. They suffered degradations without number and occasionally were victims of massacres or pogroms, usually instigated by the government. But they had the consolations of their religion, their own schools and community institutions. Despite persecution and grinding poverty, the Jews developed a rich and distinctive literature and culture of their own. Except in military and tax matters, their communities exercised local autonomy. They were not deterred from espousing Zionism or from emigrating—several million of them migrated to the United States in the last decades of the nineteenth century and the first of this century.

Non-Russians, being the most oppressed, inevitably and understandably were attracted most strongly by revolutionary hope and organization. This was true of the Ukrainians, Poles, Georgians, Armenians, and Moslems. But the Jews especially, as the most discriminated against, played roles beyond their numbers in the population not only in the Bolshevik but in Menshevik and other more moderate groupings.

As a result, non-Russians were conspicuous in the Soviet leadership, particularly in the early years. Trotsky and Zinoviev were Jews, Stalin was a Georgian, Mikoyan is an Armenian. Most of them, in their times of revolutionary zeal, considered themselves internationalists, citizens of the One Communist World to be.

This was especially true of the Jews, for some of whom communism seemed also an escape from the alienation and penalties of race and religion.

The prominence of a handful of Jews in the communist hierarchy proved to be a misfortune for all Russian Jews, who in large measure became scapegoats in the mass revulsions against the crimes of communism. Anti-Semitism had always been deep-rooted in Russia, in particular in the Ukraine and the Polish provinces. Now, as popular hatred of the Red regime deepened, much of it was turned irrationally against the Jews. I recall trying, and failing, to convince my simple-minded peasant house-worker that Lenin and Stalin were not Jews: to her they were hateful communists, and therefore Jews. This stupidity was so widespread, in fact, that until the rise of Hitler the Kremlin conducted campaigns against anti-Semitism, correctly identifying it as an indirect expression of anti-regime sentiment.

Somewhere along the line, however, Stalin apparently decided to join the anti-Semitic tide instead of fighting it. His inborn anti-Semitism had been exacerbated by the bitter struggle with Trotsky and his chief associates, many of them also Jews. He came to abhor intellectuals in general and Jewish intellectuals in particular. His alliance with Hitler was marked by the immediate expulsion of virtually all Jews from high office in the diplomatic and military services and from the higher reaches in the Soviet elites generally. Essentially this condition still prevails.

After the defeat of Nazi Germany, Stalin took over the vanquished Hitler's anti-Semitism along with other German reparations. Disguising it as a campaign against "cosmopolitans," "rootless persons," and other euphemisms for Jews, the Kremlin systematically demoted or purged Jews from sensitive positions in government, the party, education, science, and culture. (There were and there remain enough exceptions to sow confusion on the thorny issue—men like Lazar Kaganovich in the Kremlin, Ilya Ehrenburg in journalism, Yevsei Liberman in economics.) Military, diplomatic, and other elite schools excluded Jews altogether, and the universities fixed narrow quotas for admission of Jewish students.

This was one area in which the death of Stalin produced not even the illusion of a new moderation. Khrushchev made little effort to conceal his notorious personal anti-Semitism. He retained all the Stalinist restrictions on the race. His drive against "underground capitalism" gave him a welcome opportunity to pillory Jews by underlining their complicity in illegal private trade. In 1964, a book called *Judaism without Embellishment,* by one Trofim Kichko, as foul a concoction as anything produced by Julius Streicher in Hitler Germany, was published and widely distributed in the Ukraine; in a country where publishing and distribution are carefully guarded government monopolies, the regime could not easily disown responsibility.

Any expression of sympathy for Zionism or Israel continues to be treated as counterrevolution. In the Stalinist decades alleged Zionism put thousands of Jews into concentration camps, where some of them no doubt still languish. It can still bring long terms of exile in "corrective labor colonies." Even in East European communist countries, there are Jewish schools and theaters, newspapers and communal organizations, but not in Soviet Russia, with more Jewish population than in its entire European bloc.

The Kremlin appears committed, at this time, "to deprive corporate Jewish life of the means to preserve its collective existence and the denial to individual Jews of any opportunity to learn the meaning of their Jewish identity." The quotation is from an analysis of the subject by the American Jewish Congress published in December, 1966. The Yiddish-American novelist, I. B. Singer, in reviewing the Elie Wiesel book in the *New York Times,* added up the facts:

"They clearly show that the aim of the Soviet leadership is once and for all to root out Jewishness: to make their Jews forget Hebrew, Yiddish, Jewish literature and their religious and cultural heritage—an effort in which no one has succeeded in the two thousand years of Jewish exile."

Third-rate citizens under the Romanoffs, the Jews are at best second-rate citizens under communism. It makes nor more communist logic than it made tsarist logic. Now, as then, it is mindless race prejudice.

The assumptions behind the American doctrine of "building bridges" to communist governments, in particular the belief that the cold war is over or expiring, were rudely shaken up by the Mideast crisis in May-June, 1967. "Lyndon's bridges falling down," some Washingtonians quipped. Even the *New York Times,* so ardent in its zeal for accommodation, editorially decried the "adventurism" of the USSR. "The theory that the Soviet Union no longer would risk involvement in a conventional war," it sadly conceded, "must now be revised, along with all the illusions about the possibility of détente."

The beleaguerment of Israel by Arab nations equipped with billions of dollars' worth of Soviet arms could not have taken place without Kremlin consent and encouragement. In the aftermath of the Israeli victory, Moscow disdained concealment and prudence in its drive to retrieve dominance in the area. At once it began to rearm the losers for another try, while mounting a diplomatic offensive against the victor. Premier Kosygin, in the United Nations and in his talks with President Johnson, was grimly unyielding. Soviet militancy in naked pursuit of imperialist purposes was again in the open.

With respect to the cold war, Kenneth Crawford of *Newsweek* wrote: "The Middle East has dashed ice water in the world's face, banishing in an instant the stupor of illusion so long fostered by the wishful and the woolly." Returning from a meeting of the International Labor Organization, at which he met many Soviet delegates, Representative John Ashbrook of Ohio could report: "At all levels of talk, the communist leaders are proving that the administration's talk of peaceful co-existence and accommodation is a subject of contempt and ridicule. . . . Never have they withdrawn from their determination to dominate the world."

To sum up: In terms of the number of non-Russian countries and ethnic minorities directly and indirectly under its iron dominion, Soviet Russia is today incomparably the largest empire in the world. It is the only one (except for other communists) actively and unswervingly committed to world hegemony and engaged in expanding that empire. Its pretensions to leadership in the "liberation" of colonial and semi-colonial peoples—in roughly the sense that Red soldiers liberated watches and fountain-pens in defeated countries after the war—are insulting to the intelligence of humankind.

17 / War and Peace

The myth that Soviet Russia has been a champion of world peace.

Soviet Russia's self-image throughout its long life has been of a country encircled by predatory enemies poised to strike. Its domestic and export propaganda alike assumed imminent assault by "capitalist imperialism" and was designed to frustrate the plotted aggressions. The Kremlin has seen itself, with a Dostoievskian touch, as the injured and insulted party, cornered and badgered by "war-mongers" about to wreck its world-liberating mission.

Yet from the end of its civil war period to date, the Soviet Union has been attacked *only once*, in June 1941, and that by another totalitarian nation in the midst of a war they had launched in partnership twenty-two months earlier. And on that occasion the "imperialist West," identified always as the obsessed enemy of the "socialist fatherland," rallied at once to its defense, unreservedly and without seeking any *quid pro quo*.

In its every other involvement in war, directly or by proxy, Moscow has been the instigator and aggressor.

While the civil war was still under way, in 1920, Lenin rejected the peace offered by Poland on favorable territorial terms. He chose instead to "break the crust of Polish resistance with the bayonets of the Red Army." The Soviet pursuing forces reached the outskirts of Warsaw, where they were decisively thrown back.

Meanwhile independent governments had been set up in the largest non-Russian nations of the old Russian empire, the Ukraine and Georgia. They were officially recognized by the Kremlin, which negotiated diplomatic and consular relations with Georgia and a formal alliance with the Ukraine. Then the Red Army proceeded to crush them both. Soon thereafter the new Moscow masters, through subversion backed by Soviet troops, imposed a communist regime on Outer Mongolia, where they did not have even the excuse of prior Russian possession.

Thus the pattern of military dynamism was set early, and it has been followed consistently. As yet weak and in need of time to consolidate its rule, the Kremlin understandably agitated for peace, while using every opportunity that arose for aggrandizement by force or the threat of force.

The Red Army invaded Manchuria and defeated China in 1928–1929. From 1925 to 1937 it negotiated a series of non-aggression pacts, each of them stage-managed to enhance its reputation as a peace-loving neighbor. In due time it swept them aside without notice or alibi.

Without Soviet communist help, it should be remembered, Nazism probably would not have come to power in Germany, after which it was a Moscow-Berlin deal for dividing the spoils that touched off history's most devastating war.

On the authority of a secret clause in the Moscow-Berlin pact of collaboration, Soviet Russia invaded Poland, Lithuania, Latvia, Estonia, and Finland. Following the Allied victory, Soviet forces of occupation were converted into forces of permanent imperial domination throughout East-Central Europe.

The Kremlin deliberately engaged in indirect aggression by provoking and supporting civil wars in northern Iran and in Greece in the immediate postwar years. In 1950, it instigated the war of aggression against South Korea, together with Red China (at that time still under Moscow influence), and later in that decade communist attempts to seize power in the Middle East. Then, by the secret installation of Soviet nuclear weapons in Cuba, it brought the world to the brink of its first nuclear showdown. Every Western defensive reaction to these forays—the Truman Doctrine, NATO, the Korean War, the Eisenhower Doctrine, President Kennedy's insistence on the removal of the missles from Cuba —was damned by Moscow as offensive "war-mongering."

Coincident with such overt Soviet blows to peace, the USSR nurtured a climate of crowding dangers. Repeatedly it mounted "crises" in West Berlin. With scores of vetoes it virtually paralyzed the peace-keeping functions of the United Nations, refused to abide by U.N. decisions that did not suit Soviet purposes, and stymied nearly every hopeful effort for arms reduction and control of nuclear force, by the U.N. or in bilateral negotiations with the United States. Meanwhile its persistent bad faith in violating treaties and pledges sowed fears and suspicions that further deepened the climate of crisis and accelerated the arms race.

"The simple fact," Professor Strausz-Hupé has written, "is that the Soviet conflict managers have either instigated or aggravated almost every international dispute which has gripped the postwar world." Through it all, however, Soviet communism and its foreign extensions have held fast to the legend that Soviet Russia is a peace-loving, law-abiding nation "threatened" by "bourgeois madmen." Rarely has the primacy of theory over fact been more strikingly demonstrated. No matter how often and anxiously the democratic powers pleaded for détente and a "world of diversity," the communists professed to see only a West "lusting" for war.

The theory, basic to Marxism-Leninism, is that class war within nations and between nations is a permanent and irreconcilable condition. "World imperialism cannot live side by side with a victorious Soviet Union," said Lenin, and his successors and disciples without exception have played variations on that theme. Not once in these fifty years has a Soviet leader conceded the possibility of a permanent settlement short of total communist victory.

From their doctrinal vantage point, the major democratic nations, at times when their military superiority was overwhelming, should have made war on their sworn enemy. In failing to do so— worse, in aiding the survival and economic fortification of the Soviet state—they were behaving eccentrically, in stubborn defiance of Marxist-Leninist laws. But the refusal of the other side to play the game as prescribed did not affect Soviet faith in their doctrine. Massive propaganda against the theoretical war-makers never ceased, along with prodigious world-wide "peace campaigns."

The Bolsheviks did not originate the ploy of accusing the enemy of what you are yourself about to do—it is as old as history. But never has any nation used it so often and so effectively. While proudly proclaiming permanent war against the non-communist world and precluding compromise, the communists have posed as champions of peace beleaguered by ruthless enemies. In the light of their fifty-year record of aggressions, and in the light of their force-oriented philosophy and program, only the blind can fail to see the pose as a cynical hoax. Peace, for communists, is not a humane objective but a slogan of expediency—a propaganda "ruse," to use Lenin's word.

It is a measure of mankind's yearning for peace that millions at various times have fallen for the rawest Soviet trickery in its name. It did not occur to them that a regime which killed millions of its own citizens, engaged in kidnapping people in foreign countries, tried to starve West Berlin into submission, trained and equipped thousands of terrorists for operations all over the world—that such a regime could hardly be opposed to war on principle.

In the lexicon of communists, of course, peace has nothing in common with idealistic or religious pacifism, which they have always ridiculed and despised. Their literature candidly describes peace as a continuation of war by other means, while gearing for the violent conflict to follow. They have employed the potentials of peace slogans for specific purposes of their own: to gain time or to terrify their own subjects with a spectre of war; to mobilize sympathizers and innocents, including true pacifists, for "defense of the Soviet Union." Their slogans are never directed against war as such, but only against wars that might endanger the USSR. Indeed they always specify support for "just" wars, so-called wars of liberation—in fact, those conflicts provoked or approved by communists.

• *Road to Surrender*

Karl Marx taught that "war is the midwife of revolution"; that "the last word of social science on the eve of each general reconstruction of society will always remain: 'struggle or death, bloody war or nothingness.' "

Lenin concurred. "Great historical questions can be solved only by violence," he declared.

Mao Tse-tung has written: "Every communist must grasp that political power grows out of the barrel of a gun. . . . In fact, we can say that the whole world can be remolded only with a gun."

No communist leader or theoretician, past or present, has questioned that conflict, violence, war are inherent in their ideology.

On the contrary, "militancy" is a matter of revolutionary pride and honor. They think and plan in the vernacular of struggle: strategy and tactics, fronts, enemies, encirclements.

This does not imply that they seek war on their own soil. Naturally the Soviet Union and its associates would like to achieve their "inevitable victory," One Communist World, with the least risk and at the smallest price to themselves. Hence they prefer proxy wars, civil wars, and best of all, capitulation to communism without resistance. To avoid the costs of direct confrontation with powerful adversaries and its potential of defeat—*this is the whole content and meaning of their peace propaganda.*

Nikita Khrushchev, whose reign coincided with the recognition of his country as the second largest nuclear power, was explicit in this connection. An apocalyptic world war, though likely, was no longer inevitable, he announced. The capitalists now had a choice of non-violent "transition to socialism." Whether violence will be necessary, he explained again and again, "depends on the resistance of the exploiters: If the ruling classes counter revolution with force and are unwilling to bow to the will of the people, the proletariat must break their resistance and start a resolute civil war."

But their ultimate defeat and submission being historically predetermined anyhow, the non-communist countries would be "mad" to turn down Moscow's "peaceable" offer to accept unconditional surrender. On a vast historical scale he was merely repeating the age-old challenge of highwaymen: "Money or your life!" He pointed to Czechoslovakia, with a straight face, as an apt example of the kind of peaceful surrender he had in view.

Actually there was nothing novel in the Khrushchevian proposal, hailed so happily by the West. Lenin, too, gladly accepted surrender without battle from non-Russian peoples too weak or disorganized to resist the Red Army. Stalin, too, preferred the "peaceful" capitulation by the Baltic republics to the firm resistance he met in Finland. If Lenin and Stalin did not offer to the major nations the privilege of submission without fighting, it was only because the Soviet power position was still too weak. Unlike Khrushchev and his successors, armed with the ultimate weapon, they could not have hoped to obtain by threats more than the piecemeal concessions that they did exact.

There has been no significant change in communist conflict

theories, strategy, and goals. The only new element in the equation is nuclear power. The Kremlin can now hope to soften and intimidate a world demoralized by dread of nuclear annihilation and willing to pay a high price to evade the catastrophe.

That hope is not as farfetched as it may seem at first blush. Thousands of men and women in the free world, with the nonagenarian Lord Bertrand Russell as their chief ideologist, have in fact already resigned themselves to peaceful surrender, under the rubric, "Better Red than Dead." They are exhorting the world to hand over its money—their freedom and independence—to the highwaymen in exchange for life. Fortunately they are still a small if noisy minority. But Soviet leaders have nothing to lose by continuing to dangle their invitation to surrender before the eyes of a disoriented humanity. At the least they can count on extorting concessions, accommodations, economic aid, more leeway for their legions of subversion around the world.

What Moscow has opened is a *road to surrender*. Astonishingly, it has been mistaken by a broad segment of world opinion, led by reputable statesmen and Kremlinologists, as a *road to peace*. They have read their own hopes into communist double-talk about peaceful transitions to socialism, and especially into the renewed and refurbished Stalinist slogan, more than forty years old, of "peaceful coexistence." It is a propaganda gambit that is in truth, as the communists themselves have endlessly told us, a rededication to conquest and victory under the new conditions of a "balance of terror." But wishful thinking usually finds what it seeks; in this case, evidence of "mellowing" and "fundamental transformation."

• Peace Campaigns

"Peace campaigns" have been standard weapons in the communist arsenal of political and psychological warfare. No sane comrade anywhere has taken them literally. To guard them against the marginal chance of such delusion, the Communist International at a Moscow Congress in 1928 spelled it out for the faithful: "The peace policy of the proletarian state certainly does not imply that the Soviet state has become reconciled with capitalism. . . . It is merely another, and under present conditions, *a more advantageous, form of fighting capitalism*."

I have underlined the key words because they are pertinent to the present Kremlin policies. Thirty-three years later another world conclave of Communist parties in Moscow would say: "Peaceful coexistence . . . is a form of class struggle between socialism and capitalism. In conditions of peaceful coexistence favorable opportunities are provided for the development of the class struggle in the capitalist countries and the national liberation movement of the peoples of the colonial and dependent countries."

Moscow thus rates good marks for consistency. Always the objectives of its peace drives have been, not peace, but tactical advantage for its revolutionary wars. Always they have been couched in the bellicose language of "unmasking aggressors . . . delivering death-blows . . . crushing enemies." Always they have been devices for unlimited hate-mongering against the putative enemies of peace at a given time: Western imperialists, fascist beasts, social fascists (Aesopian for liberals and non-communist socialists), the United States, and so on.

Space permits no more than a summary panoramic view of the phenomenon. The Anti-Imperialist League of the mid-twenties evolved into the World Congress Against War in Amsterdam in 1932, which planted anti-war leagues, committees, congresses in nearly all countries, each of them with false-fronts of famous names behind which communists pulled the strings, wrote the manifestoes, and recruited innocents for purposes beyond their comprehension. Then Stalin made his deal with Hitler and all the movements were washed out.

Deserted by the string-pullers, the millions in many countries who had for years been engaged in what they supposed was a crusade for peace were left bewildered and humiliated. But they had learned nothing from the debacle. A few years after the war they, or others like them, were ready for the next round of ardent self-deception, started by Stalin and continued by his heirs.

There was the Congress of Intellectuals for Peace in Wroclaw, Poland, in 1948, the Cultural and Scientific Congress for World Peace in New York a year later, then a World Peace Council presiding over an array of national peace organizations. The great enterprise, first called Peace Partisans and then the World Peace Movement, was climaxed by the Stockholm Appeal in 1950, and the clamorous ingathering of signatures to a petition for outlawing the atom bomb—the American quota was five million names. Whether 400 million people did in fact sign, as the managers claimed, became an academic question. The whole gargantuan project faded away after Soviet Russia had stockpiled enough nuclear force to dispense with the anti-atom comedy.

It was quite a show while it lasted. Those who refused to join the parade were castigated throughout the world as "war-mongers" and "enemies of peace." They included "the old hangman Churchill" and that "Labourite cannibal" Prime Minister Attlee. In Norway, where the appeal was headquartered, 109 writers, in rejecting Ilya Ehrenburg's invitation to sign, noted that he "did not find on his five-page letter a single space to mention at least once the word peace." The works of the British novelist J. B. Priestley and others who snubbed the Stockholm Appeal were proscribed in Russia.

The appeal and its ancillary documents, those who bothered to read before signing would have seen, were crudely anti-American and pro-Soviet. The only palpable threat to the peace as the movement got started was posed by the Soviet blockade of West Berlin. At the height of the campaign, in June, 1950, the communist aggression was unleashed in Korea. But common sense had no role in the hysterical world-wide denunciations of "American warmongers." The top-echelon American communist leader, Gus Hall, was crying out against "murderous aggression by the profit-greedy, war-mad Wall Street monopolists."

The premise was that Americans were hell-bent for war—but no one explained why the United States, since it still had a virtual monopoly of the atom bomb, hadn't already attacked. Nor did anyone explain, though the question was pressed by critics, why the appeal was limited to the bomb, with nary a word about reducing or outlawing armies—the largest of which happened to be the Red Army. The absolute Moscow control of what was the largest "peace" crusade in history was confirmed by the instant expulsion of Yugoslavia from the World Peace Movement as soon as Stalin excommunicated Tito.

In the United States the sham peace movement was a conspicuous feature of the 1930's, remembered as the Red Decade. It took the form, around 1933, of a League Against War and Fascism, directed primarily against the United States itself. Stalin was then neck-deep in trouble, his tormented land beset by famine and all-embracing discontents; the Nazis were gaining strength in Germany; Japan was massing its forces on the Soviet-Manchurian frontiers. According to his Marxist logic this was the time when "Western imperialists" would attack him. By the simple device of labeling them "fascists," he planned to channel Western anti-fascist feelings against the great democracies.

Although the communist initiative and control was quite open, the word "peace" worked its magic. Thousands of individuals and scores of organizations—political, religious, social, trade-union, cultural—quickly made common cause with the known communist fronts in the sprawling league. Conventional pacifist groups joined up. Eventually even some Young Democrats and Young Republicans, through association with the American Youth Congress, entered this Red catch-all. The ten-point program of the league was geared to cripple American defense efforts, propagandize against preparedness, sabotage war industries, and infiltrate the armed forces.

But in a few years Stalin decided that the "main danger" was not from the democracies after all. The anti-communist Berlin-Rome-Tokyo Axis had come into being. In 1934, the USSR joined what it had long castigated as the "imperialist" League of Nations, and the people's-front period took shape. In the United States, communism by 1936 was redefined as "Twentieth-Century Americanism." Accordingly the League Against War and Fascism was rechristened, more positively, as the League for Peace and Democracy.

The members and affiliates may not have added up to seven and a half millions, as the league officials claimed; they came to several millions in any case. But they were consulted neither about the revised name nor the revised program—suddenly switched by 180 degrees. Now they assailed the West for its complacent moods in the face of the rising fascist dangers and the United States in particular for neglecting military preparedness and failing to react with force to the Japanese invasion of Manchuria and China. In the retrospect of history there is grim humor in the fact that one of the new slogans was "Hands off Poland!" "It will be necessary to clear away all remnants of the pacifist rubbish of opposing war by surrender to the war-makers!" Earl Browder, then the American party leader, thundered, and the pacifist outfits in his league applauded that sentiment.

The league, brightest star in the vast constellation of communist fronts, was at the peak of its activity and influence when the mortal blow descended. Within a few months after Moscow and Berlin announced their pact of friendship, the gigantic peace crusade was arbitrarily liquidated by decision of a few communist agents. The next orgy of peace-mongering for the Kremlin did not come until the late 1940's. But in America at least, it is pleasant to record, it never quite attained the dimensions of its Red Decade forebears.

It is not an accident, as communists phrase such matters, that the overall effect of the assorted peace campaigns generated by Moscow through forty years has been to aggravate the fears and suspicions of their time. Far from relaxing tensions, they deepened distrust and hatred of the alleged enemies, while rallying support for the Soviet side. Under the spurious flags of peace, they have therefore promoted what amounted to mobilizations for war. (How genuine pacifists could go along with the bogus campaigns surpassed understanding, but go along many of them did.)

In terms of their true, as distinct from professed, objectives, the drives have been successful. Inside Soviet Russia, by spreading fear of imminent war, they served to explain and justify difficulties, intensified exploitation, and stepped-up terror. In the rest of the world they served to identify the concepts of communism and peace in the public mind, at the same time dividing opinion and undercutting national patriotism.

18 / Peaceful Coexistence

The myth that the coexistence slogan means what it says.

Whatever the main theme of a Soviet peace campaign, an almost constant sub-theme has been peaceful coexistence.

The idea, sparked by Lenin, was frequently reiterated by Stalin. The German ambassador to Moscow, Count von Schulenberg, has recorded that Foreign Minister Molotov told him reassuringly in August, 1939, at the time the infamous Pact was being negotiated: "The principle of peaceful coexistence of different political regimes is a principle long established in the foreign policy of the USSR." But the apotheosis of the principle came in the reign of Khrushchev, when it was promoted from a lowly "tactic" to a primary "strategy." In communist conflict management the distinction is vital.

The Twentieth Party Congress, it should be recalled, met in early 1956, about half a year after the Geneva Summit Conference, where the Western nations projected and the Soviet delegation accepted the concept of a "balance of terror." With direct war thus ruled out for the foreseeable future, the Kremlin saw its hands untied for other varieties of conflict.

Khrushchev's enthusiasm for the exciting horizons was overshadowed in the world press by his "secret speech" against Stalin, but it is in the record. Cutting through the glutinous communist prose, what he said was: 1. That revolutionary history was entering its final phase, "the transition from capitalism to socialism on a world-wide scale." 2. That the communists were moving from the *defensive* to the *offensive*. 3. That the final showdown with "imperialism" must be put off as long as possible, hence peaceful coexistence. 4. That the interval of stalemate must be utilized for indirect attack, through the weaker nations and colonial areas.

The essence of the new strategy, as molded in the following years, was decidedly not a truce, but a reaffirmation of revolutionary goals and methods. This was not understood by a world yearning for normalcy. Year after year, Khrushchev and his associates have tried to set us straight, but with only indifferent success. They have even charged that our refusal to understand was deliberate, intended to blur the Kremlin's true revolutionary image. Whether or not the capitalists understand it, however, the communists promised to attack, attack, attack.

In the course of a visit to Hungary in 1958, Khrushchev said: "We have always declared and declare now that we do not want war, but we do not renounce class war. . . . Capitalism is at its ebb, heading for collapse. This does not mean that it is already lying down with its legs stretched out. Much work has yet to be done to bring about such a state." Peaceful coexistence, as he saw it, by providing insurance against a major war, opened dazzling opportunities for activating that "work."

He put the whole issue crudely but frankly at another time: "We must realize that we cannot coexist eternally. One of us must go to the grave. We do not want to go to the grave. They do not want to go to their grave either. So what can be done? We must push them to their grave."

An analysis of the strategy behind the Soviet slogan was made in 1960 for a Congressional committee by the Foreign Policy Institute of the University of Pennsylvania. In his address to the Supreme Soviet in October, 1959, it said, Khrushchev wanted all communists to understand "that his peaceful coexistence policy is based on hard calculations of winning vital advantage in the struggle with the West, and not any softening of either the heart or the ideology"—that the game is to be played by the old rule for the same ends that Lenin had laid down.

Khrushchev's policy has been taken over intact by the new bosses. Brezhnev made this clear at the Party Congress in the spring of 1966. The Soviet Union, he emphasized, regards peaceful coexistence "as a form of class struggle between socialism and capitalism." The capitalists, he went on, "will never give up their power of their own free will. It is only through tenacious class struggle that the working class and the rest of the working people will achieve victory. . . . Naturally there can be no peaceful coexistence where internal processes of class and national liberation struggle in the capitalist countries or colonies are concerned."

This was standard for all communist exegesis on the strategy of peaceful coexistence from 1956 forward. There would be no ideological truce, Khrushchev had said during his American visit—not "until shrimps learned to whistle." But ideological warfare, to communists, is not a philosophical debate. It means action.

In a militant speech on January 6, 1961—the famous speech which President Kennedy, according to the *New York Times,* called "a Red blueprint for eventual world domination"—Khrushchev again addressed himself to the core of the new strategy. "The policy of peaceful coexistence, as regards its social content," he said, "is a form of intense economic, political and ideological struggle of the proletariat against the aggressive forces of imperialism in the international arena." There will be more and more uprisings "against rotten reactionary regimes, against the colonizers," he promised. "The communists fully support such just wars and march in the front ranks with the peoples waging liberation struggles."

On July 14, 1963—while American and British delegates were in the Soviet capital in connection with the nuclear test-ban treaty —the Moscow press tried to tell them the facts of international life in the wondrous era of peaceful existence. "We fully stand for the destruction of imperialism and capitalism," it said. "We not only believe in the inevitable destruction of capitalism but we are doing everything for this to be accomplished as soon as possible."

Writing in the October, 1965 issue of the *World Marxist Review,* the Kremlin's American gauleiter, Gus Hall, also put the matter clearly enough: "The policy of peaceful coexistence . . . has never been a policy based on the acceptance of the *status quo* in world relations. It has been and remains a weapon of struggle—a struggle in which both hands are used. With one hand, the aggressive forces of world imperialism and world war are held back; with the other, full support is given to the forces fighting for national independence and to the peoples moving toward a socialist goal."

A few more verbatim quotations, all drawn from communist leaders and publicists in the 1960's, leave no margins for doubt that the policy at its core is one of intensified and more self-confident belligerency:

> Some try to reduce the notion of peaceful coexistence to the renunciation of war. But peace and peaceful coexistence are not one and the same thing.

> In the past, peaceful coexistence has been understood and at least tacitly implemented as a respect for the *status quo*, which means: what is controlled by the West must remain under Western control. . . . We cannot accept this kind of interpretation.

> Peaceful coexistence . . . is certainly not a passive process . . . but an active and intense struggle, in the course of which socialism irresistibly attacks, while capitalism suffers one defeat after another.

> Peaceful coexistence not only does not exclude the class struggle but is itself a form of the class struggle between victorious socialism and decrepit capitalism on the world scene, a sharp and irreconcilable struggle, the final outcome of which will be the triumph of communism throughout the entire world.

> The class struggle . . . cannot be dissolved by international agreement. For this struggle to cease, the causes eliciting it must be eliminated, *i.e.* capitalism must be liquidated.

One communist writer described the new strategy as "a well-thought-out and well-founded policy to bring us victory over imperialism." A Soviet ideologue named Melnikov underlined that "peaceful coexistence is directed toward making social progress and accelerating the inevitable collapse of imperialism." The authors of a Czechoslovak book asserted bluntly: "*Peaceful coexistence means maximum support to the oppressed nations, including arms.*"

In Moscow, on September 7, 1966, one Y. Arbatov wrote: "The various forms of direct aid by socialist countries to the revolutionary movement—that is to say, armed intervention—are by no means excluded." A few weeks later, on September 30, a party theoretician, Professor M. Rozental, made the same point: "Where no other possibility exists to smash the obstacles which stand in the way of the gathering forces of socialist change except by force of arms, a Marxist party will follow this path with all determination, boldly raising the banner of armed insurrection at the opportune moment."

This repeated stress on armed help and armed insurrection in both top newspapers in a single month, Arbatov in *Izvestia* and Rozental in *Pravda*, was significant. In Moscow such things are planned. No doubt it was intended to impress the outside world with the Kremlin's combative spirit; but the great democracies were far too busy building the bridges of détente to pay any attention.

In the euphoric mood generated abroad by the de-Stalinization ploy, it is forgotten that in downgrading Stalin, his inheritors upgraded Lenin, today the main mentor for Kremlin policy. And if Lenin was unambiguous on one precept it was his certainty that there can be no peaceable solution of relations with the non-communist world. "As long as capitalism and socialism exist, we cannot live in peace," he said. "In the end, one or the other will triumph—a funeral dirge will be sung over the Soviet republic or over world capitalism." Also: "The existence of the Soviet republic side by side with imperialist states for a long time is unthinkable. One or the other must triumph in the end. And before that end supervenes, a series of frightful collisions between the Soviet republic and the bourgeois states will be inevitable."

• Decades of Aggressions

Plainly, peaceful coexistence *à la* Kremlin holds no encouragement for those who profess to foresee a viable détente between the two worlds. The era of coexistence, taking 1956 as the starting point, has been far from peaceful. It compasses the Soviet bloodbath in Hungary, a series of Moscow-managed crises in the Middle East, installation of Soviet missiles in Cuba, Soviet arming of the Simbas for Congo rebellion, the Kremlin-led Tricontinental Conference in Havana and the subsequent terrorist activities in Latin America by the Military Directorate there set up. On May 21, 1967, *Pravda* pinpointed the targets of the moment, promising support to the "Armed Forces of Liberation" in Guatamala, Venezuela, and Colombia, as well as guerrillas in Peru, Haiti, and Paraguay. It has been an era of undiminished communist hate propaganda against the West and especially the United States.

Peaceful coexistence, moreover, has not deterred nuclear bomb-rattling by the Kremlin. Few countries have been spared its threats of attack. Between 1956 and the end of 1960, according to General C. P. Cabell, then deputy director of the CIA, Soviet leaders "have on more than forty occasions threatened fifteen countries with destruction by rockets with nuclear warheads." The list grew a lot longer in the following years.

Boasting of the first manned satellite flights, in a speech on December 9, 1961, as reported by Tass, Khrushchev added: "If we could send up Yuri Gagarin and Gherman Titov, we could of course send up other payloads and land them wherever we wanted." His nuclear blackmail continued so persistently that the *U.S. News & World Report* could put this headline on a round-up story: "Is Khrushchev 'Dr. Strangelove'?"

To equate all of this with a new, more pacific mood calls for exceptional powers of self-deception. But many, too many, have shown themselves equal to the challenge. For nearly half a century, as already noted, every verbal shift in the Moscow "line" has produced a new mirage of optimism in the desert of free-world fears. Recently Bertram D. Wolfe made a partial compendium of these hopes, every one which in turn proved false:

> Each maneuver and slogan has been greeted as the long-awaited "fundamental transformation"; "the sobering that comes from the responsible exercise of power over a great nation"; the "response to the pressure of reality"; the modification of totalitarian power by the growth of a "rationalist technocracy"; the "sobering effect of privilege upon a new privileged class"; a "feeling of national responsibility to Russia as against the aim of World Revolution"; "the quiet digestion period of a sated beast of prey" no longer on the hunt; the "diffusion of authority which could lead to a constitutional despotism"; the "mellowing process that sooner or later overtakes all militant movements"; the "sober second thoughts" which have come at long last "from a recognition of the universal and mutual destructiveness of nuclear war"; the "erosion" or even "the *end* of ideology."

Each of the opinions in quotation marks, Mr. Wolfe pointed out, came not from amateurs but "from the writings of some highly respected specialist in Russian history and Soviet affairs." To his compilation I would add one of my own favorites to this fascinating record of Western wishful thinking. As the Geneva Summit Conference approached in July 1955, R. A. Butler, then

Britain's Chancellor of the Exchequer, declared: "There is in the international scene today a feeling of spring after a long winter of discontent." It proved to be, alas, one of the shortest political springs on record.

Despite Soviet candor about its real revolutionary and violent content, peaceful coexistence has produced its own rose-tinted mirages. Perhaps the most fantastic is the theory of "convergence," advanced in all seriousness, according to which Soviet totalitarianism and our open societies are moving toward a middle ground of idyllic cooperation.

The theory has moved the communists to both laughter and fury. A typical comment, by one A. Solodnikov in *International Affairs:* "The concept of a future in which capitalism and communism will 'converge' on an 'equal footing' is utopian through and through. . . . Life will always *smash* the advocates of ideological compromises and their bleak illusions and attempts to find a 'third way' in the struggle of the two systems. . . . Our socialist work is definitely helping capitalism in one thing: *to dig its grave more quickly.*"

Unambiguous communist rejection of the various theories of accommodation, however, does not discourage the one-sided love affair. In Western ears peaceful coexistence sounds like a promise to "live and let live." The wooing supplicants find it hard to grasp that to communists it means "live and *don't* let live."

The hard truth was summed up by Professor Stefan T. Possony, an American scholar and historian: "The traditional goal of communism, the conquest of the entire world, is not only reaffirmed but is held far more strongly and hopefully than in the past. It is 'unthinkable' that communists will abandon their goal of world domination regardless of the price they have to pay." It has been acknowledged by other Americans:

- President John F. Kennedy in his first State of the Union message in 1961, referring to the USSR and China: "We must never be lulled into believing that either power has yielded its ambitions for world domination."
- Secretary of Defense Robert McNamara, in the *Washington World* in 1963: "There has been no change in the policy of the Soviet Union to encourage what Mr. Khrushchev calls wars of

national liberation, or popular revolts—what we know as covert armed aggression, guerrilla warfare and subversion. And the Soviet Union has not diminished its efforts in any area."

- Secretary of State Dean Rusk, in an address to the Council on Foreign Relations in 1966: "The leaders of both principal communist nations are committed to the promotion of communist world revolution—even while they disagree bitterly on tactics. . . . We should not forget what we have learned about the anatomy and physiognomy of aggression. We ought to know better than to ignore the aggressor's openly proclaimed intention. . . ."

But Secretary Rusk credits too uncritically the assumption of Sino-Soviet disagreement on world-revolutionary tactics. True, Peking constantly inveighs against Moscow's coexistence slogan. For obvious forensic advantage, in its struggle for primacy in world communism, it chooses to misunderstand the slogan precisely as it is misunderstood in some Western statements on accommodation and "convergence," as "proof" that the Kremlin has joined the capitalist world. But an examination of Soviet and Chinese pronouncements, slight semantic differences aside, reveals nearly absolute agreement on methods and goals.

In 1965, Marshal Lin Piao, Defense Minister of Red China, presented Mao Tse-tung's view of the current world. He defined North America and Western Europe as "the cities of the world," with Asia, Africa, and Latin America as the "countryside." The contemporary world revolution, he said, "presents a picture of the encirclement of the cities by the rural areas." By conquering the countryside, the cities will be surrounded, weakened, and overcome. The "colossus of U.S. imperialism," he argued, "can be split and defeated. The people of Asia, Africa, and Latin America and other regions can destroy it piece by piece, some striking at its head and others at its feet." *

Except for his cities-and-countryside metaphor, what Lin Piao said was exactly what Khrushchev, Brezhnev, and their confreres

---

* This contraposition of "world town" and "world village" is not a Chinese inspiration. Dr. Karl A. Wittfogel, director of the Chinese History Project at the University of Washington, writes: "The terms themselves are not new. They had already been used by the young Lenin; and they were used, in a somewhat different sense, by Bukharin."

have been saying. Peking and Moscow alike now see the West "encircled" by the less developed nations and regions. Both, for the present, rule out direct war with "U.S. imperialism" but concentrate on wars of liberation, guerrilla terror and subversion in Asia, Africa, and Latin America. Both are thus equally committed to indirect offensives through the soft underbelly of the non-communist world. Lin Piao merely restated the basic revolutionary strategy of Soviet Russia under its shield of peaceful coexistence.

Yet the very people who have discounted or ignored the Soviet strategy have been deeply alarmed by its Chinese equivalent. This curious reaction again reflects the perennial free-world dream of easy solutions of its dilemma. By dividing the enemy into "good" and "bad" communists, it is easier to believe in détente, convergence, and other such comforting prospects. No matter what the Soviet Russians say and do to disown the label, they remain "good" communists to those promoting the one-sided love affair.

While touring Africa in the latter part of 1963, Chou En-lai, Mao's Premier, declared: "If anything unusual happens, the Soviet Union and China will stand shoulder to shoulder, arm to arm. . . . Remember, both China and Russia belong to the socialist camp." Because such rock-bottom realities do not fit into their stubborn hopes of Soviet-American détente, those eager to believe that the cold war is over, dismiss and forget them.

The consoling claim nowadays is that communist unity is a thing of the past—that "this Humpty Dumpty will not and cannot be reassembled," as George Kennan phrased it. This is far from established and in any case is irrelevant in practical terms. There have been a few exceptions (notably in India) but overwhelmingly, in the clinches, the communists show remarkable cohesion as against their common foe. They have been absolutely unified in support of North Vietnam, on the Dominican issue, on support of communist-brewed mischief anywhere. In Havana they sit together on the central strategy board for Latin America.

The all-important "gimmick" in peaceful coexistence *à la* Kremlin, though implicit or explicit in all Soviet statements, is rarely comprehended or even mentioned in the West. It is that the USSR remains free to incite and arm "liberation wars," guerrilla movements, subversion in *our* world, whereas the democracies are debarred from similar liberating activities in *their* world.

Suppose the unthinkable happened: suppose the non-communist nations staged a conference exactly like the one in Havana in 1966 and set up a Military Directorate to plan and direct liberation wars in the communist countries. The howls from Red capitals would be equaled only by the howls of anguish from appeasers and "bridge-builders" in the free world. We have meekly accepted the strange, self-paralyzing, and self-defeating principle that communist nations and colonies are inviolate, regardless how openly and savagely they violate other nations and regions.

This shocking disparity in rights of maneuver under the doctrine makes peaceful coexistence a trap for the West. Perhaps one fine day the free world will desist from nibbling at the bait long enough to assert reciprocity. It need only decide to be as resolute in promoting "transition *from communism to freedom*" as the communists in promoting "transition *from capitalism to communism.*" The least we deserve, in simple political logic, is the same freedom of action against Red imperialism that its masters not only claim but exercise against what they call Western imperialism.

What is probably the best study of the Kremlin slogan was written by Dr. Richard V. Allen of Georgetown University (now with the Hoover Institution) for the Standing Committee on Education Against Communism of the American Bar Association. First published in 1964 under the title *Peaceful Coexistence: A Communist Blueprint for Victory*, it was reissued in an enlarged and updated version in 1966 as *Peace or Peaceful Coexistence?*

"The specific function of peaceful coexistence" it found, "is not the establishment of a period of relative calm. It is to provide conditions favorable for waging a many-pronged offensive against and within the non-communist world." In the communist understanding of the slogan, Dr. Allen underlines, "one does not *practice* peaceful coexistence, one *wages* it. Peaceful coexistence is to the communists a unilateral strategic doctrine imposed upon the 'inevitably doomed' adversary. . . ."

His conclusion applies not only to the latest variation on the theme of peace but to all previous Muscovite tunes:

It is clear that when communists employ the language of "peace" they do so to mask their true strategic purpose: the isolation, encirclement, weakening and final destruction of the free world and its way of life. The cold war has not concluded, but has entered a new and still more complex phase in which the spectrum of psychological, economic and class warfare will be radically expanded. Such classic techniques as subversion, espionage, propaganda, sabotage, terrorism, deceit and incited disorder will remain and be refined; but the new techniques of nuclear blackmail are also to be employed wherever feasible. . . .

The great paradox of our time may well turn out to be our inability to recognize that the cold war has in reality become more intense despite the increasing appearances of peace. It need not be emphasized that the overwhelming sentiment of the free world is to live in peace. But to mistake the illusion of peace for genuine peace would be a profoundly dangerous, perhaps fatal mistake.

• *Chinese Puzzle*

For nearly a decade the deepening struggle between Red Russia and Red China has provided Westerners addicted to political daydreaming with blissful visions. The "good" communists in Moscow would be neutralized by the "bad" communists in Peking, and perhaps driven into alliance with the democracies against that common danger. Then came the locust plague of Mao Tse-tung's Red Guards, wrecking all previous calculations and hopes.

As we go to press the turbulence in China is still running wild, like a hundred rivers that have broken through their levees. Anything may happen. I am aware of the dangers of casting in type even hypothetical judgments. But the developments are important enough to justify the risk.

In passing we should note that the standard argument for admitting Red China to the United Nations was that "we can't ignore 700 million Chinese." Now it is clear that the Peking regime, far from representing those millions, doesn't even represent the Chinese communists. Its vaunted monolithic stability turns out to be a fairy tale.

The internal struggle has been erroneously described as factional. More precisely, Mao Tse-tung, Marshal Lin Piao, and their associates, backed by brainwashed and know-nothing youth, have unleashed a revolution against their own governing apparatus, against the great majority of power-holders in party committees, administrative organs, social organizations. The role of the Chinese Red Army, which may prove decisive, is as yet ambiguous, with segments throwing their weight now on one side, now on the other.

What are the possible outcomes?

First: The authority of Mao may be restored, perhaps on the basis of a face-saving compromise. That would mean, at least as long as he remains alive, a freezing of the old Sino-Soviet enmity. The USSR might well exploit the disordered transition period to seize vulnerable border territories—possibly Inner Mongolia, where anti-Mao leaders appear to have the upper hand, but especially the province of Sinkiang (Chinese Turkestan), to which Russia has historic claims and which is now the site of Chinese nuclear testing. Given its overwhelming military superiority and logistical advanages, Russia probably could make such grabs, camouflaged to be sure as local rebellions, without real danger of war.

Second: The opposition elements, in general the entrenched party and government beaureaucracy, may triumph over the Mao-Lin group—if not now, then later, with the death of Mao. The most significant effect would be a restoration of the "fraternal unity" between the two communist powers.

The Kremlin has made clear from the beginning that its sympathies are with Mao's more reasonable and pragmatic foes. Acting President Liu Shao-chi, the acknowledged leader of the anti-Mao alignment, has always been regarded as pro-Soviet. That Moscow's self-interested sympathy is translated into material and strategic collaboration against Mao can be taken for granted.

The re-establishment of the great communist monolith, from the Elbe to the Pacific, would cancel out all the paralyzing delusions of those who want desperately to believe that the communist danger is over. It would be a death-blow to Western theories of convergence and détente.

Third: The vast Chinese empire may collapse into its traditional condition of "war-lordism": regional military governments, conceivably giving lip-service to a weak central authority but ruling on their own. This outcome, of course, would mark the end of Chinese communism and would give a black eye to the entire world communist movement. To Moscow it would therefore be decidedly distressing, almost as distressing as a victory for Mao Tse-tung.

The possibility of Soviet intervention at some point cannot be ruled out. Whether or not it involved formal declarations of war, war it would be. For the Kremlin this would have the great advantage of galvanizing its citizenry in old-fashioned patriotism at a time when the Soviet regime craves national unity. The Russians have always disliked and feared their Chinese neighbor—in part a heritage from the long Mongolian occupation of their country. They could be welded for conflict with China far more readily than for war with the democratic West.

We need only suppose, for speculation's sake, that there is a Sino-Soviet war to realize the absurdity of talk about a Western alliance with Russia against China. The Soviet objective would be to reinstate a communist government of its own kind and under its own control. If attained, it would make international communism stronger and more dynamic than ever before. The hopes of the West, unless it had been reduced to idiocy by commitments to "building bridges" to communist regimes, would be to give the Chinese people another chance for ordered progress in relative freedom. Far from coinciding, the purposes of the USSR and the West would be diametrically opposed and an alliance utterly senseless.

What of the seven hundred millions, the gray masses in whose name all contenders pretend to speak? One of the most knowledgeable of the China-watchers in Hong Kong, Robert Elegant, posed this question to recent escapees from the tormented country. "The mood of the masses of Communist China," he then reported in his syndicated article on January 25, 1967, "is one of revenge—revenge for years of humiliation, repression, deprivation and above all, revenge for the communists' violent attempts to reshape the nature of every individual."

The masses neither understand nor care about the ideological disputations. The peasants, and that is nearly the whole of the population, want an old-style family farm. The workers want more wages and more food. The intellectuals, except the minority embroiled in the struggle, want only to be let alone to think and study and work without whips at their backs.

By the time these words see print, the pieces in the tantalizing Chinese puzzle may have fallen into place. Whatever the pattern that emerges, it will have a profound effect on Soviet Russia.

19 / Science

The myth that Soviet communism has fostered progress in science.

The last fifty years have compassed more scientific progress than the preceding five centuries. Man's capacity to absorb the crowding new has been strained by the flood of discoveries and inventions in physics and chemistry, electronics and aeronautics, psychology and medicine, in every other department of knowledge and inquiry.

In this burgeoning world of science, Soviet Russia's share has been lamentably meagre. The country has made worthwhile contributions on the fringes—such as equipment for suturing severed arteries, to mention one of many—but not one of the truly epoch-making discoveries and inventions of the half-century. Its citizens have been awarded a number of Nobel Prizes, but none of them represented a historic breakthrough in its field.

Illusions on this score have been bred by the launching of the Sputnik and Lunik before the United States orbited a satellite. These feats will long and deservedly remain a source of Russian national pride. They involved important engineering work—in the build-up of engine thrust, in particular. But on the whole, they reflected an early and speeded-up concentration of effort, an act of political will, rather than any new scientific principles or inventions unknown to the outside world.*

* In June, 1965, at a university symposium, Dr. Richard Porter, a consultant in Aerospace Science and Technology to the General Electric Company, in comparing American and Soviet space programs, said at one point: "The Soviet work is good but has less variety and depth of original data to work with than is available in the U.S. program and, apparently, is not so advanced in data handling and analysis techniques or, perhaps, does not find modern electronic data-handling equipment so readily available as it is in the United

The Soviets drew on the common reservoir of knowledge in other advanced countries. Moreover, no outsider can estimate how much their space spectaculars owed (1) to the harvest of massive espionage in the United States, Canada, and Britain, and (2) to German scientific and technical brains; hundreds of German specialists, along with installations and prototypes, had been brought to Russia after the war.

One of these German scientists, Professor H. Barwich, worked on the development of Soviet atomics for a full decade, from 1945 to 1955, and drew a Stalin Prize for his contributions. Writing in a German magazine in 1965, he declared that the espionage activities of Klaus Fuchs alone saved the Soviets two years of research, "quite possibly it was more." The Kremlin, he said, captured the entire German groundwork in rocket, power unit, and radar knowledge, together with the equipment and key personnel.

The Russians are naturally creative people. On the basis of their record before the advent of Bolshevism, the world had every reason to look to them for seminal thought in science, for pacesetting in mathematics, biology, medicine, and other disciplines in which they had shown special aptitudes in the nineteenth and early twentieth centuries.

These expectations have been largely disappointed. One can attest this without the slightest disparagement of Russian abilities. On the contrary, given the oppressive anti-intellectual atmosphere under communism, even the marginal contributions speak volumes for the inherent genius of the people.

There is little, if anything, in the area of science that the West has obtained from Soviet Russia. It has not been hampered or impoverished by Soviet refusal to permit access to its accomplishments. Moscow, by contrast, has been so avid for Western science and technology that it has engaged in economic espionage abroad on a scale without precedent anywhere anytime, determined to steal what it could not buy.

Despite itself, in dread of possible consequences, the Kremlin is being driven by the imperatives of technology to tolerate more ra-

---

States. There is a noticeably greater tendency for Soviet authors to use U.S. data in their analytical work than the other way around." But he also noted that "the Soviets have enjoyed a considerable margin of superiority in booster capability."

tionality in science and research. A point was reached in the 1950's when the economic penalties of dogmatic ignorance were becoming too alarming. While holding steadfastly to its absolute supremacy in decision-making, the regime gradually authorized more sensible approaches to science and a larger degree of autonomy in research.

In the exact sciences, the new freedom is extensive, but the more directly a discipline affects politics and ideology—philosophy, psychology, jurisprudence, history especially—the greater the remaining restrictions.

And in some fields distortion and falsehoods are as mandatory as ever. Political science is out of bounds for obvious reasons—uninhibited study of open societies is inconceivable. Facts about the non-communist world are twisted or invented in line with Marxist-Leninist preconceptions.

A brochure by one E. Kolman, titled *Is There a God?* and published three years after Stalin's death, said at one point: "In the capitalist states even today scientists who do not believe in God are persecuted. . . . They persecute and starve lecturers who teach the truth about the origin of the earth, of life and man. It often happens that scientific books are publicly burned." This kind of cynical nonsense about the infidel democracies, and it is one quotation out of thousands, scarcely jibes with a genuine scientific spirit. In the clinches, propaganda and indoctrination still have the right of way over ascertainable truth.

Even the partial retreat from obscurantism has been made slow and difficult because of a heritage of monstrous persecution of science and learning in the recent past, including the physical destruction of thousands of first-rate Russian minds. Every major purge, it should be remembered, took a larger toll from the educated minority than from the population as a whole. In the 1930's, climaxed by the blood-purges, the best brains were removed from the national, republic, and affiliated Academies of Science, the universities and research institutions.

It is doubtful that "the greatest scientist of our epoch, Comrade Stalin," as *Pravda* called him, and his cohorts knew specifically why they were so frightened of these men and women. It was a conditioned reflex against knowledge and reason, as sources of possible doubts about communism and its works. As for the victims, most of them could only surmise what "crimes" were imputed to them from the fantastic "confessions" they were tortured into signing. No scientific field was exempt from police depredations. "Saboteurs" by the hundred were turned up in medicine, anthropology, linguistics. "Diversionist wrecking" was exposed in astronomy; a normal mind finds it difficult to imagine why an all-powerful regime should be wracked by fears in the astronomic heavens.

Another devastating wave of purge washed over the country from 1946 forward and continued unabated as long as Stalin lived. It is known as the Zhdanov period, after Andrei Zhdanov, Stalin's ideological and cultural tsar, who initiated the horror for his boss. The havoc it worked among intellectuals was as tragic as in the thirties. Along with the standard charges of heresy and sabotage, the persecutions were now directed with special cruelty against newly-minted crimes like "rootless cosmopolitanism" and "kowtowing to the West."

Stalin was determined to wipe out the memories of his pact with Hitler and the role of the capitalist West in winning the war and saving his regime. He was haunted by the knowledge that millions of his subjects, soldiers and civilians, had caught a glimpse of life without communism in Eastern and Central Europe. He became psychotically dedicated to isolating his country, especially intellectually, from the rest of humanity.

As proclaimed by Zhdanov and thousands of lesser Zhdanovs, the USSR, "the world's most advanced country," had nothing to learn from the jungle of ignorance, religion, "reaction" and lust for war beyond the Soviet frontiers. Any sign of interest in the culture or science of other nations became *prima facie* evidence of treason. Correspondence, let alone personal contacts, with American or European universities and learned societies, even in the distant past, meant arrest, concentration camp, sometimes execution as a spy.

The xenophobia was not new—distrust of foreign thought was deep through all the Soviet years—but it was now intensified. The Kremlin eagerly reached out for technology. What it called "Fordism" became in the time of forced-tempo industrialization almost an object of worship. But paradoxically the rulers shied away in horror from Western abstract ideas and discoveries in pure science in which that technology was rooted.

Thus the theories of Albert Einstein, Sigmund Freud, and Nor-

bert Wiener, the American father of cybernetics, were denounced
out of hand as capitalist frauds. In more recent years, they have
been grudgingly "rehabilitated" but they are still handled with care
as anti-Marxist booby-traps.

Relativity was arbitrarily denounced by Lenin; not until the mid-
fifties did it become entirely safe for physicists to treat Einstein
seriously. As recently as 1963, a book on philosophy issued by the
Academy of Science began its chapter on Freud with these words:
"Freudianism is one of the most widespread and reactionary movements in contemporary capitalist double-talk."

For years cybernetics was fiercely assailed as a bourgeois black
art. A *Philosophical Dictionary*, published in 1954, still stated:
"Cybernetics is a reactionary pseudo-science, emerging in the
United States after the war and spreading widely to other capitalist
countries as well." Belatedly, the USSR developed what amounted
to a mania of faith in cybernetics, but the time-lag could not be
made up. Soviet technology was utterly unprepared for the computer age and continues to pay for the folly in backwardness.

• *The Reign of Lysenko*

Perhaps the best way to convey the appalling tragedy of men of
learning is to tell briefly the incredible story of Trofim D. Lysenko,
who for some thirty years dominated Soviet biological sciences and
related fields, such as genetics, histology, embryology, zoology. It is
by all odds the greatest scandal in the scientific domain in our century. Already there is a substantial literature on the fantastic business—none of it in Soviet libraries—and doubtless it will be examined in the future by students of the pathology of communism.

Whether Lysenko is a fraud or a fantastic ignoramus is open to
debate. Practically that is of little importance. What is important
is that his reign of terror over a vital scientific area lasted, with one
brief eclipse from 1955 to 1958, from the early thirties until
Khrushchev was ousted in 1964. In this period the police-state imposed his theories on the entire country, inflicting damage on the
nation's agriculture, forestry, and science as a whole.

Lysenko first appeared on the national scene as a disciple of
Michurin, sometimes called "the Russian Burbank." Unlike both
Michurin and Burbank, he was not content merely to develop new
species of plants and fruits. He preached his own system of gene-

tics, according to which the whole civilized world was mistaken in accepting the laws of heredity and mutations established by the Austrian monk Gregor Mendel in the previous century and confirmed by thousands of biologists thereafter.

Lysenko denied the existence of genes. He renounced theoretical experimentation in favor of "practical" hit-and-miss tests. He insisted that acquired characteristics could be transmitted to new generations in both plant and animal breeding. Eugenics, being tied to Mendelian findings, he ruled out entirely.

Two outstanding Western geneticists visited Lysenko in his early years of notoriety. Dr. S.C. Harland, a Briton, reported: "I found him completely ignorant of the elementary principles of genetics and plant physiology." An American colleague, the late Dr. H. J. Muller, a winner of the Nobel Prize in biology, declared: "Lysenko's writings on theoretical lines are the merest drivel. He obviously fails to comprehend either what a controlled experiment is, or the established principles of genetics." On another occasion, Dr. Muller wrote: "In the light of modern scientific knowledge, Lysenkoism must be termed a superstition, as much a superstition as belief that the earth is flat." Nearly all reputable Russian biologists, including Professor Nikolai Vavilov, one of the world's most respected authorities, were amazed that this half-educated amateur was being listened to seriously.

But the greatest scientist of all, Comrade Stalin, was thoroughly captivated by Lysenko's half-baked and flamboyant claims. The newly collectivized agriculture was then in grievous trouble, famine was mowing down millions. The worried politicians proved easy targets for wonder-working horticultural nostrums.

In Lysenko they hailed a "practical agronomist" in contrast to the fancy theorists with their genes and laws of heredity. He promised great leaps foward, to use a later Chinese slogan. He refused to be frustrated by the slowness of nature and would bend it to his will—revolution instead of slow-poke evolution! Besides, the established laws of heredity seemed a kind of eternal predestination and vaguely un-Marxist, though Marx had never written a line on the subject. Lysenko's award of priority to environment, again vaguely, seemed to offer greater hope of engineering the "new Soviet man" of the Marxist-Leninist theology.

Stalin latched on to Lysenko, threw the whole weight of the

dictatorship behind him. This he adhered to until the end of his life, after which Khrushchev became Lysenko's chief patron. By 1938, the upstart displaced Vavilov as head of the Lenin Academy of Agricultural Sciences, and the Central Committee of the party ordered all Marxists to embrace the Lysenko magic, like it or not. By 1940, he was director of the Institute of Genetics of the Academy of Science.

He was not only the undisputed tsar of the entire empire of research and education in agronomy and biology, but had emerged as a political power in the land. Mendelian principles of heredity were "abolished." Genes were turned into a counterrevolutionary word, erased from all science textbooks.

Unable to convert Vavilov and other serious specialists, Lysenko, supported by the party, equated disagreement with treason and increasingly resorted to purges. Opponents were castigated as "rotten liberals," stooges for the West waging a struggle against Soviet progress. Because the great Mendel had been a monk, the charge of "clerical reaction" was added to the catalog of sins.

Professor Albert Parry wrote in 1960:

Scores of reputable Russian scientists lost their jobs, and many their liberty and their very lives when they dared to oppose Lysenko even mildly.

The ugly record began in 1932 when two cystologists, G. A. Levitsky and N. P. Avdulov, were sent to concentration camps. It drew its first blood in 1935 when I. J. Agol and L. P. Ferry were executed by the Soviet police, the first two Russian geneticists to be put to death.

Two years later Avdulov was shot, and so was S. G. Levit, former head of the celebrated Moscow Institute for Medical Genetic Research. In 1940 the great Prof. Nicholas Avilov himself, for decades the guiding light of Russian biology and the pride of the world's genetics, was arrested by the Stalin-Lysenko police. Two years later, a prisoner in Siberia, Vavilov was dead. Nor is this numbing list complete; whole staffs of anti-Lysenko scientists died similarly, in prison or labor camps, of bullets or slow mistreatment.

Lysenko's power reached its peak in the postwar Zhdanov period. His hatred of Western science fitted neatly into the Russian chauvinism of that time. The incredible part of the affair is that Lysenko accomplished nothing except to extend the botanical work pioneered by Michurin and Burbank. He had a green thumb, a way with growing things, the persuasiveness of a fanatic or a charlatan, but not a trace of the scientific mentality.

During his brief eclipse, the Soviet *Botanical Journal* in 1955 wrote of his work: "It has now been conclusively demonstrated that the entire concept is factually unsound and theoretically and methodically erroneous and that it is not of practical value." Reputable Russian scientists charged in print that he had falsified reports to bamboozle the party. Nevertheless, Khrushchev restored him to favor.

Why did Stalin and his successors cling to Lysenkoism through all the years in the face of overwhelming scientific opinion against him? Was it sheer stubbornness? Or a godlike feeling that they could dictate to nature as ruthlessly as to man? No one, in the nature of the case, can give full answers to such questions.

"Laws of heredity," Bertram D. Wolfe has written, were "passed by the Politburo." In the view of Dr. David Joravsky of the Harvard University Research Center (*Problems of Communism,* November-December 1965), Lysenkoism "simply carried [the] anti-intellectual attitude to its ultimate absurdity." He quoted an old botanist to whom he spoke in Russia as exclaiming: "Lysenko is the Rasputin of Soviet biology!"

"It was science which paid the most immediate and heaviest price for the authorities' support of Lysenkoism," Dr. Joravsky declared. "Genetics, cystology and evolutionary theory were driven out of educational and research institutions, first from those concerned with agricultural applications, then from secondary schools and ultimately, from 1948 to 1953, from the universities and research laboratories."

By this time it is generally conceded in the USSR that Lysenkoism was without any validity—precisely as all non-Soviet biologists had known from the outset. The gene is being "rehabilitated"; millions of textbooks are being junked and a hundred thousand biology teachers are being retrained. Intelligent Soviet people are frankly ashamed and embarrassed. Lysenko himself apparently has not been punished and many of his disciples are still entrenched in some scientific institutions—presumably they still enjoy the patronage of powerful Kremlin caliphs.

The thirty-year Lysenko saga tells us nearly all we need to know about the fate of science and intellect under an ideological autocracy. It reduces to self-evident absurdity the pretense that communism has helped science to flourish. Such a gross imposture sustained by police force would not have been possible in a free society. Even if Lysenko were right in his revolt against reason, the suppression of dissenting voices would have indicted the USSR as an enemy of intellect. There can be no genuine science without freedom of thought and inquiry, without autonomy for the searching mind.

20 / Culture

The myth that the Soviets have promoted
the arts and culture.

The last fifty years have also witnessed great change and great
achievement in the arts and pure thought. Novel approaches to
philosophy and religion, sociology and historiography, have been
matched by exciting experiments with new styles, forms and materials in painting, sculpture, music, letters.

In those areas Soviet Russia has been not merely passive but
actively reactionary, hostile to everything fresh, innovative, experi-
mental, unorthodox. The mercenaries of a state theology have
crushed every assertion of individuality at home and blocked its
infiltration from beyond the frontiers.

Intellectually the nation was sealed off and isolated as thoroughly as Japan before it was pried open by Western gunboats.
The guardians of a vulgar materialism have invented cultural
crimes—"formalism," "cosmopolitanism," "idealism"—rating suppression, banishment to Siberia, even death. Ideas and forms unacceptable to the total state, or simply beyond the mental grasp of its
rulers and gendarmes, have not merely been attacked as "wrong,"
they have been punished as heresy.

For nearly half a century a great nation has had only one permissible truth, Marxism-Leninism, and only one permissible mode of
thought, Dialectic Materialism. Merely to suggest that there might
be other truths and methods made one an "enemy of the people."
Actually to stray beyond the confines of the prescribed verities as
defined by their custodians at any given time, brought anything
from ostracism to death.

All art and culture was squeezed into strait jacket called "socialist realism," which required the representation of Soviet life as happy and heroic, and that in styles so simplistic that even a Stalin or Khrushchev could understand them and whistle their tunes. Socialist realism—still the official doctrine, reaffirmed by the last Party Congress—is plainly a dishonest formula: there is nothing socialist or realistic about coloring or denying the facts of life. At bottom it is a propaganda device, limiting art to poster-like chromos and literarture to political advertising, above all prohibiting free self-expression. Creativity was thus stultified or driven underground.

Max Eastman wrote in 1955, in his *Reflections on the Failure of Socialism*:

Instead of liberating the mind of man, the Bolshevik revolution locked it into a state's prison tighter than ever before. No flight of thought was conceivable, no poetic promenade even, to sneak through the doors or peep out of a window in this pre-Darwinian dungeon called Dialectic Materialism. No one in the western world has any idea of the degree to which Soviet minds are closed and sealed tight against any idea but the premises and conclusions of this antique system of wishful thinking. So far as concerns the advance of human understanding, the Soviet Union is a gigantic road-block, armed, fortified and defended by indoctrinated automatons made out of flesh, blood and brains in robot-factories they call schools.

Earlier, in 1951, a Russian concert violinist who had known the Soviet music and theater worlds from the inside, Juri Jelagin, by then with the Houston (Texas) Symphony Orchestra, wrote a remarkable book, *Taming the Arts*. It is a moving personal and political account of what happens when thought and esthetics are totally subjected to a vulgar state. In the concluding chapter he wrote:

The Soviet government inherited from the old Russia a great culture and a magnificent modern art which was among the most brilliant in the world. Russian art showed every indication of maturity: a high development of form and technical perfection; a large variety of artistic styles, directions and schools. . . . Within a short period of time this great development in art was on the verge of annihilation. Everything that is created in the Soviet Union, including music, has a distinctly backward, primitive character; everything bears the unmistakable second-rate stamp of pauperization and degradation of technique.

And so in the arts, as in science, few works of surpassing originality, let alone genius, have come out of Soviet Russia. The one novel worthy of standing beside Tolstoy or Turgeniev, Chekhov or Gorki, *Doctor Zhivago* by Boris Pasternak, was written in secret ("for the drawer," as Soviet writers say) and, though available to the rest of the world and awarded the Nobel Prize, has been denied publication in its native land. Shostakovich and Prokofiev, composers ranking with great forebears like Tchaikovsky and Mussorgsky, were repeatedly attacked, humiliated and silenced for periods, their work twisted by official pressures and some of it outlawed.

The old Russia had been a cornucopia of creative works even under the limitations of Romanoff absolutism. Its Russian Ballet and the Bolshoi Opera, and to a more limited extent Stanislavsky's Moscow Art Theater, are still the main adornments of Russian culture. As long as writers avoided overt attacks on the monarchy, they could explore any ideas and pull apart any institutions. Russian literature was then openly committed to reform, liberty, and a compassionate humanism. Tsarism had constrained free expression —Soviet communism choked it off entirely.

The propaganda claim that the Soviets have fostered intellectual and artistic progress is fantastic on the face of it. The country has produced no significant Soviet philosopher or inventor, lamentably few men in the arts comparable to those of the preceding half-century. The life of the mind and spirit has been arid and sterile. The dictatorship, with the rise of Stalin to its apex, turned deeply anti-intellectual, suspicious of those who, because they think, may think differently.

Since the demise of Stalin, of course, there has been a thawing and a stirring of talent—so remarkable and newsworthy after the decades-long drought that its scope and its quality have been unduly magnified. But the regime still deals with the intelligentsia as if it were an alien power, to be tranquilized or intimidated into

The Kremlin had few more obedient servants and stalwart deconformity.

fenders among writers of talent than the novelist Alexander Fadeyev. An enthusiastic communist, he repeatedly figured as the regime's spokesman at international conferences and in polemics
with Western writers. His war novel, *The Young Guard,* which
appeared in 1945, was hailed and rewarded by officialdom and circulated in huge editions. Some years later, however, it came under
delayed criticism for an alleged lack of emphasis on the role of the
party in his story. Submissively he rewrote it to correct the "errors"
in a new version in 1951. But in 1956, at the age of fifty-five, he
shocked the country and the party by committing suicide.

Three years after the passing of Stalin, soon after the launching
of de-Stalinization, even a Fadeyev cracked under the continuing
pressures. Surely the "new freedom" for the creative minority has
been grotesquely overrated.

• *Progress in Education*

The one aspect of cultural life where the Soviet regime has
achieved greatly is education—not in quality, to be sure, but in
quantity. Nearly the entire population has learned to read and
write; 95 per cent, to be exact, a figure exceeded by only twenty
other countries. Although the number of students in higher education generally is smaller, in proportion to the population, than in
Sweden, Canada, or the United States, the Soviets hold first place
for graduates in engineering, science, and agriculture—a reflection,
of course, of their extreme specialization.

Russian women have made enormous progress in education, representing, as of 1960, some 40 per cent of the total enrollment in
the institutions of higher learning. This percentage is not significantly different from what it is in other advanced nations, but
more of the women students take degrees in science, engineering,
and especially in medicine and pedagogy than in the West. Relatively few, considering their great numbers, occupy top posts in
scholarship, engineering, and science—a pattern of male domination very much as in the rest of the world. Even fewer women
reach leadership levels in the party and in government. While they
make up 50 per cent of the country's work force, they constitute
only 20 per cent of the party membership. There are only five
women (2.6 per cent of the total) in the Central Committee, and
there has never been a woman in the Politburo.

None of this, of course, detracts from the credit due to the regime, against the background of their relative retardation before 1917, for the education of women. It should be noted, too, that the Kremlin has brought its own brands of culture, such as propaganda plays and cinema, to millions in the provinces. Even second-echelon cities now have local theatrical groups and are visited by major companies on tour—very much as in the United States.

The authentic achievements in education, however, have been deeply impaired by the restraints on free thought inherent in a totalitarian society. In the nature of the case, the coersions prevailing in intellectual life generally affected the schools. The humanities have been neglected. What passes for "social science" has been, certainly until the most recent years, no more than indoctrination by rote in Marxism-Leninism.

Large areas of knowledge and inquiry are still blacked out. Education has been almost wholly functional, without room for the free mind and spirit, geared to prevention of independent thinking rather than its encouragement. At every point where they might conflict, the premises of the state ideology have foreclosed uninhibited inquiry and discussion in the educational process.

It is not true, as so many nowadays appear to believe, that Russia before the revolution was almost entirely illiterate. The compulsory schooling law of 1910, geared to embrace the entire population by 1920, was being earnestly implemented when war and civil war intervened. Professor S. Timasheff, with Fordham University in New York and a leading authority on Russian history, wrote in *The Great Retreat*, published in 1946: "If the peaceful development had continued, from 1920 on, all Russian children would have had access to the primary school." He rejected the Soviet figures on illiteracy under tsarism. "It is possible to make an estimate which yields the index of literacy as 40.2 per cent in 1914," he wrote.

In the youngest generation, the one subject to military service, the index was much higher. According to official records for 1914, 67.8 per cent of army recruits, the young men of twenty-one, were literate—a percentage above that in some American states at that time. It was the exceptional extent of illiteracy among peasant women that pulled down the national average as calculated by Professor Timasheff. He cited a census of industrial workers only taken in 1920 that showed a literacy index of over 77 per cent among those between fourteen and twenty, evidently reflecting the compulsory schooling law of 1910.

This is a far remove from the nearly complete illiteracy implied by communist propaganda. The fact is that there was a great recession in schooling in the early Soviet years, due to war and civil war, famine, and dislocation of life in general. The boastful Soviet percentages of increase in literacy take that low point as their base, rather than true pre-war figures.

More important, the values of literacy have been vitiated by the state monopoly of the printed word. As Professor George S. Counts of Columbia University wrote in a book on Soviet education, the drive to end illiteracy "was designed, not to liberate the mind of the individual but to hold it captive. . . . Literacy without a free press can scarcely be a truly liberating force in society." Under communism mere literacy in the first place gives the regime readier channels for polluting minds with official lies. Its goal is not enlightenment but indoctrination. What would be the advantage of a state monopoly of all reading matter, if the people couldn't read?

In the old Russia, there was a small highly-educated class; in the new Russia there is a large half-educated class. From kindergarten to university, the worst sin Soviet teachers could commit was to cast doubts on prescribed ideas and facts. Being human, they played it safe, no matter how outraged they may have been in their secret minds by the curriculum and textbooks. Meekly they taught that "everyone knows the irresistible, shattering power of Stalin's logic, the crystal clearness of his intellect, his iron will, devotion to the party, his modesty, his artlessness, his solicitude for the people and mercilessness to enemies of the people." The quotation, from the *Short Biography* of the dictator, was prescribed for classroom use by the *Teacher's Gazette* in 1947.

The prime duty of teachers, the journal *Pedagogica* declared, is "instilling in children hatred for the enemies of the people." Eastman's indictment of the "robot-factories they call schools" is justified by perusal of any Soviet textbook for the young, even now.

There has been only marginal improvement in this connection under Stalin's successors. Not only children but college and university students are still taught a version of the history of the revolution and the civil war that doesn't mention Leon Trotsky. The story of industrialization and collectivization is told in classrooms without mentioning the unspeakable horrors of those processes. In history books the USSR still won the war, not only against Germany but against Japan, practically single-handedly and despite betrayals by the Western Allies. Now school books produced in the Khrushchev years are being busily edited to reduce or oblitrate *his* stature.

The intention here decidedly is not to underrate the potentials of education and literacy, even under totalitarian conditions. Reading provides access to the treasure-house of classic Russian literature, replete with mental and spiritual stimulation. As John Scott of *Time* magazine wrote not too long ago on returning from another trip through Russia: "The human mind cannot easily be fettered, even in the Soviet Union. You cannot teach a young man or woman to read, to make mathematical analyses and scientific instruments, to use computers and other complicated instruments— without having him learn to think." The deep-reaching restiveness of Soviet youth today and its increasing defiance of authority confirm that he was correct.

• Persecution of the Arts

Russians, I remarked earlier, are a naturally creative people. Even during the civil war, amid general slaughter, hunger and epidemics, their country experienced a burst of artistic energy. The world repute the USSR long enjoyed for theater, cinema and literature, indeed, rested chiefly on works in the first dozen years or so, before the Stalin era went into full stride.

Those involved in that minor renaissance for the most part had already been active under the old regime but drew new inspiration from the revolutionary upheavals. The names and achievements upon which Soviet culture has nourished its self-esteem even to the present all date back to that first period. Stanislavsky, Meyerhold, Vakhtangov, Nemirovich-Danchenko, in the theater; Eisenstein and Pudovkin, in motion pictures; the poets Pasternak, Yessenin, Mayakovsky, Mandelstamm, Akhmatova; the prose writers Zamyatin, Pilnyak, Bulgakov, Babel, Alexei Tolstoy, Zoshchenko; Prokofiev and the young Shostakovich in music—the list is heartwarming.

But their relative freedom was short-lived. Yessenin and Mayakovsky, in the end were unable to adjust themselves to the new Soviet life and committed suicide; Yessenin in 1925, Mayakovsky five years later. Another talented writer, Andrei Sobol, took his own life in 1926.

A few, like Pasternak and Akhmatova, remained alive and free but reduced to virtual silence. Many gifted Russians, of course, had escaped to the West where, despite the material and psychological limitations of life as *émigrés*, they made or continued brilliant careers; men like Bunin, Nabokov, Merezhkovsky, Mark Aldanov, Leonid Andreiev, Mikhail Artzibashev, Konstantin Balmont, in literature; Rachmaninoff and Stravinsky, in music; Diaghilev, in ballet; Sikorsky and de Seversky, in aeronautics. Dozens of Russian exiles attained positions of eminence in the most important Western universities.

The rest, along with thousands of their fellow artists, were driven to barren conformity or physically destroyed in the eclipse of thought and culture that came with industrialization and collectivization. The hacks, the sycophants, the politicians of the arts took over. It was not enough to refrain from attacking the regime; the luxury of neutrality was denied them. To remain alive, as Pasternak would say in *Doctor Zhivago*, you had "to praise what you most hate and to grovel before what makes you unhappy." A fog of mediocrity settled over the land.

At the time Hitler was burning books, an outrage that drew horrified protests from the civilized world, Stalin in effect was burning authors. But the same world hardly noticed and many of its intellectual spokesmen even applauded rapturously. A double standard of judgment, one for communists and another for other brands of despotism, had by then become fashionable.

Persecution of the arts and intellect was no less fierce in the postwar Zhdanov years. The cruelties were as savage, the regimentation as total. Again there were waves of suicide among intellectuals. The excitement churned up by the "thaw" after the demise of Stalin is less a measure of the "new freedom" in the arts than it is of the deep-freeze that was being defrosted, but freethinking, especially where it touches on the political system and its ideology, is still kept within narrow limits.

The posthumous "rehabilitation" of writers after the so-called de-Stalinization in 1956, incidentally, reminded the Soviet public of how many hundreds of gifted men and women—now officially declared innocent of any crime—had been destroyed. Among them, to mention only a few, were Alexander Voronsky, one of the truly great Russian literary critics; Isaac Babel, novelist and short-story writer; the poet Pavel Bespalov. The rehabilitated also included a striking number of literary men in the national-minority regions, creating in their native languages: Abdulla Amantai, a Bashkir poet; Rukhula Akhudnov, an Azerbaijan journalist and scholar; David Bergelson, who wrote in Yiddish; the Armenian, Aksel Bakuntz. The executioners did not discriminate—they exterminated Russian and non-Russian innocents alike.

Novels like *The Thaw* by Ilya Eherenburg; *Not by Bread Alone* by Dudintsev; *One Day in the Life of Ivan Denisovich* by Solzhenitsyn; the poetry of Yevgeny Yevtushenko, Andrei Voznesensky, Robert Rozhdestvensky, Bella Akhmadulina, Bulat Okudzhava, and many others—these have electrified the Soviet people and the world. Truth-speaking authors, and poets in particular, are all but deified by Soviet students and the youth generally. They turn out by the thousand to hear their favorite poets. For a time, until the police intervened, they gathered for open-air readings.

Without derogating their literary quality, however, it must be said that as artists these men and women are hardly in a class with the Russian masters of the past. Their fame derives not only from literary merit, but from the social and political overtones of their work. The most popular writers are those who show most valor and skill in defending humanist values and virtues, and not necessarily the most gifted. To a people long tormented by thirst, good clean water can be as intoxicating as champagne.

Some fourteen thousand people, overwhelmingly youngsters, jammed a sports stadium outside Moscow on the evening of November 30, 1962. They were noisy and excited, like fans anywhere gathered for a major event. Thousands more were milling around unhappily outside. It was not a sports event, but a Poet's Evening that had drawn this multitude, which greeted the three writers, two men and a woman, with thunderous applause.

The enthusiasm had less to do with the quality of the poetry, though all three are first-rate artists, than with their boldness in dissecting and indicting aspects of Soviet existence. It was in essence a political demonstration, and no one knew this better than the men in the Kremlin. Probably it was not coincidental that Khrushchev chose the very next day for a violent attack on unorthodox art and artists that marked a new period of toughness against the dissident moods in culture.

The new writers, and older ones emboldened by their example, dared write of love, justice, mercy, conscience, the soul, and other long outlawed themes—especially about truth. They dared complain of drab and regimented lives. New heroes appeared in their works—or rather the old heroes of the old Russian literature: sensitive men and women concerned with private conscience and happiness. Small wonder that the enthusiasm evoked was unbounded.

It is, in fact, close to a miracle that after decades of absolute suppression and the virtual destruction of two generations of artists, the fountains of sincere emotion and creativity had not dried up. This seems to me the most meaningful aspect of the new period. Assuredly it holds out hope for a genuine rebirth of Russian genius once the yoke of autocracy has been thrown off.

But it would be a factual error—and a disservice to the intellectuals straining against state controls—to suppose that the yoke has already been removed. Socialist realism remains the only "safe" doctrine. Those who speak out still risk loss of their livelihood and worse, particularly if they are on the lower rungs, without the shield of national and international fame. Abstract and other unorthodox painters and sculptors still cannot be exhibited, despite a few brief token shows through the years.

Even the limited permissiveness in culture continues to be anxiously policed by a hectoring, threatening state, and the trend at this time is toward less not more freedom. The areas of the permissive are not expanding but shrinking. The new rights stop short where they might challenge the official truths. Writers and artists are jailed more rarely than in the Stalin era, but punitive measures against free spirits have not been ended. Surveillance of non-conformers has been increased under the Brezhnev-Kosygin regime; young writers have been more often interrogated by the police. The ugly practice of committing recalcitrants to mental institutions has not been called off. The inquisitors are ubiquitous and tireless.

A recent Czechoslovak defector, Jan Lukas, described as his country's leading creative photographer, said on arriving in America: "Whenever the regime feels that the danger point has been reached, the door is promptly and unreservedly slammed in the artist's face. The artist therefore often feels akin to a yo-yo—manipulated openly or covertly, depending on his stature." This is no less true for Soviet Russia.

Joseph Brodsky, a modernist poet, was imprisoned a few years ago as a "parasite"—full-time dedication to the muse was defined by the authorities as wilful idleness. About ten days after Sinyavsky and Daniel were convicted in a blaze of world attention, the young poet Vladimir Batshev was sentenced to five years in a labor camp without benefit of publicity at home or abroad. Only the authorities know how many more have suffered such martyrdom in total darkness. In the summer of 1966 at least seventy Ukrainian writers were arrested, at least twenty of them shipped to labor camps; whatever the formal charge, their real crime was excessive pro-Ukrainian sentiment. Many others have been repressed on other pretexts. Most authors, including some of those who get their work published, still write also "for the drawer"—works they know have no chance of passing the censors. After all, there is only one publisher, the state, and it is sensitive to every nuance of direct or elliptical criticism. Writers who get published in foreign countries, with or without their connivance, are at once visited by "literary critics in plain-clothes."

"Many writings are not being published at the moment," Max Frankel reported to the New York *Times* after a visit to the USSR in 1963. "Films are being made but not shown; canvases are completed but not displayed. Ordinary people here still do not dare to write an honest letter abroad, not to mention a politically sensitive statement at home."

There was a measure of relaxation in the last year of Khrushchev's reign, but by the summer of 1965 harsh winds were blowing again and are becoming more biting at this writing. The new weather was signalized by the dismissal of the chief editor of *Pravda,* A. M. Rumyantsev, who had written a couple of editorials on the temperate side. In 1966, the reaction was in full blow. Brezhnev and Kosygin obviously had decided that the intellectuals needed a taste of the whip.

The trial of Sinyavsky and Daniel, now serving seven- and five-year sentences at hard labor, was to be the demonstrative whipping. Their sin was that they had permitted their novels and essays, unpublishable at home, to be published abroad under pennames, "Abram Terz" and "Nikolai Arzhak" respectively. Their arrest, according to a New York *Times* dispatch, drew a bitter comment credited to the poet Yessenin-Volpin. The men were lucky, he said, because "there were so many others about whom the world knows nothing—as little as people know of a rabbit eaten by the wolves in the forest."

Clandestine poems, stories, essays are circulated in typed or handwritten copies on a scale amounting to another, unauthorized literature challenging the published literature. Within the country some of the best known and most widely recited poems, especially those of the late Boris Pasternak, are precisely those the government has denied publication. A spiritual cult has developed around Pasternak's memory; people, mostly the young, make pilgrimages to his grave in a Moscow suburb and it is a matter of self-respect to know his proscribed poetry by heart.

Even celebrated authors enjoying vast reader demand find much of their new work prohibited. The foremost Soviet prose writer, Solzhenitsyn, for example, has been refused publication of two novels and many stories and as a result is known to be in serious economic straits. One of these novels, *The Cancer Ward,* slated to run in *Novy Mir,* failed to appear, but its content became known in the West and illicit copies are being passed from hand to hand in the Soviet Union. *Novy Mir* and another literary magazine, *Yunost,* have published daringly, sometimes close to the political danger line. The tenure of the editors is uncertain—the Kremlin may fire them without notice, as happened to their predecessors.

(These words were barely off my typewriter when news came through that the two editors who were running *Novy Mir* during the illness of Alexander Tvardovsky, the chief editor, have been removed, as the United Press phrased it, "in an apparent blow at the country's liberal literary movement." The rumors were to the effect that it was punishment for having accepted the Solzhenitsyn story.)

The important point is that none of the supposed new freedoms are permanent or confirmed by decrees. They are exercised on sufferance subject to good behavior. The Kremlin gives and the Kremlin takes away.

• *Note on a Poet*

Yevgeny Yevtushenko is no Pushkin—in fact, he is no Yevtushenko. I mean that for all his literary glibness and youthful charms he does not measure up to the inflated fame that has come to him. All his instincts are deeply humanist, and his writings abound with evocations of long-forbidden values. That is enough to make him an idol of Russian youth. Yet his personal situation is not without an aspect of pathos, for his fate is typical of the badgered intellectual in a totalitarian society.

The sad truth is that Yevtushenko, at home or on his foreign tours, has never uttered a line critical of communism as a faith or as a way of life. Its superiority over non-communist nations is implicit where it is not explicit in all his works and lectures. "I am proud because they cannot break me down or force me to my knees," he exclaimed in one of his earliest poems. But "they" could and they did. Following Khrushchev's denunciation of the new tendencies in December, 1962, Yevtushenko was among those who "recanted" his alleged sins. For a year or two thereafter he was in the "doghouse," silent and denied the foreign travel he loves.

Unlike more outspoken colleagues who end up in forced-labor camps or lunatic asylums, he knows the limits of his new freedom and exercises caution in safeguarding his career and comfort. He has not said a word in defense of, or sympathy for, Sinyavsky and Daniel, or other recent victims of literary suppression.

In a curious way, given his fame as a truth-speaker, he serves as a court poet. The Kremlin knows that it can trust him to go to the bourgeois infidels of the West; that he will limit himself always to fine poetic flights without reflecting on the Soviet regime and its oligarchs. At his American lectures his worshipful audiences sometimes asked embarrassing questions with political implications, and always Yevtushenko evaded them with wisecracks. The Kremlin can count on him also to return home to attack and ridicule the world of freedom which had lionized him. America, he informed his Soviet admirers in early 1967, on getting back from a much-publicized tour, is a land of "frozen lies," its skyscrapers about to skid on the slippery frauds.

Yes, the masters can depend on him confidently. He is their talented press agent, a showpiece of the bogus freedom so dear to liberal hearts abroad. But one wonders what is really in his own heart. Does he enjoy his celebrations of truth and justice, knowing as he must that he dare not go beyond the limits set by thought-police? More courageous Soviet writers, those willing to take more chances, do not hold him in great esteem, literary tests aside—and they are not allowed to go abroad.

• Revolt of the Intelligentsia

It would be a mistake, given these facts, to believe that the arts and sciences and education have been liberated. They seem free only in contrast to the total blackout that preceded. Compared with open societies or pre-1917 Russia, they remain in dire bondage. Yet many intellectuals venture far more than is strictly allowed, apparently gambling that the dictators will hesitate to make martyrs of them, or simply in a mood to take the medicine of punishment if they must. *Their new self-confidence is the most fateful element in the cultural equation.*

Confirmation of this fact has come, of all people, from the daughter of Stalin, Svetlana Alliluyeva. On arriving in the United States as a refugee in April, 1967, she explained that she was seeking the freedom of expression and of conscience denied in her native land. "I can say," she declared in a press conference, "that I *lost hopes which I had before that we are going to become liberal somehow.*" Other intellectuals, she indicated, shared her despair and are producing honest works in defiance of the authorities.* Many of the men who now rule the Soviet world, she emphasized, were as guilty as her father of the "crimes" they hypocritically charge against him alone. The blame, as she saw it, must be put where it belongs—on "the regime and ideology as a whole."

Her testimony, one hopes against hope, may awaken those abroad who have mesmerized themselves into the belief that "liberalization" has come to the Soviet Union. The New York *Times* (April 30) called her declarations "the most devastating critique of

---

* In the June, 1967, issue of *The Atlantic* magazine, Mrs. Alliluyeva wrote about the "martyrs of Russian literature" in the past and at present: "As before, it is given to gendarmes and policemen to be the first critics of a writer's work. Except that in Russia under the Czars neither Gogol nor Shchedrin was ever brought to trial for the sharpness of his satirical fantasies, and they were not punished for laughing at the absurdities of Russian life. But now you can be tried for a metaphor, sent to a camp for figures of speech!"

communism and the Soviet system heard since the denunciation of Stalin and Stalinism." But evidently they were not devastating enough to dislodge consoling delusions, even in that newspaper. It continued editorially to plug for American foreign policy resting on the assumption that the USSR has undergone a fundamental change.

No one would denigrate the moral courage and mental clarity of Stalin's daughter. Yet it should be made clear that other defecting intellectuals, dozens of them, have said approximately what she did, sometimes in almost the same words, only to be ignored in the free world.

People habituated to life in freedom do not find it easy to understand the heartbreak involved for a Soviet citizen in fleeing to the West. How many of us, under similar circumstances, would abandon the earth we love, our families and friends, our language and careers, to start life anew—often in middle age—in alien countries frightening in their sheer strangeness? Always the elation of escape is mixed with feelings of guilt for having found sanctuary while others are facing the challenge of totalitarian oppression back home.

Another recent defector, Yury Krotkov, whom I quoted in an earlier chapter, conveys this touchingly in the introductory chapter to his book, *The Angry Exile*. A successful writer in his homeland, with prestigious "credits" for conformist plays and film scenarios, he was tormented by the price of success and comfort. "All I have ever written," he exclaims, "is a lie, dishonorable fabrications of situations, images, conflicts, pseudo-values, nothing but hackwork and propaganda."

Krotkov points to "the struggle that is going on in literature, the arts, and all fields of intellectual endeavor in the Soviet Union," and expresses admiration for colleagues "who are risking their careers, perhaps their freedom, in the cause of artistic emancipation." But for himself, he felt unequal to such heroism—he is no Pasternak, he says sadly—and chose the easier course of flight. Like so many other émigrés, he hoped to make the West aware of the battles for human and artistic values under way today in his native land. And like them, alas, he found the free world indifferent or worse, steeped in self-deceptions about a "new freedom" in the USSR.

The chief value of Svetlana Stalina's defection is that because of her identity, because of the drama of truth-telling by the daughter of Stalin, her voice could be heard above the babble of Western confusions. Perhaps, as a by-product of the drama, some of the unknown Krotkovs, too, will now be listened to. Free-world opinion has worked itself into a sad misunderstanding. It supposes that the Kremlin masters are willing, even eager, to "liberalize" life in their country, when in fact they are thoroughly alarmed by the process and are resisting it at every turn. As a result the outside world awards credit for victories of the human spirit to the dictators, though the credit belongs solely to valiant men and women who risk all in defying the regime.

In underlining the lack of creative freedom which impelled her to seek asylum, Svetlana mentioned the harsh punishments meted out to Sinyavsky and Daniel. The true significance of that case is not in the prosecution itself—standard in a police-state—but in the reaction of the Soviet intelligentsia, of which hers is typical. The arrest and the ferocious sentences were clearly planned by Brezhnev and Kosygin as a warning to others, but they failed to intimidate. On the contrary, they touched off a bold show of sympathy for the victims.

The only major writer asked to address the 1966 Party Congress was Mikhail Sholokhov, recent winner of a Nobel Prize and a "dogmatist" or Stalinist. He not only defended the conviction of the two men but said that the sentences were too mild. In the good old days, he exclaimed, "these renegades would have received a different measure of punishment, let me tell you!" He meant execution, of course, and he drew wild applause in the Kremlin hall: a sufficient indication of where the ruling party stands in the war on intellectual liberty.

But the result of Sholokhov's lynch speech, according to an American observer on the scene, is that he is "probably the most hated man in Soviet letters today." A noted woman writer, Lydia Chukhovskaya, addressed an open letter of rebuke to Sholokhov, an eloquent defense of the free mind that was as much a rebuke to the regime as to the novelist personally. The Soviet press ignored it, of course, but later it was included in an illicit "white book" on the Sinyavsky-Daniel case, circulated inside Russia and widely republished abroad.* According to an Associated Press story from Moscow on January 24, 1967, the young poet who compiled the "white book," Alexander Ginsburg, was arrested.

One of the youthful leaders of a demonstration against the arrest of writers, Vladimir Butovsky, was locked into an insane asylum. Others were arrested for "plotting" an anti-Stalin demonstration in Red Square to mark the anniversary of the despot's death. On January 22, 1967, a group of students demonstrated in Moscow's Pushkin Square, at the base of the statue of the national poet, against the law under which writers were being convicted. One of the organizers, Victor Khaustov, was condemned to four years of hard labor.

The danger of police repression, however, does not seem to deter the more spirited critics of cultural policies. In late 1966 a compilation of unpublished materials, what Russians call a "literary almanac," was circulated in manuscript form in Moscow and presumably elsewhere under the title *Phoenix 1966*. Copies reached Europe and parts of it have seen print there. Demonstratively, it included two of the essays by Andrei Sinyavsky which had brought his imprisonment.

The most remarkable feature of the illicit journal was an editorial addressed to the rulers. Referring to a decree of September 16, 1966, setting more drastic penalties for anti-regime writings and activities, it charged that "the authorities wanted to create a legal base from which to repress the democratic spirit that is beginning to emerge," and added: "You may win this battle but all the same you will lose the war, the war for democracy in Russia." The youthful editor of *Phoenix 1966*, Yuri Galanskov, and at least two collaborators, Vera Lashkov and Piotr Rodzievsky were duly arrested, as no doubt they expected to be. The rock-bottom importance of such episodes, and they are numerous, is in their spirit of defiance. *What is under way is not, as supposed abroad, a change in the essential nature of the Soviet system, but a historic struggle between the intelligentsia and the rulers.* The deepest significance is not artistic but political.

Tensions are not yet at the breaking point, perhaps will never reach that point. But there are no signs of conciliation on either

* The full text was published in the New York *Times*, November 19, 1966.

side. The Kremlin gives some ground, then retrieves it, swinging uncertainly between moderation and toughness. It mollifies, threatens, and negotiates with the communities of mind and spirit as if they were alien forces to be contained if not conquered. A British observer who has made many trips to the USSR and uses the pseudonym Timothy McClure concluded a recent survey of cultural life there with the words: "The leaders have demonstrated that the party's bias remains anti-intellectual, resistant to change and distrustful of the arts."

On that celebrated occasion, on December 1, 1962, when Khrushchev threw a tantrum at an exhibition of modern art, he stalked out of the place with a final exclamation: "Gentlemen, we are at war with you!" The heartening fact is that the "gentlemen" have not been too frightened. A number of writers, and artists (among them Yestushenko, as already noted) did recant their "errors," but most of them, including some of the recanters, after lying low for a while, resumed their heretical ways with renewed courage. Actually the authorities carry on their offensive in the war so cautiously, by Soviet standards, that it looks more like defensive action.

After an interval of eight years and many postponements, the Fourth Congress of the Union of Soviet Writers finally met in Moscow in June, 1967. The delays were needed to assure that the gathering would be "disciplined" in the party sense. And it was—controlled from above, and obedient. Of the 473 delegates, 403 were party members. Only eight were under thirty—suggesting the exclusion of or a boycott by youth. The regime wanted no rebellion in its "jubilee year."

The whole thing seemed tame, arid. Yet something exciting did happen—the only dramatic event being discussed in the Soviet Union. Alexander Solzhenitsyn, denied the right to speak, disseminated a bold letter among the delegates in which he accused the Union of cowardice, denounced literary censorship, and recounted his own persecution by the police. (The full text has been published in the Paris *Le Monde*, the *New York Times* and other foreign papers, but not, of course, inside the USSR.) Not only did the authorities not dare arrest him but scores of the seemingly tame delegates have publicly joined him in demanding an end to censorship.

Valentin Katayev, best known abroad for his comedy of some

forty years ago, *Squaring the Circle*, could write in 1966 (in fiction, to be sure), "Break down the barriers, let the people see clear light and magnificent open spaces!" His message was that people must "patiently, heroically build bridges from man to man, because human corpses clutter the path and stone monuments obscure the horizon." No one, least of all the Kremlin hierarchs, could fail to understand that he was pleading for broad, humane approach.

Alexander Yessenin-Volpin, son of the Sergei Yessenin who took his own life in 1925, wrote in a book published in America in 1961:

Actually, only a morally and mentally defective person can fail to reach a stage of extreme indignation in the Soviet Union. If this were not so, the communists would have no reason to seal up their borders. . . . Now the methods have changed, but not radically. The main point is that even the relative freedom which we have gained (a level of freedom which would seem to a person from another country to be the most shameful slavery) was not won by our society itself, but was granted to it by the government, or more accurately, by the communist "church," as a sort of cat-and-mouse game with the people, rather than for the sake of more civilized rule. . . . There is no freedom of the press in Russia, but who can say there is no freedom of thought?

That was from one of the essays which, predictably, led to his temporary confinement in an insane asylum. Yessenin-Volpin, it seems to me, underrated the role of "society itself"—the "church" did what it did not as a cat-and-mouse amusement, but in the hope of easing dangerous tensions. They have not been eased. The struggle between the total state and the majority of the intelligentsia becomes more embittered. Despite its overwhelming advantages of physical force, it is by no means a foregone conclusion that the state will win in the long-run.

Judgments on the milder cultural climate since Stalin and on its portents for the future naturally will differ. But any implication that it somehow cancels out the thirty-five years of appalling inclemency would be, to put it mildly, extraordinary—a cruel affront to the millions of victims. The fifty-year record clearly shows that the Russian peoples, under a more open government, would have achieved infinitely more and better. As for those who cling to the myth that Soviet communism has actually *fostered* culture, one can only marvel at their historical ignorance.

21 / Underdeveloped Nations

The myth that communism is a rational model for underdeveloped countries.

According to orthodox Marxism, socialism or communism was to have come first in the advanced, most fully industrialized nations. Instead it came only in backward and largely agrarian countries: Russia, China, Cuba. Out of this historical accident has grown a theory which in effect stands Marxism on its head, namely that the more backward or primitive a nation, the more fit it is to embrace socialism.

The theory is not only false, it is grotesque. It implies the socialization of functioning industry that does not yet exist, the collectivization of agriculture when there is no industrial base to supply the necessary machinery and chemical support.

Communists have succeeded in taking over relatively underdeveloped countries precisely because they were retarded, especially in terms of political experience and sophistication. "Lenin seized power not in a land 'ripe for socialism' but in a land ripe for seizing power," as Bertram D. Wolfe put it. Soon enough Lenin realized that Marx was right on this score, that socialism did not flow from power alone. When his hope that Germany or some other advanced capitalist nation would go communist and balance Russia's backwardness did not come true, Lenin sadly reverted to the private enterprise of the NEP period.

This is a piece of Soviet history pertinent to the plight of Afro-Asians and Latin Americans tempted to embark on a communist course. Socialist catchwords may enable them to come to power, but they will not enable them to introduce a viable socialist life. Admittedly Ghana or Peru or India could fall to the communists more easily than, let us say, Belgium or Canada, but their socialism would be at best a caricature of the real thing.

In nearly all of the emerging or industrially backward nations there is a minority, organized in open or clandestine parties, pressing and intriguing for the imposition of their ready-made Moscow or Peking pattern. As groups, though not as individuals, they are too rigidly committed to be accessible to reason.

But that is not the case with the largest part of the radical and progressive elements who think themselves, in a vague way, "socialists." They are not bound to a hard-and-fast program but are under the spell of a diffuse socialist mystique, convinced that they can do what existing communist systems have failed to do—that they can reconcile their cloudy visions of economic equality and abundance with the freedoms, civil liberties, and human rights they crave for themselves and their countrymen.

It is to them, in the first place, that any plea for study and understanding of the fifty-year experience in the USSR should be addressed. The fact that Russia, in its attempt to "build socialism," quickly became totalitarian cannot be attributed to specifically Russian conditions or historic background. All other communist states are totalitarian, including Czechoslovakia and East Germany, which were industrially advanced and had democratic experience and traditions.

In theory, fully industrialized and technically advanced nations like England or the United States could undertake full socialization and retain basic political freedoms. That is the hope which sustains sincere socialists and communists in such countries. It has been said that only the most affluent capitalist nations could *afford* communism with its built-in economic fallacies and wastes. But in practice, as Czechoslovakia for one has demonstrated, political freedoms cannot survive under economic dictatorship.

The Afro-Asian and Latin American countries should be forewarned that involuntary labor, however trimmed with collectivist phrases, is uneconomic in the modern world and doomed to defeat in competition with free labor.

They should be forewarned, on the political level, that collaboration with communists always carries with it the threat of political annihilation. Communists declare openly, proudly, that they "cooperate" only in order to capture and destroy temporary allies. In the Spanish Civil War, the Loyalists accepted communist help and in due time paid for it with submission to Soviet dictation, murderous divisions in their ranks and ultimate defeat. The postwar governments of Poland, Czechoslovakia, Hungary, Rumania began as coalitions in which communists were minorities, and ended up as totalitarian satellites of Soviet Russia.

History is our warrant that a country or a movement cannot go just a little communist, any more than an individual can put just a little poison in his soup. Though men engaged in the revolutions of rising expectations are often in desperate need of guiding, training, money and weapons from outside, would they awarely accept it from fascist sources? *Yet communists, even more than fascists, are committed to ruining what they cannot rule.*

Above all, the educated, thinking elites in the underdeveloped world should be forewarned that communism and democracy, communism and humanism, simply do not mix. They are stark opposites. Attempts to combine them are exercises in futility. Whatever the verbal camouflage, communism is a revolt *against* democracy, against liberalism, against social and cultural pluralism. Its high-priests ridicule humanist principles and aspirations—at least until some apocryphal future when their communist utopia prevails in the whole world—as *"petit bourgeois* liberalism." They deride ethical values as "idealism"—a word of abuse in the communist lexicon—and the religious heritage of mankind as "superstition."

Soviet Russia in its half-century has left no room for doubt that the costs of "building socialism" are higher than any people would knowingly agree to pay. This is what countries being propagandized to follow the Soviet road have to recognize. Even their willingness to pay the price in long-term deprivations and totalitarian regimentation is not in itself a guarantee that they can duplicate the Soviet record, sorry as it may be. They need, in addition, the advantages with which the Bolsheviks started in 1917: a substantial economic base, existing scientific and technical elites, national resources and population gigantic enough to permit profligate investments without going bankrupt—and a citizenry that can be beaten into enduring incalculable sufferings for forty or fifty years.

I am not inveighing against rebellion as such, as justified in the Declaration of Independence of the thirteen American colonies in

1776. It is usually the product of injustice and despair. In many countries today rebels are staking their lives for causes they consider noble, idealistic, well worth the supreme sacrifice—and that includes rebels in the socialist-bloc countries.

But to the extent that they identify their goals with communism and submit to communist leadership, they are the victims of a grand deception; in the measure that the truth is available, it is self-deception. Victory may then be a worse fate than defeat, for they will have won serfdom in new dimensions, colonial dependence in some Red empire. Victory would not only lead to their personal "liquidation" more surely than defeat but, as in Cuba, would make renewed rebellion infinitely more difficult.

Alexander Kerensky, who headed the Provisional Government when it was smashed by Lenin, is alive and residing in the United States. "The Russian people," he wrote in his recent autobiography, "cannot be blamed for falling into the Bolshevik trap for, at that time, the world had had no experience with modern totalitarian techniques. But there is no such excuse for the millions of workers, farmers, and intellectuals in the democratic West who are offered the bait today. To them the frightful experience of my native land should serve as a grim warning."

He need not have limited himself to the West. The traps are all set, the bait pungent, everywhere on this planet. Before swallowing it, those sincerely concerned for the future of their peoples owe it to their intelligence and their conscience to take a hard, clear-eyed look at the Soviet realities under the communist claims and to examine the alternatives. They should compare what they see in Soviet Russia, again with eyes unblurred by propaganda clichés, with the open, democratic, prospering societies.

These do not claim perfection and they fall far short of it. The press and literature in the democracies run over with criticism and protest against defects, against real and imagined injustices and corruptions. Indeed, the social progress, the ever wider distribution of material goods and amenities, the almost universal access of youth to education, the fundamental liberties of speech and press, thought, and religious faiths, mobility at home and travel abroad, judicial protection of the individual against the state and the tyranny of majorities—these tend to be taken for granted, like the air one breathes.

The existence of imperfections in democratic countries does not prove that communism is or can be more satisfactory, any more than the existence of an ailment in the body proves that a particular nostrum will cure it. This is the essential illogic of communist preachments, emphasizing the evils of the *status quo* in the free world but ignoring or misrepresenting the infinitely greater evils in the communist lands. Tsarist absolutism unquestionably obstructed the full unfoldment of a modern industrial society—which hardly proved that another and more rigid absolutism would open the road to modernization.

Despite their inadequacies, I submit, the advanced free nations offer more promising models than any of the closed, monolithic societies for rational men and women engaged in the contemporary revolutions of rising expectations.

PART III

What Price Communism?

*An assessment of the Soviet half-century, as has been underscored
in preceding sections of the book, cannot evade consideration of
the exorbitant price paid by the Russian peoples and the world.
Many of the costs have been put on record in examining the principal myths with which the subject is encrusted. But a summation
is in order, to complete the balance sheet. This unavoidably in-
volves some repetition; and the six groupings under which the costs
are organized of necessity overlap and intermesh.*

1 / The Costs in Life

A British journalist, D. G. Stewart-Smith, in his book *Defeat of
Communism*, attempted an estimate. International communism
from 1917 to 1964, he found, was directly responsible for eighty-
three million deaths—more than the deaths in the two World
Wars. This did not include the loss of life in the second of these
holocausts, although Moscow's role in the triumph of Hitlerism
and in unleashing the war cannot be underestimated. Of the
eighty-three million, according to his analysis, more than forty-five
million were in Soviet Russia proper, through civil war, famines,
"liquidation of the *kulaks*," purge executions, the high mortality
rates in concentration camps, and so on.

Such figures, any figures in this grim context, are open to challenge in both directions. He puts the dead in the man-made famine of 1932–1933, for instance, at six million—I would scale it

down to four million. (Yet a British historian, J. N. Westwood, in his recent book, *Russia 1917–1964*, writes: "About 10 to 15 million people died in the 1932–34 famine and its attendant epidemics"; possibly he had in mind also the toll of life in the deportations of those years.) Deaths in forced-labor areas and prison "isolators," Mr. Stewart-Smith reckons at eleven million—most estimates are substantially higher. At Yalta, Winston Churchill was voicing sympathy for the high Russian casualties in the war. Stalin shrugged. Collectivization, he told his guest, had cost the USSR more lives than the war. If he was right, Mr. Stewart-Smith's total in that column is probably too small.

In his monumental study *The Growth of Industrial Production in the Soviet Union*, released in 1962, Professor G. Warren Nutter aligned Soviet statistics revealing "a deficit of some 40 million people between 1941 and 1945." Since the highest estimate of loss of life in the war is 20 million, at least that many more had been lost through other causes. In 1913 the population within the present boundaries of the Soviet Union was more than 60 per cent higher than that of the United States, but by 1962 it was only 20 per cent higher. In this Soviet shrinkage demographers see evidence of the tens of millions of lives destroyed.

A young Yugoslav educator, Mihajlo Mihajlov, returning from a long summer sojourn in Russia in 1964, was jailed for publishing an uninhibited account of his experience and findings. Apparently Tito had acted under pressures from Moscow: the main charge was giving offense to a friendly foreign government. Tito himself, of course, had said things a thousand times more devastating about the USSR. Speaking in Zagreb on November 3, 1952, for instance, he exclaimed: "Millions of Soviet citizens languish in *death* and forced-labor camps." It was no secret that what Moscow found most distressing in Mihajlov's account was his revelation that the Soviets early in their career had operated extermination camps, thus canceling out another "first" in the Nazi obscenities.

"The Soviet press is writing less and less about fascist and Nazi camps, to avoid comparisons with the Soviet camps," Dr. Mihajlov wrote. "This is quite understandable. The first 'death camps' were not founded by the Germans, but by the Soviets. In 1921, near Arkhangelsk, they set up Kolgomor camp for the sole purpose of physically destroying the prisoners. It operated successfully for many years and swallowed up many of the Bolsheviks' former allies —members of the non-Bolshevik revolutionary parties."

But one blushes at the quibblings about figures and comparative sadisms. It is like insisting that only five million Jews perished in Nazi gas chambers, not six million as commonly believed. What are a few million corpses more or less in the statistics of the Caligulas and Genghis Khans, the Hitlers and Stalins of history?

Millions of the victims, in the torture chambers and in the slave camps, were denied the solace of a quick and easy death; they died slowly, excruciatingly, from physical abuse, overwork, undernourishment and exposure. The Soviet killings of individuals and of groups "as a class" were not committed in a frenzy of anger or panic. For the most part they were carried out in cold blood, deliberately: calculated destruction not only of enemies but of potential enemies, or simply to be rid of the superfluous and unwanted.

2 / The Costs in Terror

It is even more difficult, actually impossible, to reckon the costs of half a century of terror generally, spanning as it does the spectrum from harassments to executions, from purges to mass deportations. No one was exempted, not even devoted communists and heroes.

The vastness of the Soviet state's machinery for internal spying and repression is in itself an index to the extent and ubiquity of terror. Never before, not even in a world that included German Nazism and Italian fascism, has a regime spawned such gigantic organs of surveillance, denunciation, punishment, censorship, and intimidation. No government in modern times, except perhaps Communist China, has invented so many "crimes against the state" or applied the death penalty so extensively. In former revolutions, terror and brutality subsided with victory. In Soviet Russia, uniquely in the history of revolutions, persecution and punishment grew in scope and ferocity after the safety and power of the new masters was assured.

As a matter of course, the authorities read the citizen's mail and listen in on his phone. The secret police maintain branch offices on the premises of the larger factories, mines, farms, universities, libraries, hotels, railroad stations. Little agents inform on bigger agents, like vermin on vermin. Every functionary important enough to rate a secretary or chauffeur takes it for granted that they are reporting not only his conduct, contacts and opinions, but his "political mood" for evaluation by the police. Not even the topmost leaders are exempt from this round-the-clock attention.

Every janitor reports on the tenants and every tenant is encouraged to watch and report on his neighbors, his fellow employees, local officials. Children are taught to report on their parents. In the years since Stalin, especially in Khrushchev's time, millions of young people have been organized in local vigilante brigades to check on the personal and political morals of their neighborhoods. Under beguiling names like *Druzhiny* (state guards), these youngsters, mostly teen-agers, may invade private homes, stage "trials" and hand out punishments. In some ways they resemble the Red Guards unloosed by Mao Tse-tung in China in 1966.

Victor Kravchenko, a Soviet defector, wrote in his celebrated book, *I Chose Freedom* (1946): "Multiple webs of espionage by the party and of the party, by the GPU and of the GPU, pooling information at some points, competing at other points, covered Soviet life from top to bottom. We lived in a world swarming with invisible eyes and ears." He was depicting the 1930's, but basically this system still prevails.

On January 11, 1918, Lenin, commenting on the blood-letting already under way, added: "We are still far from *real* terror, because for the time being we are stronger than they are." They—the foes of his regime—must have grown stronger with every month and year, since the "real" terror was applied on an ever larger scale.

Estimates of the number of slave laborers, by former camp inmates and scholarly researchers, range from ten to twenty-five million. Brooks Atkinson, in 1946, after his return from a six-year assignment in the USSR for the New York *Times*, put it between ten and fifteen million. A conscientious study made for a Commission of Inquiry into Forced Labor, published in 1951 as a book (*The Soviet Slave Empire*, by Albert Konrad Herling) said: "There is no doubt that in the last decade the prison camps and forced-labor camps had a minimum of eight million workers, and at various times a maximum of twenty million."

Some 90 per cent of this humanity being men of working age—only about 10 per cent of the victims were women—this represents

about 15 to 30 per cent of the country's total male working population. But when we take into account the large turnover in the
camps and exile regions—the mortality rate in the worst camps has
been estimated as high as 30 per cent a year—it is a fair guess that
no fewer than fifty million Soviet citizens in the aggregate experienced the Gehenna of the slave-labor system for periods of a year
(for those lucky enough to die quickly) to twenty-five years.

After all discounts are made, it is clear that almost every family
in the vast Soviet empire gave at least one member to the insatiable
beast. During and after the war, of course, millions of non-Soviet
prisoners—Germans, Balts, Poles, and other East Europeans, as
well as Japanese and many Americans—swelled these legions of the
damned. Statistics do not begin to suggest the sufferings involved
for the direct victims and their broken families. It would take the
genius of a Dante to describe the purgatory and the hell in which
men, women, and even children lived like so many animals, in filth
and vermin, worked literally to death, chronically starved, abused
and insulted.*

---

* For those interested to delve more deeply into the grim facts about Soviet
concentration camps, there is a rich literature in many languages. Here, ar-
ranged chronologically, are a few of the books available in English:

Letters from Russian Prisons, edited by Roger N. Baldwin. Albert & Charles
Boni, 1925.

Escape from the Soviets, by Tatiana Tchernavin. Dutton, 1935.

I Speak for the Silent, by Vladimir V. Tchernavin. Hale, Cushman & Flint,
1935.

Prisoner of the OGPU, by George Kitchin. Longmans Green, 1935.

Escape from Russian Chains, by Ivan Solonevich. Williams and Norgate,
1937.

The Woman Who Could Not Die, by Julia de Beausobre. Viking, 1938.

Forced Labor in Soviet Russia, by David Dallin and Boris Nicolaevsky. Yale
University Press, 1947.

The Dark Side of the Moon, preface by T.S. Eliot. Scribner's, 1947.

Tell the West! by Jerzy Gliksman. Gresham Press, 1948.

Soviet Gold: My Life as a Slave Laborer, by Vladimir Petrov. Farrar, Straus,
1949.

Slave Labor in Russia. Presented by the American Federation of Labor to the
United Nations, 1949.

Under Two Dictators, by Margaret Buber. Gollancz, 1950.

The Soviet Slave Empire, by Albert Herling. Wilfred Funk, 1951.

Eleven Years in Soviet Prison Camps, by Elinor Lipper. Regnery, 1951.

Stalin's Slave Camps: An Indictment of Modern Slavery. Confederation of
Free Trade Unions, Brussels, 1951.

A German woman, Elinor Lipper, came close to conveying the horror in her book, *Eleven Years in Soviet Prison Camps*, published in 1951. "A Soviet camp," she wrote, "is an incubator for all the vilest human instincts. Its name, 'correction labor camp,' is a mockery. . . . Not only does the camp provide no educational work; it gives the criminal the finest opportunity to practice his profession. The thief steals, the speculator speculates, the prostitute sells herself. The normal person is perverted, the honest man becomes a hypocrite, the brave man a coward, and all have their spirits and bodies broken." The fact that political offenders, the vast majority, are herded together with ordinary criminals is one of the worst afflictions of camp life; the "politicals" are literally at the mercy of killers and perverts, who wield more power than the official warders and guards.

Contrary to widespread misconceptions deliberately spread by the Kremlin and its friends abroad, the camp system has not been abolished since the passing of Stalin. Its dimensions have been reduced, although current victims must still be counted by the hundreds of thousands—by millions, according to some estimates. The treatment of inmates has become more lenient. But the institution itself is intact, and additional "crimes" punishable by exile to "corrective labor colonies"—in many cases the old camps *renamed* for easier swallowing—have been announced by the authorities from time to time.

Then there was the malignant process of collectivization. According to the pro-Soviet Sidney and Beatrice Webb, British Fabian Socialists, one million peasant families were liquidated. This is the most moderate estimate. At least five million human beings, that is, from babes in arms to the aged, were stripped of all possessions and transported in cattle cars to the Siberian *taiga*, the Arctic tundra, and Central Asian deserts, to live or die. Three or four times as many fled from the unfolding horrors in their ancestral villages, abandoning their homes and goods; most of them found work at new construction and industrial sites, the rest ended up in slave camps and exile regions.

As Far As My Feet Will Carry Me, by Josef M. Bauer. Random House, 1957.
I Was a Slave in Russia, by John H. Noble. Devin-Adair, 1958.
Years of My Life: The Memoirs of a General of the Soviet Army, by A. V. Gorbatov. Norton, 1965.

Their ordeal was only part of the incalculable agonies of the entire peasantry—at that time more than three-fourths of the population—most of them despoiled of their earthly goods and herded by raw force into the hated *kolkhozes*. Ever since, they have been subjected to a new species of serfdom, tied to the land, exploited without mercy in the interests of the state, their fate even bleaker by far than that of the so-called proletariat in factories, mines, and offices.

The testimony of Isaac Deutscher, a British writer, is pertinent because he has been consistently pro-Soviet, excusing the most obscene crimes in terms of historical necessity. In his book *What Next?* (1953), he wrote about collectivization: "The terror matched the resistance which those policies encountered. Only with scorpions could tens of millions be driven into collective farms, multitudes be shifted to new industrial sites, and the vast majority of people forced to toil in misery and suppress in silence the fury evoked by the privileges of a minority."

After a brief relaxation of pressures in the mid-thirties, the terror zoomed to new peaks in the time of the blood-purges, from 1936 to the coming of the war. The world to this day has not realized the real magnitude of that great carnage. It could know directly only the publicized butchering of leading communists, military men, professors, writers. The melodramatic Moscow treason trials in the foreground tended to shut off the view of the all-embracing purges behind them. Actually the whole population was affected.

In the ruling party, 1,800,000 members and candidates for membership were expelled, more than half the total, and that meant for them anything from concentration camp to shooting. At least eight million more, non-communists, were subjected to liquidation, implying anything from loss of their jobs and homes to loss of their lives. Executions and suicides have been estimated by Soviet defectors involved in the holocaust as high as two millions, and one million would probably be a moderate guess of the total. The late Moshe Pijade, one of the three of four leading communists in Yugoslavia, raised the ante in his polemic anti-Stalin zeal. "In 1936, 1937, and 1938," he said "over three million people disappeared from the earth's surface in the Soviet Union."

A purge of some ten million men and women staggers the imagination. Including their families and friends, whose lives were shaken up and often wrecked, we come close to a quarter of the whole population! And in truth no one escaped the tragedy, living amidst the thunderous fears of the time. Millions not actually involved in the purge remained psychologically crippled by the sheer waiting and dreading.

During the war, the inhabitants of entire "autonomous republics" were torn up by the roots fron their ancestral soil, deported and dispersed, like the supposed *kulaks* a decade earlier. These victims included the Volga Germans, the Crimean Tartars, the Buddhist Kalmyks, Chechen-Ingush, Balkars, and Karachais. Millions of Ukrainians received the same treatment; Khrushchev himself, one of the top engineers of this mass exile, would explain in 1956: "The Ukrainians escaped this fate only because there were too many of them and because there was no place to exile them to." The peoples deported in mass—not even members of the Communist Party and the *Komsomols* were spared—were not "rehabilitated" until 1957. By that time, their ancient homes had been preempted by Russians and others, so that the belated right to return was largely meaningless.

The nationwide purges were resumed after the war, in the so-called Zhdanov period (named for Stalin's ideological inquisitor, Andrei Zhdanov). In scale, duration, and malevolence, they matched the abominations of the 1930's. Those subjected to the greatest pressures were then the educated classes: scientists, writers, artists, and intellectuals generally.

Having touched on the most conspicuous episodes, we must again make clear that these, and others like them, do not encompass the whole terror in its myriad dimensions. There was the premium put on hypocrisy and lying, the shattering of family life by sudden arrests and by the ravages of denunciation. There was, and remains, the systematic persecution of religious faith and practice, the most sacred beliefs and holy objects of the greater part of the population —Christians, Moslems, Jews—mocked and mangled. Like people trapped on battlegrounds in war, everyone in Soviet Russia, from the lowliest to the highest, lived in an atmosphere of unremitting fear, blood, sudden evacuation and sudden death, but with refinements of danger and dread unknown in mere military wars.

Every student of the Soviet times has his own little list of what he considers the worst or most revealing elements in the terror. Dr. Lin Yutang, for example, cites his three "favorites": (1) making children of twelve subject to capital punishment; (2) sending women to work in under-surface coal mines; (3) harassing workers in their lunch recess with threats of prison for lateness in returning to work.

The overwhelming majority of Soviet citizens now alive were born into an all-pervasive atmosphere of terror, grew up in it, absorbing its nerve-wracking hates and poisons. They have lived under the constant surveillance of a colossal secret-police organization, with its own specialized army for internal repressions, supported by great contingents of professional and volunteer informers—an establishment for detection of heresy and swift punishment second in size only to the regular armed forces.

They have known the panic of the after-midnight knock on the door; the anguish of denunciation by close friends and relatives, including one's adored children; the awareness that their most innocent conversations, their mail and phones might be monitored and bring disaster. Arbitrary terror encompasses more humiliations, persecutions, punishments without crime, than language can convey. This was the haunting memory that moved Yevgeny Yevtushenko to recall the loss of "twenty million in war, and millions in the war on the people."

The defense of the horrors has become standard in communist apologetics. It is to the effect that capitalist industrialization in the nineteenth century, marked by sweatshops and child labor, was also cruel. The argument is both specious and stupid. Private entrepreneurs did not deliberately and arbitrarily, as a matter of state policy, murder millions and condemn tens of millions to slave labor in hideous concentration camps. Moreover, in Western Europe and the United States, under relatively democratic systems, the evils could be exposed, opposed, and ultimately eliminated.

Let no one suppose that terror on this scale over such a protracted period can be canceled out in the national memory and from the national conscience by a few years of moderation. Its scars are on every mind and heart. Although they have never been published, the heartbreak songs of camp and prison, the haunting laments of the homeless children, are sung by the new generation, secretly among themselves or defiantly in schools and at demonstrations. The wounds are unstitched, unhealed—gangrenous with guilt among the mighty, a festering fury among the humble.

3 / The Costs in Thought Control

Having sealed the country as hermetically as they could against foreign printed matter and radio, the oligarchy rationed information stingily through absolute control of the flow of news and ideas. The content of everything in print and on the airwaves was limited to authorized "truths," which is another name for official lies. Multiple censorships guarded against the leakage of forbidden thoughts through the press, books, scientific papers; on the stage and screen and on the air; in schoolrooms and lecture halls. Folk songs and fairy tales were examined for dangerous overtones. Not even the Holy Writ of Marx, Engels and Lenin was exempt from censorial editing and suppressions.

Textbooks, from kindergarten up, were crammed with half-truths and full lies. Every discipline, from economics to agronomy, from biology to philosophy, was narrowed and mangled to conform with dicta from Marx and Lenin and the propaganda line of the masters. Areas as seemingly remote from Kremlin interests as astronomy and psychiatry were sown with booby-traps for careless practitioners. The marauders were especially ruthless in the fields of history. Everything that did not fit into their arbitrary mythology was thrown into what has been called the Memory Hole. Past events were revised or blotted out. Historical "facts" and biographical data were simply invented, then deleted or restored periodically as the party "line" changed.

Reflecting the occupational hazards of callings involving the mind, the proportion of professors and students, scientists, historians and such was especially high, in relation to their numbers, among the "liquidated" and the inmates of slave camps. In literature and all the other arts, music included, the creative urge became the shortest road to economic penury or physical extinction. At the same time the treasure-houses of Russian poetry, prose, music, philosophy were "purged" insofar as censors could do it with so great and vast national heritage.

Lord Bertrand Russell, the British philosopher, though he was at the time sympathetic to the Russian Revolution, wrote in a book on Bolshevism in 1920: "If a more just economic system were only attainable by closing men's minds against free inquiry, and plunging them back into the intellectual prison of the Middle Ages, *I should consider the price too high.*" The exorbitant price was paid but it did not buy the more just economic system. Said André Gide, after his journey through the USSR which cured him of his illusions about communism: "I doubt that in any country of the world, even Hitler's Germany, is thought less free, more bowed down, more terrorized."

Those who have read George Orwell's fantasy-novel, *1984,* have some idea of what it means to have your every thought and gesture and facial expression watched by Big Brother. Some parts of his prevision of thought-control carried to its extreme were chillingly close to what was actually happening in Stalin's empire.

The other side of suppression and censorship has been large-scale and systematic indoctrination. Veritable armies of lecturers have been engaged in molding two hundred million minds to conform to preconceived patterns. Enormous funds and manpower—a million full-time and part-time indoctrinators, it has been estimated— were assigned to this job of "brainwashing." William Benton, publisher of the *Encyclopaedia Britannica,* after a study of the subject in Russia, wrote in 1956:

"Throughout the Soviet Union, there are about six thousand special schools maintained by the party and devoted exclusively to training professional propagandists. . . . Above these schools are 177 regional 'propaganda colleges' to train 'alumni' of the local schools. And above the regional schools are a dozen high institutions giving 'graduate training' to several thousand advanced students."

Never before in history has there been such a stupendous enterprise in shaping the thought of a nation—in "selling" a regime on a twenty-four-hour schedule to its captive subjects. The pressures of nagging, hectoring slogans, clichés, exhortations, boasts, and threats are so relentless that they have amounted to a form of psychological torture. Some people have cracked under the strain, most have bowed meekly. Yet amazingly, unauthorized thoughts and feelings, memories and intuitions, somehow did survive in the underground of minds and hearts and now, more than ever before in the fifty years, rise to the surface to taunt and frighten the rulers.

4 / The Political Costs

These are inherent in the formula of "dictatorship of the proletariat." The self-anointed and self-perpetuating dictators, a few hundred or a few thousand, have exercised absolute power over the small ruling party and through it over the rest of the citizenry. The rank-and-file communist has various privileges and opportunities but no more political rights than his non-party neighbors. The tight oligarchy operates through appointed proconsuls and agents of all degrees. The authority each of them wields is strictly delegated from the top and he is accountable only to his superiors in the pyramid, never to the people under his tutelage.

Soviet communism has stamped out free speech, press, and assembly, even in the restricted measure that they existed under the monarchy. The reader need only think of the political rights he enjoys—no matter how inadequate he may consider them—and realize that he would not have them if he were a Soviet citizen. "Elections" are limited to a single list of names, drawn up by the party or by organizations under party control. The whole process of "voting" is a compulsory totalitarian charade, implying not the slightest degree of popular participation in government. It does not differ from elections under Mussolini and Hitler, who in fact merely copied the Soviet model.

As a practical matter, it is unimportant how the Soviets or "legislatures" are "elected" and who "represents" the constituency, since these bodies have no governing function whatsoever. They meet so rarely and so briefly that the very pretense of a role in running the nation is farcical. The Supreme Soviet of the USSR, the national parliament, meets only once or twice a year *for a few days, a week at most*. Only mentally retarded children could believe the fairy tale that it disposes of the law-making business of a great and complex empire in this time. The "parliament" does not even have the time to rubberstamp all the decrees and plans theoretically submitted for its approval. It has never rejected any law or plan submitted by the bosses or approved it by less than unanimous vote. From the ballot box to the gala annual speech-making marathon in the Kremlin, the exercise is spurious.

Despite the beating of drums around so-called de-Stalinization, the country still lives under the Stalin constitution—not that it makes any difference, since it is ignored in practice insofar as political and civil rights are concerned. That extraordinary document was modestly presented in 1936 as "the most democratic constitution in the world" and duly hailed abroad at the time as evidence of Stalin's "new liberalism." It added insult to injury by listing on paper the fundamental civil guarantees denied in actuality, then and now. It assigned autonomous functions to an array of social and governmental organizations, with the mere proviso that all of them must remain under control of the Communist Party.

From time to time, as at present, there has been a supposed "return to legality." But it appeared soon enough that there can be no real rule of law under a regime that is itself lawless, that extracts "confessions" to invented crimes by torture, violates its own constitution, disposes of its enemies by secret administrative action, issues decrees affecting the entire citizenry by arbitrary decision of the uppermost clique.

Where political sins are involved—and nearly everything is "political" in the totalitarian world—the judicial system is a travesty of justice. The accused has no right to defense counsel until after the police and investigatory machine has prepared him for trial. Even then, the defense lawyer, unless he has an urge to political suicide, can do nothing to embarrass the prosecution or expose its deceptions. In the infamous demonstration trials, in particular, the supposed defenders sometimes outdid the prosecutors in zeal to destroy their "clients."

Exoneration of citizens brought to trial under "political" statutes is exceedingly rare; to be accused by the all-knowing, all-seeing state is proof enough of guilt. Failure to denounce others who may harbor sinful views, whether relatives or strangers, is a punishable crime. Wives are obliged to testify against husbands, husbands against wives, and of course no one is exempted from testifying against himself.

Everyone knows that in Soviet Russia there is no *habeas corpus.* Few outside the country know that there is not even *habeas cadaver.* No non-official witnesses can confirm an execution and the body of the executed is not returned to the family for burial. The suspicion that a relative or friend whose death has been officially announced may in fact be alive, rotting in some isolator or concentration hell, adds mortifying uncertainty to the tragedy. Instances of "executed" persons who years later turned up alive are not unknown in the Soviet Union.

The individual has no semblance of any role in government, in law-making and decision-making, and most important, no protection against the will and whims of an arbitrary, all-powerful state. A differing value is placed on political and civil freedoms in different civilizations, but no matter how low the price-tag, their total denial to more than 200 million people for five decades is a decisive element in the balance sheet.

5 / The Costs to the World

Directly and through its international apparatus and extensions, the damage Soviet communism has done to the world is incalculable.

There is hardly a major crisis anywhere on this globe—from Southeast Asia to the Caribbean, from Africa to the Middle East—in which the territorial and ideological ambitions of Moscow are not deeply involved. The turbid tides of anti-Western and anti-American demonstrations, riots, arson—even in America and the West—are almost always communist-instigated, communist-led or, at the least, exploited by the communists.

And this has been true ever since Bolshevism seized a base of operations in Russia, along with the country's colossal material and human resources. The world since 1917 has been in a continuous turmoil of bloody conflicts, ferocious civil wars, competing propagandas, nearly all of them fomented or encouraged by communism. At bottom the history of these fifty years has been a struggle between free nations and those aspiring to freedom on one side, and a dehumanized totalitarianism on the other. Directly or by its example, as already observed, communism has spawned other types of totalitarianism, while itself enduring as the strongest and most menacing.

It happens that I was present, as a very young free-lance reporter, in late 1920 at the Livorno (Leghorn) congress of the Italian Socialist party. I watched how the communist faction, with Moscow agents present openly directing the strategy of demolition, split that powerful organization and its trade unions. It was this split that opened wide the road to Mussolini and his castor-oil brigades. In the same fashion, more moderate Marxist and other Leftist forces in the rest of the world were splintered from within on Kremlin orders. The parties which local adherents of the Moscow faith could not take over, they systematically destroyed.

The most disastrous consequences of this effort—disastrous, it turned out, for Russia too—was the triumph of National Socialism in Germany. In the climactic years of Hitler's rise, Stalin and his Communist International identified the moderate socialists and liberal reformers as "social fascists" and "the main enemy." Against them even collaboration with the Hitlerites was certified as smart tactics. In 1931, on Kremlin instructions, the German Communist party joined the Nazis on certain issues to defeat the non-communist Left. Thus the opposition, which might have headed off the obscenity, was fragmented and the Nazi movement had the unimpeded right of way.

The Kremlin stuck to its blunder even after Hitler was enthroned and slaughtering German communists. As late as April, 1934, the Communist International still declared solemnly that Nazism "by destroying all the democratic illusions of the masses and liberating them from the influence of Social Democracy, accelerates the rate of Germany's development toward proletarian revolution."

Earlier that year the communist chieftain in the United States, Earl Browder, ridiculed those who feared Hitlerism. Fascism, he explained, "destroys the moral base for capitalist rule, discrediting bourgeois law in the eyes of the masses; it hastens the exposure of all demagogic supporters of capitalism, especially its main support among the workers—the socialist trade-union leaders. It hastens the revolutionization of the workers, destroys their democratic illusions and prepares the masses for the revolutionary struggle for power."

The Stalin-Hitler pact that unleashed World War II astonished only those who had forgotten the Kremlin's ambivalence on Nazism. The two dictatorships had plenty in common. It was easier for communists willing to serve Hitler to join his party than for most other Germans. After the war, Ulbricht in East Germany repaid the compliment by enlisting thousands of ex-Nazis in his communist apparatus.

The evil went deeper. Communist ideology, by disorienting the minds of several generations of men, contributed to a world-wide erosion of traditional intellectual and ethical standards, the decay of idealism and democratic preferences. It provided a rationale for inhumane practices under "revolutionary" labels. Red intrusion and subversion weakened or destroyed progressive and radical movements, trade-unions, democratizing trends.

Starting with one hundred and sixty million subjects in one country, communism has spread to take in a third of the human race. Because it was unloosed in Russia, its extension propagated and financed by Lenin's Third or Communist International, the sufferings in all other Red nations, from China to Cuba, may justly be charged against Soviet communism.

The conquest of unwilling poeples was begun by the Lenin-Trotsky regime with the re-imposition of Russian imperial domin-ion over racial-national minorities that had broken away in the civil-war period. Gruzia (Georgia), the Ukraine, various Central Asian areas that had set up their own governments were brutally beaten into submission. Then, in due time, Lenin's successors went on to crush one neighboring nation after another: Outer Mongolia be-fore the Second World War, Central and Eastern European na-tions during and after the war. And the end, as Soviet propaganda and official programs make clear, is not yet.

In an era when old-style colonialism has been virtually ended, Red imperialism has emerged as the largest colonial system extant. It is today the only dynamic, *expanding* imperialism on this planet. Korea, Vietnam, the horrifying toll of death in averting a commu-nist take-over in Indonesia, are merely episodes in the permanent totalitarian offensive against the rest of the world.

As the Second World War was drawing to its end, Winston Churchill, in a burst of optimism he was to regret, said: "I know of no government which stands to its obligation, even in its own de-spite, more solidly than the Soviet Union." President Truman matched this faith in "good old Joe." But the echoes of the last battles had barely died away when Moscow returned with renewed energy to its systematic assaults on free societies.

Again Stalin was denouncing the Allies without whom he could not have saved his regime from obliteration. One after another the Kremlin's solemn undertakings for postwar occupation and normalization of the defeated lands were broken. One after another the hopes that Soviet Russia would cooperate for a peaceful world, nurtured by President Roosevelt's and Prime Minister Churchill's reassurances, were punctured.While the West hurriedly demobilized, the Soviets held their military strength at wartime levels and used it to intimidate neighbors and yesterday's allies. In brief, everything was back to abnormal.

In Bulgaria, Poland, Berlin, the Soviet Zone of Occupation in Germany, the three- and four-nation interim authorities were displaced by all-Soviet controls. Finally a Red puppet regime was nailed down on Czechoslovakia. Through the United Nations, Washington offered one of the most generous gifts in history: an equal share for the USSR in a multi-nation control of the nuclear power that was still an American monopoly. Stalin turned it down. Similarly he turned down a part in the Marshall Plan and stopped his new colonies from participating in it. Then came Soviet-made crises in Berlin and the sudden invasion of South Korea.

Muscovite obstruction and aggression were back on history's agenda. Hesitantly, reluctantly, the United States, Britain, France, Turkey had begun to rearm and to build NATO and other regional defensive alliances. By the deliberate, world-revolutionary choice of the Soviet hierarchs a debilitating armaments race was forced upon a world struggling to repair the devastations of the war. Moscow was fishing in troubled waters in Africa, the Middle East, Latin America—and diligently troubling waters that were still calm.

Soviet contempt for treaties and its own pledged word are a matter of public record. In 1955, a fully documented analysis of nearly one thousand Soviet treaties made public by a U.S. Senate committee showed that the USSR "had broken its word to virtually every country to which it ever gave a signed promise." Subsequently a special committee of the American Bar Association found that in twenty-five postwar years the United States had 3,400 meetings with communists, and that "all this talk led to fifty-two major agreements and Soviet Russia had broken fifty of them." The strength and the prestige of the United Nations have been undermined by more than a hundred Soviet vetoes, and by refusal, when it suited Kremlin purposes, to abide by U.N. decisions.

The Red blight is everywhere. Every nation and colonial region, from the most advanced to the most backward, has its legal or underground communist contingents—usually both brands—working to disrupt the existing or emerging order. Every major social or religious organization, every vital labor and peasant movement, every national-independence movement, is already infiltrated by communists or in the process of penetration.

Because it is consciously at war, international communism endlessly prepares the necessary leaders and experts in the use of all political, psychological, economic, and revolutionary weapons. The campaigns are planned and manned by professionals, painstakingly trained for their jobs. According to NATO intelligence files, Henry J. Taylor reported in the American press in September, 1966, the Soviet regime "runs African-Asian communist indoctrination programs in about 177 colleges and six thousand secondary schools in Iron Curtain countries, a trade-union institute for Africans in Budapest, and terrorist training centers in Prague, Warsaw and in East Germany."

If anything, these NATO intelligence figures understate the magnitude of the "educational" networks for preparing guerrilla leaders, propaganda specialists, social sappers, terror cadres from all continents, then deploying them in their native lands to explode legal governments, to capture or ruin non-communist revolutionary movements. Other such training centers operate in Red China and Cuba.

None of this is recent or accidental. Years before 1917 Lenin set up study centers for followers in Bologna and Capri in Italy, and a third near Paris. Schools for communist revolution were established in Russia and non-communist countries soon after the Bolshevik *coup d'état* and multiplied steadily thereafter. Textbooks for the trainees in treason cover a wide range of skills. Typical subjects include "Preparation for Armed Insurrection," "Ideological Penetration of Armed Services," "The Tactic of the United Front."

In the half-century, the schools have graduated scores of thousands of agents, masters of the arts of softening free peoples and sapping their self-confidence, setting class against class and race against race. The fact that there are today more such schools than ever before should give pause to those who would like to believe that the cold war is over. Revolutionary cadres on such a scale are not being trained for the fun of it.

The communist blight, I repeat, is everywhere. The havoc it works has not been limited to governments and institutions. Its poisonous effects have been even wider and deeper on the minds of men the world over. Sincere progressives in all countries, as I have already pointed out, have been disoriented and corrupted by support of, or flirtation with, communist doctrines and practices. Men and women of intellectual and moral stature—among them educators and religious leaders who influence young minds—not to mention the millionfold Lumpen-intelligentsia in the non-communist world, found themselves defending slave labor, glorying in the Big Lie, shouting "Hoorah for murder!" when the killers were communists.

Communist propaganda generated the kind of cynicism that could applaud Kremlin blood-purges and genocide; that could side with the enemy against one's own country in Korea or Vietnam; that could argue self-righteously, "What if a few more million die" —in Russia, that is, or China, not in their own country. Unlimited violence and crime were a down-payment on the utopia of their fantasy world; though the advance payments already come to more than eighty million lives, a usurious fanaticism can take more and yet more in its stride.

6 / The Costs in Moral Values

A deep immoralism has marked the Soviet years from the start. It turned the person into an object, a bloodless statistic, and shrank respect for the living to the vanishing point. In pursuit of its purposes, it has demeaned or outlawed truth, honor, kindness, personal loyalty, and other such "petty bourgeois prejudices." No appraisal of the Soviet half-century makes sense if it evades these staggering costs in moral terms.

History, of course, is replete with evil governments and cruel individual tyrants, but usually they gave lip-service to some code of ethics even while violating it. The USSR was the first totally immoral state, so proclaimed by its founders, so maintained by their successors. It has treated immoralism as a positive virtue, derided ethical scruples, boasted of its capacity for what others call evil, acknowledging no limits on action beyond its own will and expediency.

Communists, one Martin Milligan instructed readers in the January, 1965 issue of *Marxism Today*, "must regard themselves as free, indeed morally obliged, to violate *the principles of truthfulness, respect for life*, etc. when it is absolutely clear that a great deal more harm would be done by adhering to such principles than by violating them." The killer thus sets himself up as the sole judge of when he is "morally obliged" to kill! This has been a continuous, inviolate principle. Forty-four years earlier a certain I. Duzcinski explained:

"Communist ethics makes it the highest duty to accept the necessity of acting wickedly. This was the greatest sacrifice the revolution asked of us. The conviction of the true communists is that evil transforms itself into bliss through the dialectics of historical evolution."

With continued indulgence, however, acting wickedly ceased to be a sacrifice and became itself a source of bliss—the psychotic thrill of power to inflict pain and death with complete impunity. The willingness to hurt or kill for the cause was hailed in the communist incantations as "Bolshevik firmness" and "Leninist courage." By that perverted logic, the firmness and courage proved by slaying a million were multiplied tenfold in slaying ten million. The very categories of Good and Evil were outlawed as sentimental weakness. Vyacheslav Molotov was entirely in Soviet character when he said off-handedly, while the Germans were raining death on Poland, that one's opinion of Nazism was just "a matter of taste."

A hostage system made the whole family punishable for the political crimes of any relative. The arrest and conviction of a man almost always brought some punishment, at the least exile, to his wife and grown children; invariably they were dispersed to different prisons and camps in different parts of the country.

Other regimes may have induced young children to spy on their parents—it remained for the Soviets to erect a monument to Pavlik Morozov, a little monster who informed on his father and mother and got them executed. The Pavlik episode occurred in the 1930's in a village in the Sverdlovsk area. Peasant neighbors were so infuriated by his action that they killed the boy, thus creating a martyr memorialized in metal in that village and held up as a model for all good little communists.

Other tyrants may have robbed their citizens—it remained for the Soviet secret police to round up tens of thousands suspected of hiding a few dollars, jewels or other *valuta*, and to subject them to medieval tortures for weeks and months until they handed it over. The police in every district had a production quota to fulfill in this "gold-mining in torture chambers"—those victims who did have something to hand over were the lucky ones.

Jean Jacques Rousseau, who warned that "nothing on this earth is worth buying at the price of human blood," could never have made the grade as a Bolshevik. Lenin and his brethren laughed at such sentimental nonsense as "bourgeois liberalism." For Good and Evil they substituted expediency. Thus released from the moral restraints on normal men, they could compound any monstrosity not merely in good conscience but in pride.

Lenin, it is important to recall, had found Sergei Nechayev, the apostle of absolute immoralism, even before he found Marx. In 1868, Nechayev wrote his celebrated *Catechism of a Revolutionist,* in which he renounced all norms of civilized behavior and prescribed every imaginable depravity in the pursuit of the "ideal." It is as fanatic, hate-packed a document as the human brain has ever produced. The revolutionist, he wrote, "knows only one science, the science of destruction," which does not stop at lying, robbery, betrayal and torture of friends, murder of his own family. His central dictum, that "everything that contributes to the triumph of the revolution" is moral, has been echoed by Lenin and his disciples to this day and, indeed, figures in every communist pronouncement on morality.

"Thus before he became a Marxist," Max Eastman has summed it up, "Lenin had arrived by an emotional road at the rejection of moral standards which Marx deduced from a pretended science of history. The confluence of these two streams of thought [Nechayev and Marx] is one of the greatest disasters that ever befell mankind." [2]

It was pure Nechayevism, in almost the master's original language, when Lenin wrote: "Morality is that which serves the destruction of the old exploiters' society. We do not believe in eternal morality and expose the deceit of all legends about morality." This precept was in due time enshrined in the *Soviet Encyclopaedia:* "The only scientific criterion of morality is the defense of the victory of communism." Thus the wisdom of time and the genius of moral philosophers through the millennia were discarded in the name of a distant vision of the perfect society.

Let no one suppose from his reference to deceit that Lenin ever opposed it in principle. On the contrary, deception was a matter of tactics, a primary tool for rule, when practised by "the vanguard of the proletariat," meaning himself and his henchmen. He chose hate, arrogance, mass murder, in the boundless ego-mania of men possessed by the conviction that they are the destined saviors of Humanity, the destined instruments of History.

Now that Soviet communism has vaulted over a quarter-century of Stalin dominance to rest its claim to legitimate succession on Lenin alone, there is a tendency to romanticize his character. It is argued, even by some opponents of communism, that he was humane, idealistic, and so on. Yet there is little that Stalin did, except in its scale, that was not done first by Lenin. Stalin simply carried to insane extremes the crimes first sanctified by Lenin.

It was Lenin, it should not be forgotten, who devised the first terror machine, the Cheka, and put a sanctimonious sadist, Felix Djerzhinski, at its head. It was Lenin who ordered the murder of thousands of innocent "hostages"; dispersed the first and only democratically elected legislative body after the Bolshevik seizure of power, the Constituent Assembly; crushed the Kronstadt revolt of his own Red sailors; raised lies and falsification to prime virtues in his system.

Messianic delusion as an alibi for immoralism is an old, old story. In *The Blithedale Romance,* a novel about the communistic experiment in Brook Farm in the 1840's, Nathaniel Hawthorne depicted its leaders, men obsessed by a vision of perfection:

"They have no heart, no sympathy, no reason, no conscience. They will keep no friend, unless he make himself the mirror of their purpose; they will smite and slay you, and trample your dead corpse under foot, all the more readily, if you take the first step with them and cannot take the second and the third, and every other step in their terribly strait path."

Whatever brand of beatitude those in the grip of such obsession may be pushing, they wind up in utter depravity. Dazzled by hallucinations of some golden future, convinced that they and they alone can bring it into being, any means seems to them haloed by the envisioned end.

The dilemma of ends and means is central to an assessment of communism. After all, both a highway robber and an honest workman have the same objective: to acquire money. The difference is in the means each uses to attain that end. Brutal means invariably brutalizes those who use them as well as those who are its victims. Milovan Djilas, the Yugoslav ex-communist, in his celebrated book, *The New Class*, was right, of course, when he wrote:

"Throughout history there have been no ideal ends which were attained with non-ideal means, just as there has been no free society which was built by slaves. Nothing so well reveals the reality and greatness of ends as the methods used to attain them."

Another writer, Professor W. W. Kulski, in 1957 posed one of the basic questions in his book, *The Soviet Regime: Communism in Practice:* "Is it worthwhile to inflict death and untold suffering on individual human beings for a dream of future happiness of mankind?" People who live by the accumulated wisdom of the ages and the sages, he believes, cannot hesitate in giving their answer:

"No end and no dream of future happiness could make them feel free to use any and all means. Soviet experience proves that means may become ends in themselves, while the millennium of future happiness recedes beyond human vision and reach."

Yet their profession of noble intentions leading ultimately to a perfect society has been the only argument advanced by communists for their savage terror. Five hundred years ago, in 1441, the nominal Bishop of Verden, Dietrich von Nieheim, set down a statement which helps explain the excesses of the Inquisition. "When its existence is threatened," he wrote, "the Church is freed of moral edicts. Unity as an aim blesses all means: perfidy, treachery, tyranny, simony, prisons and death." The words sound as if they had been uttered by a zealous communist today in defense of *his* "church." False confessions extracted by torture, mass homicide, universal spying, man-made famine, genocide—everything goes, until the very memory of decency, love, justice fades out.

That in the Soviet Union the means have all but expunged the professed ends is all too clear. The ends were the creation of a just society of equals. Industrialization—which Marx had taken for granted as a heritage from the displaced capitalism—in Russia became the unavoidable means. And inevitably that evolved into a supreme end in itself, so compelling that it was used to explain and justify the most vicious means. The initial ends continued to be recalled in ritualistic oratory, but they lost relevance to real life, dominated by the regime's obsession with the new end of industrialization at any cost. What is more, the seizure and retention of power, which was at first regarded as a transitory means for the attainment of communism, also turned into a supreme end in itself.

Thus in the name of humanity, the Soviets have cheapened and insulted human life. They have "scientifically" sacrificed the living generations for the supposed benefit of generations yet unborn, inflicted real horrors today for highly problematical happiness in some far-off tomorrow.

That, too, violates our ingrained moral intuitions. Anyone who decided to torture and murder one man or woman for the good of the victim's unborn great-grandchildren would be adjudged insane. Is he any less insane when he decides to torture and exterminate millions of men and women for the good of their unborn posterity? Have only the unborn a right to happiness, so that the anguish of the living is a trifling investment for their great-grandchildren?

A thousand accidents may snatch the theoretical happiness from the coming generations; they may even have a different concept of happiness than the group now brandishing "the sword of history" in their behalf. Only the torment of the living is real and indubitable. If it is morally permissible to wipe out a sector of Humanity for the sake of History, then there is no sensible reason for drawing the line at five million or five hundred million. Drown them all, comrades, leaving only a he-Stalin and a she-Stalin in their monolithic ark to start things over again from scratch!

By 1934, when I departed from Russia, nothing was left of the high mood of dedication, traces of which I had still found among communists six years earlier. The very vocabulary of idealism had been outlawed. "Equality" was lampooned as bourgeois romanticism. Excessive concern for the needs and sensibilities of ordinary people was punished as "rotten liberalism." Terror was no longer explained away as a sad necessity. It was used starkly and glorified as "human engineering." Means had blotted out ends and have held this priority ever since.

The Marxist theory of permanent class struggle rules out compromise, reform, truce, common humanity, mutual respect, family loyalties. "Marx's great crime" Eugene Methvin writes in an as yet unpublished book, "was that he dethroned man's civilizing emotion—love and the spirit of cooperation—for his more primitive, monstrous emotion, hate. In man's ambivalent Jekyll-Hyde nature as the civilized savage, Marxism is a throwback philosophy, anti-civilization and anti-*homo sapiens*."

Any doubts on this score have been removed by Marxism as practised under Soviet communism. Philip Spratt a former British-Indian communist leader, stated: "The communist movement runs on hate—the leading theorists are quite frank about it—and hate is a potent fuel." Hate not merely of capitalism as an abstraction, but of capitalists as people; hate of entire nations is preached in school books for Soviet children. The American poet, e.e. cummings, after a sojourn in Soviet Russia, wrote in his quaint style: "every kumrad is a bit of quite unmitigated hate."

In the Congo in 1965 hopped-up Simbas, armed and inspired by Moscow and Peking, went on a murderous spree that shocked the world. Witnesses testified that they attended scenes in which men and women were dismembered, disembowled, and their hearts used for ritual food. Far from apologizing for its established complicity in such barbaric cruelties, spokesmen for the Kremlin in the United Nations demanded that the United States be condemned for rescuing some of the trapped victims, black and white, from this fate.

As a practical matter, on its own terms of expediency, the official rejection of ethical standards has taken a heavy toll from the Soviet regime itself. Lacking a moral compass, the Soviets have written a record of blunders and depravities paid for in economic losses, destruction of irreplaceable brains and skills, loss of popular respect, loathing for the system on the part of the new generations.

A corrupt autocracy, both by example and from the need to escape its exactions, has bred corruption in the people. By falsifying statistics, concealing and lying about simple facts, it has taught its subjects to lie and falsify. Hence the shocking dimensions of theft of state property, bribery, faked bookkeeping, disregard of law: matters that are constantly exposed and bewailed by the Kremlin's own press. Hence political and moral decay within the ruling party, likewise admitted and inveighed against in this press. Day after day the leaders plead for discipline and dedication among their followers, attacking (to quote a recent Soviet document) the "schizophrenics, hypocrites, self-servers, windbags, eye-washers, demagogues" in the party concerned only with "their own personal well-being."

In a time of ferocious purges, Maxim Gorki was implored to intercede with the Kremlin, where his influence was enormous, for literary friends dying in dungeons or awaiting execution. Not only did he refuse but he used the occasion to express publicly his sympathy for the prison wardens and executioners. "People whose historical duty it is to kill some beings in order to save others," he wrote, "are *martyrs*, and my conscience will never allow me to condemn them." It was a degrading affair: the champion of the denizens of the "lower depths" championing the police and firing squads! If the once warm-hearted humanitarian could be so corrupted in the climate of immoralism, what did it do to lesser men?

Indeed it is proof of the underlying moral potential of the Russian peoples that, in the fifth decade of life under Nechayev-Leninist oppression, they still harbored "old-fashioned" human feelings. As soon as the Stalin terror subsided a little, after the despot's death, we saw it in the writings of young poets and in the eagerness with which the new soul-searching was taken up by youth generally. The instincts for decency had not atrophied; they were thawing out. In endless ways the more articulate and more daring showed, and continue to show, that they have hearts attuned to love and charity and respect for life.

Inevitably the reign of immoralism in one country, its rationale for "acting wickedly," spilled over into the surrounding world. Once they accepted communism in theory, men and women managed to accept and even defend its excesses in practice. This was true not only of outright party members but of a broad periphery of sympathizers, those whom Stalin called his "useful idiots" abroad.

And that, too, must be listed, along with the orgies of savagery in the name of good causes in so many places. Communism has fed and fattened and spurred on "the monster of violence that stalks the unhappy twentieth century," as Allen Drury calls it in his latest novel.

Such are the appalling costs of fifty years of Soviet dictatorship— a sketchy and inadequate summary, yet sufficient to underline the folly of evaluating supposed "progress" without considering the price paid by the Russian peoples and all mankind.

The new "moderation" has been so blown up by wishful hoping that it has induced waves of euphoria in some quarters. There is loose talk of "liberalization," though the Kremlin mocks the word and dreads the idea. In truth the Soviet Union remains a closed and maximally policed society. Not a dent has been made in the regime's monopoly of political power.

The dictatorship itself, eager to establish the continuity of its reign from Lenin to date, does not rest its claims of "miraculous success" on the post-Stalin or post-Khrushchev period, but on the entire half-century. The judgment of history, similarly, will be based on everything that has transpired in these fifty years.

PART IV

Whither Russia?

When measured by its costs in life suffering and moral depravity Soviet communism is demonstrably the most tragic failure on this scale in all history. This would be true even if it had succeeded in providing more material satisfactions than any other system, but even on that elementary level it has not succeeded.

In the last few years the Kremlin has reduced its police terrors and thought controls and has sought to inject a few limited free-market principles into its command economy: a process the outside world hopefully hailed as "liberalization." But this the dictatorship has done under the duress of assertive unrests and piled-up economic troubles, thus in effect *confirming* the overall failure. Besides, to applaud a homicidal regime for having cut down the number of its murders does seem like carrying tolerance for evil to an irrational extreme.

Is this verdict "objective"? The real question is whether it is true. Once an honest judgment has been reached, whether it be right or wrong, a pose of impartiality becomes hypocritical. Accuracy, yes; objectivity, no. Those who have written about Hitlerism were not expected to pretend a lofty objectivity in the face of its fiendishness. Writers on communism cannot evade the same kind of moral involvement and commitment.

There was a time when critics of fascism, to show that they were not biased, cited Mussolini's alleged success in making the trains run on time and Hitler's in abolishing unemployment and building magnificent auto-highways. That kind of objectivity, it is now apparent, was both cynical and fatuous.

It makes no more sense, I submit, to balance the score of Soviet crimes and oppressions with the arithmetic of literacy, blast furnaces, and space hardware. Flocks of satellites do not compensate for the execution of twelve-year-old children as "enemies of the state"; the Kremlin's gold hoard does not make up for the fact that it was mined by legions of prisoners under inhuman conditions; universal censorship of reading matter makes a mockery of universal literacy.

In a foreword to a book in 1948 indicting Stalin and his regime, a brilliant French scholar, Suzanne Labin, defended the moral passion she had brought to the writing. "I claim that I have studied communism with total objectivity," she explained, "and this very objectivity leads me to a total condemnation. I am objective but not neutral."

Dr. Lin Yutang, the Chinese-American educator and philosopher, took the same view in his anti-communist book, *The Secret Name*, about ten years ago. He, too, disdained neutrality in documenting "the life of fear and poverty and degradation" lived by hundreds of millions under the communist yoke, once he had "come to the conclusion that the whole experiment was not worthwhile."

Those authors have been asked, and doubtless this one will be: Isn't there anything good you can say about communism in practice? The truthful answer is No. A great deal of good can be said about the Russian people, the first and worst victims of communism, both in admiration and compassion. But out of respect for their long martyrdom one should not strain to discover minor virtues in a system guilty of major sins. Nor should one credit to the Soviet oligarchy with accomplishments by the Russian peoples despite the fallacies of communism and the exactions of totalitarianism.

I would have been close to a miracle if a great country with enormous resources and an industrious population of more than two hundred million had failed to make impressive progress in many directions. Not one item in that progress, however, is the direct result of communism. Its equivalent can be found in other countries, attained with less brutality and without preposterous claims to "achievements unmatched in all history."

Let's have the gist of the fifty Soviet years made clear: *Never before have so many paid so much for so little.*

Golden Anniversary

At the half-century mark, Soviet communism presents a dismal spectacle, from any vantage point. Soviet Russia is mired in a welter of economic, ideological, and political crises. It is on the defensive, against critics at home and in its postwar appendages, against social groups pressing for some share in decision-making and government.

The communist world, of which Russia is still the heart and center, is ringed with walls and mined zones and electrified barbed-wire to imprison its inhabitants, but thousands continue to risk their lives to break out to freedom.

The sad and sullen land is washed by tides of popular discontent, articulated more and more boldly by an awakening intelligentsia of poets, students, technocrats, scientists.

The peasantry, still close to half the population, remains openly hostile, fixed in a mood of "non-cooperation" bordering on conscious sabotage, still clinging to its dream of family ownership of the land they work.

The youth is skeptical, alienated and increasingly defiant. The regime no longer tries to conceal the hostility of the new generation—it is too vast and takes too many different forms to be concealed.

The non-Russian national regions, nearly half of the Soviet population in the aggregate, are more restive, more insistent on greater political, economic, and cultural autonomies.

At the same time the world communist movement is in serious disarray, Moscow's patent to leadership widely challenged, its satraps in Eastern Europe compelled to court their own masses with gestures of defiance against the Kremlin.

As for the people generally, they are fed up with slogans, calls to yet more sacrifice, threats and abuse for the failures of their masters. Drained of patience, they no longer muffle their angers over pervasive shortages, poverty, foreign adventures.

The thinking minority, even within the ruling shifts, sees in the allegedly accomplished socialism only, in Dr. Lin Yutang's phrase, "a satire on Marxism." The dreams of the early period, even among the communists, has been reduced to ashes, presided over by a decadent party.

A new class, the bureaucracy in the party, government, and economy—arrogant, well-fed, flaunting its "status symbols," its power and privileges, guarded by secret police and censorships—rides roughshod over the masses.

The mirage of bliss and plenty beyond the horizons of time is being treated as just that: a propaganda fantasy. The promise that the living generation will see "true communism" has lost all credibility. Khrushchev's blunder in fixing a date for its arrival—1980—is no longer mentioned, having been junked with his other extravaganzas.

After five decades of anti-God campaigns, so often marked by terror, the press continues to complain about failure on the antireligious front. The renewed search for ideals to live by, in particular among the young, has spiritual overtones.

The fifty-year landscape is disfigured by dump-heaps of innocent dead, now haunted by the ghosts of thousands of terror victims "rehabilitated" posthumously. The horrors no one dared talk about are today in the open. A great weight of guilt and bitterness presses down on the national conscience.

Soviet Russia has a history without heroes to warm the old or inspire the young—the list begins and ends with Lenin—but teeming with ex-heroes "exposed" as villains. (And even Lenin, as a man who surrounded himself almost wholly with traitors, spies and maniacs, is open at the very least to implications of stupidity.)

Each of his successors has vilified those who went before, to be vilified in turn by those who followed, thus reducing the past to a shambles of depraved leadership. Twenty-five of the fifty Soviet years were dominated by a "power-mad maniac," Stalin, and ten more by a "hare-brained schemer," Khrushchev. The masses and their overlords look back on an unbroken chain of "traitors" like Trotsky, Zinoviev, and nearly all the other founding fathers; paranoiac killers like Stalin, Yagoda, Yezhov, Beria; "anti-party" plotters like Molotov, Kaganovich, Malenkov; blundering clowns like Khrushchev.

This is not a summation by an unkind outsider. It is official Soviet history certified by the top rulers. What, in the light of this self-indictment, becomes of the party's vaunted "infallibility"?

At the half-century mark the dictatorship is as fearful as ever before of allowing elementary civil freedoms and access to competing ideas. It holds the so-called trade-unions in bondage as state agencies for squeezing more labor out of the working classes. Strikes, which break out here and there notwithstanding, are punished as rebellion.

The statute prescribing the death penalty for an attempt to escape from the Soviet paradise is still in force. Angels with fiery swords did not permit Adam and Eve to return to the Garden of Eden; communists with firing squads do not permit their Adams and Eves to *leave* the Red Eden.

The nation is governed by a handful of men devoid of the charisma of those whom they have discredited but in whose name, like it or not, they are compelled to govern. There are no more giants in the land, not even giant monsters. The present bosses have been described by the most knowledgeable Westerners as a "regime of clerks" and "an elite of uninspiring technicians." It is doubtful that they possess the intellectual force and the personal prestige to prop up an aging regime tied to a decomposing ideology.

In 1966, the Institute for the Study of the USSR, in Munich, published a revised *Who's Who in the USSR*. It contained 5,500 biographies, the cream of the upper classes; but only 133 of those listed were under forty years of age, and nearly half of these were sports celebrities—a statistical commentary on the Kremlin's inability to recruit youth into its elites.

The Soviet system is scelerotic, the memories of its ardent years so many fossilized formulas. By its own admissions, in connection with efforts to revive the old spirit, the reservoir of beliefs is running dry. "The waning of revolutionary zeal," in the words of Dr. Robert Strausz-Hupé, "has been accompanied by a hardening of liturgical ideology."

The latest Party Congress, in the spring of 1966, mirrored the creeping demoralization. "To non-communist observers all over the world," the *U. S. News & World Report* summed it up, "this Moscow gathering appeared to be a spiritless affair offering no new ideas and little comfort to the communist rank-and-file."

On the material "fronts"—one of the liturgical words—matters are in no better case. The growing of food is the most important enterprise in any great nation. But Soviet agriculture is in permanent crisis. Collectivized farming, imposed at such an awesome cost in life, is close to bankrupt.

The country has been saved from hunger by the thin margin of farming on a private basis and by large purchases of grain from capitalist growers. An exceptionally good harvest, like that in 1966, may ease conditions for the moment, but it doesn't solve the larger problem of peasant passivity and low output.

Despite the impressive industrial growth—in considerable measure *because* of it—the elephantine economy staggers from one crisis to another. Reality is presenting its bills for the fallacies of totalitarian economics.

The Kremlin managers are disoriented by the advent of modern technology. Their political forebears could erect steel mills, dig mines and hack out canals by the brute force of cheap, unskilled, almost unlimited manpower, but the complexities of automation, subtle tools, cybernetics, do not yield to crude coersions.

After fifty years of bloody experimenting with socialism, its masterminds are reaching out gingerly, on a timid scale, for the despised free-market controls. Thirty years after the announcement of "full socialism," they are re-discovering simple facts of economic life like profits, market prices, demand and supply.

At this writing only a small fraction of the Soviet working force has been affected by the so-called economic reforms, and in any case the hope of combining totalitarian economic monopoly with a few selected capitalist techniques appears foredoomed to failure.

Soviet industry is dangerously out of balance, and Moscow is begging for capitalist machinery and credits to help overcome confusions. The old boast of "overtaking and outdistancing" the West has not been heard since Khrushchev was silenced.

The workers, the common man, in whose name the laboratories of the Great Experiment and its abattoirs have been run, are not concerned with economic theory. The "classless society" of the official documents is sufficiently visible to them in new classes of graded economic and social privilege.

Differences in income are as wide or wider than in bourgeois industrial societies, plus extras for the privileged groups that do not show up in statistics. Economic equality survives only in future-tense rhetoric; in real life *uravnilovka*—equal earning and living norms—has become a dirty word in the communist vocabulary.

In an earlier phase in American industry, so long outlived that few remember it, the country had a social abomination known as a "company town." It was deservedly execrated as virtual slavery. Those were towns, mostly in certain mining areas, in which the company owned and controlled the local government and police, the homes, shops, schools, everything and of course kept out the labor unions.

The best way to visualize Soviet Russia is perhaps to see it as a single "company town," rigidly dominated by the state-employer. Worse, in that there is no escape for the worker; there is only *one* employer, the state, which is equipped with armies, security police, prison camps, and arbitrary decrees to deal with recalcitrants.

The inhabitants are hardly consoled by the fiction that they "own" all industry—and they do, in the same sense that a prisoner owns his prison cell. The fiction, when alluded to by a less-than-bright tourist, draws a horse-laugh from workers.

Along with their other headaches, the Kremlin must contend with colossal pilfering of state property, diversion of state funds into private pockets through fraudulent bookkeeping, a vast underground of illegal private business, an array of "economic crimes" so widespread that in recent years some of them have been made punishable by death.

It is not an epidemic of criminality—Russians are as honest as other peoples and usually more law-abiding. No, it is a conditioned reflex to the pains of an all-embracing state and at bottom another species of political resistance. The state is the enemy, to be tricked, robbed, defrauded wherever possible. The old Bolshevik commandment, directed against capitalism, "expropriate the expropriators," has come home to roost.

A leading Russian historian, V. O. Klyuchevsky, writing about seventeenth-century Russia, indicted it in a phrase that became famous: *"The state swelled and the people shrank."* It applies accurately to the half of the twentieth century we are dealing with here. The state assuredly has swelled, in territory and population, in military power and political influence, but the people as individuals have shrunk.

On its fiftieth anniversary the Soviet oligarchy has little more than naked power with which to confront a citizenry more and more defiant and demanding—and it is uncertain and fearful of how far it dare use that power.

Around the world, wherever communism prevails, its regimes face the telltale contrasts between life—in both material terms and by standards of freedom—on opposite sides of the various "walls" and "curtains"; between East Germany and West Germany, East Berlin and West Berlin, Russia and Finland, North and South Korea, Taiwan (Formosa) and the China mainland.

This, in brief, is the pile of poverty, confusion, agrarian peonage, oppression, and frustration being presented to the world on the golden anniversary of Bolshevism as "socialism victorious," "Marxism triumphant," and an object of emulation to peoples and nations around the globe. The extraordinary part of it is among all those peoples and nations there are minorities not only willing but zealous to buy the same bargain. They no longer have even the excuse of ignorance.

Evolution or Revolution?

"Wither Russia?" As the half-centennial approached, the old conundrum was asked again, among others by *Problems of Communism*, a bi-monthly journal of high academic quality published in Washington. Answers were given by an array of top scholars and journalists in the field (and a few lesser lights like myself). They ran as a symposium beginning with the last issue in 1965 and into 1967.

The contributors, of course, differed widely in their *prognosis* for the Russian future, but they were almost unanimous in their *diagnosis* of the present condition. The very titles of some of the articles tell the story: "The Beginning of the End?" by Michel Tatu; "The Soviet System—Transformation or Degeneration?" by Zbigniew Brzezinski; "Notes on an Agonizing Diagnosis" by Wolfgang Leonhard. And in examining symptoms they used, as a matter of course, words like "crisis . . . demoralization . . . decay . . . degeneration."

With only variations in emphasis, virtually all of these long-time students of Soviet affairs agreed that the patient was in a bad way:

1. The regime has failed completely to win "legitimacy" in the eyes of the people in general and of the elite groupings—in the arts, sciences, technologies—in particular. The rulers are still regarded by the ruled as a kind of internal occupation force, besieging and besieged.

2. There is an open and deepening struggle between the bureaucracy and the dynamic social elites, the technical-cultural intelligentsia, which neither need nor want party dictation.

3. The *apparatchiki* or party functionaries, top to bottom, will grow more obstinate, less rational, in opposing deeper changes that might cut into their privileged roles. "The most conservative Western bourgeois," in M. Garder's words, "is a revolutionary next to the *apparatchik*."

4. There is a sharp decline in the vitality of the Soviet leadership, which is incapable of fundamental reforms, especially in the all-important political areas, called for by its mounting troubles. The initiating pressures and specific proposals for the limited non-political revisions already adopted have all come from outside, not from within the top leadership.

5. The regime is no longer able to draw adequate "creative and innovative talent" into its top echelons, losing it by default to the very groups which are trying to shake off party domination. Communism is no longer a wave of the future but "a spent wave of the past."

6. For all these reasons decay has set in and threatens the survival of the aging system. The country, several of the writers specify, is in a typically *pre-revolutionary condition,* like that in France before its great Revolution, in the last stage of tsarist absolutism, or in Hungary before the October, 1956, uprising.

7. The decay is too far gone for superficial therapies. It demands deep-reaching changes in doctrine, thinking and institutions, probably beyond the capacities of the rulers. "The party leaders," to quote Dr. Tatu, "now know that the grant of partial freedom only whets the appetite of those to whom it is given," yet this hardens the determination of the bureaucracy to hold on to its vested advantages.

The symposium was launched with a review of a significant French book: *L'Agonie du Régime en Russie Sovietique (The*

Death Struggle of the Regime in Soviet Russia) by Michel Garder, a military man who has long specialized in Soviet studies. The death agony, he declares, is evident in "the conflict between a decaying regime that no longer has any justification other than the personal interests of those who profit by it" and "the upper strata of the technological intelligentsia."

It is a contest, M. Garder argues, that cannot end in a compromise. There is not enough flexibility in the dictatorship. He therefore sees a collapse—probably a non-communist and perhaps anti-communist take-over with the help of the military elites. "Recognition of the hare-brained absurdity of a Marxist-Lennist religion," he believes, "has long ago become inevitable for the true elite of the country and is from day to day dawning upon millions of average persons." There will come a moment—he sets the date, imprudently, as 1970—when the technological masses "will feel impelled to seize power."

The reviewer, Michel Tatu, disapproves of the "apocalyptic character" of such a forecast and is almost apologetic for treating it seriously. Yet he goes along with its factual premises. He concurs that there is "the loss of political impetus" in the dictatorship and that it has ever less room for maneuver:

"The known aspirations for individual freedom in the USSR, particularly among the young people, the 'radicalization' found among their conservative opponents, the general lassitude, to say the least, toward worn-out slogans, and the dissatisfaction with the prevailing standard of living—all this is abundant evidence to lead one to conclude that the day everybody is left to himself in the Soviet Union the situation will soon be out of control. The fact that accounts have not yet been settled for the 'excesses' committed during the Stalinist era only adds to the uncertainty."

If compromise between the dictators and the country cannot be achieved, Dr. Tatu concludes, "there remains the possibility of a transfer of power to the military and the police," with communism and the communists as scapegoats. Which is pretty much Garder's view, except that unlike Garder he grants a one-in-three chance that the party may still contain the situation for a long time.

Dr. Hans J. Morgenthau of the University of Chicago analyzes several types of inertia that may prolong the regime's life, but he is not optimistic on this score. In the past, when under fire, "the regime could fall back upon its doctrine," but now "the erosion of that doctrine heralds the crisis of the regime."

The Kremlin, he writes, "has only been able to control the challenge because it has the power to set relatively narrow limits to open dissent. . . . When a totalitarian regime reaches a stage when it can afford neither to suppress dissent altogether nor to give it free reign, the tendency of the leadership is to fluctuate narrowly between relative permissiveness and relative oppression."

The question, then, is how long can it maneuver in this tight squeeze? Professor Morgenthau sees a "great chance that the regime will be forced either to revert to Stalinist methods to maintain itself, or else to destroy itself by submitting to competition for political power."

Professor Frederick C. Barghoorn of Yale also dismisses the Garder book, as "the latest in a long line of apocalyptic predictions of the collapse of communism." He warns that "great revolutions are most infrequent and that successful political systems are tenacious and adaptive." But by his own diagnosis, Soviet communism can hardly be rated as a "successful political system"; its lack of "legitimacy" in the eyes of its subjects, if nothing else, refutes that assumption. In any case, he goes on to cast doubts, if not on the tenacity of the regime, then on its potentials for adaptiveness.

"When political structures and the belief systems which legitimate them cease to be 'functional,' " he explains, tensions develop, and the Kremlin has been slow and crude in meeting the challenge. While "there has recently been an encouraging revival of rational and empirical thinking in many fields," creative transformation is obstructed: "The dominant political culture . . . is still characterized by a great deal of arbitrary administrative behavior, cloaked in secrecy and justified with sacrosanct dogma and official lies."

The post-Stalin gains, he underlines, "are still not protected by firm legal guarantees or even by explicit revisions of the obsolete and stifling dogmas." The party, that is, refuses to give an inch of its political monopoly. "Soviet liberal intellectuals and their well-wishers abroad," Barghoorn cautions, would do well to realize that the "partial reforms" and the "reluctant, possibly temporary concessions" are grudging loans subject to call, not fixed new rights.

Interestingly, he asserts that "the Russian political tradition is woefully defective in gradualism." But if not gradualism, then what? Presumably its opposite—impetuous, precipitate outbursts. Yet he cannot bring himself to consider such non-gradualism seriously. Having in effect made out a good case for the potentials of explosive developments, he concludes that "the Soviet political system will continue to adapt itself more or less successfully" notwithstanding.

This reluctance to consider the possibility, if not the likelihood, of revolution in Russia is understandable, in the temper of academic prudence. It is even more striking in the brilliant analysis contributed by Professor Brzezinski of Columbia University, at this writing with the State Department as a foreign-policy adviser.

He paints perhaps the most convincing picture of a regime in decline. The party has lost most of its relevance for the new period; in fact, "Soviet history in the last few years has been dominated by the spectacle of a party in search of a role." But officialdom isn't budging: "The *apparatchiki* are still part of an extremely centralized and rigidly hierarchical bureaucratic organization, increasingly set in its ways, politically corrupted by years of unchallenged power. . . . Institutional conflict combined with mediocre and unstable power makes for ineffective and precarious power. . . . The youth could become a source of ferment, the consumers could become more restless, the scientists more outspoken, the non-Russian nationalities more demanding."

In short, "decay is bound to set in" and "the stability of the political system may be endangered." Already he discerns a "reopening of the gap that existed in pre-revolutionary Russia between the political system and the society, thereby posing the threat of the degeneration of the Soviet system." He identifies in the USSR today some of the same "indicators" of explosion that marked France, tsarist Russia, Chiang Kai-shek's China and Rakosi's Hungary just before their respective revolutions.

The logic of this analysis points clearly to potentials of collapse. But Brzezinski stops well short of such an "apocalyptic" conclusion. Should the Kremlin choose increasing dogmatism and unleash violence against dissenters, he says, "the possibility of revolutionary outbreaks could not be discounted entirely." But that is as far as he pursues the thought.

Instead he prescribes a basement-to-garret reorganization of the regime: "The progressive transformation of the bureaucratic com-

munist dictatorship into a more pluralistic and institutionalized political system . . . seems essential if its degeneration is to be
averted." He spells out the indispensable changes. He doesn't
argue that such far-reaching reform, amounting to the advent of a
parliamentary-constitutional government, *can* be peacefully attained. Given his own picture of a decaying, half-paralyzed master-
class confronting a pre-revolutionary threat, hidebound by dogma
and vested interests, it would seem more "apocalyptic" to expect
his suggested transformation than to foresee a nervous breakdown
such as Russia experienced several times in this century.

A German specialist who was brought up in Soviet Russia,
Wolfgang Leonhard, like the others, stresses "the contradiction
between economic objectives and political power interests." Should
the 314,000 local party organizations devote themselves to ideological tasks or to guiding the economy? The question is urgent and
the Kremlin hasn't answered it, perhaps cannot answer it without
surrendering its power. However senseless the Marxist-Leninist re-
ligion-plus-economy becomes in practice, Leonhard says, "it is not
likely that the party will ever abandon a doctrine which so conven-
iently justifies the party's role in Soviet society as well as its position within the international communist movement." In effect he
poses the question—"evolution or revolution?"—without attempting to answer it.

Perhaps the most persuasive prognosis is set forth by Robert
Conquest, the British student of Soviet affairs. He, too, finds "the
conditions of a classical Marxist pre-revolutionary situation," but
he is less sure that the regime can muddle through. Random patch-
ing will not suffice, he believes: "It therefore appears inevitable
that the pressures will continue to build up. The question that
remains to be answered is whether the political integument will be
destroyed explosively or will erode away gently."

But he does not seem convinced that the present leaders can
take adequate measures in sufficient time to forestall explosion and
adds that "in the USSR today one would not expect a great deal of
time to be still available." On balance he must warn that we
"should not fall into the temptation of believing the *status quo* to
be as stable as it may appear to the superficial glance."

This is substantially my own feeling. I dare not predict a revolution in Russia, much less set a date for it like M. Garder. But we

should not rule it out. It seems to me more reasonable to expect a violent upheaval than to guarantee the stability and durability of the present regime. There is no conflagration but an abundance of materials so inflammable that a spark might ignite them.

Revolution has always seemed "impossible" until it occurs, after which everyone sagely agrees that it had been "inevitable." In the last months of 1916 and the first of 1917, foreign correspondents in Petrograd, including the most anti-regime among them, were still warning that the talk of revolution was premature. A week before the 1953 uprising in East Germany, not one political specialist would have ventured to forecast such an event. The rash of bloody rebellion in Vorkuta and other Soviet concentration camps certainly had not been foreseen by the Kremlin or anyone else.

In both Poland and Hungary, we were assured by Western journalists and diplomats until the moment of the uprisings, all elements of potential revolt had been liquidated. Their Red Armies had been thoroughly indoctrinated, large percentages of their officers corps were party members. Soviet forces were stationed in both countries. The former bourgeoisie had ceased to exist and youth had been brought up by Marxist-Leninist teachers.

After the event, I made a limited survey of published comment on the satellite area during the preceding year by foreign tourists, reporters, and diplomats. While many of them noted grumbling and other signs of ferment, not one mentioned the possibility of popular rebellion, or mentioned it only to deny it. On the tenth anniversary of the Hungarian revolt, Robert Murphy, who had been Deputy Undersecretary of State at the time, told an interviewer, Bob Considine: "We were caught completely by surprise. Sure, we had CIA people in there. I know: I was on the State Department's CIA board. But there was no hint from them of what was about to break out so spontaneously, so emotionally."

Given the conditions described in the "Whither Russia?" symposium, it would be an egregious error to assume that the Soviet rulers had wide, let alone limitless, choices. The problem is not merely how far they are willing to go to meet the people's aspirations and satisfy the demands of new social groups, but how far they *can* go without risking their power and their lives.

The Lessons of Hungary

A much-quoted saying attributed to Mao Tse-tung runs this way: "In the last analysis, all the truths of Marxism can be summed up in one sentence: To rebel is justified." But this is a concept that cuts both ways—the justification applies to communist societies no less than to others.

Mao himself learned it the hard way when his so-called cultural revolution through young Red Guards ignited a civil conflict which at this writing is still burning violently. In early 1966, the Chinese communist system seemed the most thoroughly regimented, stable, monolithic structure on this planet. A few months later, it was in flames beyond the control of the bosses, the loyalties of top mandarins and even of the army in doubt. Whatever the outcome, the events in Red China serve as a further warning against taking the "finality" of any totalitarian system for granted.

"At the top everything is peaceful and smooth, but below the top, in the depths, and even in its ranks, new thoughts, new ideas, are bubbling and future storms are brewing." These are the words of Milovan Djilas, himself for years second in command of a communist country.

While this ferment under the monolithic surfaces was generally admitted, it had long been argued that successful revolution against totalitarian regimes is inconceivable, a thing of the past. An effective rising, it was taken for granted, calls for revolutionary organization and leadership, with an ideology or program around which the masses can be rallied—pre-conditions made impossible by the size and ubiquity of the communist police and security systems. There could be no undergrounds and conspiracies. In addition, the totalitarian tyrannies always have immense military might and the latest weapons at their disposal.

There are still a few theorists who hold this view, insisting therefore that the Soviet dictatorship can never be overthrown from within. But they can adhere to this belief only by ignoring or underrating the experience of the Hungarian revolt in October, 1956, and in lesser degree the uprisings in Poland about the same time and in East Germany in 1953. In these countries there was only negligible organized resistance, if any, and no known leadership. The rebellions were completely unexpected and spontaneous: less "movements" than explosions, unplotted, unplanned, unled, galvanized by the simplest and most basic ideas—freedom, justice, independence.

And in Hungary, it is of prime importance to recall, *the revolution was successful*—successful within its own frontiers, so that it could be defeated only by force from outside.

Probably modern history holds no precedent of a revolution that triumphed so overwhelmingly so quickly. Within three days after its outbreak, the power passed to the people, actively or passively supported by all social groupings. Initiated by students, poets, journalists—by the numerically small intelligentsia—it was joined almost at once by the factory workers, the peasantry, the remnants of the middle class, the armed forces, and a large part of the ruling Communist Party itself. Leadership emerged from the ranks, some of it from the liberated political prisoners. The discipline was truly remarkable; there was virtually no looting, no factional wars, no terror except against the security police.

Hungary, and this is its great historical importance, provided the proof that revolution against a totalitarian state is possible. It cancelled out the assumption that the new species of despotism, because it can prevent organization and atomize opposition, is invulnerable to the forces of internal unrest. In effect it established a new pattern, what might be called revolution by concensus, fundamentally unlike the classic examples of the French and Russian revolutions.

If and when there is a mass uprising against the Soviet regime—not a palace revolution but a true popular revolt—it may be expected to follow the lines of events in Hungary in the fall of 1956. It will come not through plotted arson but through spontaneous combustion, and its leadership will spring also from the ranks of communism and its elites, including the military. Consequently it is necessary to comprehend the major lessons of the Hungarian events—thus far the only successful revolution against a totalitarian state.

The first of these can be fairly stated as a law: When the time is ripe, when the climactic hour has struck, the size of the government's military establishment, the number and quality of its weapons, becomes irrelevant. Hungary demonstrated that not only are the armed forces, and those who man the weapons, swept along by the national tide, but in the measure that they retain some discipline and leadership, these are placed at the disposal of the revolution.

Whether and when a real uprising on a nationwide scale will take place in the USSR is open to argument, but the magnitude and power of the Soviet military machine is no longer pertinent to the inquiry. Not the dimensions but the loyalties of the military set-up will tell the story. If it sticks by the regime, even a small, old-fashioned army can crush a rebellion as effectively as a huge modern army. The larger the army, in fact, the closer it is to the people, the more likely to share its angers and aspirations. A small elite army (such as the special KGB force) may identify itself with the regime longer than the huge conscript army and may even find itself fighting the main military establishment until the issue is resolved.

A second Hungarian fact seems tremendously significant for all communist countries, Russia included. This is the swift and thorough disintegration of the ruling political party under the impact of a popular eruption. Almost at once the Hungarian people discovered an extraordinary truth: that there were few communists in their country, in the sense of fanatically dedicated supporters of the regime. There were bureaucrats, time-servers, groups with material or power stakes in the established order, but remarkably little of the dedicated communist faith-unto-death that can withstand the hammer-blows of a popular revolt: the kind of faith that is still found among communists in the non-communist world.

Hundreds of formerly enthusiastic communists, among the two hundred thousand who fled the country, have given witness to the special disillusionment and anguish among their kind. They included men and women of high reputation and earning capacity, who had everything to gain from playing with the regime, yet found themselves sparking and leading the revolution. I have read and talked to many of them—their words seemed to echo those of the Soviet intellectuals among whom I lived in the early thirties. Again and again Soviet journalists, writers, actors who outwardly were "sincere communists," trusted by the Kremlin and living a good life by local standards, talked to me in just that vein.

In many cases they posed for years—not only to me but, more important, to themselves—as true believers, but always a time came when the pose collapsed. Sometimes it was in vodka that they suddenly found the courage to protest their fate. More often it was some new excess of official ghoulishness that moved them to break silence. And always I knew that it was not to educate a foreigner that they risked frankness but to assuage their own inner despairs.

Of this I am sure: that, by and large, support of the Kremlin rests on self-interest, the patriotism that fears a weakening of the country, dread of the vacuum that would be left by the overthrow of the regime, on cynicism and hopelessness and sheer inertia, but not on faith. These are powerful bulwarks and may sustain the weight of the dictatorship for yet a long time.

One more aspect of the Hungarian experience is particularly relevant to Soviet Russia. As you listened to or read the personal stories of escaped Freedom Fighters, in the first years after the Soviet invasion, you realized that none of them had planned to revolt or to join revolt by others. It "just happened." Mostly they were not even conscious of being rebels, certainly not to the degree of staking their lives, until they found themselves shouting slogans and shooting guns and throwing Molotov cocktails.

An intelligent Soviet fugitive has described this phenomenon of unconscious rebellion, common to the subjects of all totalitarian states, as "double-mindedness." A Soviet citizen, he explained, as a matter of almost biological necessity develops two nearly unrelated minds. There is the public mind, obedient, conformist and even honestly enthusiastic for the *status quo*—a mind stocked with the safe slogans and doctrines. And there is the inchoate secret mind, where suppressed doubts, wrongs, resentments, and frustrations breed and fester, where dangerous knowledge and moral intuitions are filed away.

What happened in Hungary, without planning or leadership, was that the hidden mind erupted to the surface and took command. The Petoefi Circle in Budapest, where it all started, was an all-communist organization. The chain of events began with an "egghead" discussion about the role of free thought in Marxist-Leninist ideology. More and more of the participants—not against communism but in the hope of salvaging it—questioned the ortho-dox position and demanded a place for intellectual truth, creative freedom in the arts, exposure of faked trials. Not one of them dreamed that he was stirring up a great revolution.

The rulers and the resident foreigners and the experts were utterly astonished when the explosion came, but *most astonished of all were the rebels themselves.* A few apparently minor incidents crystalized the atomized resistance into a mighty unanimity. This is what can be expected in Soviet Russia, too, if and when the time is ripe. It may be touched off by student-led demonstrations of the sort that are constantly taking place; or by a mass protest against new economic burdens, such as occurred in Novocherkassk in 1962; or by some seemingly trivial episode that mysteriously, unexpectedly, lights a fuse to long-accumulated emotional dynamite.

Perhaps the greatest source of strength for the dictatorships today, in Hungary and in all communist countries, is the remembrance of the West's failure to intervene, if only to the extent of a timely warning to Moscow not to intervene. Call it prudence or fear or a failure of nerve, the passivity of those they had accounted as friends killed the illusion among the masses and the intelligentsia that the democratic world cared and would come to their aid in case of an open conflict with the despots. The heritage of Hungary, for opponents of the task-masters in the communist world, is a bleak sense of isolation and abandonment.

In the USSR, however, this new knowledge that they stand alone is balanced in part by the realization that in the event of a revolt in Russia there will be no outside power able or willing to crush it. In theory China, if still in communist hands, might attempt a rescue operation, but practically geography is most unfavorable to such an intervention.

More than a century ago one of the most percipient of modern political thinkers, Alexis de Tocqueville, made an observation highly pertinent to the Soviet scene today:

"Experience suggests that the most dangerous moment for an evil government is usually when it begins to reform itself. . . . The sufferings that are endured patiently, as being inevitable, become intolerable the moment it appears that there might be an escape. Reform then only serves to reveal more clearly what still remains oppressive and now all the more unbearable; the suffering, it is true, has been reduced, but one's sensitivity has become more acute."

No doubt Tocqueville had in mind the French Revolution. It erupted not when conditions were at their worst in his country but when there had been a measure of improvement portending further progress. The uprising in Red Hungary, too, came at a time when there had been some loosening of controls, a marginal but real moderation of terror. In the USSR at this writing, through no one denies that the political weather is milder, moods of discontent and protests are more open and vocal.

The so-called reforms and concessions to the people and in particular to intellectuals who reflect popular feelings may postpone a showdown with the regime—or they may provoke one. The present stalemate is so tense on both sides that it is unlikely to endure indefinitely. At some point the Kremlin will be driven to act. Either it must carry reform far beyond the present half-measures, to the degree of diluting its political monopoly, or it must again resort to terror. In either case it will be putting its survival on the line in a life-or-death gamble.

Index